POSTWAR AMERICAN FICTION AND THE RISE OF MODERN CONSERVATISM

AF614384

Bryan M. Santin examines over a half-century of intersection between American fiction and postwar conservatism. He traces the shifting racial politics of movement conservatism to argue that contemporary perceptions of literary form and aesthetic value are intrinsically connected to the rise of the American Right. Instead of casting postwar conservatives as cynical hustlers or ideological fanatics, Santin shows how the long-term rhetorical shift in conservative notions of literary value and prestige reveal an aesthetic antinomy between high culture and low culture. This shift, he argues, registered and mediated the deeper foundational antinomy structuring postwar conservatism itself: the stable social order of traditionalism and the creative destruction of free-market capitalism. Postwar conservatives produced, in effect, an ambivalent double register in the discourse of conservative literary taste that sought to celebrate neo-aristocratic manifestations of cultural capital while condemning newer, more progressive manifestations revolving around racial and ethnic diversity.

BRYAN M. SANTIN obtained his PhD in English from the University of Notre Dame in 2017. He is Assistant Professor of English at Concordia University Irvine, where he teaches courses in American literature, world literature, and composition.

CAMBRIDGE STUDIES IN AMERICAN LITERATURE AND CULTURE

Editor
Leonard Cassuto, Fordham University

Founding Editor
Albert Gelpi, Stanford University

Advisory Board
Robert Levine, University of Maryland
Ross Posnock, Columbia University
Branka Arsić, Columbia University
Wai Chee Dimock, Yale University
Tim Armstrong, Royal Holloway, University of London
Walter Benn Michaels, University of Illinois, Chicago
Kenneth Warren, University of Chicago

Recent Books in this Series

185. ALEX MENRISKY
Wild Abandon: American Literature and the Identity Politics of Ecology
184. HEIKE SCHAEFER
American Literature and Immediacy: Literary Innovation and the Emergence of Photography, Film, and Television
183. DALE M. BAUER
Nineteenth-Century American Women's Serial Novels
182. MARIANNE NOBLE
Rethinking Sympathy and Human Contact in Nineteenth-Century American Literature
181. ROB TURNER
Counterfeit Culture
180. KATE STANLEY
Practices of Surprise in American Literature after Emerson
179. JOHANNES VOELZ
The Poetics of Insecurity
178. JOHN HAY
Postapocalyptic Fantasies in Antebellum American Literature
177. PAUL JAUSSEN
Writing in Real Time

(Continued after the Index)

POSTWAR AMERICAN FICTION AND THE RISE OF MODERN CONSERVATISM

A Literary History, 1945–2008

BRYAN M. SANTIN
Concordia University Irvine

Shaftesbury Road, Cambridge CB2 8EA, United Kingdom

One Liberty Plaza, 20th Floor, New York, NY 10006, USA

477 Williamstown Road, Port Melbourne, VIC 3207, Australia

314–321, 3rd Floor, Plot 3, Splendor Forum, Jasola District Centre, New Delhi – 110025, India

103 Penang Road, #05–06/07, Visioncrest Commercial, Singapore 238467

Cambridge University Press is part of Cambridge University Press & Assessment, a department of the University of Cambridge.

We share the University's mission to contribute to society through the pursuit of education, learning and research at the highest international levels of excellence.

www.cambridge.org
Information on this title: www.cambridge.org/9781108932202

DOI: 10.1017/9781108961974

© BryanM. Santin 2021

This publication is in copyright. Subject to statutory exception and to the provisions of relevant collective licensing agreements, no reproduction of any part may take place without the written permission of Cambridge University Press & Assessment.

First published 2021
First paperback edition 2023

A catalogue record for this publication is available from the British Library

Library of Congress Cataloging-in-Publication data
NAMES: Santin, Bryan Michael, author.
TITLE: Postwar American fiction and the rise of modern conservatism : a literary history, 1945–2008 / Bryan M. Santin, Concordia University Irvine.
DESCRIPTION: Cambridge, United Kingdom ; New York, NY : Cambridge University Press, 2021. | Series: Cambridge studies in American literature and culture ; [186] | Includes bibliographical references and index.
IDENTIFIERS: LCCN 2020046991 (print) | LCCN 2020046992 (ebook) | ISBN 9781108832656 (hardback) | ISBN 9781108961974 (ebook)
SUBJECTS: LCSH: American fiction – 20th century – History and criticism. | Conservatism in literature. | Right and left (Political science) in literature. | Politics and literature – United States – History – 20th century. | Conservatism – United States – History – 20th century. | United States – Politics and government – 20th century. | United States – Intellectual life – 20th century.
CLASSIFICATION: LCC PS374.C59 S26 2021 (print) | LCC PS374.C59 (ebook) | DDC 813/.54093581–dc23
LC record available at https://lccn.loc.gov/2020046991
LC ebook record available at https://lccn.loc.gov/2020046992

ISBN 978-1-108-83265-6 Hardback
ISBN 978-1-108-93220-2 Paperback

Cambridge University Press & Assessment has no responsibility for the persistence or accuracy of URLs for external or third-party internet websites referred to in this publication and does not guarantee that any content on such websites is, or will remain, accurate or appropriate.

For my wife, Julianne

Contents

Acknowledgments

Thanks, first and foremost, to the staff at Cambridge University Press, particularly Ray Ryan and Leonard Cassuto. They believed in this book and their feedback and guidance have made its publication possible. I am also grateful to my scholarly mentors at the University of Notre Dame who offered advice and critical insight at various stages of this project: Sandra Gustafson, Kate Marshall, Matthew Wilkens, Michael Zuckert, and Elliott Visconsi. Thanks also to my colleagues at Concordia University Irvine, whose supportive fellowship sustained me throughout the revision process, particularly John Norton, Kristen Schmidt, Katharine Borst, Philip Broadbent, Jessica Danger, Camelia Raghinaru, Kerri Tom, and Keith Garton. I am grateful to two provosts at Concordia University Irvine, Peter Senkbeil and Scott Ashmon, who authorized multiple faculty research grants for me to finish this project.

Finally, always, and impossibly, I am thankful to my parents, Michele and Bryan, and to my entire family.

Introduction

American Fiction and Movement Conservatism

By the second decade of the twenty-first century, the robust linkage between highbrow literary fiction and progressive liberalism was virtually axiomatic. In a 2014 cover story for *National Review*, "Let Your Right Brain Run Free," Adam Bellow, son of Saul Bellow, exemplified the typical conservative lament when faced with this fact. Unusually, though, Bellow transformed his complaint that a liberal ethos dominates the major institutions of the US literary establishment into an argument for why "conservative fiction" should be "the next front in the culture war" (A. Bellow, 26). Using the left-brain/right-brain metaphor, Bellow claimed that for too long "conservatives have favored the rational left brain at the expense of the right," making the proverbial conservative mind "hyper-developed in one respect, completely undeveloped in another" (30). By the left side of the conservative mind, Bellow meant the postwar creation of "a network of think tanks, foundations, magazines, and publishing houses" that were the institutional and intellectual underpinnings of the modern conservative movement (30). To grow the right side, Bellow believed, conservatives essentially ought to recreate that massive organizational effort to produce American literature instead of political power: "We need our own writing programs, fellowships, prizes, and so forth. We need to build a feeder system so that the cream can rise to the top, and also make an end run around the gate-keepers of the liberal establishment" (30). With partisan rhetorical flourish, Bellow predicated that fiction might very well become "the beating heart of the new counterculture" (29). My book is concerned not with Bellow's improbable predication of a new conservative literary counterculture, but with the implicit literary-historical assumptions which formed the foundation of his prophecy regarding the use of literature to acquire prestige. In other words, how did it become such a widespread cultural assumption that highbrow postwar US fiction was so tightly associated with liberalism, and how has that assumption distorted contemporary perceptions of American literary history? Essentially, the aim of *Postwar American Fiction and the Rise of Modern Conservatism* is not just to unravel the perception that highbrow literature is a natural, virtually inexorable, ally of post-sixties progressive liberalism, but also to show how that connection is a historically contingent development shaped in part by deeper arguments within movement conservatism about the purpose and acquisition of literary cultural capital.

An influential conservative intellectual and editor best known for guiding several controversial conservative books to publication – including Dinesh D'Souza's *Illiberal Education* (1991), Richard Herrnstein and Charles Murray's *The Bell Curve* (1994), and Jonah Goldberg's *Liberal Fascism* (2008) – Bellow tells a familiar story of how post-sixties liberalism and highbrow fiction came to be interwoven that is decidedly flawed, but it is precisely his story's flaws that illuminate the problem. Bellow's story is straightforward and causally mechanistic: Never truly investing much time or resources into postwar American literature, members of William F. Buckley, Jr.'s "conservative movement" worked incessantly to attain power via the Republican Party. Bellow assumes that the intersection between postwar literature and politics was a dynamic debate, to be sure, but one whose dynamism was largely between major institutions, writers, critics, and scholars on the liberal and Left side of the political spectrum. The modern American Right, largely indifferent to aesthetics and devoid of agency in the realm of high culture, was the static background to an intellectually rich and vibrant foreground of argumentation and debate. However, Bellow's story indicates a basic misconception of two different, though connected, historical phenomena: the postwar conservative movement's early paradoxical orientation toward highbrow literature vis-à-vis race, and several major literary writers' own evolving understanding of modern American conservatism. Indeed, one of my central claims is that while a variety of factors have shaped the aesthetic-political tastes that undergird much of the post-1945 US literary field, these tastes cannot be sufficiently understood without a better, more rigorous contextualization of the rise of modern conservatism and its evolving positons on race.

In its attempt to contextualize the important relationship between American literature and modern conservatism, this book steers away from the tempting, though ultimately fruitless, question: Whither is "conservative fiction" in the postwar United States? Since its inception in the wake of World War II, the modern conservative movement in the United States has rarely, if ever, been viewed as an important factor in postwar American literature, especially prose fiction. This typical viewpoint is persuasive if one treats postwar conservatism as a uniform bloc of writers and thinkers clustered around the influential magazine *National Review* and its founder William F. Buckley, Jr., whose early rise to fame before the launch of *National Review* (November 1955) was due to two controversial books: one arguing that students were being indoctrinated into secular collectivism at his alma mater Yale University (*God and Man at Yale*, 1951), and the other asserting that Joseph McCarthy's crusade against supposed communists in the United States was not just defensible but commendable (*McCarthy and His Enemies*, 1954). As Macel D. Ezell pointed out in *Unequivocal Americanism: Right-Wing Novels in the Cold War Era* (1977), the first book-length study investigating the intersection between postwar conservatism and American fiction: "Imaginative literature constitutes only a small part of the mass of right-wing materials published in the Cold War era. . . . This is in keeping with the very limited number of novelists who publicly identify with right-wing causes" (1). While organizing *National Review*'s fifth anniversary celebration, Ezell notes, Buckley advertised a formal dinner in a fall sixties issue by listing the names of prominent conservatives who would be in attendance. He named only two self-identified "conservative" fiction writers: John Dos Passos and Taylor Caldwell (1). When *National Review* launched the "Conservative Book Club" in 1964, just one of the twenty-nine sponsors, Dos Passos, was a fiction writer (1). Though a valuable piece of early literary analysis on the modern conservative movement, Ezell's book reproduced a flawed assumption regarding the philosophical coherence of postwar conservatism: That Buckley's effort at *National Review* to combine traditionalists, ultra-capitalists, and aggressive cold warriors was a natural synthesis of compatible positions, producing an ultraorthodox metric for aesthetic judgment. Until the veritable explosion of historiographic scholarship on postwar conservatism in the American academy beginning in the last decade of the twentieth century, it was routine for scholars to emphasize the conservative movement's ideological rigidity, intellectual shallowness, and as a corollary, its comparative irrelevance within the sphere of American culture.[1] But in casting movement conservatism as a monolithic intellectual undertaking spawned by *National Review*, earlier literary scholars such as Ezell tended to construct aesthetic categories that produced rather anemic inquiries concerned with defining "true" conservative writers as understood through the narrow aperture of an ideologically inflexible definition of modern conservatism.

I should stress that I do not regard Ezell's accounts, or even more recent accounts, of this relationship between the chimera "conservative fiction" and the conservative movement itself as poorly argued or simply unpersuasive. On the contrary, the paltry accounts of American conservatism and literature correspond to, what seems in the current discourse like, an already tenuous relationship. Writing for the *Daily Beast* in 2012, James McGirk sums up well, if somewhat hyperbolically, the longstanding consensus explanation for the lack of "serious literary fiction for Republicans," stating that the American "right has been radicalized by a ridiculous ideology that would be outrageous if expressed in literature" (McGirk). McGirk assumes that conservatives understand novels as political tools that are different in degree but not in kind to, say, a campaign stump speech or a late-night Fox News diatribe. The cluster of assumptions that underpin such a viewpoint looks something like this: Conservative fiction in the postwar United States is produced by conservative authors who meet the peculiar definitional criteria of "conservative" if they have been accepted by, or positively affiliated with, the modern conservative movement. When conceptualized in this way, the absence of a significant body of conservative fiction appears so self-evident that it hardly requires further research.

In his more recent scholarly essay "The Plight of Conservative Literature" published in the celebrated anthology *A New Literary History of America* (2010), Michael Kimmage runs into precisely this kind of definitional dead-end. Kimmage conceptualizes the "conservative novel" as a work that not only essentially adheres to the conservative movement's sacred trinity of traditionalism, capitalism, and anti-communism, but one which also has had an impact on the movement itself and American culture more broadly. "The challenge, for conservatives," Kimmage writes, "has been to sponsor literature as a living branch of contemporary culture. The conservative emphasis on precedent and experience, the anti-utopian cast of the conservative mind, leads conservative authors to autobiography, to a nonfiction reckoning with the dilemmas of history, politics, and the self" (949). It is only when one enlarges the category of literature to include highly stylized memoirs like Whittaker Chambers's *Witness* (1952) that fictional techniques can be said to "have had substantial influence on the conservative movement" (951). Kimmage points out, in other words, that postwar movement conservatives have not been able to rally around American novelists who are at once "authentically" conservative, culturally relevant, and canonically important according to literary critics and professional scholars. Kimmage provides us, then, with an account of what seems self-evident in contemporary literary studies: postwar conservatives have not been able to marshal support for their movement in the semiautonomous field of high literary culture. Insofar as "literature" retains any aesthetic-cultural value in this account, the phrase "conservative literature" approaches the oxymoronic. It appears, in short, that American literature has not been very important to the emergence of postwar conservatism, and that postwar conservatism has not had much to do with "serious" highbrow American literature.

My overarching argument hinges on the premise that this standard conceptualization of "conservative fiction" is not so much wrong as categorically reductive, which is to say grounded in a set of discourse norms that discourage critics from interrogating the dominant narrative which has, by now, ossified into the commonplace notion that modern American conservatism has little to do with highbrow literature. By returning, in the early chapters of this book, to the origins of the conservative movement and reexamining the importance its thinkers placed on American literature as an ambivalent form of cultural capital, I construct a new contextual account of post-1945 literary production that clarifies not only the stale category of "conservative fiction" but, more importantly, a few of the basic assumptions regarding the cultural politics of postwar American fiction. For my purposes, then, the category of "conservative fiction" is not an especially interesting or fruitful object of scholarly analysis in itself; rather, it is one of the seemingly insignificant stray threads that unravels the fabric holding together the discourse of contemporary literary politics in which highbrow literary fiction seems like a natural ally of progressive liberalism. Toward the end of this book, I show that this prevailing notion that "conservative fiction" is just another media arm of the conservative movement – that is, the view that novels such as Ayn Rand's *Atlas Shrugged* or Tim LaHaye and Jerry B. Jenkins's *Left Behind* series belong to the same insular conservative media universe as Rupert Murdoch's Fox News Channel – is a rather recent invention. During the early years of modern conservatism, several of the movement's most prominent intellectuals did not equate "conservative fiction" with literary works that were essentially propagandistic vehicles for partisan political issues. The use of literature for blatant political activism, traditionalist conservatives such as Russell Kirk, Whittaker Chambers, Robert Nisbet, and Peter Viereck believed, was a trademark of revolutionary socialism. For them, to posit a relationship between one slice of Western literature called "conservative" and another slice called "leftist" would amount to a false dichotomy. Although they certainly recognized a genre like Soviet realism as leftist literature, they did not acknowledge a one-for-one correspondence with a similar body of "conservative literature."

For conservative thinkers such as Kirk and Chambers, to regard conservative literature as just another instrument of partisan politics would have been to accept the sociopolitical framework of the Left. Instead, they identified the "great" works of Western literature in general, and American literature in particular, as de facto conservative in their depth, complexity, and tragic profundity.[2] According to these conservatives, while leftist literature aimed to cause the ideological scales to fall from the eyes of proletarians around the world, great Western literature went about its noble task of interrogating what T.S. Eliot called the "permanent things," those enduring human problems whose complexity had always exceeded – and always would – the shallowness of political parties, electoral campaigns, and all of the trivial accouterments of redistributing formal power in society (Eliot, 76). As the preeminent theorist of traditionalist conservatism in the fifties, Russell Kirk and his allies defined "conservatism" as a broad mood or disposition that did not privilege partisan politics, and they placed a high value on literature, embracing its formal nuances and complexities, which manifested in their championing of literary titans like Dostoevsky, Hawthorne, Eliot, and Faulkner. By interrogating the "nature of man" in light of the immense upheavals of the first half of the twentieth century, these authors were not writing doctrinaire conservative literature so much as writing "great literature" that inevitably expressed conservative themes. The most important theme to be gleaned in the postwar moment, for Kirk and others, was the rupture of tradition ushered in by the radical changes wrought by totalitarianism, most notably Soviet Communism and German Nazism, both of which they saw as monstrous ideological twins of the collectivist Left, and the rising threat of a uniquely leftist "American Fascism." Thinking within the broad historical terms furnished by the Western liberal arts tradition, conservative traditionalists insisted on the superiority of high literary culture to guard against the looming totalitarian terror unleashed, in their minds, by state-enforced progressive liberalism – most notably and problematically, the civil rights movement's post-*Brown* v. *Board* fight for desegregation and full enfranchisement. Ultimately, though, the early conservative movement's commitment to the cultural capital associated with formally difficult literature was inextricably bound up with a staunch defense of Jim Crow segregation, and the conservative movement's later shift in racial politics (from de facto support for segregationist policies to colorblind, neoliberal individualism) triggered a deeply conflicted aesthetic shift in conservatives' perceptions of literary value from modernist literary fiction to mass-market commercial fiction.

By focusing on the historical development of the conservative movement's ambivalence about highbrow literature as a form of cultural capital, I hope to avoid another reductive line of argumentation based on the notion that postwar American conservatives have used the discourse of high literary culture *purely* for cynical and meretricious ends. In that kind of account, the post–World War II conservative movement was, at its core, little more than a group of revanchist culture warriors raging against postwar liberalism's expansion of rights, especially in relation to racial minorities. Instead, I argue that the political strivings of conservatives – some motivated cynically, others sincerely – cannot be so easily separated from their long-time admiration for highbrow literature. In my retelling, then, conservatives are not one-dimensional, diabolical antagonists in postwar literary and cultural history, but actors in an under-theorized narrative of American literary history who formed alliances and shored up ideological disputes in ways that estranged them, at times unwittingly, from the very forms of highbrow literature they sought to preserve and protect.

Far from being apathetic about the culture capital afforded by literature in the early postwar period, movement conservatives had not only routinely tried to recruit serious novelists to bolster their movement's intellectual and cultural reputation; they had also positioned themselves as the true guardians of highbrow culture, American literature in particular, with a hybrid discourse that combined early twentieth-century New Humanism of the Irving Babbitt variety, New Criticism, Southern Agrarianism, and a neo-Burkean traditionalism that looked favorably upon Jim Crow segregation. Beginning in the sixties, though, conservatives found it increasingly difficult to position themselves simultaneously as the disinterested champions of complex, morally ambivalent literature *and* as the populist defenders of aggrieved white innocence, laissez-faire capitalism, and aggressive American nationalism. By the end of the century, movement conservatives never stopped sincerely thinking of themselves as the custodians of American high culture – as their fierce, though sometimes unsophisticated, defenses of the Western canon attested – but their determination to create a constellation of partisan organizations and policy institutions while deploying a mixture of neoliberalism and racially coded populism distanced conservatives ever further from the literary institutions, major novelists, and even habits of mind that nourished highbrow literature. In my account, then, the roughly half-century shift in the literary tastes of American conservatives does not simply unmask conservatives as cynical, bad faith actors (though, to be clear, some polemical conservatives occupied just those roles); instead, I show that they were largely members of a hybrid, political-philosophical insurgent movement that deployed concepts of literary prestige and cultural capital in contradictory ways over time that formally mimicked their unique ideology of neo-aristocratic traditionalism, reactionary cultural populism, and neoliberal capitalism.

Scholarly Context

Before delving any deeper into the nuances of my overarching argument, I need to contextualize the extant scholarship on contemporary American fiction, especially as the field intersects with postwar American politics and the rise of movement conservatism. Although this book's *raison d'être* is that few wide-ranging, chronological accounts of postwar fiction and movement conservatism exist, I do not mean to imply that there is not already a great deal of valuable scholarship on specific dimensions of literature and "conservatism," an expansive term that encompasses everything from broad definitions of conservative aesthetic forms to specific, real-world conservative politics. Specifically, scholars have examined roughly four (sometimes overlapping) areas: first, the well-established connection between conservative, even authoritarian, politics and the reactionary modernism of writers such as T.S. Eliot and Ezra Pound; second, the emergence of the reactionary branch of New Criticism and its members' influence on conservative writers such as Flannery O'Connor and their institutional role in professionalizing post-1945 literary studies; third, the ways in which the post-seventies conservative Christian resurgence realigned parts of the literary and cultural fields while much of the Western world was supposedly undergoing a process of public secularization; fourth, the occasional analysis of American conservative writers or movement conservative ideology in literary scholarship that examines the relationship between American fiction and postwar progressive liberalism.

Since the chapters that follow deal mainly with American culture after World War II, the latter two areas of scholarship are especially important to this book.[3] Thus far, the most systematic scholarly work on postwar American fiction and a specific dimension of the modern conservative movement has emerged from the subfield of religion and literature. In the same year that the philosopher Charles Taylor published *A Secular Age* (2007) – his magisterial tome critiquing the "subtraction story" at the heart of modernity's "master narrative of secularization," which mistakenly contends that religious authority and experiences have simply receded in the face of Enlightenment reason and technology – Lawrence Buell inquired into the under-theorized nature of conservative Christianity in the field of literary studies in ways that echoed Taylor (Taylor, 530). Was American literary studies "in danger of being 'left behind' like the characters in LaHaye and Jenkins' [*Left Behind*] series," Buell asked, pointing out that one of the most conspicuous disparities between contemporary literary studies and "the drift of mainstream US culture is that religiocentric frames of explanation started to go out of fashion at about the same time evangelical Christianity began to seize control of public culture to a degree unprecedented since colonial times" (32). In the wake of Buell's warning, more scholarship began to emerge that focused wholly or in part on the intersection of evangelical Christianity, conservative American politics, and contemporary fiction.[4] Undoubtedly, though, the most significant piece of book-length scholarship to emerge in this area has been Christopher Douglas's *If God Meant to Interfere: American Literature and the Rise of the Christian Right* (Cornell University Press, 2016). In the best book-length treatment of postwar fiction and political conservatism to date, Douglas argues that major liberal-leaning novelists were routinely confounded by the post-seventies conservative Christian resurgence because of the way this resurgence functioned "both in terms of a religion extending its universal and metaphysical claims to everyone and a kind of descent-based cultural identity within the broader frame of American multicultural reality" (135). Declaring that the conservative Christian resurgence "has been the unrecognized religious context for US literary production since the 1970s," Douglas traces a surprising network of linkages between the Christian Right, postmodernism, and multiculturalism (3). The Christian Right, Douglas contends, should not be viewed as a movement that stood in simple opposition to either postmodernism or multiculturalism; rather, evangelical-based Christian conservatism routinely borrowed intellectual forms and concepts from these seemingly progressive movements. The double register of American conservative religious discourse – that is, a universal theology open to everyone *and* a specific, white cultural identity – produced the very conditions that allowed the conservative Christian resurgence to become complexly intertwined with postmodernism and multiculturalism. This book concurs with Douglas on several points, especially the notion that conservative discourse often speaks in a variety of double registers, and aims to build on his groundbreaking scholarship in a few ways. Most significantly, I add a fuller chronological exploration of the relationship between postwar fiction and modern conservatism, stretching from the World War II era to the early twenty-first century. In addition, while Douglas focuses almost exclusively on liberal-leaning novelists, I analyze novelists, critics, and intellectuals who are affiliated to varying degrees with both postwar liberalism and conservatism.

Notably, the methodological principle of selection that undergirds the catalogue of liberal-leaning novelists that Douglas draws upon in *If God Meant to Interfere* dovetails with the last area of literary scholarship

I outline earlier: the intersection between postwar American fiction and progressive liberalism. Over the past few decades, when literary scholars have examined the relationship between post-1945 literature and politics, they have often concentrated on the relationship between literature and politics *on the political Left*, and only occasionally included a writer affiliated with movement conservatism.[5] However, perhaps the most fascinating way that postwar American conservatism has manifested in recent literary scholarship is through, what I would describe as, a kind of shadow presence. Without identifying and analyzing it in significant historiographic depth, modern conservatism is sometimes tacitly invoked when scholars write about, and against, the deep entrenchment of white supremacy, neoliberalism, hetero-normativity, patriarchy, and bellicose American foreign policy. In these accounts, the apparent absence of modern American conservatism is a pseudo-absence that recalls the discourse surrounding Victorian sexuality in Michel Foucault's famous account of the "repressive hypothesis": ostensibly repressed but constantly debated and discussed in coded language (*History of Sexuality*, 12–15).

For instance, in their influential 2005 essay "Do You Believe in Magic? Literary Thinking and the New Left," Sean McCann and Michael Szalay reconstruct a persuasive narrative about the political implications of post-sixties American literature by emphasizing a constellation of aesthetic disputes between the technocratic rationality of the old New Deal Left and the anti-authoritarianism of the New Left. Pinpointing 1967 and its much-publicized "Summer of Love," McCann and Szalay argue that this pivotal year marked "a decisive turning point in the history of oppositional politics in the US – a shift, years in the making, away from the organizational thinking of the Old Left to the meliorism of mainstream liberalism" (436). Essentially, for McCann and Szalay, organizational collective politics receded in the face of an increasingly individualistic culture of personal freedom, for the New Left put its faith in "the spontaneous, the symbolic, and ultimately, the magical" (436). Noting that major American novels since the social upheavals of the sixties have tended to echo the New Left's critique of bureaucratic faith embedded in the ideology of the Old Left, McCann and Szalay argue that writers such as Don DeLillo, Thomas Pynchon, and Toni Morrison embraced not just an anti-government stance but an anti-politics stance characterized by "a fascination with the limits of calculation [that ran] hand in hand with a sacralization of the sublimely irrational," leading to the implicit thematic notion that "the most appropriate attitude toward mundane political conflict or social tension is the effort to transcend it" (449; 447). While they provide valuable and penetrating insights, McCann and Szalay reproduce a familiar framework in which the literary events and debates that have truly mattered since the sixties have centered on intra-ideological disputes between post–New Deal liberals and various strands of the New Left, even though the heart of their argument regarding the possibility of progressive political change depends on an implicit shift in the tactics and strategies of movement conservatism. As Adam Kelly points out, McCann and Szalay read "postmodern experimentation as [a form of] proto-libertarianism" that is either ineffective at challenging the rising neoliberal ethos or, worse yet, perhaps even congruent with capitalist exploitation and thus complicit in the eventual rise of Reaganite American capitalism (50). Tacitly, McCann and Szalay accuse major American novelists such as Pynchon and Morrison of not fully grasping how conservative modes of oppression have shifted over time, even though McCann and Szalay do not offer a substantial theorization of this conservative shift themselves. As in other influential books of literary scholarship on the postwar era, the legibility of American literature here posits a sociopolitical background that obscures, while not totally erasing, the ascent of modern conservatism in the second half of the twentieth century.

Szalay reiterates this framework in his otherwise brilliant book *Hip Figures: A Literary History of the Democratic Party* (2012), wherein he argues that the concept of hipness was an essential element of the postwar Democratic Party as it strove to reconcile the white, liberal professional-managerial class and African Americans. Forged most conspicuously in postwar American fiction, Szalay claims, this "range of predominately white fantasies about hip have animated the secret imagination of postwar liberalism and, more concretely, organized the Democratic Party's efforts to redress 'the brutal legacy of slavery and Jim Crow'" (2). As an introductory framing device to the book, though, Szalay notes that Republicans have always remained "attached at their grass roots to the modern conservative movement crystallized by Barry Goldwater, committed to consolidating white supremacy, concentrating wealth, and privatizing the New Deal welfare state" (1). While Szalay is not entirely mistaken, the static, unambiguous portrait of conservative ideology he draws upon as he moves from the immediate postwar period to the end of the century lacks a certain degree of historiographic nuance. As in his joint article with McCann, Szalay's *Hip Figures* locates too many of the causal mechanisms of post-1945 political and cultural change within the intra-ideological conflicts of modern liberalism and the Left. Since Szalay ignores the extant historiography on the post–World War II American conservative movement, the causal dimension of his major claim about sociopolitical change – that is, the role race played in the fracture of New Deal liberalism in the sixties – narrows his gaze to one story with one hydra-headed character: the political Left. Like a tragic figure undone by his own virtue, the splintering American Left in Szalay's narrative destroys itself in pursuit of equality for racial minorities and the oppressed, but gains (partly hollow) forms of cultural distinction and prestige through its association with hipness, coolness, and highbrow literary fiction.[6] Inadvertently, the American Right plays the role of the antagonistic usurper who undeservingly enjoys the fruits of the slain noble hero at play's end in the form of real political power. Essentially, Szalay echoes Todd Gitlin's appealing, though ultimately misleading, quip that American liberals and leftists marched on English departments in the eighties while conservatives marched on Washington and took the White House (*Twilight of Common Dreams*, 126). The reigning liberal cultural politics of postwar fiction, Szalay's account implies, are essentially the compensatory byproduct of modern American liberalism's political failure to marry racially progressive policies with the electoral victories that would have produced formal political power and, perhaps, challenged the looming neoliberal orthodoxy of post-sixties American politics.

Essentially, I wish to highlight how the scholarly frameworks of McCann and Szalay, though valuable in many respects, are at times rooted in a set of under-theorized literary-sociological questions that revolve around postwar movement conservatism. Moreover, the largely tacit way these questions are formulated give them that uncanny spectral "shadow presence" I mentioned earlier. In *Cool Characters: Irony and American Fiction*, Lee Konstantinou illuminates my fundamental point when he critiques McCann and Szalay by noting that in their accounts "culture takes on a mystifying – and arguably mystified – power to block 'real' politics" (34). Similarly, Walter Benn Michaels engages in a comparable kind of mystical reification, Konstantinou notes, when Michaels declares that progressive political "culture" – which Michaels defines as the liberal "dramas of inclusion and exclusion" about individual identity that leave class-based inequality intact – has morphed into "a primary technology for disarticulating difference from disagreement . . . [and] for disarticulating difference from inequality" (Konstantinou, 34; Michaels, 16–17). It is ironic, Konstantinou concludes, grouping together McCann, Szalay, and Michaels as post-countercultural critics, that in "a discourse that sometimes seems to hope to dispense with culture in the name of politics, culture can take on a ghostly power" (34). What I want to stress is that the specter of "culture" haunting this post-countercultural discourse has a great deal to do with tacit assumptions about movement conservatism. These post-countercultural scholars, in essence, are accusing liberal-leaning novelists and progressive intellectuals of misunderstanding that a particular strategy (New Leftist-inspired symbolic rebellion on the level of culture) that is often used to attack one form of oppression (explicit midcentury manifestations of racism or sexism) unwittingly strengthened another form of oppression (the solidification of neoliberal economic structures that perpetuate inequality). But another, more revealing, way to put this accusation is to say that most New Leftist–inspired attacks on one strain of postwar movement conservatism (traditionalism as manifested in the early aftermath of World War II) strengthened another strain of postwar movement conservatism later in the century (Reaganite neoliberalism). The problem for this brand of post-countercultural discourse, and a small but significant gap in contemporary literary studies more broadly, is that its practitioners do not offer sustained theoretical accounts of movement conservatism in the relatively autonomous field of postwar American culture.[7] My key intervention is not to stake out an exaggerated role for the influence of movement conservatism on American literature, but merely to point out that the American Right has not received the amount of serious attention from literary scholars that its role in postwar American politics and culture seems to suggest it should. In short, some of the best extant literary scholarship has examined the intersection between American literature and postwar liberalism to produce good models for showing how the cultural and political fields have impacted one another. By expanding our focus to the intersection between American literature and postwar conservatism, I hope to contribute to the production of such models.

Imagining the American Right

The impetus for this book begins with a crucial hypothetical question: if the basic trajectory of the postwar literary field saw highbrow fiction become increasingly associated with progressive liberal politics, even though the simultaneous trajectory of postwar American politics saw the fall of New Deal liberalism and the rise of a historically unique form of modern conservatism, then what insights about literary taste and perceptions of aesthetic value could a book-length reconstruction of these dual literary-historiographic narratives produce? Since that question posits a complex relationship between the literary field and the larger sociopolitical context, this book adopts a literary-sociological method inspired partly by the sociology of Pierre Bourdieu. Famous for radically historicizing the sacred aura of high culture, Bourdieu argues that the seemingly untainted "aesthetic disposition" is determined by a class-structured society that produces relatively autonomous fields of social practice that are themselves preconditions for the production, exchange, and consumption of various kinds of "capital" – for example, economic, social, and cultural (*Distinction*, xxiv–xxv). However, this book's deepest influences cannot simply be traced to Bourdieu alone, but to a recent line of sociology-minded literary scholars that includes John Guillory, Alan Liu, Mark McGurl, and James English who do not regard Bourdieu's *oeuvre* as inerrant sociological scripture. While Bourdieu's system of thought can be reductive in relation to the literary field, English points out in *The Economy of Prestige: Prizes, Awards, and the Circulation of Culture Value*, it has nevertheless been a key theoretical system in "the more general attempt over the last two decades to rethink the relationships among culture, economics, and sociology" (8). The clearest benefit of this method is not only that it forestalls cruder theoretical approaches that posit a reflective, mechanistic relationship between some reified "base" (socioeconomic reality) and mirror-like objects in a passive "superstructure" (literary texts); it empowers scholars to understand literary texts as carriers of cultural capital that circulate within the semiautonomous field of culture, to be sure, but also other fields such as economics and politics, ultimately producing strong explanatory frameworks that can account for unanticipated cultural shifts in literary tastes or artistic prestige.[8]

Within this strain of literary-sociological scholarship, two specific scholarly accounts have furnished the most useful forms of analysis for my present study: McGurl's examination of how literary prestige became embedded in the "art-novel" and Guillory's interrogation of how cultural capital operated implicitly in the canon wars. In tracing how the formally difficult modernist novel came to be conceived of as art, and "thus as a bearer of cultural capital," McGurl argues that one of the most notable features of the art-novel was that its roots in "some of the aristocratic and intellectualist emphases of the romance tradition" caused it to privilege "*intellectual* virtue – smarts – above all other forms of virtue" (*The Novel Art*, 29; 12). Mastering formal aesthetic difficulty, then, became a key way to gain a sense of cultural distinction for an intellectual elite within the rising "professional-managerial class," whose bourgeois professionalism suggested "that there might be pleasure *in* work and, specifically, in the kind of intellectual work that reading the difficult modernist text is said to require" (*The Novel Art*, 11). Essentially, McGurl's study of the modernist art-novel sets the stage for the early chapters of *Postwar American Fiction and the Rise of Modern Conservatism*, since his socio-literary history anticipates precisely how movement conservatives in the mid-twentieth century would conceptualize the value and purpose of highbrow literature. If, as Thorstein Veblen famously theorized, someone born into the leisure-class could prove his inherent nobility by engaging in the "conspicuous leisure" signaled by studying the humanities, then McGurl notes that the rise of the professional-managerial class blurred the distinction between aesthetic waste and aesthetic intellectual labor (Veblen, 257; *The Novel Art*, 17). In the early stages of their movement, as I detail in later chapters, when William F. Buckley and Russell Kirk were championing novelists like Faulkner and O'Connor, or when Whittaker Chambers was praising the sublime difficulty of James Joyce's *Finnegans Wake*, postwar conservatives were essentially valuing literary texts for the quasi-Veblenian sense of honor and distinction that resided within the category of "literature," since it was associated with a form of intellectual labor that could justify the political power of an elite, capitalist ruling class. In the later stages of the conservative movement toward the end of the twentieth century, as John Guillory argues in his seminal work *Cultural Capital: The Problem of Literary Canon Formation*, this neo-aristocratic conception of literary value would prove to be at the heart of the conservative movement's grievance about the supposed "devaluation" of the Western canon. While interrogating the frequent slippage in conservative discourse between two uses of the word of "culture" – at times, an American "national culture" existing within the imagined paradigm of Western civilization *and*, at other times, a refined aesthetic disposition that allows one to possess the knowledge capital of highbrow "culture" – Guillory makes a noteworthy point:

> The apparent failure of the university's cultural project of constituting a national culture elicits from the New Right the clamorous demand for a return to what was after all the *bourgeois* school, the institution enabling the old bourgeoisie to identify itself culturally by acquiring the cultural capital formerly restricted to the aristocratic or clerical estates. This capital consisted of nothing other than the "great works" of Western civilization. (Guillory, 41)

For Guillory, the upshot of this insight is that the modern conservative position in the canon wars was founded on a deep contradiction. Reaganite conservatism "rest[ed] on the unshakeable foundation of the free market," Guillory writes, but it was "the market itself which produces the effect of cultural flight" (46). Since the profit-oriented "professional-managerial class has made the correct assessment that . . . the reading of great works is not worth the investment of very much time or money," Guillory concludes, then the conservative lament over "the devaluation of the humanities curriculum is in reality a decline in its *market* value" (46). Ironically, movement conservatives were bemoaning the growing obsolescence of an older form of cultural capital within the very neoliberal economic agenda that, insofar as any one movement can be held responsible at all for large-scale socioeconomic shifts, they themselves helped to actualize.

Although one obvious argumentative move here would be to cast the postwar conservative movement as rife with either cynical hustlers or ideological fanatics, I want to insist that neither of those caricatures would truly illuminate the complex relationship between conservative perceptions of literary value and conservative politics. At the argumentative core of this book is the notion that shifting conservative visions of literary value reveal an aesthetic antinomy between high culture and low culture that registered and mediated the deeper foundational antinomy structuring movement conservatism itself: the stable social order of neo-Burkean traditionalism and the creative destruction of free-market capitalism. Initially, traditionalist intellectuals spearheaded the early postwar conservative movement, and they advanced a market-based economic agenda that aligned with the wealthiest class, the byproduct of which prompted conservatives to speak the neo-aristocratic language of both elite wealth and elite high culture. As Peter Kolozi points out in *Conservatives Against Capitalism: From the Industrial Revolution to Globalization*, traditionalist conservatives believed, of course, that social inequality was merely a reflection of natural human inequality, but they also "believed that the organizing principle of capitalist hierarchy founded exclusively on economic laissez-faire was debased" (11). What united traditionalist conservatives across generations, Kolozi argues, "is their belief that laissez-faire capitalism has [usually] undermined an established social hierarchy governed by the virtuous or the excellent," continually causing traditionalists to search for ways "to reconfigure the ruling class and cultural values away from the exclusive rule of economic calculation" (11). Although Kolozi does not explore the literary field at any length, his work sheds light on my socio-literary contention that what traditionalist conservatives saw as a hierarchy of the virtuous elite was founded on a fantasy of literary cultural capital drawn from high culture.

By the mid-sixties, though, as more libertarian-minded conservative activists, intellectuals, and politicians increasingly tried to attract voters in earnest, movement conservatives began to configure a populist ideology with a different kind of language, the language of aggrieved rebellion on behalf of ordinary, God-fearing white Americans. The potential problem, of course, was that populism usually needs a villainous elite, a powerful faction or class that exercises power so unethically that it delegitimizes its fundamental authority to rule. Conservatives found a solution in the rhetorical construction of a supposedly monolithic "liberal cultural elite," a loose amalgamation of university intellectuals, activists, writers, and government officials who were arrogantly lording their power over the mass of ordinary Americans. As the political scientist Corey Robin notes, this solution illuminated the central "task of right-wing populism: to appeal to the mass without disrupting the power of [economic] elites or, more precisely to harness the energy of the mass in order to reinforce or restore the power of elites" (55). Fortunately for conservatives, this rhetorical strategy coincided with two other powerful social currents: the emancipatory activist movements of the sixties *and* a dramatic expansion of the professional-managerial class, a social faction – as Alvin Gouldner theorized in *The Future of Intellectuals and the Rise of the New Class* – which not only posed serious challenges to traditional leftist frameworks of class analysis but also made the conservative culture war legible and, for many people, convincing.[9]

I argue that by villainizing liberal cultural elites, postwar conservatives produced, in effect, an ambivalent double register in the discourse of conservative literary taste that sought to celebrate specific neo-aristocratic manifestations of cultural capital while viciously condemning newer, more progressive manifestations revolving around racial and ethnic diversity that were celebrated by those liberal elites. The former manifestation, which conservatives championed, is the kind of cultural capital associated, following Guillory's account, with the old bourgeoisie, its frequent association of high culture with whiteness, and the implicit corollary assumption that naturalized the marriage between political power and elite wealth; the latter, which conservatives condemned, is the kind of cultural capital associated with, what McGurl in *The Program Era* dubs, "high cultural pluralism," a style of creative writing which "joins the high literary values of modernism with a fascination with the experience of cultural difference and the authenticity of the ethnic voice" that American universities canonized in the wake of the emancipatory movements of the sixties (32). As I show throughout the book, one of the most remarkable and paradoxical features of this double register of taste operating within conservative discourse was how it both retained the mystique of the "aesthetic disposition" outlined by Bourdieu *and* deployed a quasi-Bourdieuan critique of the stereotypical liberal's quest to garner cultural capital. At times, conservatives would easily adopt the aesthetic disposition themselves when waxing philosophical about the sacredness of great literature, perfectly illustrating how the aesthetic disposition participates in "cultural consecration," a process which confers on high cultural objects "a sort of ontological promotion akin to transubstantiation" (Bourdieu, *Distinction*, xxix). But at other times, conservatives would just as quickly condemn liberal cultural elites for their hip affectation of high cultural forms, accusing liberals of consuming high culture precisely to affirm their supposed superiority over the vulgar, ordinary (conservative) masses, and thus legitimating their status and power through the sneaky aesthetic disposition of taste. When one reads, for instance, the barrage of criticism that conservatives leveled at the rapturous celebration of difficult literary texts by minority writers such as Toni Morrison, one can hear an echo of Bourdieu's famous critique that status accrues to those with the (politically) correct tastes: "Taste classifies, and it classifies the classifier" (*Distinction*, xxix). Because of their occasionally crude Bourdieuian approach, conservatives imagined that this liberal cultural elite operated in the institutions and organizations that produced and legitimated highbrow literature, especially the postwar American university and prize committees such as the Pulitzer Prize Board and the National Book Foundation. From the perspective of conservatives, these actors helped shape the literary field in politically meretricious ways, elevating literary texts for the wrong aesthetic-political reasons. By the onset of the twenty-first century, the ultimate effect was a vicious, ongoing cycle of *conservative self-exclusion* from the literary field of high culture that looked something like this: conservatives had created a robust collective identity around the notion that high literature was hopelessly written, criticized, and culturally consecrated by a liberal elite, which led conservatives to engage in a kind of quasi-rebellious self-removal from the literary field, while continually vocalizing their obsessive disdain for high literature, which in turn reinforced the notion that the literary field was not a viable vocational space for movement conservatives.[10]

In the chapters that follow, then, I narrate a story about how modern American conservatism detached itself – but only partially – from the field of highbrow literature. Over the second half of the twentieth century, movement conservatives shifted their orientation toward what Bourdieu calls collective belief in the "literary *illusio*" – that is, the fundamental, "originating adherence to the literary game which grounds belief in the *importance* or *interest* of literary fictions" (*Rules of Art*, 333). In the immediate postwar period, conservatives enthusiastically supported the *illusio* and the stakes of the highbrow literary game, imagining great works of genius to be repositories of unmediated aesthetic value, largely exempt from the desecration of both financial and cultural economies. In the aftermath of the sixties, though, conservatives could not sustain this unequivocal belief in the *illusio*, for in their eyes the literary field was increasingly controlled by a virtue-signaling, white liberal cultural elite who were transforming, in Bourdieu's words, "the literary or artistic enterprise into a cynical mystification or a conscious tricky" (*Rules of Art*, 274). Essentially, conservatives found themselves suspended between belief and disbelief in the *illusio*, "between the impulse to see art as a kind of Ponzi scheme and the impulse to preserve it as a place for out most trusting investments" (English, 216). On the one hand, conservatives never abandoned their T.S. Eliot–inspired fantasy that "literary culture is the site at which the most socially important beliefs and attitudes are produced, the site at which those beliefs and attitudes are generated which *unify* the culture" (Guillory, 152). As their perennial defenses of the Western canon attest, conservatives saw this process of cultural unification occurring in a literary cultural field which, in Bourdieu's famous phrase, represents "the economic world reversed" since it largely disdains mass popular praise and commercial success, ultimately presenting high culture as a superior reality untouched by the very free-market pressures that defined the increasingly dominant strain of modern American conservatism (*Field of Cultural Production*, 29). But, on the other hand, conservatives were disillusioned with the specific trajectory of post-sixties literary culture in the United States, conceptualizing it as a dubious liberal game of cultural competition – just another site, in other words, of hegemonic ideological struggle.

From the perspective of my sociological-literary account, we should reject the one-dimensional argument that the entire conservative movement cynically recognized that the discourse realm of highbrow literature was not the best social space to win political arguments, and that they ceded high culture to liberals once it no longer served their crass electoral interests. Instead, as they helped reshape the dominant political order away from New Deal liberalism, key members of the conservative movement continually switched registers between a sincere belief in the cultural capital generated by highbrow literature and an aggrieved disbelief in the cultural capital generated by the highbrow literature of a liberal-dominated literary field. By the end of the twentieth century, although the framework of this conservative double register would manifest itself most notably in the "canon wars" debate – that is, conservatives' sincere belief in the "great" literature of the past versus their cynical, mocking distrust of the contemporary literary field – it has a much deeper historical and philosophical remit in modern American conservatism than most scholarship has analyzed heretofore. I contend that the postwar conservative movement, though only one catalyst in a much larger set of socio-aesthetic catalysts, should be recognized as an under-theorized group of agents who contributed to the reshaping of normative assumptions about literary form, cultural capital, and high cultural prestige associated with literary fiction. To flesh out this literary history, I interrogate how major American novelists associated with liberalism and the Left (e.g., Ralph Ellison, James Baldwin, Thomas Pynchon, and Toni Morrison), major American novelists associated with various strains of the political Right (e.g., Flannery O'Connor, Norman Mailer, and Saul Bellow), and postwar novelists celebrated almost solely by modern conservatives (e.g., Ayn Rand, William F. Buckley, Jr., Tom Wolfe) registered the conservative movement's partial, though important, contribution to the realignment of the literary field, and how they responded to the American Right as site of political, cultural, and literary contestation. In approaching postwar American literary history in this way, I aim to reveal why movement conservatives at midcentury positioned themselves as elite traditionalists who supported Jim Crow segregation and defended high culture against the masses, but then after the sixties began to embrace both laissez-faire capitalism and coded racial populism in ways that generated the institutional conditions for the eventual presumed linkage between liberalism and highbrow literary fiction.

Throughout the postwar era, I demonstrate that the literary trope of "American Fascism" was one of the most salient ways in which anxieties surrounding both political and cultural capital manifested in postwar political and cultural debates, for it was a remarkably durable device deployed by a politically diverse group of novelists, including Rand, O'Connor, Baldwin, Mailer, Bellow, Pynchon, and Morrison. In terms of cultural currency, the trope of American Fascism peaked in the years between 1965 and 1972, arguably reaching its apex in 1968. After the Democratic Party campaign apparatus successfully portrayed Barry Goldwater as a quasi-fascist in 1964, politicians and critics from across the political spectrum – from staunch movement conservatives to Southern States' Rights segregationists to Cold War liberals to New Left student radicals – saw the utility of the uniquely potent political slur. Although historians and scholars have always highlighted how the label "fascist" was often pinned on conservatives in the sixties, many tend to overlook conservatives' similarly frequent usage of the epitaph.[11] As the New Deal coalition collapsed in the late sixties, and the authority of Cold War liberalism was undermined from forces on the Right and Left, the "fascist" insult functioned not as a precise term drawn from political theory, or as a reference to historical fascism, but as an all-purpose indicator of legitimacy or illegitimacy in the changing discourse of American society. Since Americans had never lived through the reign of an overt fascist government, the nature of the "fascist" accusation was almost always comparative: Ronald Reagan or Malcolm X was *like* a Nazi, by which the accuser commonly meant the indescribable evil of *Nazi-ness*. In this sense, to call someone a fascist was an inherently imaginative act, a conscious fiction derived from the realm of American literature itself, descending from novels like Nathanael West's *A Cool Million* (1934), Sinclair Lewis's *It Can't Happen Here* (1935), and Robert Penn Warren's *All the King's Men* (1946).

In the late sixties, this trope of fascism became bound up with the way literary fiction challenged the very definition of America and its broader meaning. Was America, as New Leftists claimed, already a profoundly fascist state rooted in racism and violent oppression? Or was America an unprecedented model of virtue for the rest of the world, "the last best hope of man on earth," in Reagan's famous stump speech for Goldwater, and the cultural revolutions of the sixties dark harbingers of nihilistic fascism to come ("A Time for Choosing")? For many Americans, cultural values and preferences functioned as proxy answers to these sensational questions, especially literary preferences. In the literary field, fascism became a trope that was associated with a historically unique reduction of cultural capital, since the Cold War struggle between the United States and the Soviet Union distinctively politicized the notion of literary prestige. In the literary sphere of the "cultural Cold War," as Frances Stonor Saunders has called it, although Soviet social realism was pitted against Anglophone modernism, the symbolic scapegoat in that discourse was usually fascism and fascist aesthetics (Saunders, 56).[12] In his path-breaking book on the Nazis' plans for cultural hegemony, *The Nazi-Fascist New Order for European Culture*, Benjamin G. Martin argues that the Axis-led European nations had such a hard time yoking highbrow literature to their authoritarian cause because they failed to understand that unique cultural fields are relatively autonomous with specific types of internal prestige or cultural capital (9). In the eyes of the Western Allied–led nations, it was obvious that the "autonomy offered to artists and intellectuals by the Nazi-Fascist New Order was a sham," Martin writes, "undermined by the grasping state control that German and Italian officials pursued with growing brutality over time" (10). In the postwar American political field, then, to call someone a fascist was to accuse that person of politicizing highbrow literature in an especially diabolical way, desecrating the semiautonomous nature of high culture with vulgar emotional appeals that sought to trigger an impulse toward human sadism, and thus capture power illegitimately. But the most fascinating and paradoxical feature of this trope in the postwar US literary field, as I anatomize in later chapters, was the precise inversion of the source of the imagined fascist menace in conservative versus liberal discourses. For liberals, American Fascism threatened to emerge from the combination of a wealthy reactionary elite and the (right-wing) populist masses. For conservatives, American Fascism was always on the brink of emerging from the combination of a liberal culture elite and the perverse, often racialized (left-wing), populist masses.[13] In this book-length study of the over half-century intersection between American fiction and postwar conservatism, the trope of American Fascism is one major thread that I utilize to trace the shifting racial politics of movement conservatism to show how specific contemporary literary forms and perceptions of aesthetic value are more bound up than we have previously imagined with the rise of the American Right.

In the first half of the book, from the birth of the postwar era to the end of the sixties, I reconstruct the widely held critical view that even though New Deal liberalism was the dominant political order in the United States, the most celebrated literature of the period was derived from Anglophone modernism, an aesthetic movement embodied by writers including T.S. Eliot, William Faulkner, and Ezra Pound, whom prominent critics such as Lionel Trilling perceived as anti-liberal at best and reactionary at worst. Focusing on the literary output of Flannery O'Connor, Ayn Rand, and Ralph Ellison in the fifties, I show how traditionalist intellectuals such as Russell Kirk in the early conservative movement used the vocabulary of New Criticism to celebrate the formal complexity and moral ambivalence in works by Ellison and O'Connor, but favored O'Connor for her implicit Southern racial politics, while scorning Rand's popular didactic fiction and colorblind individualism. As Goldwater-Reagan conservatives started gaining power within the Republican Party in the sixties, though, modern conservative ideology hardened, especially in the face of the civil rights movement, and the literary forms they valued began to reflect their increasing drive for ideological purity. Turning to the works of James Baldwin and Norman Mailer, I detail not only Baldwin's struggle with those earlier normative assumptions about race, political didacticism, and the novel form, but the contemporaneous belief among conservatives that Mailer was an ex-radical echoing their own racial anxieties via New Journalism and the "nonfiction novel," innovative genres conservatives temporarily sought to elevate above the novel.

In the second half of the book, from the 1970s to the early 2000s, I examine how the realignment of electoral politics in the United States toward conservatism coincided with the assumption that highbrow literary fiction had become a cultural form associated with post-sixties liberalism and the American Left. I posit a matrix of causes responsible for this shift in literary sensibilities across the political spectrum, ranging from ideological changes in political discourse to large institutional shifts, such as the New Right's populist attacks on college-educated elites and Affirmative Action, to the explosion of conservative think-tanks beginning in the seventies during the simultaneous rise of what Mark McGurl has called "the Program Era." Concentrating on the mid-career works of Saul Bellow and Thomas Pynchon, I reconstruct conservatism's embrace of neoliberal capitalism and the racialized populism of the New Right to explain Bellow's isolation as a culturally conservative highbrow novelist and Pynchon's reevaluation of the supposedly radical politics of postmodern form. I then examine how conservatives unwittingly contributed to the dramatic ascent of Toni Morrison, who was using formal modernist aesthetics for racially progressive ends at the precise moment when conservatives were simultaneously decrying the dissolution of the Western canon and championing the conventions of mass-market realism epitomized in the new social realism of Tom Wolfe. The book concludes with a brief inquiry that historicizes the conventional "highbrow-literature-equals-liberalism" view associated with the politics of literary form in the early twenty-first century. Toward this end, I examine the curious case of Marilynne Robinson, one of the most decorated living American novelists who seems like she would easily be aligned with American conservatism, but is not, for reasons that are intertwined with the perceived anti-intellectualism of the political Right. In short, Robinson epitomizes the prevailing, though flawed, assumption within the literary field that the cultural capital associated with highbrow literature is inevitably aligned with progressive liberalism.

CHAPTER 1

US Literature and the Modern Right at Midcentury
Conservative Modernism, Race, and the Cold War, 1945–1960

1.1 Introduction: Literary Guerrilla Warfare between Russell Kirk and Lionel Trilling

In the early postwar years, the most significant intersection between movement conservatism and American literature was Lionel Trilling's famous claim in the preface to *The Liberal Imagination* (1950) that liberalism in midcentury America constituted "not only the dominant but even the sole intellectual tradition" (xv). While Trilling readily admitted the existence of conservative and reactionary "impulses," these impulses, he said, did not generally "express themselves in ideas but only in action or in irritable mental gestures which seek to resemble ideas" (xv). Although frequently referred to in the following years as an epic insult, Trilling's remark did not come from a place of boastful superiority. Trilling was concerned that liberalism's desire to rationally order society strengthened an "organizational impulse" whose chief unintended consequence was that well-intentioned government bureaucrats forgot "that the world is a complex and unexpected and terrible place which is not always to be understood by the mind as we use it in our everyday tasks" (xx). To counteract the liberal imagination's penchant for superficiality, for seeing problems in the social world as a string of technical problems and solutions, Trilling argued that liberals had to engage with the kind of literature "that takes the fullest and most precise account of variousness [*sic*], possibility, complexity, and difficulty" (xxi). Here, Trilling followed openly in the intellectual footsteps of John Stuart Mill, who urged nineteenth-century liberals to absorb the disconcerting conservative implications of Samuel Coleridge's poetry (xvi). While it would be absurd, Trilling knew, to predict anachronistically Coleridge's positions on partisan issues in midcentury America, the point was that Coleridge's "powerful conservative mind" threw up a fundamental challenge to the general liberal belief that injecting rationality into society could, in large part, cure the social ills caused by irrationality (xvi). For liberal readers in the postwar United States, modernist literature fulfilled the same function that Coleridge's poetry once did, since it tested liberal assumptions. Anglophone modernists, Trilling wrote, "demand of us [liberals] a great agility and ingenuity in coping with their antagonism to our social and political ideals" (301). The liberal imagination, Trilling believed, posited a social–clinical framework trading in metaphors of diseases and cures. But as a close reader of modernists like Joyce, Eliot, Faulkner, Woolf, Stein, and Hemingway, he also saw that the complexity of social problems might not be legible within this framework.

Upon the publication of Trilling's book, the young, unknown conservative scholar Russell Kirk took Trilling's declaration as an intellectual challenge. Kirk began his counterattack by highlighting the tension in Trilling's thought between liberalism and "great" canonical literature. As Kirk liked to point out, Trilling confessed that midcentury American liberalism was fundamentally at odds with the modernist giants of the twentieth century. "Our liberal ideology," Trilling conceded in *The Liberal Imagination*, "has produced a large literature of social and political protest, but not, for several decades, a single writer who commands our real literary admiration" (98). Kirk agreed wholeheartedly with this sentiment, seizing upon it and quoting it, along with similar remarks by Trilling, repeatedly throughout the fifties. "In Europe, the leading writers of the age," Kirk wrote, "reject the dogmas of liberalism and democracy" ("English Letters in the Age of Boredom," 13). To support this weighty declaration, Kirk quoted Trilling, who acknowledged: "No connection exists between our liberal educated classes and the best of the literary mind [*sic*] of our time. And this is to say that there is no connection between the political ideas of our educated class and the deep places of the imagination" (*Liberal Imagination*, 98–99). If Trilling had the gall to claim that liberalism constituted the sole intellectual tradition in the United States, Kirk thought, but could not smoothly integrate the most important literary minds into that narrative, perhaps the conservative intellectual counterattack should be mounted from inside the American literary tradition itself.

A year before publishing his iconic book for the conservative movement, *The Conservative Mind: From Burke to Santayana* (1953), Kirk provided a rough sketch of this thesis in a short piece entitled "The Moral Conservatism of Hawthorne." Implicitly alluding to Trilling, Kirk opened the essay with the following sentence: "Conservatism in America, though so often defeated at the polls, always has held its head high among men of letters" (361). Hawthorne, like Flannery O'Connor roughly a century later, challenged the optimistic liberals of his day, most notably Ralph Waldo Emerson and the transcendentalists, by reminding them of the importance of the past and the inescapability of original sin (362). With novels like *The Scarlet Letter* and *The Blithedale Romance*, Kirk argued that Hawthorne secured his place in American history as a conservative of abiding importance, for he "chastened American optimism by declaring that sin . . . is virtually constant; that projects of reform must begin and end with the human heart; that our real enemy is not social institutions but the devil within us; that the fanatical improver of mankind through artificial alteration is, commonly, in truth a destroyer of souls" (363). Although Kirk regarded Hawthorne as one of the strongest links in a long historical chain of American conservatives, he believed that the core of Hawthorne's thought was inspired not directly by an American-born thinker but indirectly by Kirk's own favorite archetype of Western conservatism, Edmund Burke (364).

The linkage Kirk made between Hawthorne and Burke in this essay prefigured the larger framework of *The Conservative Mind* and its central contention that the beating heart of conservatism was imaginative highbrow literature.[1] Synthesizing political treatises and literary works, Kirk constructed his breakout book as an extended response to Trilling's claim regarding the absence of a conservative intellectual tradition. Calling his tome a "prolonged essay in definition," Kirk hoped to answer the question: "What system of ideas, common to England and the United States, has sustained men of conservative instincts in their resistance against radical theories and social transformation ever since the beginning of the French Revolution?" (3). The answer was that Burke had invented what Kirk called "conscious conservatism" in response to the French Revolution, and that ever since, the conservative intellectual tradition in America had patterned itself off Burkean philosophy and its nineteenth-century British descendants who emphasized tradition, prejudice, custom, and organic social order (5). But whereas the British conservative tradition, according to Kirk, featured a consistent stream of prominent political statesmen, the record of noteworthy conservative politicians in the American tradition was spotty. For this reason, Kirk turned to numerous American writers of humane letters in *The Conservative Mind* to bolster his argument. Contra Trilling, a conservative intellectual tradition did, in fact, exist – but it resided in the high cultural canons of American literature.[2]

For Kirk and other traditionalist conservatives, the lack of American politicians whom they could deem properly "conservative" was a minor problem, not a mortal threat to American conservatism. Throughout his life, Kirk tended to deemphasize the importance of practical politics, as he was known to quote George Gissing's aphorism that politics was a vulgar arena for the "quarter educated" (Birzer, *Russell Kirk: American Conservative*, 9). While movement conservatism under Buckley's leadership would eventually put a high value on gaining electoral power in the ensuing decades, the early movement tended to interpret – perhaps even willfully misinterpret – its exile from the halls of power as a beneficial augmentation of perspective. Formal political power was trivial when compared to the titanic ideological struggle playing out on the global battlefield of ideas. "Men of ideas, rather than political parties, determine the ultimate course of things," Kirk wrote in the introduction to *The Conservative Mind*, "and I have chosen my conservatives accordingly" (9). In his equally influential book *God and Man at Yale* (1951), Buckley made a similar declaration that would come to acquire axiomatic authority for postwar conservatives: "I myself believe that the duel between Christianity and atheism is the most important in the world. I further believe that the struggle between individualism and collectivism is the same struggle reproduced on another level" (xvi). Movement conservatives were embarking on a crusade, in their own minds, that was more profound than electing a conservative president or achieving a congressional majority; they were combatting twentieth-century totalitarianism by returning to the wisdom of their Anglophone ancestors, and their first line of defense in the battle was the Western literary canon. The major upshot is that in the immediate postwar moment, movement conservatives valued (what they imagined to be) the historical resilience imbedded in cultural capital acquired from the literary field over the seemingly transient nature of political capital gained through the electoral process.

1.2 Highbrow Literature as Cold War Weapon

Beginning with Kirk's efforts to uncover a living conservative intellectual tradition, conservatives in the postwar period stressed the importance of grounding that tradition in humane letters because their battle against totalitarian collectivism was rooted in a sharp distinction between traditional wisdom in the humanities and the mere technical knowledge that they believed undergirded materialist ideologies. In his confessional memoir *Witness*, the ex-communist-turned-conservative Whittaker Chambers lamented: "Men have never been so educated, but wisdom, even as an idea, has conspicuously vanished from the world" (506). For Chambers, the central doctrine of Christianity was a source of wisdom that went deeper than everyday politics. While Christian wisdom could be found in the works of theologians like Sören Kierkegaard and Karl Barth, Chambers consistently identified Fyodor Dostoyevsky as the greatest conservative thinker of modern times (*Witness,* 506). In his definitive biography of Chambers, Sam Tanenhaus notes the deep influence that Dostoyevsky's novels, especially *The Possessed,* had on Chambers in the late forties and early fifties. After reading that novel half a dozen times, Chambers discovered the basic premise of his opposition to communism: the conflict between Christianity and atheism (Tanenhaus, *Whittaker Chambers: A Biography,* 333; 453).

The problem with postwar American liberals, Chambers and Kirk believed, was that they refused to grasp in these precise terms the existential crisis brought on by every form of totalitarianism, and thus liberals had assumed the role of unwitting accomplices in the slow slide toward global oppression. Instead of seeing conflicts through the aperture of great literary narratives, modern liberals continued to see conflicts through the lens of technocratic knowledge that Trilling had warned was too narrow. Toward the end of *Witness*, Chambers retells a moment during the second Alger Hiss trial when a liberal congressman had asked him about "the economic problem of Communism" (711). Avoiding a meaningless academic debate, in his eyes, about the materialistic differences between capitalism and communism, Chambers writes: "I answered, citing Dostoevsky [*sic*]: 'The problem of Communism is not an economic problem. The problem of Communism is the problem of atheism'" (712). Chambers's frustration with this kind of partisan shallowness is a reoccurring theme in *Witness.* Modern liberals, thought Chambers, could never quite bring themselves to believe that an ex-communist spy wasn't an overzealous political hatchet man. To see the Chambers–Hiss affair "as a manifestation of partisan politics," Chambers believed for the rest of his life, was to be "influenced by the traditional pattern of American politics at a time when that traditional pattern no longer holds . . . The explanation lies deeper" (741). The spatial metaphors Chambers employs here and elsewhere virtually always privilege depth over surface, and the "deeper" Chambers probed with his prose, the more he uncovered tragic Dostoyevskian dilemmas that revealed the irrational psychic forces that his one-time friend Trilling claimed were associated in "the literary mind with the dark unconscious and with the most primitive human relationships" (*Liberal Imagination,* 293).

In a frequently quoted passage from *Witness*, Chambers describes just such a tragic dilemma. Liberals, in their well-meaning desire to assuage human suffering, have failed to comprehend how their ideological commitments represent a step in the wrong direction concerning the larger struggle between good and evil. As Chambers writes, these "men who could not see that what they firmly believed was liberalism added up to socialism could scarcely be expected to see what added up to Communism. Any charge of Communism enraged them precisely because they could not grasp the differences between themselves and those against whom it was made" (472–73). Though they may not have realized it yet, midcentury American liberals had become, for all intents and purposes, revolutionaries because they had placed their faith in man-made solutions over the wisdom of the Christian tradition. Any man should be called a "revolutionary," Chambers writes in the introduction to *Witness*, who is put "to the challenge: *God or Man?*," and he responds with "the answer: *Man*" (13). For Chambers, this insight could not be reached through the structural logic of thirties dialectical materialism or any other materialist method; instead, it was primarily a metaphysical insight gleaned through literary form, which explains why the entire structure and theme of *Witness* is derived from Dostoyevsky's late novels.

With this Dostoyevskian template undergirding his memoir, Chambers hoped to offer a vision that would reorganize the entire political spectrum in the postwar United States. Following World War II, American politics had settled into an ideological consensus, at least according to prominent liberal intellectuals. In *The Vital Center* (1948), Arthur Schlesinger, Jr. offered the most potent articulation of this viewpoint, contending that the liberal welfare state was an infinitely better form of government than right-wing fascism and left-wing communism. Liberalism, as Schlesinger's guiding spatial metaphor suggested, was the sane middle ground between these two insane totalitarian systems on the Right and Left. By rooting himself in the Dostoyevskian novel, Chambers sought to show that the firm distinctions liberals made between postwar liberalism, German Nazism, and Soviet Communism were wish-fulfillment fantasies. Although Chambers failed to convince Leftists and liberals that the dominant political spectrum was categorically incoherent, his views were profoundly influential on the burgeoning conservatism movement, especially the connection Chambers drew between communism and fascism as manifestations of the Left. While reviewers like Philip Rahv routinely took issue with Chambers's conflation of "liberals, socialists, and party-line communists," they tended to ignore the larger point Chambers was making about fascism as the ultimate endpoint ("The Sense and Nonsense of Whittaker Chambers," 137). Reflecting on the Soviet purges of the thirties and their reverberations in the American Communist Party, Chambers stated that at the time he believed he was just witnessing "the imprint of the peculiarly malevolent character of Joseph Stalin, his personal perversion of what in itself was good" (*Witness,* 248). Eventually, though, Chambers had a startling literary-style epiphany that triggered his break from communism. "The important point was not the character of Stalin, but the character of Communism," Chambers writes, for "Stalin was carrying [communism] to its inevitable development as the greatest of the fascist forms" (249). Later in *Witness*, Chambers put it even more bluntly: "The fascist character of Communism was inherent in it from the beginning" (460). For Chambers, the Dostoyevskian memoir-novel afforded him a bird's-eye view of this oncoming apocalyptic drama playing out on the stage of twentieth-century history. In short, Chambers inverted the classic Marxist teleology of history: Postwar liberalism was drifting toward communism because it shared the same materialist essence as Soviet Communism, which was itself always in the process of maturing into fascism as its final stage of development.[3]

Following the publication of *Witness*, Russell Kirk not only made the same claim regarding the basic continuity between communism and fascism but also stressed the importance that literary form played in seeing such a connection. Writing about Trilling and other liberals of the literary establishment, Kirk claimed that they were so "naïve" as to "maintain that the Fascist and Nazi regimes were inspired by 'conservative' elements and constituted 'reaction'" (*Conservative Mind,* 425). Only fellow conservatives like Chambers "understood that the Fascist and Communist systems were simply parallel afflictions from out the winter of our discontent" (426). A fascist heart resided at the core of communism, Kirk maintained, due to the secular-materialist foundations of both systems. Like Chambers, Kirk contended that this insight was best understood through a literary framework, specifically what Kirk called the "moral imagination," a phrase he borrowed and adapted from Burke. Although Burke mentioned the moral imagination only once in his writings, Kirk appropriated this term and used it as the starting point for his own expansive aesthetic theory. In *Reflections on the Revolution in France*, Burke invoked the moral imagination while lamenting the destruction of social norms wrought by French Jacobins: "All the decent drapery of life is to be rudely torn off. All the superadded ideas, furnished from the wardrobe of a moral imagination, which the heart owns, and the understanding ratifies, as necessary to cover the defects of our naked, shivering nature, and to raise it to dignity in our own estimation, are to be exploded as a ridiculous, absurd, and antiquated fashion" (171). On the one hand, according to Kirk, Burke was fully aware that the moral imagination was a social fiction, a genteel instrument of civilization that obscured the true "naked, shivering nature" of humanity. But, on the other hand, the development of the moral imagination via literature and the arts raised humans above their basest needs and desires, orienting them toward the higher emotions of empathy, ethics, and love. Once reason was cut off from older Christian sources of wisdom, Kirk believed, the justification was in place for killing naked, shivering humans in the name of progress.

However, if traditionalists regarded materialist ideologies like communism and fascism as deeply flawed because they reduced human beings to their basest desires in the name of material progress, that worldview also undermined the basic premise of capitalism beloved by libertarians in the conservative movement. Capitalism for traditionalists like Chambers, Kirk, and Peter Viereck was not an absolute good. For Chambers, an ex-communist still thinking in long-term historical stages, capitalism represented social change so transformative that it could practically be called "revolutionary." In a series of personal letters to Buckley in the fifties, Chambers wrote that he had even determined that capitalism was intrinsically incompatible with any definition of conservatism. "Conservatism is alien to the very nature of capitalism," Chambers declared, "whose love of life and growth is perpetual change" (*Odyssey of a Friend,* 229). While Chambers felt that he must "uphold capitalism in its American version," he could not in good faith equate conservatism with capitalism, writing: "I claim that capitalism is not, and by its essential nature cannot conceivably be, conservative" (228). According to this traditionalist position, to posit capitalism as the foundation of postwar conservatism, as Rand and other libertarians would, was to root conservatism in the same materialist essence as communism and fascism.[4]

Similarly, Kirk and Viereck saw capitalism not as a constitutive ingredient of conservatism, but as an economic system that was relatively better than other systems, but then only if capitalism could be harnessed to aid the preservation of a traditional society. In Peter Viereck's *Conservatism Revisited: The Revolt against Ideology* (1949), a book generally credited with reviving the very word "conservatism" in postwar American academic circles, Viereck rejected the purely economic definition of conservatism for the same reasons as Kirk. "The core and fire-center of conservatism," Viereck asserted, "is a humanist reverence for the dignity of the individual soul. This is incompatible with the fascist or Stalinist collectivism; incompatible with a purely mechanistic view of man; incompatible with a purely economic view of history" (71). In *The Conservative Mind*, Kirk was especially troubled by the social changes wrought by industrial capitalism. After the invention of the automobile and Fordist manufacturing practices in the early twentieth century, Kirk claimed that "before long, men would begin to see that the automobile, and the mass-production techniques which made it possible, could alter national character and morality more thoroughly than could the most absolute of tyrants" (325). The deeply anti-conservative product of Fordism, Kirk summed up in a dramatic phrase, was a "mechanical Jacobin" (325). In his follow-up book *A Program for Conservatives* (1954), Kirk directed his critiques at laissez-faire economists like Ludwig Von Mises, the famous Austrian School philosopher-economist and libertarian hero of the postwar Right, writing: "Theirs is a doctrine which destroys itself in proportion as it is generally promulgated: once supernatural and traditional sanctions are dissolved, economic self-interest is ridiculously inadequate to preserve order. Prescription and prejudice are the defenses of justice and peace" (144). Shifting into his typical jeremiadic discourse, Kirk argued that if economists like von Mises failed to recognize that the free market does not itself create order, but rather thrives as a consequence of a traditionally ordered society, a totalitarian catastrophe would ensue: "Laugh them away [i.e., prescription and Burkean prejudice], and in come those forces of delusion and unrest which Marxism exemplifies today; men refuse to live by economic reasonableness alone" (144). Both Kirk and Viereck made use of the Dostoyevskian literary drama, outlined by Chambers in the late forties and the early fifties, to warn against a coming collectivist dystopia that would begin with the egalitarian collectivism of socialism but end inevitably with the horrific collectivism of fascism.[5]

From the beginning of the postwar era, the central rift between libertarian and traditionalist conservatives was about how much emphasis should be placed on capitalism versus tradition – summarized sometimes as "freedom versus order." From this perspective, postwar American conservatism was a historically contingent, makeshift alliance between Burkean traditionalists emphasizing social order, custom, and deep communal and religious bonds, and neoclassical liberals emphasizing liberty, limited government, and free-market capitalism. Although conservatives would eventually praise this alliance as a successful "fusion" of traditionalism and libertarianism brought about by the ex-communist and *National Review* writer Frank Meyer, the conservative movement's early documents show that this pseudo-synthesis remained philosophically contradictory, albeit pragmatically beneficial, as thinkers on both sides engaged in bitter intellectual battles for roughly half a century. Ironically, Meyer made every effort to distance his ongoing intellectual project from the notion of fusionism, casting himself as a "libertarian conservative" who refused to accommodate American traditionalists descended from Burke. Instead of "abstractly 'fusing' two positions," Meyer wrote in a 1962 article entitled "Why Freedom" for *National Review*, "What I have been attempting to do is to help articulate in theoretical and practical terms the instinctive consensus of the contemporary American conservative movement. ... That consensus simultaneously accepts the existence of an objective moral and spiritual order, which places as man's end the pursuit of virtue, *and* the freedom of the individual person as a decisive necessity for a good political order" (223). For Meyer, traditionalism shared the same ideological essence as "collectivist" ideologies like Nazism and Soviet Communism: All three ideologies "had a vision of how men ought to live and was determined to force that vision upon those subject to their will. If the state is endowed with the power to enforce virtue, the men who hold that power will enforce their own concepts as virtuous" (224). It is no coincidence, in light of this claim, that Meyer chose "Collectivism Rebaptized" as the title for his critical review of Kirk's *The Conservative Mind.*

Instead of labeling this "fusionism," it would be more accurate to say that Meyer sought to imbue libertarianism with the traditionalist concept of "virtue" in the hopes of restraining the potentially revolutionary implications of classical liberalism – namely, the principle of equality. In perhaps his most important essay "Freedom, Tradition, Conservatism" (1960), Meyer argued that conservatives "must draw upon those who called themselves conservatives in [the nineteenth century] but also those who called themselves liberals" (26). In Meyer's writings, conservatives found the theoretical core of postwar conservatism: it was a not just a "fusion" of a small band of relative political unknowns hostile to the New Deal but a much more curious combination of Burkean conservatism and classical liberalism. Put another way, if one accepted the conservative truism that the American and French Revolutions inaugurated modern politics, Meyer's postwar conservatism was something like a grand fusion of a premodern defense of inherited privilege and a modern defense of individual liberty.

In the best of all possible worlds, Meyer claimed, politicians and intellectuals would "distinguish between the *authoritarianism* with which men and institutions suppress the freedom of men and the *authority* of God and truth" (24). By "authoritarianism," Meyer meant eighteenth-century Europe's neofeudal nobility class, the suppression of a free-market economy, and the royal refusal to recognize natural rights and the doctrines of limited state power. But what, one may ask, did Meyer mean by the morally superior "*authority* of God and truth"? Didn't King Louis XVI regard the doctrine of the divine right of kings as the authority of God and truth, whereas Robespierre did not? Who decided what constituted illegitimate authoritarianism and legitimate authority? Meyer implied that what should be conserved was not only the political achievements of classical liberalism but also many of the most retrograde social customs embedded in the historical setting that produced classical liberalism. According to Meyer, an unqualified commitment to classical liberalism risked a collectivist revolt from the proletarian class in the name of equality, while an unqualified commitment to Burkean traditionalism risked an authoritarian collectivism descending from the class of political elites. Early postwar conservatives would find a provisional solution to this problem in the literary trope of "American Fascism," which allowed them to label any kind of emancipatory uprising "collectivist," especially the civil rights movement and the legal abolition of segregation.

While scholars on the Right and Left typically frame Meyer's philosophical synthesis as a struggle over the negative freedom of libertarianism versus the positive freedom of traditionalism, the heart of the conflict concerns the polysemic word "collectivism" in early postwar conservative discourse. It is vital to understand that "collectivism" in this discourse was not simply a synonym for "communism" but a densely metaphorical term simultaneously connoting American progressivism, New Deal liberalism, European socialism and anarchism, Soviet Communism and, most importantly, the fascist impulse supposedly underlying each one of these ideologies. Scholars commonly account for the uneasy synthesis between traditionalists and libertarians by emphasizing how deeply both camps were committed to fighting "collectivism" in all its forms. Moreover, they point to the anticommunist American Right – led by *National Review* contributors like James Burnham, William S. Schlamm, and Erik von Kuehnelt-Leddihn – as the third strand of postwar American conservatism that allowed the movement to cohere around the figure of William F. Buckley, Jr., the quintessential postwar American conservative who claimed membership in all three camps. Buckley, in this sense, was the glue that held together the three different pieces of the philosophical conservative puzzle.

What has been overshadowed in previous scholarly articulations of postwar conservatism was not only the Right's invocation of fascism as a literary and cultural trope that consistently underpinned their anticommunism but also the racial anxieties and fantasies that were bound up with that trope.[6] If the perceived mortal threat of collectivism in all its guises was the bridge that united traditionalists and libertarians, as George Nash claimed in his seminal hagiography *The Conservative Intellectual Movement in America Since 1945* (1976), then the key support beam of that bridge was a rhetorical conflation of totalitarian collectivism with the means – and sometimes, wittingly or unwittingly, the ends – of totalitarian fascism (Nash, 165). As I demonstrated earlier, traditionalists were quick to link European Fascism and Soviet Communism by positing a causal relationship between the rise of totalitarian collectivism and the overthrow of venerable social customs, political institutions, and religious rituals. But libertarians were equally apt to link fascism and communism for reasons that had very little to do with the traditionalist concerns about preserving an organic community. In his important book *The Road to Serfdom* (1944), Friedrich Hayek argued that "the rise of fascism and Nazism was not a reaction against the socialist trends of the preceding period but a necessary outcome of those tendencies" (6). Ludwig von Mises, Hayek's intellectual mentor, argued in *Omnipotent Government* (1944) that what he called "Etatism," or "the trend toward government control of business," was the main cause of Nazism in Germany (6). In this line of libertarian argumentation, collectivist "fascism" was primarily the result of a strong central government meddling with decentralized free markets and trampling over individual rights.

For movement conservatives, no matter which intellectual camp they were most strongly affiliated with (i.e., traditionalism, libertarianism, or anti-communism), the term "fascism" was both menacing and malleable enough to bind them to other conservatives in their fight against collectivism at home (New Deal liberalism) and abroad (Soviet Communism). But their notion of collectivist American Fascism, which was far from a theoretically coherent or historically precise invocation of twentieth-century European Fascism, was largely an imaginary rubric that aimed to alert white, upper-middle-class Americans to the supposed cabals of liberal cultural "elitists" planning, on behalf of the unruly racial masses, to take over the United States. Adopting the rhetoric of paranoia and fear in the late fifties, conservatives warned Americans of well-meaning liberals in the federal government who would eventually, indeed inevitably, turn to violence as a last resort to enforce their utopian schemes, especially regarding desegregation and issues of race. In a now infamous *National Review* article "The Right to Nullify" (1956), Forrest Davis used a profoundly odd fascist analogy to frame white Southerners' resistance to desegregation as a battle between "Washington vs. The Deep South," comparing federal intervention to Nazism in a way that posited white Southerners as the "non-Aryan" victims of liberal cultural elites in the government: "Socialism, in practice in the Soviet Union, or its spawns, Nazism and Fascism, characteristically has developed into hierarchic societies with elites and untouchables ... in Nazi Germany the non-Aryans were declassed and denied many privileges, including more often than not the privilege of living" (11). The basic issue, Davis asserted with a breathtaking disregard for African Americans as full citizens, was about "where the rights and prerogatives of the central authority leave off and the rights of the citizen begin" (11). The peculiar twists of logic exemplify the anxious conservative belief that postwar liberalism's extension of rights to African Americans shared a fundamental, though enigmatic, connection with fascism as the heart of collectivism.

A major problem for conservatives, of course, was that progressive liberalism was so popular in the aftermath of World War II that conservatives struggled to convince large swaths of the electorate that liberals were clandestine collectivists. In light of this difficulty, movement conservatives implemented a rhetorical style that obscured the source of agency and responsibility for the coming collectivist takeover of the United States. In an anonymous October 1957 article published in "The Week" section of *National Review* entitled "Bayonets and the Law," the author conflated federal intervention in Little Rock, Arkansas, in September 1957 with latent American Fascism: "For this is the way of the Welfare state. Behind that bland and smiling mask is set the coercive jaw ... And if you get far enough out of step, friend, take a look at that line of bayonets in Little Rock. Those bayonets will teach you, if nothing else will, that we are all going to be free and equal and happy" (316).[7] By adopting a style that mimicked Buckley's ironic distance and cutting wit, the author drew an intentionally murky portrait of good-hearted liberal intentions. Were liberals cold-blooded hypocrites who are only using the language of freedom and equality to crush dissent? Or was the situation more complex than that; perhaps liberals really did believe they were creating a better, more equal nation with threats of violence that shaded into authoritarianism, most notably when they were seeking to expand the civil rights of African Americans? For movement conservatives at *National Review*, the default strategy was almost always to claim the latter: that liberals were unconsciously going down the road of communist-fascist collectivism.[8]

In the immediate aftermath of World War II, of course, it was common for American officials and public leaders across the political spectrum –

from President Harry Truman and labor union leader George Meany to ex-President Herbert Hoover and FBI director J. Edgar Hoover – to conflate Soviet Communism and German Nazism, thereby conjuring up an image of "Red Fascism" (Adler and Paterson, 1046; 1048; 1060). Especially after World War II, historians Les K. Adler and Thomas G. Paterson argued that Americans "casually and deliberately articulated distorted similarities between Nazi and Communist ideologies, German and Soviet foreign policies, authoritarian controls, and trade practices, and Hitler and Stalin" (1046). Whereas postwar liberal intellectuals routinely drew a distinction between communism as an ideology that failed to live up to its ideals of improving human existence, and fascism as an ideology that sought to eliminate those deemed unworthy of human existence, postwar conservatives believed that the leftist-liberal desire to alleviate suffering, especially the suffering of racial minorities, inevitably ended in bloodshed in the very name of ending suffering. From the perspective of American literary history, what was significant about the conservative version of this claim was not so much its truth-value, which historians have long debunked, but the way in which movement conservatives arrived at this conclusion through the language and form of fiction and the rhetoric of "Western civilization." Since conservatives tended to couch their ominous warnings in the rhetoric of secret plots and imminent destruction, literary texts and allusions became vital sources for framing arguments about menacing forms of "Red Fascism" that were at once everywhere and nowhere.

To underscore the "Red Fascism" analogy, movement conservatives frequently referenced novels like George Orwell's *1984* (1949), Arthur Koestler's *Darkness at Noon* (1940), and Albert Camus's *The Plague* (1947).[9] Although Orwell's political views were notoriously complex and his influence multivalent, his major achievement in the eyes of *National Review* was his role as an unwitting conservative spokesman who merely reiterated what American conservatives had already been preaching for decades concerning the fundamental link between communism and fascism. As the conservative John Chamberlain wrote in his 1956 review of "The Orwell Reader," Orwell's putative "discoveries of parallel qualities in Fascism and Communism, sound though they may be, came long after the first disillusioned writings of William Henry Chamberlin, Max Eastman, Eugene Lyons and half a dozen other Americans . . . " ("Orwell: Prophet After the Fact," 21). Similarly, Frank Meyer argued that "the great insight" of *Darkness at Noon*, Koestler's epic political novel portraying an Old Bolshevik's show trial persecution by the Soviet government in the thirties, is that the "protean" nature of collectivist ideologies can animate both the victims and executioners of events like the Holocaust and the Soviet Purges ("Of Khrushchev, Stalin, and Sitting Ducks," 16). Finally, despite their aversion to Camus's existentialist-flavored atheism, *National Review* conservatives regarded his novels, particularly *The Plague*, as a space that defamiliarized the standard categorization of left-wing Soviet Communism and right-wing Nazi Fascism and thus reimagined the basic, brutal similarities between them. In a 1960 obituary for Camus, which was unsigned but bore Buckley's diction and stylistic tics, the author claimed that it was imperative to understand that in "*The Plague*, the African city ravaged and isolated by the rat-born disease is also Nazi-occupied France, Bolshevik-ruled Russia" ("Albert Camus," 33). Conservatives also understood that, no matter how persuasively these works linked communist and fascist regimes, they had diminishing returns for reading audiences in the United States when considered in isolation. Several common threads running through these novels made it difficult for American readers to connect those recognizable brands of totalitarian collectivism with the comparatively innocuous brand of liberal, New Deal collectivism: these novelists were not Americans, were not writing about the United States, and, in truth, were using firsthand experience of European and Soviet regimes to warn the larger world.

This peculiar literary-political phenomenon was pointed out not by a movement conservative, nor by a professional liberal critic like Lionel Trilling, but by George F. Kennan, the noted geopolitical realist and architect of America's Cold War "containment policy." In a prescient 1953 analysis of the way in which novels by major non-American authors like Orwell and Koestler contributed to the American public's distorted conflation of Soviet Communism and Nazi Fascism as identical totalitarian regimes, Kennan highlighted the novelistic foundation underpinning the "Red Fascism" analogy:

> When I try to picture totalitarianism to myself as a general phenomenon, what comes into my mind most prominently is neither the Soviet picture nor the Nazi picture as I have known them in the flesh, but rather the fictional and symbolic images created by such people as Orwell or Kafka or Koestler or the early Soviet satirists. The purest expression of the phenomenon, in other words, seems to me to have been rendered not in its physical reality but in its power as a dream, or a nightmare. Not that it lacks the physical reality, or that this reality is lacking in power; but it is precisely in the way it appears to people, in the impact it has on the subconscious, in the state of mind it creates in its victims, that totalitarianism reveals most deeply

> its meaning and nature. *Here, then, we seem to have a phenomenon of which it can be said that is both reality and a bad dream, but that its deepest reality lies strangely enough in its manifestation as a dream* . . . ("Totalitarianism in the Modern Word," 19–20, emphasis added)

Unlike Kennan, movement conservatives took the dream-like quality of "Red Fascism" prevalent in American culture one step further, using highbrow American fiction to stress the basic continuity between what they saw as several variations of collectivism, linking liberalism with other forms of collectivism by stressing the common thread, and frightening specter, of African American civil rights. The reality of postwar liberalism, in the eyes of conservatives, was not found simply on the surface of American politics – that is, in national campaigns, the dry facts of public policy, or machine party politics in the Democratic Party outside of the Old South – but in the high cultural literary dreams of the nation. To understand the ostensible mortal threat posed by modern liberalism, conservatives believed, one had to engage in literary hermeneutics.

From the very beginning of the conservative movement, despite the lack of renowned novelists affiliated with their movement, conservatives themselves always maintained the importance of fiction in American culture. Conservatives valued fiction not because they believed it revealed that liberalism and totalitarian collectivism were indistinguishable, nor that liberals were just authoritarian fascists in sheep's clothing, but because American fiction created a respected, prestigious imaginative space within which readers could see how liberalism – notwithstanding the best intentions of liberals – systematically created the necessary conditions for a collectivist state that would descend into fascist collectivism. In the manifesto-like document "Our Mission Statement," published in the inaugural issue of *National Review* (November 19, 1955), Buckley explained global Cold War politics by invoking "satanic utopianism" and "the growth of Big Brother government," making an obligatory reference to Orwell's *1984* ("Our Mission Statement"). But Buckley was also adamant about the cultural component of domestic liberalism, noting that the "largest cultural menace in America is the conformity of the intellectual cliques which, in education as well as the arts, are out to impose upon the nation their modish fads and fallacies, and have nearly succeeded in doing so." To underscore the frightening ease with which cultural conformity translated into political conformity, Buckley alluded to Sinclair Lewis's *Babbitt* (1922), the classic novel by the first American Nobel Prize-winner critiquing the emptiness of bourgeois conformity and material security:

"Clever intriguers are reshaping both parties in the image of Babbitt, gone Social-Democrat" ("Our Mission Statement"). From Buckley's perspective, the thematic takeaway from a work like *Babbitt* was that progressive liberalism's specious promise of providing material comfort for all, including African Americans, quickly devolved into not just the growth of "Big Brother government," but into a form of vulgar populism that failed to recognize the tragic complexity of the human condition, for which there was allegedly no possibility for political solutions, only political disasters.

In an article published in *National Review* just three months later, the noted Southern Agrarian Richard Weaver reiterated the unforeseen link between liberalism and fascism by referencing another Sinclair Lewis novel, *It Can't Happen Here* (1935), a dystopian narrative charting the rise of American Fascism. Grounding his critique in the infamous conservative axiom that poverty is "ennobling," Weaver declared that twentieth-century advertising "faithfully reflects the modern, 'liberal' deceiving mind," for it is an ideological side effect of that central liberal creed that material security trumps the kind of hard-won virtue achieved through struggle ("The Best of Everything," 21). Blaming innovations in modern advertising on the changing expectations wrought by New Deal liberalism, Weaver claimed that liberals, in their attempts to bring material comfort to the masses, blithely ignored human evil throughout history. Modern advertising, premised on forgetting the dark side of history and revolutionary uprisings that have gone awry, coaxed Americans into downplaying the horrors of history only to have those horrors reappear in their own country: "From 'it couldn't really have happened' it may be only a step to 'It Can't Happen Here'" (22). Weaver suggested that, although starkly clear to conservatives how modern liberalism created the conditions for a collectivist state, it was difficult to convince everyday Americans who indulged in material comforts, especially those made possible by federal programs, and thus could not bear to acknowledge the suffering necessary to endure poverty with tragic nobility.

The language of high culture adopted here by Buckley and Weaver, which movement conservatives deployed only strategically, assumed that great literature revealed how materialism for the (typically) undeserving multitude debased American society. In the broader history of American cultural canons of distinction, this neo-aristocratic cultural discourse echoes a major point in Lawrence Levine's *Highbrow/Lowbrow: The Emergence of Cultural Hierarchy in America*, who shows that an elite American "highbrow" culture emerged in reaction to mass immigration, carving out a space of cultural distinction by defining itself against the "lowbrow" cultures of the unruly masses (8–9). Eventually, movement conservatives would drop this language in their populist campaigns when appealing directly to blue-collar white voters, but they would always retain it when attacking liberal cultural elites who sought to improve the material conditions of racial minorities.

1.3 The Racial Specter of Collectivism and Highbrow Literary Form

By the late fifties, as the controversy over desegregation in the South became acute, movement conservatives found that raising the issue of integration, and the dark attendant fear of miscegenation, was the single best way to convince Americans that the federal government was sliding toward collectivism. In one *National Review* article, pointedly titled "Integration is Communization," Richard Weaver returned to this theme and claimed that Southerners and other "common people" possessing common sense "have been right in identifying this [integration] as the opening tactic of Communism in this country" (67). In an unsigned editorial dated January 1956, Buckley's magazine took the position that the *Brown* decision was "one of the most brazen acts of judicial usurpation in our history, patently counter to the intent of the Constitution, shoddy and illegal in analysis, and invalid as sociology" ("Segregation and Democracy," 5). Essentially, Buckley and *National Review* claimed, segregation was "a problem that should be solved not by the central government, but locally – in the states and their local subdivisions, and in the hearts of men" (5). The phrase "in the hearts of men" shows that, despite Buckley's admiration for individualism and capitalism since his days as an undergraduate at Yale, at this point in his young political life, he still embodied the early conservative movement's traditionalist position on race. This unorthodox, neo-Burkean position emphasized social order, benign prejudice, communal cohesion, and, as an uncomfortable corollary, a tolerant stance toward Jim Crow segregation – all at the expense of basic Constitutional tenets such as the rule of law, democratic legitimacy, and equal protection.

Although the conservative movement had always contained elements of Burkean traditionalism and libertarianism derived from classical liberals like John Locke and Thomas Jefferson, its adherents leaned heavily on the traditionalist notion of prejudice when confronting desegregation in the fifties and early sixties. As the civil rights movement gained momentum in the late fifties, conservatives responded not by invoking the abstract purity of constitutional principles, as they would a decade later, but by citing the supposed practicality of Burkean prejudice that underpins civilization. In one of the most infamous articles ever published in *National Review*, "Why the South Must Prevail" (August 24, 1957), Buckley and his fellow conservatives seemed to abandon the decentralized federalism argument altogether, and instead used a traditionalist argument to defend Southern segregation and black disenfranchisement. "The question, as far as the White community is concerned," the anonymous editorial author claimed, speaking for the magazine as a whole, "is whether the claims of civilization supersede those of universal suffering" (149). The conclusion Buckley and his followers reached was unequivocal: "The sober answer is *Yes* – the White community is so entitled because, for the time being, it is the advanced race. . . . It is more important for any community, anywhere in the world, to affirm and live by civilized standards, than to bow to the demands of the numerical majority" (149). Just as Burke feared that rights-based equality would cause an organic community to dissolve "into an unsocial, uncivil, unconnected chaos of elementary principles," Buckley and his movement feared that the enforcement of equal voting rights for African Americans, founded on constitutional principles, would do irreparable harm to the "civilized," traditional order of the South (Burke, *Reflections*, 11).[10]

For postwar conservatives, traditionalists in particular, "civilization" was a term invested with an almost mystical sacredness because it was underwritten by the cultural capital generated by great Western literature stretching from Homer and Plato to Eliot and Faulkner. Another way to put this is that, for conservatives, the civilizational master theme at the core of highbrow literature revealed not just what Bourdieu famously called an inherently superior "cultural nobility," but a specifically "white cultural nobility" in the postwar United States (*Distinction*, 9). As I argue at length in Chapter 2, this perspective would explain why conservatives initially approached racial issues like desegregation not from the libertarian angle of an Ayn Rand, whose theory begins with an absolute declaration of abstract individual rights, but from the traditionalist angle of a Flannery O'Connor or a Russell Kirk, who justified inherited racial hierarchies with the New Critical language of complexity and mystery. In the eyes of many movement conservatives, the New Critical emphasis on the complexity of experience over naïve abstraction in the sphere of literature expressed a neo-Burkean philosophy that rationalized the complicated, though ultimately beneficial, traditions of racial inequality over one-dimensional calls for egalitarianism. In Kirk's words, Burke knew that liberty "had risen in consequence of an elaborate and delicate process, and its perpetuation depended upon retaining those habits of thought and action which guide the savage in his slow and weary ascent to the state of civil social man" (*Conservative Mind*, 18–19). Kirk admired the Southern Agrarians and New Critics precisely because their conception of a literary text – a multifaceted organism of relationships that could not be neatly summarized, but nevertheless possessed its own "unity" – served as a microcosm for a larger system of intricate social relationships between abstract equality and the customs of inequality that could not be articulated, or easily defended, via simple political propositions. As Cleanth Brooks and Robert Penn Warren argued in *Understanding Fiction* (1943), a sacred text of New Criticism and Flannery O'Connor's writing manual while attending the Iowa Writers' Workshop, the very definition of "propaganda literature" was the kind that "tends to state its theme abstractly and tends to insist on its 'message' at the expense of other elements in its structure. Usually it can be said that such literature tends to oversimplify its material in order to emphasize its meaning" (608). In her essay "Writing Short Stories," O'Connor echoed this principle of literary composition: "A story is a way to say something that can't be said any other way, and it takes every word in the story to say what the meaning is. You tell a story because a statement would be inadequate . . . " (*Mystery and Manners*, 96). Within this framework, social protest novels in the progressive vein of Richard Wright or John Steinbeck were inadequate because they were premised on abstractions that ignored the depth and wholeness of "lived-life." Conservatives claimed that the result of such novels was an inevitable descent, both artistically and morally, into sentimental liberal abstraction.

This discourse explains why the American novel form and the principles of New Criticism were crucial components of the early conservative movement at *National Review*: they were high cultural touchstones that could be deployed to justify the persistent necessity of unequal power relations. Conservatives knew that the basic premise for such justifications – that is, various forms of inequality are at times beneficial and, ultimately, the *least bad* social arrangement – would be difficult to articulate in the political sphere with straightforward propositions. Instead, conservatives realized that they could point to the themes of complexity, moral ambivalence, and tragic awareness dramatized by great American authors to illustrate not just the historical intricacies of injustice, but perhaps even, in true Burkean fashion, the unexpected social benefits of inequality and prejudice. In the second ever issue of *National Review*, renowned New Critic Cleanth Brooks exemplified the strategic harnessing of New Critical principles to the conservative cause of hierarchy. Reviewing Robert Penn Warren's novel *Band of Angels*, Brooks praised its lack of an intelligible (progressive) political message: "[I]t forces us to lay aside our slogans and formulae, our political and sociological diagnoses, and to contemplate freshly once more the essential human predicament" ("Powerful and Subtle," 28). Even the horrific racism experienced by one character, Amantha, was bound up with such a "complex" form of Southern racism that it should forestall the liberal reader's outright condemnation: "If what happens to Amantha provides a poignant instance of the horror involved in racial discrimination, it also provides a reminder of the complexity of the problem. For Warren is not willing to exploit his heroine as an innocent victim" (28). What a book review like this in *National Review* showed was that, in addition to evaluating how "conservative" a novel was based on content, literary form was also vitally important.

Echoing Bourdieu's point that high art forms presuppose "a sort of moral agnosticism," the fault of many liberal novelists was not so much their usage of foul language or risqué sexual scenes but their formal aesthetic deficiencies vis-à-vis New Critical principles of judgment (Bourdieu, *Distinction*, 39).[11] In this context, the ultimate formal deficiency was encapsulated in terms like "sentimentality" and "melodrama." Since the formal success of a novel or short story, for New Critics, was premised on every component in a literary work functioning together to produce a single, unitary effect too deep for explanatory words, then melodrama and sentimentality destroyed the aesthetic integrity of that work. "An effect is said to be melodramatic," Brooks and Warren wrote in *Understanding Fiction*, "when the violent or sensational seems to be used for its own sake without adequate reference to motivation of character or other elements in the story" (606). Moreover, they defined sentimentality as an "emotional response in excess of the occasion; emotional response which has not been prepared for in the story in question" (608). At *National Review*, conservatives consistently used this New Critical framework to denounce perceived liberal and leftist novelists. In his review of Norman Mailer's second novel, *The Deer Park* (1955), John Chamberlain stated that he did not necessarily oppose the novel's sexual content, but rather the way in which sex overshadowed everything else in the lives of Mailer's characters, demolishing the formal complexity which should, ideally, reflect the complexity of human experience. The result was that Mailer seemed "almost totally inattentive to their troubles as human beings in the odd moments when they are not engaged in copulation" ("Sex in the Desert," 27). At the height of the Beat Movement four years later, critic John Leonard ventriloquized the *National Review* literary line, denouncing the gratuitous sensationalism of Kerouac and Mailer and reaffirming the axiomatic importance of formal integrity. "The great American novel will be written," Leonard declares, by an author "who can't stand espresso and never heard of Wilhelm Reich – the guy who sits up all night at a typewriter and brings to his peculiar vision the discipline of form" ("Epitaph for the Beat Generation," 331). The hedonistic novels beloved by Beatniks and hipsters, in other words, were ideologically disordered in ways that paralleled their structural disorder with regard to novelistic form.[12]

For movement conservatives, the hazards of sentimentality were not confined to the back-pages of the book review section. The New Critical definition of sentimentality underpinned their conviction that the Left misread reality since they accessed it through melodramatic narratives that aimed to make audiences feel pity for the poor and the downtrodden, leaving readers rudderless and thus susceptible to dangerous swings of political (i.e., collectivist-fascist) emotion. According to Kirk, Burke had identified this tendency during the French Revolution and it supposedly held true for the totalitarian movements of the twentieth century. The French revolutionaries substituted the benign fetters of social custom, Burke wrote in a 1791 letter to Chevalier de Rivarol, with "a virtue which they call humanity or benevolence. By this means their morality has no idea in it of restraint. . . . When their disciples are thus left free and guided only by present feeling they are no longer to be depended upon for good or evil. The men who snatch the worst criminals from justice will murder the most innocent persons tomorrow" (qtd. in *The Conservative Mind*, 29). For traditionalists like Kirk who championed novels through the evaluative lens of New Criticism, Burke had hit on a literary insight. The narratives that the French revolutionaries, and radical leftists forever afterward, carried around in their heads privileged semimetal images of "friends" and "enemies" in a way that obscured the larger, complex formal structure of human experience. In the conservative mind, revolutionaries from the late eighteenth century up through the first half of the twentieth century were bad formalists on whom New Critical irony was lost. Essentially, as cultural agents, these radical revolutionaries were hopelessly lowbrow since they could not adopt "the aesthetic position," in Bourdieu's words, that "generalized capacity [of the high cultured] to neutralize ordinary urgencies and to bracket off practical ends" to see the larger formal pattern – which, for conservatives, synced up with larger formal patterns of social hierarchy (Bourdieu, *Distinction*, 47).

Despite the complicated relationship many New Critics had with contemporaneous American politics, movement conservatives were particularly drawn to their unique, literary definition of irony for two basic reasons: it accorded with not only the early conservative movement's neo-Burkean conception of empirical complexity over abstraction but also the carefully cultivated self-image conservatives had of themselves as guardians of high literary culture. In a definitive New Critical essay on irony, "Irony as a Principle of Structure," Cleanth Brooks famously argued that the crux of poetic meaning was found not in the normative meanings of words themselves but in "the pressures of context" that emerged through structural juxtaposition (738). Brooks noted that several "compelling reasons" explain why superior poets incorporated this specific kind of irony into their work, most importantly among them: the cultural dissolution of a "common symbolism," the increasing modern "skepticism as to universals," and the perversion of the English language itself "by advertising and by the mass-produced arts of radio, the moving picture, and pulp fiction" (738). At the philosophical level, conservatives seized on the notion that complex relations between words could poke holes in universal progressive abstractions such as "racial equality" or "social justice" that won over the masses. In this way, New Critical irony echoed one of Kirk's founding tenets of conservatism in *The Conservative Mind* – that is, that the follower of Burke should have an "[a]ffection for the proliferating variety and mystery of human existence, as opposed to the narrowing uniformity, egalitarianism, and utilitarian aims of most radical systems" (8). At the level of cultural prestige and literary value, movement conservatives also saw this form of irony as a sophisticated articulation of their own disdain for popular entertainment and, by extension, uninformed popular majorities. In *The Conservative Mind*, Kirk made this connection clear in the final chapter, "The Conservative as Poet," citing T. S. Eliot's famous, fearful predication in *Christianity and Culture* (1939) that liberal philistines were "destroying our ancient [cultural] edifices to make ready the ground upon which the barbarian nomads of the future will encamp in their mechanized caravans" (qtd. in Kirk, *Conservative Mind*, 493). The upshot of Eliot's warning, in Kirk's own words, was that "No high culture [was] conceivable in a society dominated by this cast of officialdom" (494). For movement conservatives, whereas progressive liberalism and lowbrow literature were natural allies whose dual tendencies toward social leveling ended in mob taste and mob rule, traditionalist conservatism was aligned with highbrow modernist literature since its forbidding aesthetic difficulty provided a high-status readerly space for conservatives to distinguish themselves from the ignorant masses.

In the early formation of postwar conservatism, the strategic embrace of difficult modernist literature for socioeconomic distinction was inextricable from the movement's de facto endorsement of Jim Crow segregation. This theme was most conspicuous in the unwavering support conservatives provided to William Faulkner in the wake of his infamous comments about desegregation a few years after the *Brown* decision. In a March 1956 essay published in *Life*, "Letter to a Northern Editor," Faulkner declared that, though he had always been "against compulsory segregation," the alarming speed of federal desegregation actions obliged him to be "just as strongly against compulsory integration," since he doubted the efficacy of using "police compulsion to eradicate that evil overnight" (51). In these sections of the essay, despite his insistence on being a "liberal," Faulkner sounded like he was making a traditionalist conservative case, arguing in textbook Burkean fashion that sentimental liberals erred in their belief that the "condition of the South [was] so simple and so uncomplex [*sic*] that it [could] be changed tomorrow by the simple will of the national majority backed by legal edict" (51). In other sections, though, Faulkner's larger argument combined anti-majoritarianism with a rationale for Southern racial oppression that more closely resembled not so much Burke as the postwar conservative revisionist embrace of John C. Calhoun. If the federal government did not "stop for a moment," Faulkner wrote, they would give white Southerners the legitimate right to question "the issue by that purely automatic sentimental appeal to that same universal human instinct for automatic sympathy for the underdog [that liberals used to arouse sympathy for African Americans]" (51–52). In *The Conservative Mind*, Kirk praised Calhoun for taking a strikingly similar position with regard to antebellum slavery. Calhoun was "the most resolute enemy of national consolidation and of omnicompetent [*sic*] democratic majorities," Kirk noted, and his stance could still teach conservatives a valuable principle: "the forbidding problem of the rights of individuals and groups menaced by the will of overbearing majorities" (169–170). In an interview Faulkner did for *The Reporter* two months later, he doubled down on this argument with an infamous remark about using violence to defend the institutions of Jim Crow, despite their profound flaws. At bottom, Faulkner maintained that the problem of desegregation was not racial, but that if Northern liberals continued to insist on dividing Southerners along racial lines, he would be willing to "fight for Mississippi against the United States if it meant going out into the street and shooting Negroes" (Meriwether and Millgate, 261). Disregarding the individual rights of Southern blacks, Faulkner pitted the oppressed individual (Jim Crow Mississippi) against the tyrannical, mob-ruled Leviathan (the federal government) in a way that resonated deeply with the early conservative movement.

In *National Review*, conservatives not only supported Faulkner's argument, a predictable move considering their ongoing negative editorials on desegregation, but they also claimed that Faulkner's comments verified his prestigious literary reputation precisely when so many liberal media outlets were trying to separate the two. In the anonymous article "Voices of Sanity" (April 7, 1956), which was either written or approved by Buckley, the author noted that Faulkner was one of the most articulate spokesmen for the corporate *National Review* position on desegregation. Though the "Nobel Prize novelist" was nominally "against segregated schooling," the author wrote, Faulkner was "convinced that the issue [was] political, not racial, and involve[d] inalienable rights of the member-states. So he declare[d] he [was] one with those who intend[ed] to resist the order of the Court" (7). Paradoxically echoing both the Declaration of Independence and John C. Calhoun's nullification theory, the author framed the issue as a dispute between the "inalienable rights" of a state, personified as an individual, and an all-powerful federal government that was illegitimate *because of its majoritarian mandate.* The validity of Faulkner's argument rested not on his sociopolitical acumen but on his literary reputation as a titan of modernism, as a formally challenging novelist playing the role of the modern-day Old Testament prophet who diagnosed cultural illnesses and spoke truth to worldly power. No matter what liberals or leftists said to "dismiss" men like Faulkner, the author concluded, "their voices count[ed]: for theirs, in respect of their dogged insistence that other things than Jim Crow [were] at stake, [were] the voices of sanity" (7). Throughout the rest of the fifties, and up until Faulkner's death in 1962, movement conservatives praised Faulkner for his "difficult," supposedly morally courageous, stance on hasty integration and connected it to his equally "difficult" fiction. In a fawning *National Review* obituary, the editors placed Faulkner among Hemingway, Fitzgerald, and Dos Passos, but implicitly elevated him as the greatest of these American modernists. Unlike Hemingway's flirtation with leftist fiction in *To Have and Have Not* (1937), Fitzgerald's emotional and cavalier flings with Marxism, and Dos Passos's famous socialist-inspired early novels, Faulkner had ostensibly never degraded his novels with politics – meaning, of course, progressive politics. Faulkner's Yoknapatawpha County was fundamentally different than those "surface worlds of the passing problem-and-thesis novel [of socialist realism], which washed out to sea with every publishing season. Faulkner wrote for the ages" ("William Faulkner, RIP," 54). Calling Faulkner a "difficult man, and very often a difficult writer," the article affirmed that this "double difficultness was, perhaps, a necessary armor against the soul-crushing assaults of the age of the masses" (54). In the conservative mind of the fifties, Faulkner's undeniable accumulation of cultural capital served as the implicit foundation of his political insight. Faulkner's greatness as a novelist proved the depth to which he understood the complexity of Southern race relations and the revolutionary monomania of progressive liberalism, for he dramatized his arguments in a challenging modernist style that was formally inextricable from its content. However, as I demonstrate in the following chapters, conservatives would abandon this explicitly racist defense of highbrow literature only a few decades later, as their theoretical rationales for Jim Crow segregation became untenable and they shifted toward a new form of colorblind individualism under Reaganism.

1.4 Conclusion: The Meaning of Ralph Ellison's (Near) Invisibility

To fortify the linkage I have been illuminating between aesthetic value and the implicit support for segregation in early postwar conservatism, I conclude by briefly sketching out the conservative movement's curious, though revealing, lack of enthusiasm for Ralph Ellison's *Invisible Man* (1952). If the high modernist aesthetics that conservatives valued were not bound up with *apologias* for racial segregation, Ellison could have been the favored novelist of the early conservative movement, despite his almost certain protestations. To be clear, I am not positing a hypothetical counter-history in which Ellison would have affiliated himself with movement conservatism, nor am I even suggesting that Ellison was a "conservative" in either a specific or a vague sense of the term.[13] Rather, I contend that Ellison, for a brief historical moment in the fifties, appeared like the perfect kind of highbrow, modernist-influenced novelist whom conservatives were desperately seeking to identify in order to lend their movement intellectual and cultural respectability. It was not Ellison's modernist aesthetics conservatives found challenging, though, but rather his anti-segregationist politics rooted in the same rhetoric of colorblind individualism that would, ironically, make him a relatively frequent point of reference for movement conservatives in the eighties.

On the surface, Ellison's *Invisible Man* had several characteristics that would have made it attractive to early movement conservatives. Directly influenced by conservative literary favorites such as Eliot and Faulkner, Ellison famously combined the techniques of Anglophone modernism, the myths of Western civilization, and various symbols drawn from American culture to produce a work of stunning formal and thematic complexity. In addition to these supposedly nonpolitical high cultural elements, Ellison also embedded critical representations of left-wing politics from communism to Black Nationalism that would have made conservatives cheer even louder. Ellison emphasized the way leftists and liberals tended to concoct stereotypes of black life as brutal and irredeemable in order to make the case for radical political change, thus obscuring the rich humanity of real black people. In *Invisible Man*, this notion of racial invisibility finds its strongest manifestations in Brother Jack and Ras the Exhorter, who represent the communist Left as a member of the fictional socialist organization "the Brotherhood" and a distinctly American brand of black nationalism, respectively. While communism remained a viable redemptive option in the end of a novel like Richard Wright's *Native Son*, Ellison's portrayal of communism was characterized by cold-blooded ruthlessness, as the Brotherhood pursues its socio-political goals with Stalinist cynicism. For many, the Brotherhood is "blind" to the humanity of the proletariat, especially poor blacks, whom the Brotherhood uses and then sacrifices – sometimes via deadly, pre-mediated Harlem riots – in the name of the greater collective good. While the accuracy of Ellison's portrayal of early Cold War–era American Communism is both controversial and outside my argumentative purview, the one-eyed Brother Jack is a nodal point in the critical literature on the implications of invisibility and blindness on the Left.[14]

After the narrator puts on an impromptu funeral for the black Brotherhood member Tod Clifton without receiving pre-clearance from the Brotherhood itself, Brother Jack scolds the narrator and reminds him that the proletariat is afflicted with collective false consciousness: "The committee makes your decisions, and it is not its practice to give undue importance to the mistaken notions of the people" (*Invisible Man*, 356). In the midst of admonishing the narrator, though, Brother Jack's fake glass eye falls out. According to the Ellison scholar Barbara Foley, Brother Jack's glass eye is an "imagistic equation" of blindness and invisibility (282). Like Foley, many critics consider the glass eye to be symbolically equivalent to the Brotherhood's blindness to the very proletariat that the Brotherhood claims to be trying to help. However, a movement conservative reading would probably emphasize an entirely different notion of blindness. For an early-fifties anti-communist like Whittaker Chambers, Brother Jack's glass eye would not be read as blindness but as a deeply probing myopia, as a tunnel vision of classical Marxist ideology critique. Ellison even drives home this point after Brother Jack picks up his eye and tells the narrator that "discipline is sacrifice," to which the narrator responds silently: "Discipline is sacrifice. Yes, and blindness" (359). Ellison suggests that leftists who are thoroughly disciplined in this kind of ideology critique are blind because, ironically, they pass off their critiques as the most acute kind of vision.

Although the Brotherhood and Ras the Exhorter both think they are enemies (i.e., the Brotherhood claims that race is just a smokescreen for class struggle, and Ras claims that socialist organizations merely perpetuate white supremacy), they both utilize the same structural discourse to misrepresent African Americans as stereotypes. The first time the narrator encounters Ras, Ras warns him: "I am no black traitor to the black people for the white people" (284). As an organization whose real motive is the strengthening of white power under different political labels, Ras believes that the Brotherhood traffics in intra-black strife. But for all his pride in the black race, Ras has no problem proclaiming that the black narrator should be lynched during the Harlem riot. In this climactic scene, the narrator realizes that Ras and the black nationalists misunderstand the narrator's ontological human-ness just like the Brotherhood:

> I was invisible, and hanging would not bring me to visibility, even in their eyes, since they wanted my death not for myself alone but for the chase I'd been on all my life . . . although to a great extent I could have done nothing else, given their blindness . . . and my invisibility. (422)

Even if the narrator is lynched, Ras will not see the narrator as human *qua* human since the narrator does not fit into his black nationalist stereotype of a black man. The movement conservative reading would point out that, just like Brother Jack, Ras is equally blinded by an abstract leftist ideology. Both leftist ideologies are characterized not by naivety and thoughtlessness, but by the hysterical repetition of a hermeneutical method that has rendered flesh-and-blood African Americans invisible because they require a fallen, pathological black culture to save and redeem. Ultimately, a conservative take on *Invisible Man* would stress not the simplistic notion of white blindness and black invisibility, but the Left's hyper-interpretation of an all-too-visible blackness.

That movement conservatives were *not* making these arguments, nor even acknowledging the cultural impact of *Invisible Man* throughout the fifties, signifies a conspicuous absence. As Kenneth W. Warren notes, *Invisible Man* was an "occasional novel" deeply inflected by the cultural transition between

Jim Crow and the civil rights era, and it bears the hallmarks of anti-communist modernism applauded by New York Intellectuals (3). The primary reason why conservatives were not engaging enthusiastically with the novel was because movement conservatives did not know how to reconcile Ellison's anti-racist themes with their own contemporaneous traditionalist defense of Jim Crow. In the novel's epilogue, the narrator decides that the only way to resolve the conflict between America's founding ideals and the country's historical oppression is to follow his grandfather's deathbed advice for dealing with white people: "I want you to overcome 'em with yeses, undermine 'em with grins" (13). As a young man, the narrator believed that his grandfather was naïve, but by the end of the novel, he understands that his grandfather meant that African Americans "were to affirm the principle on which the country was built and not the men" (433). For left-leaning critics, the narrator's commitment to the nation's abstract founding principles sounds generically conservative, making the ending a problematic site of interpretation. From Barbara Foley's perspective, the narrator reframes the moral contradiction as an aesthetic paradox; "like a New Critic, the invisible man cherishes the ambivalence that enables him to oscillate between the poles of antinomy and avoid the dull certainties of political commitment" (344). From the perspective of a midcentury movement conservative, though, any call to "affirm the principle" of individual freedom from the mouth of a black novelist was an ominous sign, as it imaginatively transformed American ideals into floating principles of equality that could disrupt the careful balance between traditional hierarchy and individual liberty that conservatives saw in their cherished ideal of "ordered liberty." The narrator stresses the imaginative leap while he continues to ponder his grandfather's advice: "Did he mean to affirm the principle, which they themselves had dreamed into being out of the chaos and darkness of the feudal past, and which they had violated and compromised to the point of absurdity even in their own corrupt minds?" (433). His approach to the American founding here is both fetishistic and pragmatic. Significantly, the narrator does not say that the nation's founders discovered a trans-historical truth, but that they "dreamed" the principle of democracy out of chaotic contingency. The result, in terms of political theory, is that the authoritative origin of American democracy resides neither in a place, nor in a group of eighteenth-century male founders, nor in a single "People" (racially defined or otherwise); it resides in a principle that the narrator knows was conceived as a grotesque fiction but would, someday, become a beautiful truth of pluralistic equality.

By examining the early conservative reception of Ellison's work, one can see the clear problem its high modernist assertion of black individuality and freedom posed for the conservative movement. In the most noteworthy critical engagement, Russell Kirk's "The Fiction of Politics and Poverty," later published in his miscellaneous collection of early literary writings *Enemies of the Permanent Things* (1969), Kirk could praise the novel's modernist form only by patently misreading its critique of twentieth-century American racism. After arguing that a significant percentage of novels "by colored authors are ferocious to the point of madness" and "distorted by ideological passion," Kirk singled out *Invisible Man* as his "chief exception to this harsh judgment" (*Enemies*, 129–30). Applauding its high modernist form, the novel was a powerful "blending of symbolism and realism," Kirk wrote, and its structural complexity demonstrated that Ellison had "fought free of ideology" (130). But when Kirk attempted to link the novel's formal brilliance with its racial themes, he twisted it into a defense for hierarchy that smacked of traditionalist conservatism – reactionary racial politics and all. Marked by the kind of bizarre preface that tended to accompany such conservative arguments, Kirk began by saying that Ellison understood that there was "*nothing* wrong about being colored or poor" (130, emphasis original). Kirk continued in a similar vein:

> [Ellison] understands that the *circumstances* of poverty, and the way in which a man bears his poverty or his color, are what matter. He is aware of what nearly everyone else has forgotten, that the poor, suffer though they may, are especially blessed of the Lord; and that some of them show it. He does not mean to whitewash the colored man, or to convert all the poor into dully affluent suburbanites. He is endowed with the tragic sense of life. (130, emphasis in original)

As a traditionalist conservative, Kirk believed, in his favorite phrase, that "political problems, at bottom, are religious and moral problems" (*Conservative Mind*, 7). For him, poverty and racism should be regarded less as political phenomena than as unalterable realities of the world ordained by God and thus designed to prepare the ground for spiritual growth. Racism especially set the stage for a metaphysical epiphany that suffering should inspire reverence for God, not interrogations of American history, a conviction that frequently conjured up sentimentalized images of stoic black suffering. For Kirk, despite all evidence to the contrary, Ellison was a great novelist because he used the idiom of high modernism to substitute colorblind individualism for traditionalism's humble equality before God alone. Any other interpretation, of course, would have undermined the conservative linkage between highbrow literary culture and reactionary racial politics.[15]

From the beginning, the conservative movement was based on the conviction that racially progressive liberalism, even Ellison's anti-communist strain, was somehow continuous with the modern phenomenon of totalitarian communism and fascism. For decades, American historians have framed this liberalism-as-totalitarianism claim by conservatives as intellectually ludicrous, as a willful misrepresentation of the facts and a flight from reality into the crudest kind of ideological fear mongering. In her comprehensive history of the party of Lincoln, *To Make Men Free: A History of the Republican Party* (2014), Heather Cox Richardson sums up post-1945 conservatism in one scathing sentence: "Movement Conservatism had always been based in ideology, not reality" (321). But what scholarly statements like this one, regardless of their validity, tend to miss is the conservative belief that the postwar political paradigm was a fantastical sociopolitical construction of liberalism. The discourse of American fiction and the genre of the novel, at the height of its cultural prestige in the mid-fifties and early sixties, provided movement conservatives with precisely what they thought they needed: a reputable foothold into the realm of political fantasy.

Conservatives were confident that the Great American Novel, even one that was antithetical to modern conservatism, was serious business.[16] Movement conservatives shared the assumption of many midcentury critics and intellectuals that, in Mark Greif's words, the novel was a uniquely important medium of cultural authority, and the crucial space in which cultural capital could be accumulated: "a vault of cultural knowledge, a tool for culturing people, and a work of art rather than an entertainment" (104). For conservatives, though, one had to add to this list that the novel could supply Americans with the symbolic ground upon which to reimagine how progressive liberalism would degenerate into a dangerous, totalitarian form of collectivism – an ominous fate heralded, most conspicuously in the fifties, by liberals who advocated for the full civil rights of racial minorities. As Kirk argued in a 1955 essay, "The Dissolution of Liberalism," the power and prestige of literature cannot be overstated: "All great systems, ethical or political, attain their ascendency over the minds of men by virtue of their appeal to the imagination" (23). Since the most profound truths take the narrative form of myth, Kirk believed, Americans needed powerful myths in the form of literature to see the process of degeneration (27–30). Indeed, this literary "myth" underpinned the entire ideological discourse structure of the early conservative movement. Once that cornerstone idea is understood, one can grasp the importance of the surprisingly high-stakes literary arguments that played out in the movement surrounding the next chapter's key literary figures, Flannery O'Connor and Ayn Rand. These two major postwar authors epitomized the divisions in movement conservatism, for their fictional works offered diametrically opposed conceptions of literary form, high cultural prestige, race, and totalitarian collectivism, and thus two radically different mythopoetic foundations for postwar American conservatism.

CHAPTER 2

The Conservative Movement's Foundational Fictions

Flannery O'Connor, Ayn Rand, and the Evolving Literary Forms of Conservatism, 1950–1964

2.1 Introduction: The Literary Aesthetic You Save May Be Your Own

In a private 1956 letter to Betty Hester, Flannery O'Connor informed her frequent correspondent that she had sold the television rights to her short story "The Life You Save May Be Your Own" to *General Electric Theater*. Noting that the show "was a production conducted by Ronald Regan [*sic*]," O'Connor expressed her discomfort with Reagan playing Mr. Shiflet, the story's conflicted protagonist who is haunted by the bourgeois nihilism of postwar American life, because she feared that Reagan would turn it into the kind of simplistic morality tale that the original story was meant to challenge: "Mr. Shiflet and the idiot daughter will no doubt go off in a Chrisler [*sic*] and live happily ever after" (*Habit of Being*, 174). Hosted by Reagan from 1953 to 1962, *General Electric Theater* was a lighthearted anthology series that General Electric used as an ill-disguised public relations outreach program. As one Reagan biographer put it, the show represented not only "the epitome of midcentury middle-brow entertainment" but also "the pivotal stretch when [Reagan's] mature political views and skills emerged … the time when his conservative ideology was formed" (Weisberg, *Ronald Reagan: The American Presidents Series*, 34). For O'Connor, the early crystallization of Reagan's so-called conservative ideology combined vulgar aesthetic taste with a shallow moral innocence underpinned by the sinful greed of corporate capitalism – an ideological combination O'Connor also saw in Ayn Rand, whose fiction O'Connor said made "Mickey Spillane look like Dostoevsky" as it championed one-dimensional philosophical "Absolutes" (*Habit of Being*, 398; 528). As a friend of Russell Kirk and a supporter of his neo-Burkean conception of traditionalism, O'Connor represented a very different vision of postwar conservatism inseparable from highbrow literature and robust moral inquiry. In this chapter, I explore these conflicting visions of aesthetic taste and political ideology in the early conservative movement, demonstrating how the internal debate influenced not only modern conservatism but also specific aspects of the broader cultural politics of postwar American fiction.

At first glance, it is difficult to understand how two authors as dissimilar as Flannery O'Connor and Ayn Rand could have been so important to constitutive pieces of the same political movement. In addition to their divergent lifestyles – O'Connor an orthodox Roman Catholic who lived essentially her entire life in rural Georgia, Rand a Russian-born atheist who immigrated to the United States and lived mostly between California and New York City – both authors developed starkly contrasting aesthetic dispositions. O'Connor, a famous alumna of the Iowa Writers' Workshop in the late forties, crafted a style rooted in the New Critical principles of nuance, irony, ambiguity, and paradox. Conversely, Rand absorbed the formal characteristics of socialist realism and then inverted them in the service of unfettered capitalism. As her recent biographer Jennifer Burns points out, Rand's novels closely mimicked the most ideologically fervent protest novels published in the Soviet Union: heavy-handed political messages, crude juxtapositions of purely good and evil systems of thought, and, most importantly, "cardboard characters in the service of an overarching ideology" (178–79). Unsurprisingly, their respective visions of conservatism seemed just as incompatible. The supreme champion of libertarian capitalism, Rand loathed Christianity, metaphysical mystery over rational thought, the concept of original sin, and the limitations on individual "liberty" imposed by historical forces and social custom. On the other hand, O'Connor was distressed by the dissolution of religious faith, the prominence of techno-scientific rationalism, the increasing materialism of American life, and the modern tendency to ignore the historical wisdom of the ancients. In short, O'Connor stood for virtually everything Rand despised, and Rand represented virtually everything O'Connor lamented.

However, like the American conservatism movement itself, O'Connor and Rand shared one crucial belief in the wake of World War II: the notion that Soviet Communism was a totalitarian, fascistic force that represented an existential threat to each of their ideological systems of thought – Christianity and capitalism, respectively. In this sense, O'Connor and Rand epitomized the larger debate in the conservative movement between Christian traditionalists and libertarian capitalists, as they offered wholly different explanations for the looming possibility of totalitarianism in

America. They also directly influenced the debate concerning the very meaning of "conservatism" because of the specific ways in which each author rendered the trope of "American Fascism" and its attendant racial anxieties differently in their respective fictional works. Traditionalists, especially Russell Kirk, embraced O'Connor as a young, emerging highbrow fiction writer who understood the revolutionary implications of secular materialism and thus helped ground conservatism in Christianity and tradition. Alternatively, despite reservations about Rand's atheism, libertarian conservatives argued for the straightforward, rhetorically persuasive nature of Rand's lowbrow fiction and acknowledged her seminal influence on libertarianism as a school of thought that permeated the conservative movement. O'Connor and Rand, each reimagining and personifying a different strand of movement conservatism, produced literary works that were not just contradictory explanations but radically incompatible antinomies. The works of O'Connor and Rand highlighted the antinomy that had always been operating at the heart of movement conservatism: The supposed descent into totalitarian collectivism in postwar America would occur either (for traditionalists) because liberal politicians were advocating for civil rights, destroying organic social order, and abandoning the wisdom of Christian tradition as they accommodated secular materialism, or (for libertarians) because politicians were not breaking up the New Deal social order *fast enough* since the "rights" of individual liberty were constantly being infringed upon by the government's illegitimate welfare schemes.

Conservatives found it difficult to solve this antinomy because it was not amenable to a neat solution. From the beginning, conservatives sought to manage the intellectual friction that was generated by different camps in the movement by emphasizing common enemies and smoothing over profound philosophical differences. If thinkers refused to adulterate the purity of their positions, which was the case with both O'Connor and Rand, either Buckley exiled them from the movement or his team at *National Review* reshaped their positions to fit within the reigning, though ever-shifting, definition of modern conservatism. This pattern suggests, in the words of George Nash, that American conservatism "in the fifties and sixties was not, in its essence, a speculative or theoretical enterprise. It was an intellectual *movement* with definite political implications. It sought not just to understand the world but to preserve, purify, even restore some of it" (171). In accordance with their increasing desire for formal political power, conservatives in the early movement were interested in winning not simply intellectual or academic arguments but cultural arguments with an intellectual vocabulary drawn from the internal prestige of high cultural fields. Between the early fifties and the rise of Goldwater in 1964, the works of O'Connor and Rand became part and parcel of a strategic shift that occurred in the rhetoric of conservatism away from the traditionalist emphasis on order and toward the libertarian emphasis on liberty. This shift was bound up with the pervasive idea on the Right that progressive advocacy via the federal government begun by the New Deal constituted the first rumblings of an undemocratic form of American Fascism. As the movement coalesced in 1955, conservatives found in O'Connor's fiction not only a powerful affirmation of traditionalist conservatism but a complex way of translating their tacit support for Jim Crow segregation into the language of religious suffering and metaphysical mystery. But when these traditionalist principles became untenable in the early sixties, conservatives began to turn to Rand's didactic literary brand of theoretical abstraction and colorblind individualism, even as they sought to exclude Rand herself from the conservative movement.

In this chapter, I examine how Kirk's early identification of Flannery O'Connor as the most important young fiction writer in 1955 epitomized traditionalist conservatism's faith in the sophisticated fiction of high culture. O'Connor was a unique type of conservative who was simultaneously an orthodox Catholic who saw totalitarian collectivism as an outgrowth of philosophical materialism *and* a disciple of the New Critics who believed that fiction, at its best, was a form of inquiry that was far too rich and complex to be wasted on ideological didacticism. I argue that shifting conservative literary tastes can also be discerned in movement conservatism's contemporaneous reception of Ayn Rand. Unlike O'Connor and traditionalist conservatives who valued aesthetic form over abstract ideas, Rand and the libertarian conservatives at *National Review* who championed her novel *Atlas Shrugged* (1957) were concerned above all with advancing a firm set of ideological principles through the medium of fiction. To disagree with these principles, in the eyes of Rand and her supporters, was tantamount to an aesthetic condemnation of her novel. While Buckley eventually ousted Rand from the conservative movement, her immense popularity with conservatives of the era foreshadowed the movement's growing distrust of literary fiction and its eventual embrace of ideological purity and cultural populism. As movement conservatives began to gain power within the Republican Party in the sixties, their ideological principles hardened and rigidified, especially in the face of the civil rights movement, and the kinds of contemporary literature conservatives valued narrowed significantly.

Following the recent work of historians and political scientists who underscore modern American conservatism's intellectual fissures, inherent discontinuities, and constant internal disputes, I highlight the extent to which postwar fiction served as an important, though still largely ignored, intellectual touchstone in the foundational debates occurring at this time between traditionalists and libertarians in the pages of *National Review* concerning the very definitional coherence of "modern conservatism" as a label and a movement. By close reading selected works by O'Connor and Rand, two fundamentally different fiction writers with material and symbolic linkages to the conservative movement, I reveal not only the importance of fiction as a crucial nodal point in these debates but also how racially fraught literary representations of totalitarian collectivism proved to be foundational for conceptualizing modern American conservatism.

2.2 O'Connorian Traditionalism vs. Randian Libertarianism: Antinomies of Literary Form and Anti-collectivism in the Conservative Imagination

What is at stake when one links, as I do, Flannery O'Connor to postwar American conservatism? Admittedly, scholars of O'Connor's fiction, and even some of her perennially loyal fans, may object to my portrayal of O'Connor and her work, especially when juxtaposed with a controversial figure like Rand, who has historically been treated in literary studies as a shoddy novelist at best and a reactionary propagandist at worst. Since O'Connor's early death in 1964, literary scholars have advocated several different models for understanding the political implications of her fiction, but practically none of them have aligned her with postwar American conservatism as closely as I do here. Scholars have always acknowledged that O'Connor's fiction, rooted in orthodox Catholicism, lends tacit support to "conservatism" in the most general and nebulous meaning of that term. In his standalone chapter dedicated to O'Connor in the *Cambridge Companion to American Fiction after 1945* (2011), Jay Watson summarized this position when he identified two guiding themes that O'Connor reiterated over and over in her work that are undoubtedly conservative in some sense:

> The first was a cosmological and epistemological emphasis on mystery, a conviction that the workings of the universe were ultimately unknowable, exceeding the limits of human perception and reason. The second was

> a deep belief in the radical incompleteness and dependence of humanity, a condition of ontological lack remediable only by and through otherness, an outside agency she identified with God's grace. (208)

Watson's observation descends from what was once largely the consensus interpretation of the significance of politics in O'Connor's fiction – which is to say, politics was hardly important at all compared to theology.[1]

It was not until the eighties that critics and scholars began to read O'Connor's work increasingly through the theoretical lenses of feminism, psychoanalysis, post-structuralism, and critical race theory. But even in those critical works, the theological dimension of O'Connor's fiction tended to be separated and privileged over the political. For several decades, this template for interpreting her fiction remained operational: Scholars acknowledged that O'Connor foregrounded sociopolitical problems in her fiction but resolved them with theological solutions because she allegedly was not interested in politics. Then they proceeded to read O'Connor mostly on her own terms, while they went about highlighting the political repercussions of her work.[2] Even more recent critics who have taken a direct interest in O'Connor's politics, such as Jon Lance Bacon and Andrew Hoberek, frame their interpretations as displacing the thematic importance of theology with politics in a way that O'Connor would supposedly deplore due to her ostensible political apathy.[3] When O'Connor wrote fiction, Bacon and Hoberek suggest, she was not very concerned with the political dimensions of postwar life, but her fiction was saturated with American politics, so critics would be remiss to ignore that inescapable fact.

However, considering O'Connor's strong material and symbolic linkages to the conservative movement, I contend that the theological and political are not so much discrete units in O'Connor's work as consciously inextricable components of a unified, sociopolitical conservative vision. Throughout most of her adult life, O'Connor reiterated this vision vis-à-vis Kirk's definition of traditionalist conservatism. Judging by her private letters, O'Connor's praise for Kirk began sometime in the mid-fifties, as her first allusion to his political thought comes in a letter to Betty Hester dated October 12, 1955, wherein she expressed her admiration for *The Conservative Mind* (*Habit of Being,* 110). Later that month, O'Connor and Kirk met in person for the first and only time in the Tennessee home of Georgia author Brainard Cheney, who had recently written a positive review of Kirk's *The Conservative Mind* in *Sewanee Review*, where O'Connor read her story "A Good Man Is Hard to Find" aloud to

Kirk, Cheney, and his wife Fanny. After this encounter, O'Connor wrote another letter to Hester about meeting Kirk, describing him comically as a man who was "about 37, looks like Humpty Dumpty (intact) with constant cigar and (outside) porkpie hat," but O'Connor also voiced her firm support for Kirk's impending bimonthly political journal *The Conservative Review*, which would eventually be renamed and published under the name *Modern Age* (112).

Less than one year after meeting Kirk, O'Connor published an enthusiastic review of Kirk's essay collection *Beyond the Dreams of Avarice* in July of 1956. Asserting that the "mainspring of any enlightened social thought" must be rooted in "the obedience to divine truth," O'Connor credited Kirk with making "the voice of an intelligent and vigorous conservative thought respected in this country" (*Presence of Grace,* 23). Echoes of Kirk's thought could also be heard in O'Connor's classic defense of Southern identity as an assemblage of conservative characteristics: "a distrust of the abstract, a sense of human dependence on the grace of God, and a knowledge that evil is not simply a problem to be solved, but a mystery to be endured" ("The Catholic Novelist in the South," *CW,* 862). It is not an exaggeration to say, bearing in mind how O'Connor usually reserved her highest praise strictly for medieval theologians, that Russell Kirk was the most influential living political theorist on her thought.

Similarly for Kirk, whose critical attention was almost always fixed on the literary and political conservatives of the past, O'Connor was the most important up-and-coming fiction writer of the late fifties and the early sixties. After meeting O'Connor, he became a strong advocate among Anglo-American conservatives for her fiction because of its deep implications for the kind of traditionalist conservatism he sought to establish in the United States. In his memoir, *The Sword of Imagination* (1995), Kirk devoted an entire chapter to the Georgia writer, "Flannery O'Connor: Notes by Humpty Dumpty," in which he recounted what happened after he had discussed literature and politics with O'Connor in Tennessee. On his trip back to Michigan, Kirk devoured O'Connor's story collection *A Good Man Is Hard to Find* (1955) and then, once at home, familiarized himself with "nearly everything that she had written" (*Sword of Imagination,* 182). Kirk was so moved by O'Connor's fiction that he wrote a personal letter to T.S. Eliot, his London publisher at the time, urging him to read her work, even though he rarely recommended new fiction to Eliot (182). Looking back on this recommendation in his memoir, Kirk stated that he was attempting to position O'Connor as the latest author in a long line of American conservatives stretching from Hawthorne to Eliot. According to Kirk, O'Connor was a descendant of these American literary figures because her fiction threw into relief the cosmic importance of "sin and redemption," making her a powerful new voice for conservatism (183). At times, Kirk even talked about O'Connor as the century's defining conservative novelist. "Without preaching and without explaining her symbols, Flannery O'Connor became the great philosophical and theological novelist – better far than Graham Greene – of this dissolving twentieth century" ("Flannery O'Connor and the Grotesque Face of God," 433). Ultimately, in Kirk's eyes at least, it was difficult to overestimate O'Connor's literary and political significance to an intellectually respectable postwar conservative movement.

At the heart of this reciprocal admiration between O'Connor and Kirk was the mutual conviction, in Kirk's words, that "political problems, at bottom, are religious and moral problems," particularly when those political problems had to do with desegregation and voting rights in the South (*Conservative Mind*, 7). As Kirk notes in his memoir, O'Connor's politics mirrored his own: "she stood with the [Southern] Agrarians – adding a Catholic element" (183). For O'Connor – as for Southern Agrarians, including Allen Tate, John Crowe Ransom, Robert Penn Warren, Andrew Nelson Lytle, and Donald Davidson – the techniques of New Criticism knotted together questions of morality, politics, and aesthetics in a way that acknowledged the complexity of lived experience born of historical custom. Instead of using literature as a blunt tool for social criticism and political change, thereby artificially bifurcating politics and aesthetics into separate categories, O'Connor and the Southern Agrarians saw literary texts as sophisticated artistic objects that punctured the illusions created by theoretical abstractions of all kinds, especially political abstractions like equality. In her essay "The Nature and Aim of Fiction," O'Connor made this sentiment clear when she criticized the ham-fisted political tendencies of young fiction writers:

> They are apt to be reformers and to want to write because they are possessed not by a story but by the bare bones of some abstract notion. They are conscious of problems, not of people, of questions and issues, not of the texture of existence, of case studies and everything that has a sociological smack, instead of with all those concrete details of life that make actual the mystery of our position on earth. (*Mystery and Manners*, 67–68)

Unlike libertarian conservatives like Rand, who began with an assertion of abstract rights, traditionalist conservatives like O'Connor and Kirk arrived at their political convictions through an aesthetic dimension bound up with concrete sense experience.

When confronted with the controversial racial problems of midcentury America, each conservative philosophical orientation produced dramatically different answers. Whereas O'Connorian traditionalism displaced the political dimension of racial issues into the realm of Christian metaphysics, and for this reason was favored by early movement conservatives in their implicit support for Jim Crow, Randian libertarianism was marked by a dogged commitment to colorblind individualism that was initially looked on with suspicion and would not become the dominant conservative position on race until the late twentieth century. For Rand, who almost always broke down an issue into a black-and-white moral absolute, racial prejudice was certainly not an existential, Faulknerian theme about white identity to be agonized over. As "the lowest, most crudely primitive form of collectivism," Rand wrote, racism was "the caveman's version of the doctrine of innate ideas – or of inherited knowledge – which has been thoroughly refuted by philosophy and science" (*Virtue of Selfishness,* 126). In typical Randian fashion, she simply weighed racial prejudice against her sacrosanct theoretical ideals of "reason" and "individualism," and found it to be another incompatible, intolerable "form of determinism" (126).[4] Conversely, O'Connor equated Rand's abstract ideals with pride and the doctrine of original sin, for they failed to take into account humanity's complex, natural inclination toward evil. Unsurprisingly, all of O'Connor's major stories dealing with racial prejudice – for example, "The Artificial Nigger" (1955), "The Displaced Person" (1955), "Everything That Rises Must Converge" (1961), "Revelation" (1965), "Judgment Day" (1965) – are ambivalent riddles that end not with horizontal, political equality between persons, a sentimental fantasy of liberals such as the pompous Julian in "Everything That Rises," but with vertical, theological equality before God.[5]

In conservative circles, the enthusiasm generated for O'Connor's work was reinforced by precisely this motif running through her fiction and essays. The concept of sentimentality, for O'Connor and traditionalist conservatives, was inextricably bound up with theological and sociopolitical implications. As one O'Connor biographer reports, O'Connor scribbled marginalia next to a pithy sentence in her personal copy of Kirk's *The Conservative Mind* that sums up the political threats posed by sentimental literature: "Abstract sentimentality ends in real brutality" (qtd. in Gooch, *Flannery: A Life of Flannery O'Connor,* 271). O'Connor developed this conservative axiom most fully in her introduction to *A Memoir of Mary Ann* (1961), a book-length account of a real twelve-year-old girl named Mary Ann, who died from cancer, written by the Dominican nuns who cared for her. First, O'Connor draws a direct historical line from Nathaniel

Hawthorne, and the conservative themes of his fiction, to the death of Mary Ann. O'Connor noted that the Dominican nuns were part of an order, Servants of Relief for Incurable Cancer, which was founded by Hawthorne's daughter, Rose. Late in life, Rose claimed that she had founded the order as a testament to her father, specifically in memory of a moment Hawthorne recounts in his notebooks when he comforted a child disfigured by scurvy with a momentary embrace in the streets of Liverpool, England ("Introduction to Mary Ann," *CW*, 825). From a theological perspective, O'Connor said that the memoir reveals how the goodness of God does not conform to anthropocentric sentimentality. Hawthorne's small gesture of Christian charity, for O'Connor, was inspirational for his daughter because it was rooted in his awareness of inherent human imperfection and the grotesque state everyone shares before God (830).

Toward the end of the introduction, what had been mostly theological reflections on O'Connor's part suddenly give way to a sociopolitical declaration that mimics the rhetorical strategy of movement conservatives like Kirk – that is, highlight a relevant conservative theme expressed by a major nineteenth-century American novelist and then use it to warn contemporary Americans about the possibility of totalitarianism. Reiterating Kirk's appreciation for Hawthorne, O'Connor wrote that Hawthorne's seemingly trivial act was a reflection of conservative restraint he had dramatized so powerfully in his short story *The Birthmark* (1843), in which a clever scientist, Aylmer, marries a young woman, Georgiana, with a conspicuous birthmark on her cheek and kills her in his monomaniacal attempt to eradicate her blemish and perfect her beauty. Unable to accept human suffering for what it is, modern liberal "Alymers whom Hawthorne saw as a menace have multiplied," O'Connor writes; "Busy cutting down human imperfection, they are making headway also on the raw material of good" (830). The meaning of suffering in Hawthorne's story is reiterated in O'Connor's Catholic theodicy for Mary Ann: Suffering is not a technical problem to be explained, but a humbling mystery to be lived through with the succor of faith. "If other ages felt less," O'Connor wrote, alluding to the abstract principle of liberal compassion, "they felt more, even though they saw with the blind, prophetical, unsentimental eye of acceptance, which is to say, of faith" (830). O'Connor laments that in "the absence of this faith now, we govern by tenderness. It is a tenderness which, long cut off from the person of Christ is wrapped in theory" (830). From this premise, O'Connor delivers a rare unequivocal political declaration, stating that once humans attempt to actualize God's love on earth without God's grace, they put into motion a process that leads to fascistic, Holocaust levels of violence: "When tenderness is detached from the source of tenderness, its logical outcome is terror. It ends in forced labor camps and in the fumes of the gas chamber" (830–31). For O'Connor, God's love was an enigmatic paradox that humans could only begin to apprehend through the formal complexity that highbrow fiction mimics and affords. Like other conservatives who subscribed to the notions of complexity and paradox espoused by New Criticism, O'Connor believed that a desire to "cure" human suffering sounded good in theory, like a tidy message in a Soviet realism novel, but that it ultimately disregarded the full range of metaphysical reality and the dark, largely unconscious motivations of the human heart steered by original sin. While liberals would object to her leaps in causal reasoning, it is important to understand how O'Connor's assertion fit neatly into the underlying politico-literary paradigm of movement conservatism. That paradigm did not privilege falsifiable historical observations so much as imaginary insights rendered visible through the medium of "great" literature that warned against synthetic solutions to intractable problems predestined in the natural order of things.

What looks, at first glance, like an unusually extreme political statement made by the supposedly apolitical Georgian recluse in her introduction to *The Memoir of Mary Ann* is actually, as revealed in her personal letters, part of a larger vision of totalitarian collectivism that mirrored the vision of traditionalists in the conservative movement. In an August 1955 letter to Betty Hester, O'Connor responded to Hester's accusation that her fiction contained a latent fascist impulse due to O'Connor's frequent reliance on violence as a narrative catalyst for enlightening her excessively proud characters. Before providing her own definition of "fascism," O'Connor chided Hester for using a term that was at once substantively hollow and emotional volatile: "Of course this word doesn't really exist uncapitalized [*sic*] so in making it that way you have the advantage of using a word with a private meaning and a public odor; which you must not do" (*Habit of Being*, 97). As an alternative, O'Connor wrote that perhaps the best definition one could find for fascism is a "doubt of the efficacy of love" (97). What appears on the surface to signify a suspicion of divine love, O'Connor claimed regarding her fiction, was ironically an expression of a Catholic writer who believed radically in God's love and wrote "fiction designed for a public with a predisposition to believe the opposite" (97). What seemed like "a negative appearance," O'Connor stated, was really the unsentimental wisdom of Christianity clashing with a thoroughly secular society.

O'Connor went on to suggest that it was precisely the same people who accused her of harboring fascist impulses who were unwittingly creating the conditions of possibility for fascist totalitarianism in America. "Another reason for the negative appearance" of her fiction that Hester associates with fascism, O'Connor claimed in a much quoted, though often decontextualized passage, was that "if you live today you breathe in nihilism. In or out of the Church, it's the gas you breathe" (97). One should note that O'Connor did not see nihilism as a synonym for atheism. While overlapping features certainly exist between the terms, in the cosmology of O'Connor fiction, atheists did not simply reject the power of God's love outright. Instead, they were usually Christ-haunted anti-saints who could not help but feel the power of God's grace and who thus wrestled with religious faith as vigorously as any orthodox believer – as exemplified by the religiously tortured protagonist, Hazel Motes, in her first novel, *Wise Blood* (1952). By contrast, the nihilist for O'Connor was someone, self-described Christian or not, who saw religious faith as a pleasant social fiction that provided all the saccharine "uplift" of a greeting card and who treated Christianity as just another supplemental ornament of bourgeois materialism.

According to O'Connor, the horrors of fascism would spring from this kind of nihilistic society foretold by Nietzsche in which God is dead because, no matter how much its members profess to believe in God, they live as if the deepest implications of religious faith do not matter. Like the traditionalist faction of the conservative movement, O'Connor saw Nietzsche as a dark prophet who predicted social revolution and the establishment of authoritarian governments. Whole swaths of postwar American society have had "the moral sense bred out of them," O'Connor wrote in another letter to Hester, just like "the wings have been bred off chickens to produce more white meat on them. This is a generation of wingless chickens, which I suppose is what Nietzsche meant when he said God was dead" (*Habit of Being*, 90). For O'Connor, this generation of "wingless chickens" had lost its moral sense because it conflated moral goodness with material gratification, sentimental "tenderness," and a form of compassion saturated with liberal clichés. In other words, postwar Americans had forgotten the ancient doctrinal insight, O'Connor said, that often "the truth as revealed by faith is hideous, emotionally disturbing, downright repulsive" (*Habit of Being*, 100). O'Connor claimed that when people were enmeshed in a nihilistic society, they could easily confuse this kind of theological truth and its traumatic impact as a tacit endorsement of fascistic violence. On the contrary, O'Connor told Hester, fascism was essentially "an offense against the body of Christ" (99). In the end, O'Connor suggested that violent suffering wrought by God, as interpreted through Christian signs and symbols, was a legitimate source of authority on earth while violence perpetrated by godless revolutionaries inevitably ended in despotism.

For many, to be sure, the line O'Connor drew here was arbitrarily thin. But the veracity of her distinction was less important than how she touched on the profound potency, and enduring anxiety, undergirding fascistic collectivism as an imaginative trope in postwar American conservatism. In a post-1945 world reeling from the horrors produced by "enlightened" secular modernity, how does one differentiate between legitimate authority and illegitimate authoritarianism? Being a fiction writer as technically skilled and philosophically thoughtful as O'Connor, it is no wonder that the richest mediations on this question appear in her mature fiction. Early in her career, though, O'Connor wrote with stark honesty about the authoritarian impulses underpinning modern liberalism through her reoccurring portraits of Rayber, the compassionate, though dangerously deluded, modern liberal who first appeared in a brief, fragmented story, "The Barber," included in O'Connor's Master's of Fine Arts (MFA) thesis at Iowa in 1947. When she submitted her writing thesis, *The Geranium: A Collection of Short Stories*, O'Connor was still honing her craft as a fiction writer operating under the principles of New Criticism. One upshot of this formal underdevelopment is that many of O'Connor's own sociopolitical assumptions as a Southern woman in her early twenties are rendered strikingly clear.[6] In the beginning of "The Barber," O'Connor forsakes the New Critical axiom "show, don't tell" and opens the story with a diegetic political assertion: "It is trying on liberals in Dilton. After the Democratic White Primary, Rayber changed his Barber" (*CW* 714). The rest of the story shows, in several clipped scenes, how the liberal college professor is unable to convince a group of unregenerate racists in the Deep South to vote for Darmon, a racially progressive candidate, instead of Hawkson, a reactionary white demagogue. After he fails to persuade the barber and his friends, who tell him never to utter the phrase "good-govermint" (i.e., "good government") in their presence again, Rayber spends hours at home crafting a speech that ends with the pretentious line: "Men who use ideas without measuring them are walking on wind" (720). But when he returns to the barbershop, Rayber can barely speak and feels ridiculous before the men's blunt "common sense," which even the young black man who sweeps up hair is convinced by, for he incredibly declares his intention to vote for Hawkson. The story ends abruptly as

Rayber, boiling with self-righteous rage, stands up with shaving cream on his face, punches the barber in the face, and storms out of the shop as blood pounds "up [his] neck just under his skin" (724).

Eliding the politics of Southern race relations, O'Connor attempts to neutralize any moral qualms about the white bigots in order to focus on Rayber's arrogance. Ever the sanctimonious liberal, Rayber cannot understand how these men are not convinced by the overwhelming power of his rationality and compassion. In the world of O'Connor's fiction, liberals like Rayber cling to a superficial "tenderness" buttressed not by God's love, but by human pride, the very source of both original sin and violence. As the final image of Rayber's blood pulsing beneath his skin suggests, under Rayber's surface-level features lies a two-pronged metaphor: his own blood symbolizing human imperfection and the blood of others waiting to be spilled by righteous vengeance. Foreshadowing a major theme in later fiction, O'Connor portrays a liberal undone by his own pride and compelled to use force in "The Barber," but this early sketch only hints at O'Connor's more complex conservative critique of racially progressive liberalism, bourgeois materialism, and latent authoritarian violence in the years to come.

2.3 Displacing Race and Class in "The Displaced Person"

O'Connor's short story "The Displaced Person," published in its final, novella-length version in *A Good Man Is Hard to Find*, is her most significant exploration of the relationship between a new, race-conscious form of latent fascism in America and the kind of social nihilism decried by traditionalist conservatives. When read within the context of O'Connor's connection to movement conservatism, the story turns into a complex warning of how fascism could emerge in America just ten years after the end of World War II. The thematic complexity, though, does not stem from a crude binary opposition between "liberals" and "conservatives," or between fascist villains and Christian heroes, but from the notion that all Americans are susceptible to the allure of totalitarian violence because they live in a society infected with nihilism. O'Connor even implies that the people most susceptible are those aligned with the conservative movement itself, the McCarthyite populists who embody the capitalist ethos of individualism, paranoid anger, and xenophobic patriotism. These so-called conservatives, for O'Connor as well as for Kirk, are reactionary in the worst sense of the word since they unthinkingly contribute to the destruction of social order and, in the process, fail to adapt and renew the traditions of a benevolent racial hierarchy.

From a sociopolitical perspective, "The Displaced Person" is about the failure of elite Southern conservatives to rule their inferiors, both white and black. Although this claim may sound reductive at first glance, I want to stress that O'Connor explores such a failure with all the ambiguity and nuance one would expect from a mature, skilled practitioner of New Critical principles. As with many of O'Connor's stories, the victims of cultural oppression and hatred, especially African Americans, are not the focal points of the narrative so much as personified indicators of social breakdown. If society were functioning properly, which is to say, according to Christian tradition and custom, the communal bonds would be organic and harmonious; the subject class would see their submission to the ruling class as mutually beneficial. Like the relationship between a Catholic priest and his parishioners, according to O'Connor, the ultimate authority of the priest rests not on dictatorial fear, but on his devotion to their welfare, the munificent surrender of his freedom to service, and their reciprocal recognition and trust. In short, the heart of the conservative traditionalist vision is not abstract self-reliance, but the complexities of mutual dependence.

It is fitting, then, that the chief antagonists in the final version of "The Displaced Person" are the widowed landowner Mrs. McIntrye, whose individual pride and financial greed blind her to true Christianity and the well-ordered society, and her lower-class white doppelgänger Mrs. Shortley, who embodies the kind of social anxiety which gives birth to authoritarian regimes. The story begins in Georgia in the late forties when Mrs. McIntrye agrees to cooperate with a Catholic priest who helps "displaced persons" from war-torn Europe relocate to the United States. The conflict arises once Mrs. McIntrye takes in the Polish family of a "displaced person," Mr. Guizac, in exchange for his work as a farmhand, even though the Shortley family, a resentful clan of lower-middle-class Southern whites, and several African Americans, Astor and Sulk, already work on the farm.

Like other O'Connor stories, Mr. Guizac is a stranger whose intrusion into an established set of hierarchical relationships does not create social instability so much as highlights the existing fragility as its base. Before Mr. Guizac arrives, the main source of tension is Mr. and Mrs. Shortley's two-pronged resentment: class-based anger directed upward at Mrs. McIntrye and race-based antipathy directed downward at the black farmhands. Mrs. Shortley's resentment becomes apparent at the very beginning of the story as she watches Mrs. McIntrye walk down her front porch steps to greet Mr. Guizac and his family. "[Mrs. McIntrye] had on her largest smile but Mrs. Shortley, even from her distance, could detect a nervous slide in it," O'Connor writes, slipping suddenly into free indirect speech, "These people who were coming were only hired help, like the Shortleys themselves or the Negroes" (*CW* 285). Beneath Mrs. McIntrye's fake smile, Mrs. Shortley knows, is not genuine Christian charity but self-interest and egotism. Instead of functioning like an organic community, Mrs. McIntrye's farm operates like a ruthless business, and Mrs. Shortley realizes that in such an arrangement she is as disposable as any "Negro."

The emphasis Mrs. McIntrye places on social distance and the exceptional nature of her own class position represents, in O'Connor's eyes, the worst aspects of secular modernity and postwar capitalism. As O'Connor writes in "The Catholic Novelist in the South," the Catholic writer in the Protestant South is in a unique position to see that "the kind of religious enthusiasm that has influenced Southern life has run hand in hand with extreme individualism for so long that there is nothing left that he can recognize" (*CW* 860). Mrs. McIntrye speaks the language of Christian libertarianism, stressing her individual rights as a property owner and her consequent power over her employees. "This is my place," she shouts in a moment of anger, "All of you are extra. Each and every one of you are extra" (323). The most deleterious effect of this kind of sinful pride, O'Connor suggests, is the dissolving of the traditional bonds that knit society together. At one point, wallowing in self-indulgence, Mrs. McIntrye explains to Mrs. Shortley why she decided to bring a Polish refugee to the farm: "A nigger thinks anybody is rich he can steal from and that white trash thinks anybody is rich who can afford to hire people as sorry as they are. And all I've got is the dirt under my feet!" (294). Instead of protecting traditional order through observation and modification, as Kirk says any true follower of Burke must, Mrs. McIntrye cultivates her own individual selfishness, causing her to become both paranoid and self-pitying, an exemplar of the decadent Old Regime in decline.

Stuck within this dehumanizing system, Mr. and Mrs. Shortley are cast adrift in the social hierarchy, certainly thankful to be white in the South, but enraged that their whiteness does not translate into the cultural privilege and economic security they feel it should. At first, through sheer imaginative willpower, Mrs. Shortley projects herself and her husband into the class upper with Mrs. McIntrye. Upon overhearing Mrs. McIntrye express the relief she feels at the presence of Mr. Guizac, since she will not have to depend on "poor white trash and niggers" anymore, Mrs. Shortley thinks to herself through

O'Connor's free indirect speech: "she knew that if Mrs. McIntrye had considered her trash, they couldn't have talked about trashy people together. Neither of them approved of trash" (293). But once Mrs. Shortley's attempt to leverage her whiteness fails, and she can no longer pretend that Mrs. McIntrye sees her as anything but white trash, Mrs. Shortley increasingly directs her anger toward Mr. Guizac, a proxy figure for the precarious class position in which the Shortley family and the black farmhands are all trapped. Reflecting on how the invention of the tractor rendered mules obsolete, Mrs. Shortley tells Astor and Sulk, "Before it was a tractor ... it could be a mule. And before it was a Displaced Person, it could be a nigger. The time is going to come ... when it won't be no more occasion to speak of a nigger" (297). As a "foreigner," in Mrs. Shortley's Southern argot, Mr. Guizac is a specter of the emerging Western capitalist order whose mere presence foreshadows the disposability of local, lower-class labor like Astor, Sulk, and the Shortley family themselves.

When Mrs. Shortley's alludes to Mr. Guizac to predict the disappearance of African Americans as a labor supply in the South, she is not only referencing her own vulnerability as "white trash" but also indirectly alluding to the evaporation of bodies in the Holocaust. For Mrs. Shortley, through whose eyes readers access Mr. Guizac during most of the story, a contagious threat of large-scale violence is mysteriously embedded in the category of the "displaced person." Soon after the arrival of Mr. Guizac, Mrs. Shortley remembers "a newsreel she had seen once of a small room piled high with bodies of naked dead people all in a heap, their arms and legs all tangled together. ... Before you could realize that it was real and take it into your head, the picture changed and a hollow-sounding voice was saying, 'Time marches on!'" (287). By presenting the newsreel footage as a collage of fragmented images, O'Connor underscores Mrs. Shortley's sense of confusion and impending dread. Thinking of the Guizac family, whom she misspells phonetically in her head as the "Gobblehooks," Mrs. Shortley has "the sudden intuition that the Gobblehooks, like rats with typhoid fleas, could have carried all those murderous ways over the water with them directly to this place. If they had come from where that kind of thing was done to them, who was to say they were not the kind that would also do it to others? The width and breadth of this question nearly shook her" (287). In Mrs. Shortley's imagination, Mr. Guizac is less an active agent of genocide than an enigmatic carrier of death, a victim of extermination transformed into an obscure omen for future victims of extermination in America.

Toward the middle of the story, as Mr. Guizac outshines Mr. Shortley with his work ethic and productivity, O'Connor makes it clear that the Shortley family is coming under the spell of a nativist paranoia that mimics the language of fascism in order to insulate themselves from Mr. Guizac's menacing aura. Feverishly imagining a "war of words," Mrs. Shortley envisions "the Polish words and the English words coming at each other . . . the Polish words, dirty and all-knowing and unreformed, flinging mud on the clean English words until everything was equally dirty. She saw them all piled up in a room, all the dead dirty words, theirs and hers too, piled up like the naked bodies in the newsreel" (300). For an experienced reader of O'Connor, the phrase "equally dirty" encapsulates Mrs. Shortley's wicked pride, since it tacitly clashes with O'Connor's own repeated declarations that we are all tainted by original sin. Instead of seeing Christianity as an all-encompassing doctrine of humility, Mrs. Shortley weaponizes religion: "Mrs. Shortley saw that the Lord God Almighty had created the strong people to do what had to be done and she felt that she would be ready when she was called" (300). Turning O'Connor's ideal of unsentimental love into the rhetoric of abstract self-righteousness, Mrs. Shortly uses coded language reminiscent of fascism – that is, "the strong people" and "do what had to be done" – in an attempt to exclude weak foreigners and then eliminate them since they are also, paradoxically, strong enough to cause great harm.

Considering Mrs. Shortley's anxieties about excess labor, Mr. Guizac *could* be read as an over-determined character who appears like a harbinger of another Nazi Holocaust, but who is really an unconscious manifestation of structural violence as a byproduct of capitalism – that is, death by dispossession and material scarcity. It even appears like O'Connor's story aligns with classical Marxist theories concerning the rise of fascism: the Shortley family represents the petits bourgeois who misinterpret the foreign Other as a shadowy racial evil instead of a systemic indicator of class struggle, and they turn toward violent methods to eradicate that foreign Other, thereby unconsciously doing the dirty work of the bourgeois ruling class.[7] The reason O'Connor's story seems so amenable to a Marxist critique is that O'Connor, though hardly a crypto-Marxist, was nevertheless a fierce critic of capitalism as a constitutive part of secular modernity, like Kirk and other traditionalist conservatives, and the way her Christian eschatological framework accounts for fascism is strikingly similar to certain Marxist frameworks.

After overhearing Mrs. McIntrye say that she intends to fire Mr. Shortley, Mrs. Shortley grows furious, urges her family to pack up their car and drive away before they suffer the humiliation of being forced to leave. On the way out, Mrs. Shortley dies of a mysterious stroke or heart attack and O'Connor's third-person authorial omnipresence declares that her eyes "seemed to contemplate for the first time the tremendous frontiers of her true country" (305). According to a Marxist reading, O'Connor instantiates the structural violence of capitalism metaphorically and Mrs. Shortley becomes its systemic victim, a disposable laborer "displaced" from the land by cheaper, more vulnerable laborers. For a Marxist critic, even Mrs. Shortley's fear – of what Mr. Guizac represents as surplus labor, not of who he is in himself – was justified, but she fundamentally misinterpreted the meaning of this anxiety, converting a potentially revolutionary insight into fascist paranoia.

As the neo-Marxist philosopher Slavoj Žižek points out, the basic thrust of fascism is to displace the inevitable excesses of capitalism onto the racial Other, typically the usurious "Jew," who is responsible for corrupting society's otherwise organic unity. The emergence of the foreign Other, then, only becomes legible against a background that conceals class struggle. As the condensation point of contradictory negative qualities, the "Jew" is simultaneously a weak parasite and a powerfully cunning saboteur, illuminating for fascists all that must be purified from the social body (*Sublime Object*, 141). Žižek argues that this racist fantasy figure is, in reality, fascist ideology's manifestation of its own impossibility. That is, society "is not prevented from achieving its full identity because of Jews: it is prevented by its own antagonistic [capitalist] nature," Žižek writes, "and it 'projects' this internal negativity into the figure of the 'Jew' ... Far from being the positive cause of social negativity, *the 'Jew' is a point at which social negativity as such assumes positive existence*" (*Sublime Object*, 143). At first glance, it certainly appears like O'Connor's story is ripe for this kind of interpretation. As a burgeoning fascist, Mrs. Shortley displaces her class-based resentment of Mrs. McIntrye onto Mr. Guizac, whom the Shortley's conflate with Jewish Holocaust victims. If only the "displaced persons" would stay in Europe, Mrs. Shortley believes, society would run smoothly. The Guizac family is the nodal point in which the impossibility of Mrs. Shortley's nationalistic ideology of "Christian America" is thrown into relief. As she leaves Mrs. McIntrye's farm, the "true country" her dead eyes seem to look upon could indicate the belated discovery of the precarious class position she occupies, along with so many others, in postwar America. The problem with this kind of politically progressive reading is not that it egregiously misinterprets the available textual evidence; rather, it fails to take into account how O'Connor frequently constructed her works with a keen awareness of their left-leaning interpretative potential, only to undermine those readings throughout the story.

In "The Displaced Person," O'Connor fashions powerful scenes of class exploitation and racial injustice, but these evils cannot be solved via political institutions since O'Connor follows Kirk in the conviction that political problems are essentially religious and moral problems. For O'Connor, as for Marxists, Mrs. Shortley is attracted to fascist rhetoric because capitalism hollows out traditional customs and arrangements of power, creating conditions that are ripe for social unrest and revolt. But whereas Marxists believe that every rise of fascism, in Žižek's memorable gloss on Walter Benjamin, "bears witness to a failed [communist] revolution," O'Connor adhered to the traditionalist conservative belief that fascism was the tragic endpoint of *all* secular revolutions, communist or fascist, since each one rejected God and sought to make, in O'Connor's words, "a religion of the state" (qtd. in Žižek, *Living in the End Times*, 152; *Habit of Being*, 347). Inverting the typical Marxist theory of fascism, O'Connor suggests that fascism is a futile attempt to solve not class struggle itself, but the metaphysical dimension of suffering that class struggle illuminates for Christians. As O'Connor notes in a private letter, the poverty of the underclass is not ideal, but she refuses to distinguish between physical poverty and spiritual poverty: "Everybody, as far as I am concerned, is The Poor" (*Habit of Being*, 103). The widespread agony capitalism leaves in its wake reveals the Christian paradox of human life – that is, that despite "all of its horror," O'Connor writes, life "has been found by God to be worth dying for" – and fascism tries to solve this problem by displacing the natural antagonism of original sin onto the foreign Other ("The Church and the Fiction Writer," *CW*, 808). From this perspective, as Mrs. Shortley's dying eyes gaze at the "tremendous frontiers of her true country," she sees her narrowly nationalistic conception of the United States dissolved and replaced by the transcendent world beyond earth. She realizes, O'Connor implies, that the "displaced person" was not a harbinger of political violence to be feared, but a sign of her own fatal reckoning with original sin, which was necessary to transform her into a displaced person in the Kingdom of God.

In the last quarter of "The Displaced Person," O'Connor completes this socio-aesthetic theory of fascism when Mrs. McIntrye invites Mr. Shortley to return to work on the farm soon after his wife's sudden death. The impetus for his rehiring is that Mrs. McIntrye is dismayed by Mr. Guizac's casual proposal to bring his sixteen-year-old female cousin from Poland to the United States to marry the black farmhand, Sulk. If

Mr. Guizac was once a proxy figure for Holocaust victims and perpetrators in Mrs. Shortley's eyes, he takes on additional metaphorical weight in Mrs. McIntrye's mind, morphing into a proxy figure for oppressed African Americans in the Jim Crow South. Mrs. McIntrye believes that Mr. Guizac's request threatens the availability of cheap labor and social control because an interracial marriage would plant the seed of agency in the minds of her black farmhands. Shouting at Mr. Guizac, Mrs. McIntrye explicitly admits her fear: "I will not have my niggers upset. I cannot run this place without my niggers. I can run it without you but not without them and if you mention this girl to Sulk again, you won't have a job with me" (314). On the surface, this late plot development looks like a rebuke of Southern racism, since it exposes Mrs. McIntrye's callous bigotry with relation to a kind of Ellisonian "invisible man" re-codified as foreign stranger, thus indirectly showing that O'Connor sides with downtrodden African Americans. But a closer examination of the story reveals that O'Connor is not opposed, in principle, to white paternalism, but to Mrs. McIntrye's haphazard and inhumane implementation of it.

What Mrs. McIntrye fails to realize, O'Connor insinuates, is that the very ideology of Christian libertarianism she supports undermines the traditional social order she wishes to preserve. On the one hand, Mrs. McIntrye privileges financial gain and the illusion of self-reliance it gives her. Mrs. McIntrye thinks of her dead husband's old business office as "a chapel," the locked drawer containing his bankbooks and ledgers as "a tabernacle," and the entire office itself as "sacred because he had conducted his business" there (312). Running the farm now, she stresses that she is above everyone else on her land, the one person who is truly independent and in charge: "You're all dependent on me," she tells one of her black farmhands, "but you each and every one act like the shoe is on the other foot" (308). But on the other hand, Mrs. McIntrye is stunned to find her own farm laborers thinking and acting within the same framework of capitalist individualism. At one point, she even claims that money "is the root of all evil," quoting her ex-husband, nicknamed "The Judge": "He said he deplored money. He said the reason you niggers were so uppity was because there was so much money in circulation" (306). The structural endpoint of this kind of atomic individualism, despite Mrs. McIntrye's angry claims to the contrary, is exemplified in Mr. Guizac's hope to have his white cousin marry an American black man. Once that traditionalist conservative notion of mutual dependency between the ruling class and the subject class is dissolved in the pursuit of the temptations promised by secular modernity, O'Connor implies, the revolutionary potential of classical liberal is loosed unchecked upon the world.

O'Connor, though, is not primarily concerned with manifestations of radical equality so much as how Mrs. McIntrye responds to the subject class's newfound agency. Instead of marrying a white Polish teenager, Sulk vanishes from the story at the end, setting "off for the southern part of the state," and O'Connor portrays this as neither a punishment for disobedience nor a celebration of his agency (326). In the final pages, O'Connor shifts her ironic gaze exclusively toward Mrs. McIntrye, tacitly criticizing her for failing to live up to the ideals of a Christian traditionalist. Mrs. McIntrye embraces this identity by listening to Mr. Shortley, who functions as a more belligerent reincarnation of Mrs. Shortley's fascist worldview. A veteran of World War II, Mr. Shortley speaks the chauvinistic language of God and country, and he feels betrayed by America's largesse to suspicious foreigners. "Gone over there and fought and bled and died and come over here," he tells Mrs. McIntrye, "and find out who's got my job – just exactly who I been fighting. It was a hand-grenade come that near to killing me and I seen who throw it – little man with eyeglasses just like [Mr. Guizac's]" (323). Mrs. McIntrye agrees with Mr. Shortley, substituting any semblance of true, O'Connorian religious devotion for a fidelity to a racially pure conception of the state, since it means she can retain her money and individual socioeconomic status.

Eventually, the Shortley's fascist rhetoric becomes a violent reality in a late scene that O'Connor uses to forge explicit allusions to the Holocaust. While Mr. Guizac works underneath a broken tractor in the fields, Mr. Shortley rides another larger tractor toward him, granting Mrs. McIntrye a final vision of the Polish refugee that harkens back to the grotesque images of bodies in the Nazi ovens that Mrs. Shortley saw in the newsreels: "She could not see his face, only his feet and legs and trunk sticking impudently out from the side of the tractor" (325). When Mr. Shortley gets off the tractor, it keeps moving, running over and killing Mr. Guizac. O'Connor obscures Mr. Shortley's precise motivations in order to highlight how he shares ultimate responsibility with Mrs. McIntrye, for when Mr. Guizac dies their eyes "come together in one look that froze them in collusion forever . . . " (326). With this scene, O'Connor engineers Mrs. McIntrye's painful epiphany, as she suffers a nervous breakdown that leaves her barely able to walk or talk for the rest of her life.

In an ironic nod to Mrs. McIntrye's self-reliance, O'Connor dispatches all the characters from the farm, leaving the Catholic priest as her sole visitor who would occasionally, in the words of the story's final sentence, "sit by the side of her bed and explain the doctrines of the Church" (327). The closing scene is significant because, unlike so many other nihilistic Christian characters in O'Connor's fiction – most famously, the Grandmother in "A Good Man Is Hard to Find" – Mrs. McIntrye does not die in the end. She is left to reflect upon her own responsibility for the death of a Christ-like displaced person. Critics usually claim that she is spared so that she may contemplate, with the help of the priest, how the sin of pride undergirds her own spiritual death-in-life and its ultimate manifestation in the physical, Holocaust-like death of the innocent refugee. As Ralph C. Wood notes, O'Connor's story is a confession "that the death camps could have been constructed in her own native Georgia as readily as in far-off Poland" (16). However, the final image of the priest explaining the doctrines of the Church is not a critique of the South's reactionary villainy, but a representation of a better model of conservatism. As an ideal model of Christian tradition maintained through centuries of continuity, the Catholic Church embodied by the priest teaches Mrs. McIntrye the core truth of traditionalist conservatism: that mutual dependence, not the extreme individualism of secular modernity, is the only sustainable system for preserving established power relations. Ultimately, O'Connor's narrative condemns Mrs. McIntrye not because she is a conservative, but because she is the wrong kind of conservative, one who fails to adapt to new postwar realities and harness those inevitable social changes back toward a balanced racial and class hierarchy.

Published in 1955 at the dawn of the postwar conservative movement, O'Connor's "The Displaced Person" epitomizes not just the traditionalist conservative idealization of the ordered Christian society, but the deeper insight that great, highbrow literature could create the very cultural conditions that would enable that tradition-based society to flourish. In this complex literary text, O'Connor's vision mimics T. S. Eliot's claim in *Christianity and Culture* (1949), a virtual master-text of postwar American traditionalists, that "the current [secular progressive] terms in which we discuss international affairs and political theory may only tend to conceal from us the real issues of contemporary civilization" (*Christianity and Culture,* 3). The solution, Eliot argues, would be the eventual establishment of a rigidly ordered Christian society whose institutions would utilize poetry to "train people to think in Christian categories and would not [therefore] impose the necessity for insincere profession of belief" (26). From a sociological perspective of literary history, what is most significant about Eliot's vision is not so much the "*excessiveness* of Eliot's fantasy of a Christian society," as John Guillory notes, but the implicit assumptions about literary prestige that ground Eliot's fantasy when "he dictates with unself-conscious pomposity a new (or old) order to society on the basis of his authority as a *literary* figure" (152). Within this framework, since the greatness of literature "consists in its claim to occupy the most important place of ideological production in the social order," traditionalist conservatives saw the cultural capital generated by highbrow fiction as an indispensable instrument to justify their vision of an ordered society. In the immediate postwar moment, according to Kirk and other traditionalists, no young writer was actualizing this Eliot-inspired vision of the wisdom of tradition better than Flannery O'Connor.

2.4 *Atlas Shrugged*: A Mass-Market Warning of Totalitarian Collectivism in America

If O'Connor's characters degenerate into American Fascists because they reject the wisdom of tradition, Ayn Rand's characters in her magnum opus *Atlas Shrugged* (1957) become fascists precisely *because* they embrace the pseudo-values of traditionalist conservatism and the wisdom of history. As she once declared with typical bombast before "the Collective," her personal cadre of student-disciples in the sixties, "I am challenging the cultural tradition of two and a half thousand years" (qtd. in Branden, 294). Although it is routinely pointed out that Rand rejected traditional ideologies and social customs, especially Christianity, because their philosophical errors supposedly laid the groundwork for communism, many scholars have ignored the imaginative framework Rand constructs in *Atlas Shrugged* that reveals how communism is merely the initial manifestation of collectivism, while fascism is the true endpoint of collectivist thought. With her bestselling novel, Rand invented a radically different literary account of the threat of fascist totalitarianism in America that movement conservatives would find appalling at first, but eventually more compelling in the following decades than O'Connor's more complex, aesthetically nuanced Christian one.

In many familiar accounts of Rand and her philosophy of Objectivism, she is portrayed as one of the most passionate defenders of political individualism in the postwar era, an avowed supporter of McCarthyism even, whose hatred of communism was matched only by her love of the free market. Today, some scholars claim, retaining the classic fascism/communism dichotomy, that Rand's loathing of communism crossed over into tacit support for fascism.[8] While many of these accounts are persuasive, they tend to obscure Rand's own stance on fascism, which mirrored the general position of movement conservatism, as the final stage of collectivism. Similar to the libertarian theories of fascism articulated by Ludwig von Mises and Friedrich Hayek, Rand's Objectivist explanation of the rise of fascism emphasized the state's authoritarian supremacy and its concomitant suspicion of market capitalism, private property, and the inalienable rights of the individual. As Rand claimed in "'Extremism,' or the Art of Smearing," an essay collected in *Capitalism: The Unknown Ideal* (1966), it "is obvious what the fraudulent issue of fascism versus communism accomplishes: it sets up, as opposites, two variants of the same political system; it eliminates the possibility of considering capitalism" (200). In her most important statement on fascism, "The Fascist New Frontier" – an essay written during the Kennedy Administration that equated its "New Frontier" programs with seemingly comparable programs in Hitler's Germany – Rand again lumped together communism and fascism, claiming that the main feature of both systems was "public ownership of the means of production, and, therefore, the abolition of property" (98). The sole difference, Rand maintained, was not substantive but rhetorical. "The socialist-communist axis keeps promising to achieve abundance, material comfort and security for its victims, in some indeterminate future," Rand wrote, whereas the "fascist-Nazi axis scorns material comfort and security, and keeps extolling some undefined sort of spiritual duty, service and conquest" (98). Since the teleological essence of collectivism is the increasing immiseration of a given population, Rand argued that a sociopolitical evolution was inevitable: modern liberalism would morph into communism on the collectivist left and then into an irrational, racist form of fascism on the *extreme* collectivist left.

A didactic novel warning Americans of a looming totalitarian threat, *Atlas Shrugged* was Rand's attempt to imagine not just how this evolution from communism to fascism occurs but also how to combat it with her own sacred trinity of reason, individualism, and capitalism. When the story begins, the United States is in a mysterious state of economic decline, the cause of which has long since mystified the American people and turned them into bitter cynics who express their undirected anger by repeating the ironic question, "Who is John Galt?" (*Atlas Shrugged*, 11). The problem, Rand implies with frequent heavy-handedness, is that the federal government is meddling with markets, hoping to redistribute the profits of successful companies like Taggart Transcontitential and Rearden Metal, each owned by the novel's dual hero-protagonists Dagny Taggart and Hank Rearden, respectively. Government officials and nefarious businessmen like Dagny's brother, Jim – a traitor to his class, Rand assures readers – frame their efforts to enforce economic equality through the soft coercion of outrageous tax rates as being motivated by public service. In an early scene between progressive officials and business leaders, Jim Taggart uses the language of altruism, reminding them that their objective is to protect people from the free market's inherently "destructive, dog-eat-dog competition" (51). This kind of collectivist logic leads Rand's villains to pass a series of laws that place arbitrary limits on competition, profit maximization, corporate mergers, and innovative business practices. In response, Rand's entrepreneurial heroes, who represent the greatest collection of talent in America, "go on strike," the best mind from each business sector systemically vanishing from society to live in Galt's Gulch, the capitalist utopia hidden deep in the Colorado Mountains founded by John Galt, a revolutionary thinker who has secretly invented a perpetual motion machine.

Up until this point in the narrative, *Atlas Shrugged* could plausibly be described as a one-dimensional anti-communist novel or, in the words of Rand biographer Jennifer Burns, "a moral fable about the evils of government interference in the free market" (166). Roughly halfway through the story, the novel appears like it could even follow a common narrative arc in the genre of tragedy: the socialist characters may realize that their adherence to the ostensible virtues of fairness, charity, and public service are, in reality, precisely the vices that ruin society, and perhaps they will see that their rational regulations end only in irrational burdens for the true "producers." It becomes apparent that this is not the ending Rand intends to write once the antagonists introduce Directive 10–289, a government decree issued in the hopes of halting the economic collapse by prohibiting all workers from changing their jobs, all companies from generating higher profits than the exact profit margin they earned when the decree was issued, and all people from inventing anything new. While government officials claim that the authoritarian order has been handed down "in the name of the general welfare [and] to protect the people's security," it clearly marks the moment in which their wickedness becomes unredeemable (*Atlas Shrugged*, 497). As Andrew Hoberek points out, Directive 10–289 is a plot device that proves that bureaucratic regulation is not merely a misguided application of instrumental reason but a disturbing manifestation of the death-drive (44). Underneath their grandiose rhetoric, these men are collectivists motived unconsciously by a form of resentment so irrational that it degenerates into what Rand defines elsewhere as the sine qua non of fascism: a nihilistic pursuit of power for power's sake, that psychic need also evident in racists, according to Rand, who wish to lord power over others and humiliate them for no direct, tangible reason ("The Fascist New Frontier," 98).

For the rest of the novel, Rand gradually reveals how socialism, left to its own inexorable nihilistic logic, will degenerate into fascism. It is not until Dagny and Rearden understand this insight, which is typified in the very title of the novel, that they can begin to let society destroy itself and then rebuild it. Rand creates the conditions of such an epiphany when Francisco d'Anconia asks Rearden what he would say to "Atlas, the giant who holds the world on his shoulders, if [he] saw that he stood, blood running down his chest, his knees buckling, his arms trembling but still trying to hold the world aloft with the last of his strength" (*Atlas Shrugged*, 422). Unable to articulate a response, Rearden asks Francisco, who delivers the dramatic answer, "To shrug" (422). Foreshadowing the title of the chapter immediately following the conversation, "The Sanction of the Victim," Rearden realizes not only that he is a victim trapped between the destructive governmental elites and the parasitical masses, but that if he refuses to assist the bureaucrats in an attempt to cleanse his guilty conscience, then their collectivist ideology will be unmasked for what it is: an absurd belief system underpinned by state violence. Once Atlas "shrugs," withdrawing from the system, the weak masses will no longer be able to exploit the strong with faux-moral condemnation, only naked force. Always thinking in tacitly inverted Marxist terms, Rand implies that the Atlases of American industry like Rearden are responsible, ironically, for interfering with what could be called the Objectivist dialectic – that is, the large-scale social process by which all leftist ideologies that regulate the free market advance in stages toward fascist collectivism.

Before the fascist system can fully emerge, the social group Rand calls "producers" must recognize that they are the architectural columns supporting society by mediating between two additional groups Rand identifies as "looters" and "moochers," the very top of society (intellectuals, politicians, government bureaucrats) and the very bottom (the ravenous, unwashed masses), respectively. While the looters and moochers are ultranationalists whose discourse draws imaginary boundaries around a communal "in-group" that emphasizes mutual sacrifice, the producers are individualists whose group identification is loose, flexible, and made up of discrete units consensually interacting, much like Rand's own romanticized vision of the cosmopolitan network of relationships formed under unregulated capitalism. The toxicity of ultranationalist discourse, Rand suggests, only becomes apparent once the producers are removed from society, and the looters and moochers are all made to live in the nationalist nightmare they have unwittingly created.

A major narrative conflict arises from the fact that, in Rand's fictional world, Marxist class categories do not neatly delineate members of each social group; at times, modest railway laborers are revealed to be natural-born producers while university intellectuals are exposed as freeloading moochers. Rand, still influenced by the socialist realist genre of her Soviet-born youth, constructs flat character-types that belong to one of these three social groups less by choice than by birthright. But whereas characters in a socialist realist novel are born into a Marxist class category, Rand's characters are born into an Objectivist category of human nature. Rand's commitment to this eccentric system of social stratification explains why *Atlas Shrugged* takes the form of popular genre fiction and, although gargantuan in size, seems to actively discourage New Critical close-reading techniques. On some level, the plot is an immense sorting and classification mechanism, staging long conversational scenes over and over to reveal who truly belongs in which social group. As that classification function approaches completion, the bloody logic of sacrifice takes over toward the end of the novel, and Rand exposes the fascist impulses residing at the core of collectivism.

In one of the last scenes designed to sort the worthy from the unworthy, Rand portrays the implicit nihilism undergirding the relationship between looters and moochers. As the elite looter *par excellence*, Jim Taggart watches his marriage to Cherryl Brooks – a smart but poor young woman who has mistaken Jim for a captain of industry like Rearden, whom she idolizes – disintegrate alongside the disintegration of the economy. Upon discovering Jim's infidelity with Rearden's looter wife, Lillian, Cherryl demands to know why Jim married her in the first place. When Jim tells her he did it because she was "worthless," Cherryl suddenly realizes the depth of depravity within Jim. "You married me, because you knew that I did not accept the gutter, inside or out," she declares, increasingly horrified, "that I was struggling to rise and would go on struggling – didn't you?" (827). For the first time, Cherryl sees that Jim has fastened himself to her because she worships producers, and he intends to devote his life to annihilating her will to work hard and "rise" because Jim could not destroy someone like Rearden. Rand suggests that Jim has also mistakenly identified Cherryl as a moocher, a young woman born into poverty who was prepared to accept the charity doled out by him, as long as he could control her. "You're a killer," Cherryl tells him in a halting voice, perfectly ventriloquizing Rand's own psycho-political theory of fascism, "for the sake of killing"

(827). Incapable of hearing the truth, Jim responds by striking her across the face. Cherryl, for her part, responds in a way that reveals her true nature as a burgeoning producer, propelling herself off a bridge with "the power of a creature running for its life" (831). Like Galt and the other strikers, Cherryl understands that she has no choice but to opt out of the collectivist social contract, and the paradoxical description of her suicide testifies to Rand's point that life in the looters' America is ruled by a kind of *thanatos* principle.

In the apocalyptic finale, the death-drive at the core of the looter identity replicates itself on a larger scale when the government deteriorates into an unmistakably fascist regime, mimicking the outward motifs of European Fascism and relying exclusively on state-sponsored force. After Galt has commandeered the national radio station and delivered his notoriously long speech on Objectivism (seventy pages in the original novel, almost sixty pages in the mass-market paperback edition), the public is immediately won over and society declines even further into anarchy. In a fleeting attempt to contain the chaos, Cuffy Meigs, formerly the Director of Unification responsible for overseeing the railroad industry, breaks into a Midwestern military base with the intention of taking control of a superweapon codenamed "Project X," an allusion to the Manhattan Project, and seize absolute power for himself. Like an American Mussolini invoking the glories of Ancient Rome, Meigs walks into the base dressed in military regalia, wearing "a tight, semi-military tunic and leather leggings," and carrying a pistol and a rabbit's foot, symbolizing his potential dictatorship of violence and superstition (1034). As Meigs argues with Dr. Robert Stadler over control of Project X, Rand's third-person omniscient voice declares that while Stadler feels "an unadmitted [*sic*] root . . . of terror" at the core of his being, Meigs's own terror "had wider roots, it embraced all of existence" (1036). Once Meigs realizes that his dream of running a fascist dictatorship will never come true, he detonates the atom bomb–like device, completing the deathward logic inherent to collectivist ethics by killing himself and thousands of innocent people with him.

In the novel's last pages, it is implied that Galt and his band of capitalist heroes wait inside their utopian community as more would-be fascist dictators sacrifice the entire country in what Rand indirectly describes as an atomic holocaust. Beyond the safety of Galt's Gulch, the catastrophe has left "only a void of darkness and rock, but the darkness was hiding the ruins of a continent: the roofless homes, the rusting tractors, the abandoned rail" (1069). With this imaginative tableau, Rand represents the final fascist stage of collectivism according to her Objectivist theory. As she writes in "The Fascist New Frontier," under fascist and communist regimes, "sacrifice is invoked as a magic, omnipotent solution to any crisis – and 'the public good' is the altar on which victims are immolated" (98). In short, *Atlas Shrugged* is a long, fantastically lowbrow illustration of this argument: When the crisis becomes too large and there are no more capitalist scapegoats to sacrifice, the collectivist government's communist mask slips off to reveal the true fascist face lurking underneath, and the logic of sacrifice grinds to its inevitable, genocidal conclusion.

At *National Review* in late 1957, Buckley quickly grew concerned when he saw that the argument embedded in Rand's novel would be compelling to certain segments of the conservative movement. Although Rand's themes of individualism and free-market capitalism meshed well with the theoretical premises of libertarian conservatives, Buckley knew that her bitter contempt toward conventional social mores, toward overt racial prejudice, and toward all religious belief systems would upset traditionalist conservatives, thereby threatening the fragile intellectual synthesis Buckley had begun to cultivate only a few years earlier. Aiming to banish Rand from the conservative movement, Buckley chose Whittaker Chambers to write a review of *Atlas Shrugged* for the final December issue of *National Review*. Entitling the review "Big Sister Is Watching You," in a typical nod by the literary-minded conservative to Orwell's *1984*, Chambers denounced Rand's novel so mercilessly that he even accused her, in the most oft-quoted line, of being no different than a Nazi. "From almost any page of *Atlas Shrugged*," Chambers writes, "a voice can be heard, from painful necessity, commanding: 'To the gas chamber – go!'" ("Big Sister Is Watching You," 594). On the surface, it seemed ironic that Chambers condemned Rand's vision in such absolute terms when both agreed on the fundamental idea that fascism was the purest manifestation of collectivism. The crucial difference, though, was that Chambers and Rand ultimately disagreed on what constituted fascism. Whereas Chambers thought that philosophical materialism, whether expressed in the form of capitalism or communism, paved the way for fascist regimes, Rand believed that the Christianized Western metaphysical tradition was the basic root of fascism.

What historians and political scholars tend to overlook about Chambers's legendary piece – one Buckley biographer has dubbed it "either the most famous or infamous book review in the history of the conservative movement" – is that Chambers believed that the question of materialism versus Christianity was inseparable from the issue of complex literary form and its tacit ability to generate cultural capital (Bogus, 208). Early in the review, Chambers points out that in *Atlas Shrugged* "everything, everybody, is either all good or all bad, without any of those intermediate shades which, in life, complicate reality and perplex the eye that seeks to probe it truly" (594). As someone who privileged the novel as a site of multifaceted inquiry, Chambers claims that such allegorical heavy-handedness must not be disregarded for the sake of some larger message. "*Atlas Shrugged* can be called a novel only by devaluing the term," Chambers writes, noting a direct relationship between the shallow quality of Rand's thought and her novelistic incompetence, "It is a massive tract for our times" (595). For Chambers, the form of a novel should not be understood as a neutral transmission mechanism for strictly partisan arguments, since that merely replicated the ideological rigidity of socialist realism. When he denigrated *Atlas Shrugged* as another naïve fable of "The War between the Children of Light and the Children of Darkness," Chamber implied that inflexible ideologies of the Right and Left made Rand a deficient novelist, to be sure, but more importantly, a deficient thinker (594). Chambers suggested that the form of the novel, especially when rooted in the aesthetic values of modernism, was just as important as the political argument; indeed, it was inextricable from the argument against philosophical materialism itself.

Essentially, the argument Chambers offered against materialism was not only, as one Rand biographer suggests, a "clash of two radically different versions of human nature," but a disagreement about literary representations of these competing definitions (Burns, 175). In the Randian vision of human nature, as in the communist one, humans were unchained from metaphysical superstition and free to fulfill their natural desires. "Thus, Randian man, like Marxian man," Chambers writes, "is made the center of a godless world" (595). It was no coincidence, Chambers thought, that the same rigid literary aesthetic flowed from two seemingly opposed godless ideologies. Following Dostoevsky, and tacitly O'Connor, Chambers believed that humans were flawed beings tainted by original sin and helplessly dependent on the awful grace of God. As a result, Chambers privileged a literary aesthetic that foregrounded metaphysical mystery, the complexity of lived experience, and a sense of moral ambiguity that confounded secular political ideology. Chambers maintained that the best fiction, in the words of O'Connor, "renews our knowledge that we live in the mystery from which we draw our abstractions" ("The Church and the Fiction Writer," *CW*, 812). When people forgot the enigma of human existence, they were left with abstract rationality grounded in materialism. Rand's novel epitomized how, Chambers argues, "in a wicked world, a materialism of the Right and a materialism of the Left, first surprisingly resemble, then, in action tend to blend with each, because while differing at the top in avowed purpose, and possibly in conflict there, at bottom they are much the same thing" (596). For Chambers, great literature worked like an antidote to ideological abstraction, and the novel form was an intellectual discourse descending from conservative modernism that should be seen as an essential ingredient in any definition of postwar conservatism truly based on Christianity and tradition. Essentially, Chambers viewed the field of high literary culture through the classic Bourdieuan "aesthetic disposition" since Chambers, in Bourdieu's words, aimed "to bracket off the nature and function of the object represented and to exclude any 'naïve' reaction ... in order to concentrate solely upon the mode of representation, the [literary] style, perceived and appreciated by compassion with other styles" (*Distinction*, 46). This aesthetic disposition, shorn of economic necessities and crude practical concerns, is what enabled Chambers not only to lump together leftist collectivist materialism and Randian capitalist materialism but also to preserve an imaginary space for conservatism rooted in high culture. What Rand's ostensible descent into the literary gutter reveals is how highbrow literature, in the minds of traditionalists like Chambers, functioned as a fantasy space outside any economy or field of desecration – financial, cultural, political, and so on – where great literature was an inherent outgrowth of genius and not a reflection of cultural capital, where the sacred value of literature was a static metaphysical given sheltered from the extreme market pressures of laissez-faire capitalism so beloved by Rand.

As scholars of conservatism note, Chambers's review sparked a conflagration on the postwar right that seemed like it may engulf the entire movement. The crux of the issue was how to balance the seemingly contradictory demands of capitalism and Christianity in the conservative movement. From the beginning of the movement, conservatives had stressed the constitutive link between atheism and collectivism in all its forms, making Christianity and capitalism unmistakable allies in the global struggle against the Soviet Union. But the Chambers–Rand dispute showed that such an alliance was far from self-evident, and that the philosophical fault line exposed was rooted in questions of literary form and aesthetic value. Dividing up into two camps over the review, the most prominent conservatives at *National Review* like Russell Kirk, Frank Meyer, Buckley protégé Garry Wills, and even Buckley himself all supported Chambers, while lesser-known writers like John Chamberlain, E. Merrill Root, and Murray Rothbard came to Rand's defense.

In a public letter published in *National Review*, Kirk claimed that his fellow literary-minded conservative Whittaker Chambers had "said precisely what I would have said – except that he said it better" (118). Similarly, Meyer accused Rand of creating fictional characters that embodied not rounded depth, but an "arid subhuman image of man" ("Why Freedom," 157). In his article "Is Ayn Rand a Conservative," the young Roman Catholic traditionalist Garry Wills noted that when John Galt "repudiates all obligations to other men, he denies history, that link with one's ancestors and with all human experience which is the first principle of conservatism" (139). In lieu of Randian propaganda, Wills pushed for a nuanced definition of conservatism that reiterated O'Connor's literary project: the true conservative "tries to keep men free, open to reality on many levels, aware of diversity and mystery" (139). Buckley disparaged the novel as ridiculous, calling its "desiccated philosophy" completely at odds with modern conservatism's "emphasis on transcendence, intellectual and moral" (qtd. in Judis, 161).

However, Rand's defenders saw not only a persuasive theoretical demonstration of the relationship between capitalism and freedom, but an epic, commercially popular novel of the postwar era. In a public letter arguing for the artistic merit of the novel, Murray N. Rothbard took issue with Chambers's claim that "*Atlas Shrugged* devalues the novel-form because it has a Message" (95). Comparing Rand to other idea-driven novelists like Dostoevsky and Thomas Mann, Rothbard asserted that *Atlas Shrugged* "is, in truth, a novel of ideas, and it is also true that purposeless novels-without-ideas have predominated in the United States ... I don't think this is something for America to boast about" (95). In the first full-length article dedicated to defending Rand, E. Merrill Root – tenured English professor, certified John Birch Society member, and former student of Robert Frost – wrote that the novel was an uncompromising exploration of moral truth, and that it would secure her place in American literature as "an artistic and philosophical Atlas" ("What About Ayn Rand?" 76). Even John Chamberlain, *National Review* book review editor and ostensible stickler for New Critical principles, offered cautious praise for Rand in an essay on the maligned "business novel," noting that *Atlas Shrugged* suggested that the genre may be able to transcend its "minor" position in American letters ("The Business Novel," 112). Unlike traditionalist conservatives who advocated for complex literary forms forged in the crucible of modernist difficulty, libertarian conservatives promoted fiction styled after popular genre novels. In their melancholic distance from power, traditionalists prized the modernist themes of alienation and civilizational decline, relishing their roles as misunderstood outsiders, J. Alfred Prufrocks measuring out their lives in coffee spoons. Regarding such fatalism as sour grapes, libertarian conservatives believed that a novel like *Atlas Shrugged*, a capitalist fable narrated in the lowbrow prose style of midcentury paperback writers like Mickey Spillane, whom Rand admired and emulated, could be an invaluable proselytizing tool for their unpopular movement. Despite the extensive philosophical disagreements prominent conservatives like Buckley had with Rand, *Atlas Shrugged* forever changed the literary dimension of movement conservatism, eventually becoming a formal template for popular conservative genre novels in the second half of the twentieth century.

2.5 The Sixties Shift: You Don't Need a Randian to Know Which Way the Wind Blows

Ultimately, the Chambers–Rand dispute was part of a larger politico-literary discourse on the postwar Right that foregrounded not *if* movement conservatives would continue to embrace their unique fusion of Christianity and capitalism – even Rand's fiercest supporters at *National Review* admitted that her atheism was problematic – but *how* that synthetic combination would fit together. In other words, the shadow rivalry within movement conservatism between O'Connorian traditionalists and Randian libertarians was a debate about how conservatives should arrive at their politics. In the traditionalist model, conservatives began with aesthetics in both senses of the word, high culture and sensuous experience, and came to political positions underpinned by mystery, humility, and organic complexity. Conversely, in the libertarian model, conservatives started with a set of general ideological principles rooted in an overarching theory of natural rights and then reached their political conclusions through abstract reasoning.

In each model, totalitarian collectivism was conceptualized as the definitive threat, but each template provided different explanations for its emergence – that is, the dangerous worship of the individual in traditionalism, the uncritical veneration of traditional community in libertarianism. Supporters of both models felt the need to identify and promote fiction writers who imagined how their respective notion of a distinctly American form of fascist authoritarianism might arise in the context of postwar liberalism. What cannot be overstated, though, is that whenever conservatives of either section alluded to the dangers of fascism, those invocations were inseparable from the emancipatory potentials of Christianity and capitalism. Whereas traditionalists were uneasy about radical equality for African Americans as a side effect of the capitalist notion of abstract individual rights, libertarians were concerned about the kind of Christian "social justice" rhetoric that Franklin Roosevelt had used so successfully to tout the New Deal.[9] In short, the conservative movement's fear of fascist collectivism and its fear of changing power relations around race were two sides of the same coin, and midcentury American novels were the interrogation rooms of these fantastical anxieties, the foundational fictions of modern conservative thought.

In the early sixties, the most compelling solution for movement conservatives was to shift their basic set of political commitments away from a predominantly traditionalist conservative model, wherein the appetites unleashed by capitalism were checked by strict Christian traditions, to the more contemporary "Christian libertarian" model that made both capitalism and Christianity absolute goods. As conservatives gained a foothold in the Republican Party in 1964 with the nomination of Barry Goldwater, the pursuit of electoral power made it increasingly appealing to use the discourse of abstract rights while also claiming to uphold America's Christian tradition. As many scholars note, conservatives were arguing for a peculiar theoretical fusion consisting of a narrow vision of individual rights situated in an equally constricted vision of Christianity, one in which "good" Christians could be unapologetic champions of the wealthy, but against both welfare relief for the poor and the 1964 Civil Rights Act.

Simultaneously, though, conservatives were also quietly fusing together the two dominant literary dimensions of the conservative movement that had developed in the first decade of its existence. From O'Connor's masterpieces of ambiguity, they appropriated the theme that fascist collectivism surfaces in a nihilistic society that abandons its traditional commitments to social hierarchy, tossing out her fundamental critiques of capitalism and individualism. From Rand's screeds of certitude, conservatives adopted the notion that the United States would turn into a dystopian collectivist state if liberals interfered with free-market capitalism, ignoring her claim that capitalism was a fully contained moral system in itself, opposed to Christian ethics root and branch. Between the inception of the conservative movement and the rise of Goldwater, this synthesis of literary visions produced not only the first glimpses of "conservative popular fiction" as an instrument of political persuasion that would emerge more fully near the end of the twentieth century but also the movement's increasingly distrustful orientation toward the literary *illusio* – that is, their fundamental belief in the game-like nature, and consequent stakes, of literary high culture.[10]

As I argue in the following chapter, the next crucial development in this shift hinged more than ever on the quintessential political conundrum of the sixties: America's "race problem." Whereas conservatives in the fifties such as O'Connor and Kirk were the ones who once claimed to begin from concrete reality, it was the great freedom movements of the sixties led by minorities and students on the Left who highlighted the injustices instantiated in the material institutions of daily social life. In the face of this challenge from below, movement conservatives had to rethink the racial positions they adopted in the fifties, which were epitomized by O'Connor's Christian vision of mutual dependencies and benevolent paternalism. Instead, to argue against someone like James Baldwin, conservatives turned toward the Randian notions of abstract rights, colorblind individualism, and the inviolate nature of private property. This shift in movement conservatism in the sixties altered not only how conservatives seriously began to hone their use of American fiction as a political tool, but perhaps just as importantly, how conservatism affected novelists like Baldwin and Norman Mailer as they conceptualized their own literary-political projects.

CHAPTER 3

The Strongbox of Custom
James Baldwin, Norman Mailer, and the Shifting Racial Logic of Postwar Conservatism, 1955–1972

3.1 Introduction: The American Novel, Cultural Politics, and the "Sixties"

"One of the most striking facts about American life," Irving Howe noted in *Politics and the Novel* (1957), "is the frequency with which political issues seem to arise in non-political formats. Instead of confronting us as formidable systems of thought, or as parties locked in bitter combat, politics in America has often appeared in the guise of religious, cultural and sexual issues" (161). For Howe, this was not only a contemporaneous insight into the United States of the fifties but also an observation of the long-standing American tendency to see politics through the prism of culture, especially during moments of social turmoil. Although uneasy as a democratic socialist, Howe was not entirely surprised roughly a decade later, during the collapse of the New Deal coalition and the rise of conservatism in electoral politics, when "culture" became the ultimate battleground for sociopolitical struggle. For scholars of the era, Howe's prophetic statement has hardened into an axiom of postwar America, as the transformative emergence of culture remains the operational assumption in most accounts of the sixties as a historical breakage point. In *Age of Fracture* (2011), historian Daniel T. Rodgers argues that the sixties represent a transitional decade in which "notions of power moved out of structures and into culture" (12). Quoting Joseph Epstein's well-known aphorism, Rodgers agrees that the sixties can be understood essentially as a "political Rorschach test" boiling down to a basic question: "Tell me what you think of that period, and I shall tell you what your politics are" (qtd. in Rodgers, *Age of Fracture,* 4). What Epstein's quip reveals, Andrew Hartman claims in *War for the Soul of America: A History of the Culture Wars* (2015), is the extent to which, during and after the sixties, "whether one thought the nation was in moral decline was often a correlative of whether one was liberal or conservative" (4). In other words, cultural tastes and preferences began to index political ideology better than party affiliation, a social change that, scholars have long argued, partly accounts for the dramatic realignment of the two major US political parties in the sixties and seventies.[1]

In the aftermath of this elevation of culture as a privileged site of political struggle, literary scholars posited that postwar US fiction after "the sixties" fell almost exclusively within the neighboring provinces of modern liberalism and the American Left.[2] This development was something of a surprise for earlier socialist literary critics such as Howe, who had always seen great canonical literature and high literary culture as sites of contestation that conservatives were routinely laying claim to, reframing literature as a high cultural field that transcended political and economic fields and revealed the eternal human condition. Major American novelists, Howe noted with consternation, often treated political ideology "as if it were merely a form of private experience," a tendency that conservative critics used in order to frame politics as subordinate to timeless universal themes, thus perpetuating the status quo (*Politics and the Novel,* 162). By the late sixties, Howe regarded the cultural turn in American radicalism, typified by the New Left, as a collection of misinformed social movements that "[adopted] a stance that seems to be political, sometimes even ideological, but often turns out to be a little more than an effort to assert a personal style" (*Steady Work,* 43). When examining the notion of the "political" in the history of the American novel, Howe implied, one should expect to find not ready-made models for modern liberalism or democratic socialism but a sociopolitical battleground where conservatives had just as much rhetorical leverage and cultural prestige as liberals.

I draw attention to Howe's vision of this relationship between politics and the novel not to advocate straightforwardly for its validity but rather to defamiliarize the contemporary truism in popular discourse that American literature and the American Left in the sixties were somehow necessary allies. In this chapter, I continue the story about American literature and politics offered in Chapter 2 to assert that this opposition between an imaginative Left and an unimaginative Right in the sixties amounts to a false dichotomy. I contend not only that American fiction changed limited, though crucial, elements of modern conservative discourse during this time but also that the conservative movement's insurgent takeover of the Republican Party beginning in the sixties had specific, under-theorized implications for the cultural politics of the American novel. To demonstrate this point, I argue that the literary projects of two of the most visible prose writers of the sixties, James Baldwin and Norman Mailer, cannot be understood fully without interrogating their engagements with the conservative movement, specifically their combative relationships with William F. Buckley, Jr., the founder of *National Review* and the paradigmatic sociopolitical figure of modern American conservatism.

In the bulk of this chapter, I pay special attention to the years between 1963 and 1968 not only because they show Baldwin and Mailer at the height of their popularity and cultural influence but also because this was the exact moment when, in the wake of the civil rights movement and the anti–Vietnam War protests, modern conservatism underwent a profound ideological shift in the pursuit of a long-term electoral strategy to court white working-class voters that reshaped the way conservatives valued highbrow literature. Whereas movement conservatives in the fifties tended to stress tradition-based hierarchies and organic social order over abstract theories of individual liberty, conservatives began to shift their emphasis in the mid-sixties toward the language of unadulterated patriotism, property rights, and colorblind individualism. In the earlier traditionalist iteration of the movement, conservatives valued more complex aesthetic formulations of the American novel – what McCann and Szalay would call "the ineffable, the extraordinary, and the mysterious" conveyed in the most sophisticated examples of the form – because that kind of literary form not only provided grounding for part of their neo-Burkean rationale for organic complexity but also combined Veblen-esque fantasies of elite financial capital married to elite cultural capital. However, in the next stage of their movement, conservatives embraced an ideologically rigid fusion of laissez-faire capitalism and cultural populism that would redirect perceptions of literary value and prestige within American conservatism toward certain conservative strands of New Journalism and, in later years, toward the one-dimensionality of mass-market genre fiction (McCann and Szalay, "Introduction: Paul Potter and the Cultural Turn" [2005], 213). In this latter stage, conservatives emphasized the "liberal cultural elite" trope with renewed vigor, constructing a monolithic stereotype of white liberal intellectuals whose racial guilt fueled their appetite for difficult, morally complex literature, a form of moral masochism that conveniently helped those same white liberals accrue "hip" cultural capital.

By close reading major works produced by Baldwin and Mailer during these years, I show that the interpretative horizon of their prose writings is inextricable from the emergence of modern conservatism as a cultural and electoral force. For Mailer, a self-identified "Left Conservative" who had recognized the allure of right-wing authoritarianism since his first novel, *The Naked and the Dead* (1948), modern postwar conservatism was a fascistic, pathological ideology that, nevertheless, represented a misguided reaction to the legitimate failures of the liberal welfare state and liberal cultural snobbery. The kernel of truth Mailer found redeemable in movement conservatism in "nonfiction novels" like *The Armies of the Night* (1968) and *Miami and the Siege of Chicago* (1968) was a romanticized form of white male individualism that occasionally overlapped with the emerging style of conservative cultural populism. Within certain strands of New Journalism, conservatives admired how writers such as Mailer and Tom Wolfe were implicitly delegitimizing – what conservatives were already calling – the "liberal media" and its so-called objectivity. In the eyes of Baldwin, the central figure in my account, Mailer's conservative turn was not just predictable but nearly unavoidable. Since his formative years as a young writer in Paris, Baldwin recognized the powerful resilience of habit and prejudice vis-à-vis race – what he calls the "strongbox of custom" in *Notes of a Native Son* (1955) – over the long arc of US history (Baldwin, *Collected Essays* [*CE*], 98). For Baldwin, "custom" was not a political buzzword signifying an inherently oppressive cultural practice; in the sixties, though, modern conservatism manifested the latest iteration of certain deeply entrenched racist habits of mind, which Baldwin interrogated most thoroughly in his supposedly failed late novel *Tell Me How Long the Train's Been Gone* (1968).[3] He understood, perhaps better than any writer of his era, that modern conservatives were advocates of a dynamic, protean ideology that toggled between a double register of highbrow elite taste and lowbrow populist grievance, which had to be reckoned with before one could seriously entertain hopes of radical social change. Ultimately, the stakes of Baldwin's insight boil down to the notion that the literary field had to reimagine the relationship between literary form and cultural prestige to deal with the sociopolitical effects of modern conservatism.

3.2 Baldwin, Mailer, and Postwar Movement Conservatism

Although Baldwin and Mailer are frequently remembered as authors connected to the epoch-defining progressive movements of the sixties, less attention has been paid to their decades-long interrogation of the rise of movement conservatism. This mutual interest in conservative thought and politics emerged out of their critical evaluations of modern liberalism, an ideology both writers regarded as naïvely committed to the notion that the kind of instrumental reason deployed by bureaucratic institutions could solve intractable social problems. What liberalism failed to account for, Baldwin and Mailer believed, was that enigmatic dimension of sociopolitical life bound up with the vision of an incoherent, irrational self that pointed toward outrageous desires and hatreds. In the late fifties and early sixties, the fullest manifestation of this dark dimension of American politics was found in the feverish discourse surrounding the "race issue," which Baldwin routinely noted was usually code for the "Negro problem." Believing that this discourse was innately resistant to the large-scale sociological analyses favored by liberal social planners, Baldwin and Mailer claimed that the novelist's skills were uniquely suited to grasping not only why the current configuration of liberalism was inadequate but also the psychic roots of the virulent white backlash.

Mailer's first significant race-based critique of liberalism and his concomitant engagement with the nascent conservative movement occur in his controversial essay "The White Negro" (1957), a long disquisition on the figure of the hipster originally published in *Dissent*, a journal cofounded by Irving Howe, which dove headlong into the great existential enigmas of death, God, orgasm, authenticity, revolution, and violence using the quintessentially "hip" vocabulary of the late fifties. According to Mailer, young white men were increasingly mimicking the language, cultural worldview, and bodily mannerisms of black men, who had always lived outside the conformist structures of white society, because black life seemed to promise an immersion in "the enormous present" of authentic selfhood (Mailer, "White Negro," 339). As an "urban adventurer," in Mailer's words, the American black male renounced "the pleasures of the mind for the more obligatory pleasures of the body, and in his music he [gave] voice to the character and quality of his existence, to his rage and the infinite variations of joy, lust, languor, growl, cramp, pinch, scream and despair of his orgasm" (339). Toward the end of the essay, Mailer maligned the liberal belief that "the Negro and even the reactionary Southern white are eventually and fundamentally people like himself, capable of becoming good liberals too if only they can be reached by good liberal reason" (357). What the liberal failed to see was what the novelist saw so clearly: the hatred and resentments swirling beneath American society. Taking school desegregation as an example, Mailer claimed that the reactionary conservative "sees the reality more closely" than the typical liberal because the reactionary understood that the true conflict was not so much about philosophical questions over civil rights and constitutional equality but the more intimate issue of miscegenation (356). "Like all conservative political fear," Mailer wrote, "it is the fear of the unforeseeable consequences, for the Negro's equality would tear a profound shift into the psychology, the sexuality, and the moral imagination of every white alive"

(356). Treating the issue of desegregation as paradigmatic, then, Mailer defined "conservatism" in a traditionalist, neo-Burkean-via-Mailer sense of the term, as an ideology that prefers gradual social change in order to prevent harmful, unforeseen consequences and anticipate the explosive forces of resentment always waiting to be unleashed from society's political unconscious.

For Baldwin, Mailer certainly offered penetrating insights into the psychic anxiety of white America, but Mailer's definition of conservatism was fundamentally flawed. Ironically, Baldwin identified this flaw by showing how the foundation of Mailer's ostensible fifties radicalism – that is, the "White Negro" as an amalgamation of the white Kerouacian beatnik and the American black male – only reinforced the very reactionary ideology it sought to undermine. Insulated from the daily realities of black life by their white, largely middle-class lifestyles, Kerouac and Mailer were novelists who could provide trenchant accounts of white bourgeois society, Baldwin believed, but they were still too deeply conditioned to see black men and women as anything more than foil characters who illuminated the hopes and fears of white men.[4] What most disturbed Baldwin in the late fifties was not that Southern white reactionaries failed to imagine the inner life of African Americans to be as rich and full as theirs, which was woefully predictable, but that these seemingly progressive radicals also seemed unable to make this imaginative leap. As a result, Baldwin experienced the profoundly ambivalent epiphany that conservatism contained an undeniable kernel of truth that would form the base of his sociopolitical vision: that the long-running traditions and corresponding prejudices that had always kept American society functioning were premised on the degradation of African Americans, and that these traditions were not simply discarded, even when they were exposed as being deeply embedded in genealogies of oppression. Baldwin's sociopolitical vision, first formed in the critical milieu of the New York Intellectuals and then refined in postwar Paris, was rooted in the notion that the historical phenomenon usually called "custom," "prejudice," or "habit" – all terms signifying the supreme principle of traditionalist conservative thought descending from Burke – was the most potent factor in the long, bloody story of American race relations, and that it had to be fully acknowledged and deconstructed before serious social change could begin. Throughout *Notes of a Native Son*, Baldwin stated repeatedly that his time in Paris taught him relatively little about France, but much about his own country, since Europe tended to alienate Americans from their familiar cultural rituals and unquestioned frameworks of meaning. Such disruptions revealed, for Baldwin, all the ways in which US history conditioned every American's understanding of race, transforming its contradictions and basic inconsistencies into a normative phenomenon.

Baldwin felt so strongly about what a traditionalist conservative would call "prejudice" that he identified its legibility as the necessary condition of possibility for starting an intelligible conversation about race in the United States. "I don't think that the Negro problem in America can even be discussed coherently," Baldwin wrote in the introductory "Autobiographical Notes" section of *Notes of a Native Son*, "without bearing in mind its context; its context being *the history, traditions, customs, the moral assumptions and preoccupations of the country*; in short, the general social fabric. Appearances to the contrary, no one in America escapes its effects and everyone in America bears some responsibility for it" (*CE*, 8, emphasis added). Before Americans, especially "radical" white Americans on the Left like Mailer, could even begin to discuss how to ameliorate postwar racism, they had to recognize that the subtle habits of mind ingrained by cultural history revealed not so much a "Negro problem" amenable to quick solutions as an intractable moral dilemma that went to the very roots of what it had always meant to be an American in the land of the free.

Later in *Notes of a Native Son*, Baldwin examined this topic head-on in his essay "A Question of Identity," a short piece that narrates the maturation process of a generic American archetype: the young (tacitly white) student in postwar Paris. Describing how the student embraces French culture with uncritical enthusiasm, Baldwin concluded that this tendency was "nothing more or less than a means of safeguarding his American simplicity" (*CE*, 98). Effectively, the student has only succeeded in placing "himself in a kind of strongbox of custom," which gave him the luxury of refusing "to see anything in Paris which can't be seen through a golden haze" (98). By locking himself inside this "strongbox of custom," the student merely repeated abroad the same process of moral disavowal that transpired for so many at home, but the fact that he experienced the process in Europe could render visible the quintessential American "assumption that it is possible to consider the person apart from all the forces which have produced him" (*CE*, 100). Baldwin thought that this unconscious presupposition "is itself based on nothing less than our history, which is the history of the total, and willing, alienation of entire peoples from their forebears ... this history has created an entirely unprecedented people, with a unique and individual past. It is, indeed, this past which has thrust upon us our present, so troubling role" (100). Unlike Mailer and some other ostensibly radical writers, who at times position the self as an atomic unit or tabula rasa that can be cut off from personal and national histories and forged anew, Baldwin believed the self to be a site of immense sociopolitical struggle influenced by centuries of oppressive cultural habituation.

In the introduction to his second essay collection, *Nobody Knows My Name* (1961), Baldwin deepened his theory of an American "strongbox of custom," further revealing the ways in which he shared a basic assumption with traditionalist conservatives regarding the power of prejudice. When Baldwin arrived in Paris, he found out that skin color did not signify the same way it did at home, for in America "the color of my skin had stood between myself and me; in Europe, that barrier was down" (*CE: Nobody Knows,* 135). At first, Baldwin experienced this cultural change as emancipatory, as a chance to discover his true self without the distorting effects of American racism, as if harvesting one's authenticity could be as easy as separating the wheat of selfhood from the chaff of culture. Eventually, though, Baldwin realized that his early search for identity was premised on a neat division between internal and external that broke down in the face of historical reality:

> It turned out that the question of who I was was not solved because I had removed myself from the social forces which menaced me – anyway, these forces had become interior, and I had dragged them across the ocean with me. The question of who I was had at last become a personal question, and the answer was to be found in me. I think that there is always something frightening about this realization. I know it frightened me. (*CE*, 135)

In Henry Louis Gates, Jr.'s notable reading of this passage, Baldwin reversed the typical, cause-and-effect understanding of American political ideology in the sixties. "For Baldwin was proposing not that politics is merely a projection of private neuroses," Gates wrote, alluding to the idea that political convictions are simply symptoms of resentment and frustration, "but that our private neuroses are shaped by quite public ones. The retreat to subjectivity . . . would lead not to an escape from the 'racial drama,' but – and this was the alarming prospect that Baldwin wanted to announce – a rediscovery of it" (Gates, "The Fire Last Time"). The upshot of this insight was that the "Negro problem" in the postwar United States was a proxy for a much larger issue regarding the instability of American identity, especially the disturbance of whiteness as a categorical absolute. In other words, the "Negro problem" was a metaphysical problem disguised as a political problem, since it disrupted the fundamental nature of white American identity. In Baldwin's eyes, this meant that *both* the modern liberal's response to racial discrimination and the radical beatnik's were inadequate because they assumed that racism could be eradicated while, at the same time, the notion of whiteness as an identity category could remain more or less intact.[5]

This insight helps explain why Baldwin and Mailer, despite their shared critiques of modern liberalism, arrived at such different definitions of, and later associations with, postwar American conservatism. For Mailer, the self-described "Left Conservative," a perplexing neologism meaning one who thinks "in the style of Marx in order to attain certain values suggested by Edmund Burke," American cultural customs and traditions retained deep value since they kept one attached to the "roots" of existence (Mailer, *Armies,* 185). The heart of Mailer's definition of modern conservatism was highlighted in his frequent deployment of the word "root," which led to the notion that conservatism was a political philosophy concerned, at base, with the preservation of certain benevolent traditions that kept one in touch with historical reality. As Mailer claimed in *The Armies of the Night,* since he identified as a conservative in some idiosyncratically Mailer-esque sense of the term, his political theorizing would always "begin at the root" (185). In his 1962 debate with William F. Buckley, Jr., Mailer stated that "the biological rage" of Goldwaterism stemmed from the feeling Barry Goldwater's supporters had "that there seems to be some almost palpable conspiracy to tear life away from its roots" ("Debate with William Buckley" [1963], 167). At its most philosophically shrewd, in Mailer's mind, conservatism amounted to Burke; at its most pathologically misdirected and misapplied, it amounted to Goldwater. Ever the unorthodox disciple of Hemingway, Mailer saw cultural traditions like hunting, boxing, bullfighting, and even certain forms of war as rituals of vitalization that naturally cultivated one's notion of "the good life" through the senses, keeping one attached to the all-important roots.

For Baldwin, though, the supposedly salutary nature of these rituals was mostly an illusion, an identity-shaping fantasy that the privileged (sometimes class privileged, other times racially privileged) reiterated back to themselves. As a result, his definition of conservatism rested on the notion that cultural traditions were complex instruments of power that legitimate unequal power relations. The despotic power of such rituals and traditions could be seen in Faulkner's insistence that desegregation was occurring too quickly, which implicitly recalled Burke's famous passage on the utility of time-tested prejudices in a moment of crisis: "Prejudice is of ready application in the emergency; it previously engages the mind in a steady course of wisdom and virtue, and does not leave that man hesitating in the moment of decision, sceptical [sic], puzzled, and unresolved" (*Reflections,* 182). According to Baldwin, the set of prejudices many white people found applicable in the crisis brought on by the civil rights movement were habits that established continuity between oppression in the past and oppression in the present, habits so ingrained that white Americans remained comfortably ignorant of their systemic operation in society. What Baldwin discovered about conservatism during these years, *contra* Mailer, was that prejudice was potent even though it had no inherent purchase on reality; indeed, prejudice derived much of its power from its lack of correspondence with the lived suffering experienced by the oppressed.

According to the quintessential traditionalist conservative Russell Kirk, Burke first theorized the term "prejudice" in *Reflections on the Revolution in France,* by which he meant the mass of "untaught feelings" furnished by generations of collective experience (Burke, *Reflections,* 182). Since any given individual's "private stock of reason" was small and his implementation of it erratic, Burke believed that "individuals would do better to avail themselves of the general bank and capital of nations, and of ages" (182). This general bank of prejudice represented an accumulation of social wisdom that had been tested and verified over time. The result, in Burke's words, was that "prejudice renders a man's virtue his habit; and not a series of unconnected acts" (182). In one of Kirk's early essays on Burkean prejudice, "Burke and the Philosophy of Prescription" (1953), he described prejudice as "the supra-rational wisdom of the species" that surpasses the meager rationality of the individual (365). Further defining prejudice as "the half-intuitive knowledge that enables man to meet the problems of life without logic-chopping," Kirk argued that the elite class's right to rule over inferior classes was not an abstract right discovered through speculation, but a "customary right which grows out of the implied conventions and compacts of many successive generations: employing these instruments, mankind manages to live together in some degree of amicability and freedom" (377). For traditionalist conservatives, prejudices were *necessary biases* that sustained the basic social order not because they were morally unassailable – Kirk readily conceded that we one could always dream up better, unachievable utopias – but because prejudices were manifestations of practical traditions that kept society functioning and Western civilization afloat.

Baldwin also conveyed this sense of necessary bias in his prominent "strongbox of custom" metaphor, but he imagined custom as a protective barrier guarding people against the whole of social reality in the interest of continuity with the repressive traditions of the past. While Baldwin and a traditionalist like Kirk both agreed that custom and prejudice were powerful mechanisms that did not necessarily map the real world with perfect verisimilitude, they disagreed on the value of these concepts as guides for managing social change, ultimately leading to their divergent definitions of conservatism itself. As Kirk pointed out, traditionalist conservatives were not against every form of change, only those changes they perceived as both radical *and* abrupt. In Burke's pithy formulation, a favorite of Kirk's, a "state without the means of some change is without the means of its conservation" (*Reflections*, 106). Reflecting on the inevitability of change in Burkean thought, Kirk wrote that change should be "a process of renewal" and should thus "come as the consequence of a need generally felt, not inspired by fine-spun abstractions" (*Conservative Mind,* 40). In this sense, Kirk claimed, traditional customs and prejudices were instruments that assisted in a slow, gradual process that allowed society "to patch and polish the old order of things" (40). The problem with this position, from Baldwin's perspective, was that many white Americans had looked upon virtually all large-scale equality movements, especially for African Americans, as too hasty and radical *no matter their rate of change.* Instead of tradition-based prejudices acting as a kind of soft brake, Baldwin believed that they halted certain kinds of change altogether and continued to distance the upper classes from the suffering of those beneath them, insulating the privileged in their innocence and making the legitimate claims of the downtrodden appear hysterical, hyperbolic, and generally implausible. The upshot of this social arrangement was that a demand for change voiced by a political movement rarely seemed, in the eyes of the ruling class, like "a need generally felt," in Kirk's words, but rather like an existential threat to civilization. Over the course of American history, as Baldwin explained to his nephew in the short epistolary section of *The Fire Next Time*, "the black man has functioned in the white man's world as a fixed star, as an immovable pillar: and as he moves out of his place, heaven and earth are shaken to their foundations" (*CE,* 294). There could be no gradual modification of the racial status quo if white identity was at stake. In short, Baldwin claimed, the true emancipation of Africans Americans in the sixties could register as nothing less than a social revolution, destroying the racial sentimentalities of *National Review* conservatives and beatnik radicals alike.

Despite their differing interpretations of the relationship between the "race issue" and the disruption of white identity, Baldwin and Mailer both agreed that whiteness in the early sixties was no longer an invisible assumption or universal given in American society, but a malleable category with increasingly intense political valences. They also knew that, in practical terms, this meant that the civil rights movement was gradually changing the basic vocabulary of political debate, throwing into relief a choice regarding racial equality that did not seem to exist before in such stark terms. During the thirties, before racial egalitarianism was a staple of American liberalism, Franklin Roosevelt courted Southern Democratic racists in congress in order to pass New Deal legislation, which effectively privileged class issues over racial issues like segregation – and even lynching – and made racial equality an optional position in the emerging paradigm of modern liberalism.[6] But roughly two decades after the Allied victory in World War II, a war supposedly fought against a Nazi regime underpinned by an overtly racist ideology, civil rights for African Americans became, slowly and painfully, a paradigmatic issue for the Democratic Party, especially after John F. Kennedy's famous civil rights address in June of 1963. It is no surprise that Baldwin and Mailer, two ambitious American novelists in the early sixties fascinated by formal and informal modes of power, found the cultural trope of "American Fascism" to be an irresistible literary device for understanding militant whiteness as one of the key lineaments of movement conservatism.

3.3 Race, Cultural Prestige, and the Rhetoric of Fascism: From Presidential Candidate Goldwater to Mayoral Candidate Buckley

Even before Barry Goldwater lost the 1964 presidential election to Lyndon Johnson in a historic landside amidst a flurry of comparisons between "Goldwater conservatism" and Nazism, movement conservatives knew they had a problem in the early sixties: their ambivalent position on civil rights made them look quite comfortable with segregation, which in turn, made them appear to some like fascists reincarnated. For Buckley and his conservative devotees, of course, this accusation was not entirely new. Although movement conservatives consistently denied the allegation, they had become somewhat accustomed to disentangling the erroneous conflation, in their minds, of conservatism and fascism. As I demonstrated in previous chapters, conservatives saw the founding of *National Review* as an opportunity to argue for the categorical similarities between fascism and communism as left-wing ideologies under the rubric of totalitarianism; but they also looked upon the magazine as an ideal platform for disassociating fascism from the American Right. Indeed, no criticism incensed conservatives of all stripes more than being called "fascists," a word they associated with an omnipotent state underpinned by a materialistic ideology of atheism, and conservatives spent a surprising amount of their time separating postwar conservatism from the taint of the fascist smear.[7] What all of their efforts to distance fifties conservatism from fascism had in common was an odd rhetorical contortion: that the main criteria for defining fascism tended to be economic rather than racial, which was a residual effect of older, pre–World War II debates that downplayed racial anti-Semitism in an early twentieth-century America still steeped in prejudices of all kinds, and emphasized the peculiar "corporate statism" structure of European Fascism. At the dawn of the sixties, conservatives found themselves almost wholly unprepared for the shift in political discourse ushered in by African American authors who employed the epitaph "fascist" as a synonym for American "racist." To the surprise of movement conservatives, the early sixties became a period when their brand of tradition-based racism, buttressed by the cultural capital of highbrow literary figures such as Faulkner and O'Connor, seemed to become *the* constitutive feature of proto-fascism in America.

The result for conservatives, as I explain below, was that the sociopolitical phenomenon labeled "the sixties" essentially began with the publication of James Baldwin's groundbreaking book *The Fire Next Time* (1963). If "the sixties" signified a fundamental challenge to the white male values of "Western civilization," as Todd Gitlin has argued, conservatives were shocked not only by its arrival, but also by James Baldwin as its messenger (*The Sixties,* xiv). Although this historical fact remains virtually unknown in literary studies, conservatives at *National Review* had praised Baldwin's abilities as a novelist at the very beginning of his career, claiming that his early fiction did not degenerate into the rigid aesthetic of grievance embedded in socialist realism. In his review of Baldwin's most financially successful novel, *Another Country* (1962), Guy Davenport noted that while he frequently chose to portray "such stock and fashionable troubles as the Negro in New York," Baldwin "neither sentimentalizes nor excuses, which is to say that he refuses to resort to either sympathy or indifference. He has settled for understanding alone" (154). Since conservatives ignored Baldwin's early essay collections, which anticipated many of the arguments in *The Fire Next Time*, they tended to see him primarily as a talented "Negro writer" in the same line as socialist-turned-conservative George Schuyler. In a profoundly ironic twist of American literary history, movement conservatives saw Baldwin, as late as the early sixties, as a promising source of cultural capital for the postwar conservative movement, and thus as a potential cultural guardian of *their vision* of American civilization.[8]

Upon the publication of *The Fire Next Time*, Buckley realized not only that conservatives had been disastrously wrong about Baldwin's politics, but also that his critical vision represented a denunciation of the racial status quo in postwar America that was more radical than the earlier critiques of Southern-based racism voiced by civil rights leaders in the fifties. Although conservatives opposed the civil rights movement at almost every turn, conservatives praised aspects of the Montgomery bus boycott, which began in December of 1955, roughly two weeks after the first issue of *National Review* was published, because of its surface-level alignment with a Christian-based capitalist worldview. "It is one thing to take the position that the government has not the power to compel integration," stated an anonymous writer in April 1957, expressing the official position of the magazine, "it is another to take the position that Negros should be made to support a legally constructed monopoly" ("How Much is it Worth?" [1957], 55). But if conservatives, who by every indication were not genuinely sympathetic to the Montgomery bus boycott, willfully misinterpreted the boycott as "Christian Negroes" arguing for their rights as consumers in an unfair market place, there was no mistaking Baldwin's fiery condemnation of America *in toto*. Buckley, hoping to expose how dangerous he believed Baldwin's book truly was, tapped his young conservative protégé Garry Wills to write an extended counterargument in the form of a review that bears striking similarities to another famous review commissioned by Buckley to tarnish the author's credibility with allusions to totalitarian collectivism: Whittaker Chambers's takedown of Ayn Rand's *Atlas Shrugged*.

Unlike Chambers, though, Garry Wills began his essay "What Color Is God?" – published in *National Review* in late May, just four days after Baldwin appeared on the cover of *Time* magazine – by acknowledging Baldwin's formidable talents as a writer. "James Baldwin is a disarming man, against whom it is necessary to arm ourselves," Wills opened the piece, for Baldwin was surely "the most sensitive and discriminating articulator of Negro suffering," and it must be acknowledged that his three novels to date – *Go Tell it on the Mountain* (1953), *Giovanni's Room* (1956) and *Another Country* – prove that "Baldwin is obviously a man who can do anything with words" (408–09). The central problem with Baldwin's latest book, Wills said, was not that Baldwin accused white America of racism, which Wills readily conceded, but that Baldwin used his talents to expose, at least in Baldwin's own mind, a kind of Nietzschean abyss at the heart of American society. Baldwin "does not attack us [i.e., white Americans] for not living up to our ideals, for lapsing, for sinning, for being bad Christians," Wills pointed out, implicitly alluding to the conservative assessment of Martin Luther King, Jr. and other Christian civil rights workers; "[Baldwin] says we do not *have* any ideals: we do not believe in any of the things our religion, our civilization, our country stand for. It is all an elaborate lie, a lie whose sole and original function is to fortify privilege" (410). Wills understood that Baldwin's almost apocalyptic discourse differed from Christian civil rights rhetoric not in degree, but in kind. Baldwin was contributing to a crucial change, Wills feared, in the basic coordinates of the "race issue" in America by upending the premise of the debate. Whereas the stereotypical "Christian Negro," in the conservative imagination, wanted to be integrated into "civilized" white society, Baldwin's real-life black characters were shrewd, jaded, and skeptical. In their eyes, white America was not the height of civilization and culture, but of cruelty and barbarism.

For Wills and others at *National Review*, Baldwin's rejection of (their formulation of) Western civilization fit neatly into a conservative discourse framework that, as I detailed at length in previous chapters, regarded root-and-branch attacks on the status quo as unwitting contributions to totalitarian collectivism. In a line often repeated by conservatives about the sixties, Wills stressed just how imperative it was for readers to grasp the profound challenge Baldwin's book posed: "So let us be clear about what is actually being said: Baldwin is asking for immediate secession from our civilization" (411). According to Wills, Baldwin's argument rested on the naïve premise that the eradication of Christianity as the beating heart of the Western tradition would inevitably herald a new, more advanced system of ethics. As a traditionalist conservative, Wills saw Baldwin not only as a base materialist on par with Rand or Marx, but as even more confused than a Randian Objectivist or Soviet Marxist since Baldwin did not have a systemic account of moral behavior. Instead, Baldwin used brilliant prose to translate his legitimate anger at American racism into the disorganized "challenge of the compulsive rebel against the present order – the White Negro of Mailer, or the anarchistic monster [of Richard Wright's] Bigger Thomas" (Wills, 410). These hypothetical revolutionaries, unmoored from the values instilled by generations of Christianity, would possess a moral calculus underpinned only by their own whims. Wills, like Whittaker Chambers before him in *Witness*, argued that this latest iteration of materialist ideology ends in the fantastical bloodlust of totalitarianism: "one never knows when, under the pressure of private vision or public disaster ... some revolutionary is going to remember that, on his own materialist principles, killing off one strain of men can be justified as analogous to the elimination of inferior offshoots in the process that produced our race and its great promise" (413). The answer, Wills claimed, was to preserve Christian ethics not because they made people perfect, but because they reminded people of how imperfect they were, and always would be.

Essentially, Wills proposed a solution that seemed to spring fully formed from the Burkean head of Russell Kirk, whose famous dictum posited that political problems were always symptoms of deeper moral and religious problems. The Christian tradition was the nation's best hope, Wills wrote toward the end of his review, because "it holds that differences between white men and black, like those between men and women, adults and children – like any of the differences that mark us out, every one – are simply manifestations of the range of the human mystery, different manifestations of the divine ... Beneath the public debate, more intimate demands upon the conscience must do their work" (416). Wills restated, in other words, the prevailing traditionalist conservative argument for racial inequality, a complex rhetorical contortion honed in the late fifties and articulated brilliantly by novelists like Flannery O'Connor that acknowledged inequality but justified it with the language of compassionate paternalism and Christian humility. The underlying premise of this position was that traditionalist conservatives recognized that the privileges bestowed upon a given race or class were a constitutive, even divinely ordained, feature of social reality. A progressive like Baldwin, from this perspective, could only be ignoring reality when he posited abstractions to pursue his grand theoretical project for radical change.

Once this foundational racial premise of traditionalist conservatism is understood, it is clear why Baldwin particularly incensed Wills when he compared white Americans, especially conservative white Americans, to German Fascists: Baldwin overturned the assumption that conservatives were hardnosed observers of reality while progressives were simply utopian dreamers. "White people were, and are, astounded by the holocaust in Germany," Baldwin wrote in *The Fire Next Time*, "They did not know that they could act that way. But I very much doubt whether black people were astounded – at least, in the same way" (*CE*, 317). Baldwin's critique went to the core of traditionalist conservatism by suggesting that the majority of white Americans were ignorant of entire swaths of social reality. For a traditionalist like Wills, this kind of statement could only register as a polemical slur rather than a legitimate observation about American society. To conflate white Americans with Nazis, Wills believed, was always to stoop to a superficial ad hominem attack, as Baldwin hoped to "dismiss with a reference to the Third Reich" a complex, thoughtful conservative argument rooted in history and tradition (Wills, 416). Wills ended his review by implying that Baldwin's Nazi insults came from a reservoir of deep, albeit legitimate, personal anger and should thus be understood as rhetorical embellishments that supplemented his more important primary arguments, which conservatives had to take seriously because they "force us to remember what our best arguments are" (417).

What makes this final assessment of *The Fire Next Time* so disjointed is that Wills, while admitting earlier in his review that Baldwin poses a unique argument and new challenge to postwar conservatism, can only muster a reply that relies on the same well-worn traditionalist position. In an ambiguous move that signaled traditionalist conservatism's inability to deal with the evolving "Negro problem," Wills failed to appreciate, or perhaps actively ignored, the fact that in order to engage with Baldwin's argument, he had to account for Baldwin's historically precise allusion to Nazi Fascism since it functioned as the linchpin of Baldwin's broader claim about white America's naïve sense of social reality. Noting that the US-led fight against Nazi Germany was a watershed moment for domestic racial issues, Baldwin wrote that the "treatment accorded to the Negro during the Second World War marks, for me, a turning point in the Negro's relation to America . . . a certain hope died, a certain respect for white Americans faded" (317–18). From here, Baldwin shifted suddenly into a prose style that closely resembled novelistic discourse, prompting readers to inhabit the imagined perspective of an African American soldier:

> You have to put yourself in the skin of a man who is wearing the uniform of his country, who is a candidate for death in its defense, and who is called a "nigger" by his comrades-in-arms and his officers; who is almost always given the hardest, ugliest, most menial work to do; who knows that the white G.I. has informed the Europeans that he is subhuman (so much for the American male's sexual security); who does not dance at the U.S.O the night white soldiers dance there, and does not drink in the same bars white soldiers drink in; and who watches German prisoners of war being treated by Americans with more human dignity than he ever has received at their hands. (*CE,* 318)

As with other passages in Baldwin's nonfiction, this reads like a series of sketches from a novel in progress – from the parenthetical aside about male sexual insecurity simulating a character's free indirect discourse to the scenic montages portraying lowly work details, segregated military dances, bar outings and, perhaps as a climactic epiphany, the depiction of white American soldiers coddling Nazi prisoners. Baldwin suggested that since

African American soldiers did in fact witness these kinds of events on a regular basis, and since the moral hypocrisy they exposed was common knowledge in black communities across the country, it should hardly be a surprise that African Americans saw German white supremacy under Hitler and white supremacy in the postwar United States as two sides of the same sociopolitical coin.

Baldwin's indictment of white hypocrisy partially accounted for the reason why movement conservatives had such a difficult time digesting Baldwin's argument in *The Fire Next Time*, since they tended to frame themselves as traditionalists with a keen awareness of the past, and liberals and progressives as future-oriented idealists who ignored the wisdom of history. Operating out of this ideological framework, conservatives saw Baldwin's statements about white American myths as part of a larger strategy that used polemical discourse to push for unrealistic notions of equality. For instance, less than a month after the lengthy Garry Wills review, Buckley provided his own critical assessment of Baldwin in his *National Review* column "On the Right," wherein he selectively misread *The Fire Next Time* as a "Call to Color Blindness." The duty for all Americans concerned about racism, Buckley wrote, reiterating the traditionalist position, "is not to try to obliterate differences which only autohypnotic color blindness could achieve, but to simulate man's capacity for love, and his toleration, understanding, and respect for other, different people" ("Call to Color Blindness," 488). Though Buckley was a self-proclaimed individualist since his time as an undergraduate at Yale, in the early sixties he still held on tightly to the early conservative movement's traditionalist position on race, which emphasized social order, benign prejudice, and implicit support for Jim Crow.

The story of how and why movement conservatives abandoned this set of traditionalist positions on civil rights is complex and uneven; however, the origins of this shift were bound up with a gradual awareness by Buckley and other conservatives that the contours of the race debate in America were changing in the sixties, and that James Baldwin was one of several major catalysts.[9] After their first incoherent responses to Baldwin's work, conservatives saw that he was configuring a far more complex and profound political vision than they had initially realized, one that went far beyond calls for abstract colorblindness and, because of its emphasis on American tradition and custom, threatened to delegitimize the conservative movement with Goldwater as its provisional leader.[10] Throughout the second half of the sixties and into the early seventies, Buckley would make it his personal mission to change the way Americans perceived race and movement conservatism, unwittingly playing a crucial part in the process of altering the way movement conservatism conceptualized the value of American literature and the prestige inherent (or not) in the literary field.

After Goldwater's crushing defeat, Buckley realized that the conservative movement's traditionalist position on civil rights had become untenable, and he slowly began testing out a new position: the colorblind "bootstraps" argument that stressed how previous generations of German, Irish, Italian, and Jewish immigrants had pulled themselves up by their bootstraps through thrift, education, and hard work. Buckley was convinced that Baldwin's writings had played a larger role than anyone imagined and he became increasingly consumed with undermining Baldwin's authority on racial issues. In February of 1965, the mutual antipathy between Buckley and Baldwin came to a head when they agreed to face one another in a formal debate before the students of the Cambridge Union Society in England, who had proposed the following debating proposition: "The American Dream is at the expense of the American Negro." Although Buckley, a former debating team captain at Yale, was much more familiar with the layout and technicalities of formal debate – e.g., Buckley knew the traditional dress code and wore a tuxedo, while Baldwin did not and wore a business suit – Baldwin's arguments were too perspicacious and his rhetoric too polished for Buckley to have a chance at winning.[11] The Buckley–Baldwin should be understood as a watershed moment in the history of movement conservatism because it reveals how and when the conservative movement's use of "small government" rhetoric as an acceptable proxy for channeling white resentment over civil rights reached critical mass, eventually displacing the traditionalist argument altogether. The crucial upshot for American literary history, though, is that it also marked the moment when the conservative culture war on behalf of American civilization began to disconnect itself from the wholesale veneration of complex moral inquiry in "literary fiction," a constitutive element of the traditionalist argument, and embrace alternative modes of prose writing like popular genre fiction and certain kinds of New Journalism that reinforce moral certitude and reflect the conservative movement's increasingly populist stance. In other words, the mid-sixties marked a significant moment in the postwar conservative movement's shifting orientation toward the *illusio* – i.e., the fundamental belief in the literary game of high culture and the prestige of its stakes – since conservatives retained some of their rhetorical respect for high culture, but vastly increased their distrustful rhetoric of the highbrow literary field.

In many ways, Baldwin's success was a result of his ability to frame the debate as a forum on postwar conservatism's unsustainable traditionalist positions on race, especially the two self-interested beliefs that conservative ideology begins by observing empirical reality, and that deep historical prejudice is benign. Baldwin opened the debate by pointing out that, even before the proposition in question could be seriously discussed, one had to realize that the very legibility of the proposition depended "on where you find yourself in the world, what your sense of reality is. That is, it depends on assumptions we hold so deeply as to be scarcely aware of them" ("The American Dream," 32). For the "Mississippi sharecropper or Alabama Sherriff," Baldwin noted, "the proposition which we are trying to discuss does not even exist" (32). Thus, the only way to honestly answer the question was to begin with the life experiences of African Americans, since they were "the people who have been most attacked by the Western system of reality" (32). When people listened to the voices of those who have been victimized by racial prejudice, Baldwin said, imagining themselves in the places of the victims, the profound sense of injustice became self-evident. Suddenly shifting into the second person in order to recreate the rhetorical power of the epistolary mode in the first section of *The Fire Next Time*, Baldwin recounted a litany of daily cruelties, what he called "the catalogue of disaster," that most African Americans have experienced by adulthood: "the policeman, the taxi driver, the waiters, the landlady, the banks, the insurance companies, the millions of details 24 hours every day which spell out to you that you are a worthless human being" (32). Baldwin argued that white Americans have learned this behavior through years of cultural prejudice, which is an insight he only began to understand while living abroad in Europe. Reiterating an abridged, though precise, version of his "strongbox of custom" metaphor from ten years earlier, Baldwin told the audience:

> It seems to me when I watch Americans in Europe that what they don't know about Europeans is what they don't know about me. They were not trying to be nasty to the French girl, rude to the French waiter. They did not know that they hurt their feelings; they didn't have any sense that this particular man and woman were human beings. They walked over them with the same sort of bland ignorance and condescension, the charm and cheerfulness, with which they had patted me on the head and which made them upset when I was upset. (33)

What traditionalist principles like prejudice and custom ensured, Baldwin implied, was the benefit of social cohesion, but only at the price of dehumanizing minorities, a political calculus whose deeply immoral assumption became visible once white Americans were removed from their society and just the dehumanizing effects of their behavior remained. Baldwin's eviscerating arguments forced conservatives into a double-bind: the only way they could plausibly believe that the philosophical principle of prejudice was a net positive for society was if they also accepted the premise that African Americans were inherently inferior to white Americans. For this reason, Baldwin turned to the equalizing logic of the market and the ostensible impartiality of labor-time, emphasizing the centuries of labor performed by black bodies to build the country and create the conditions for the so-called "American Dream": "I picked the cotton, I carried it to market, I built the railroads under something else's whip for nothing. For nothing . . . None can challenge that statement. It is a matter of historical record" (33). Baldwin found this theme of black labor so central to his argument that he ended his speech by repeating it one last time. "I am not a ward of America, I am not an object of missionary charity," Baldwin said, cutting to the racial heart of traditionalist conservatism, "I am one of the people who built the country" (88). For Baldwin, emancipatory politics was not characterized by a benevolent politician like Goldwater desegregating public schools and the armed forces at his own comfortable pace, but by African Americans attaining their own power and autonomy.

When Buckley stood up to deliver his rebuttal, Baldwin assumed that he would endorse the traditionalist argument, as he had been since the end of World War II, by saying what traditionalist conservatives always said when their backs were against a rhetorical wall: stress the inexplicable "complexity" or inescapable "paradox" of American race relations, usually with a high cultural reference to the works of William Faulkner, Flannery O'Connor, or even Mark Twain. But what Baldwin failed to anticipate was that Buckley was in the early stages of shedding the traditionalist position on race, with its increasingly toxic premise of black inferiority, for the libertarian position embodied by the emerging "bootstraps argument." The historiographic value of Buckley's speech is that it shows the conservative movement's shifting position on race in all of its unevenness and uncertainty, as Buckley sought to privilege colorblind individuality but did not realize how racial prejudice still structured his field of vision. For instance, Buckley opened his speech with a condescending proviso to debating Baldwin: that a conservative could not engage with Baldwin's arguments, "unless one is prepared to deal with him as a white man, unless one is prepared to say to him that the fact that your skin is black is utterly irrelevant to the arguments you raise" ("The American Dream," 88). On the one hand, Buckley meant to invoke the classical liberal notion of an abstract, Lockean individual to say that race did not matter; but on the other hand, Buckley could not help but equate the colorblind universal with whiteness itself.

This brief categorical misstep at the beginning of Buckley's rebuttal foreshadowed the ambivalence that structured his entire speech. At first, Buckley reiterated the same traditionalist arguments that Garry Wills launched against Baldwin in his review of *The Fire Next Time*, reductively characterizing Baldwin's argument as a simplistic cause-and-effect relationship between the "teachings of Jesus and Paul" and the Nazi creation of Dachau, which in turn would necessitate the "overthrow of our civilization because we don't live up to our highest ideals" (88). But instead of following the traditionalist harangue against Baldwin to its completion, Buckley suddenly shifted into his new libertarian, market-based position on race. Instead of "telling us to renounce our civilization," Buckley declared, Baldwin "should be addressing his own people and urging them to takes advantages of those opportunities which do exist. And urging us to make those opportunities wider" (89). In lieu of recommending a Faulkner novel or an O'Connor short story, as conservatives had been inclined to do, Buckley stated that Nathan Glazer and Daniel Patrick Moynihan provided the best analysis of the "Negro problem" in their recent sociology book *Beyond the Melting Pot*, wherein they noted that the amount of "Negro doctors" in the United States went up from 3,500 in 1900 to just 3,900 in the sixties, an increase of only about 11 percent (89). The reason was not due to racial discrimination in medical schools, Buckley said, disingenuously, but "because the Negro's particular energy is not directed toward that goal" in the same way that other ethnic groups had directed their energies toward socioeconomic improvement (89). The failure of African Americans to rise above their collective poverty, Buckley contended, did not reveal a shortcoming in American society but a shortcoming in the culture of black life, starting with the dissolution of the black family.

Concluding his speech, Buckley combined the traditionalist and libertarian positions in a new way, using colorblind, market-based language like "mobility" and "opportunity" to reimagine the familiar conservative crusade to save civilization from the barbarians at the gates. Less than ten years earlier, Buckley had warned *National Review* readers of imminent civilizational decline if African Americans were allowed to exercise their constitutional right to vote in the South; now, Buckley was saying that black people's "best chances are in a mobile society and the most mobile society in the world today is the United States" (89). In his final line, addressing the Cambridge Union audience directly, Buckley stated that "just as you waged war to save civilization, you also waged war for the benefit of the Germans, your enemies … then our determination will be to wage war not only for the whites, but also for Negroes" (89). The residue of the earlier traditionalist discourse can be heard in Buckley's implicit, and perplexing, comparison between German Fascists and African Americans, and in his belief that only white people could truly understand the best interests of "Negroes." While Baldwin had just exploded the basic premises of this traditionalist argument, his image of the laboring black individual would ironically help Buckley begin to sketch out the libertarian rhetoric of "black capitalism" so important to black conservatives in the coming decades. At this cultural moment, though, Buckley could only offer an odd, awkward mixture of racist paternalism and "pull-yourself-up-by-your-bootstraps" slogans.[12]

After Buckley's debate with Baldwin, conservatives discovered that their dream of achieving power could be won on a cultural battlefield, wherein conservatives could speak the libertarian language of freedom for all, but appeal to the deepest fears and racial anxieties of the (largely white) American electorate. This insight seriously reshaped the conservative movement's relationship to American literature, for once they saw that their quest for formal power in the late sixties hinged on accessing the psychic interiority of voters, they began to embrace ideologically rigid fiction that cemented, rather than challenged, prejudices ripe for populist outrage: welfare, urban riots, crime, Affirmative Action, the death penalty, and American exceptionalism. In response, prominent writers in the late sixties like Baldwin and Mailer were confronted in new ways with the political implications of their novels, which interrogated the most intimate and volatile prejudices in society, compelling them to reinvent their writings at the level of form to engage with the rise of modern conservatism.

3.4 The Birth of a New Conservative Aesthetic: The Electoral Rise of Movement Conservatism and the Fall of High Cultural Traditionalism

Within the conservative movement, the intense politicization of culture changed how conservatives perceived the value of highbrow literature according to a more inflexible aesthetic-political calculus. On the one hand, it compelled them to privilege literature that already accorded with their very idiosyncratic definition of conservatism comprised of traditionalism, libertarianism, and aggressive anticommunism; on the other hand, it drew them away from novels that solicited deep moral and epistemological questioning and left readers doubtful and uncertain, since those forms of inquiry were linked in the conservative mind not just with the foundation-shaking critiques of the New Left, but with a "liberal cultural elite" who supposedly assuaged their white guilt and generated more cultural capital for themselves by celebrating formally difficult, morally ambivalent fiction. For instance, whereas Whittaker Chambers once praised the formal experimentation of Joyce's *Finnegans Wake* for its implicit critique of rigid Marxist-Leninist doctrine, by the late sixties *National Review* was publishing articles by writers like Malcolm Muggeridge, who argued that "the Joycean incoherence of *Finnegans Wake*" revealed how the "great Liberal death-wish encompasses the final extinction of meaning itself" (574). But the best example of this shift could be seen in the changing reception of Ayn Rand's fiction in the pages of *National Review*. Although Buckley continued to distance the magazine from the orthodox dogma of Randian Objectivism, he still permitted the publication of articles that highlighted how the libertarian motifs in her novels meshed with the conservative movement's new libertarian slant on race. Although Rand's atheism would always cause her overall political ideology to be misguided, M. Stanton Evans argued in 1967, her "excellent grasp of capitalism" was admirable because it exposed not only "the social and political costs of welfare schemes which seek to compel false benevolence," but also the urban black "philosophical illiterates who have of late been indulging themselves in the right to riot" (1060). As the strategic deployment of white populist resentment began to bear fruit in the form of electoral victories, especially Reagan's stunning victory in California's 1966 gubernatorial race, conservatives saw that popular genre fiction like Rand's was a proselytizing tool that could be more useful than literary fiction's anguished, complex, and even "effete" moral ambivalence.

In the late sixties, this recognition accounts for the notable uptick in the number of right-wing, Rand-influenced genre novels reviewed in the "Book Section" of *National Review* that were praised for their adherence to the conservative movement's central tenets. In February of 1967, M. Stanton Evans highly recommended *The Spirit of '76: A Political Novel of the Near Future*, a dystopian screed against liberalism strongly reminiscent of *Atlas Shrugged*, and written by segregationist sympathizer Holmes Alexander; Evans called the novel "an enjoyable combination of fact, futuristic fancy, and right-wing doctrine" ("Spirit of '76," 155). Roughly a year and a half later, Clare Booth Luce applauded the novelistic talents of Stephen C. Shadegg, a close friend of Barry Goldwater and one of his chief campaign organizers in 1964. Luce approvingly called attention to the formulaic "recipe for a suspenseful yarn" Shadegg used in *The Remnant*, a novel that tells the story of a Goldwater-like US senator who sits on the "Taggert Commission," a fictional congressional commission which exposes the rampant crimes and abuses committed by major organized labor leaders and whose very name is nearly identical to the heroic libertarian "Taggart Transcontinental" company in *Atlas Shrugged* (Luce, 861). There was a stark difference between the kinds of reviews written in the early days of *National Review*, which I detailed in earlier chapters, by figures such as Cleanth Brooks who championed New Critical principles of ambiguity and paradox, and these later reviews that privileged ideological orthodoxy and were more than eager to commit, what New Critics famously called, the "heresy of paraphrase."

If one had to identify a tipping point for this new metric of literary value in movement conservatism, it would have to be a *National Review* article published in October of 1968, "The New Aesthetics of Politics," a mini-manifesto on conservative aesthetic ideology written by Jeffrey Hart, a senior editor at the magazine and a tenured English professor at Dartmouth College. While his argument begins with the familiar conservative lament that American politics had degenerated into mere "aesthetic enjoyment and spectatorial [*sic*] pleasure," a point which *National Review* staff had been making incessantly since the first televised presidential debates between Kennedy and Nixon in sixties, Hart transformed the argument into an attack on the supposed amorality of deep aesthetic reflection itself. Grounding his argument in a passage from *Reflections on the Revolution in France*, Hart wrote: "Burke commented that among the aristocrats at Versailles vice had lost half its evil by losing all its grossness" (1008). Hart contended that the aristocratic elite, which were corrupt and out of touch with the French people, were so steeped in their own solipsistic pleasures that they blinded themselves to blatant social evil, their collective moral compass honeycombed with depravity disguised as high culture. Whether Hart knew it or not, he egregiously wrenched this quote out of its proper context in *Reflections*, for Burke unequivocally meant to denounce the barbaric treatment of Marie Antoinette at the hands of the revolutionaries, saying that they had torn away the great civilizing code of chivalry, "which inspired courage whilst it mitigated ferocity, which ennobled whatever it touched, and under which vice itself lost half its evil, by losing all its grossness" (Burke, 170). While Hart's misrepresentation of Burkean thought may seem perplexing at first glance, suggesting somehow as he does that conservatives were *against* the landed aristocracy, it was actually in perfect alignment with the conservative movement's push in the late sixties to define liberals and leftists as cultural elitists, or better yet, cultural aristocrats of the highbrow. Incredibly, Hart re-conceptualized the French Revolution as a conservative morality tale about the dangers of aesthetic pleasure with the French nobility playing the role of the leftist villains and the toiling French masses cast as the proto-Silent Majority: "The aestheticization of the judgment is aristocratic in nature. It represents a shift of attention to form, to taste, to pleasure. The shift occurs because the aristocrat is free in a way that the artisan or merchant cannot be. He therefore has choice – freedom. He can make fine discriminations of quality which transcend the practical and the utilitarian. The tone, the nuance, the *je ne sais quoi* – these move into the foreground" (1008). In this passage, Hart ventriloquizes crucial components of Bourdieuan theories of social distinction *avant la lettre*, particularly Bourdieu's point that the "aesthetic disposition" that allows one to appreciate high culture "can only be acquired by means of a sort of withdrawal from economic necessity" (*Distinction,* 46). Essentially, Hart was implicitly warning his fellow conservatives that well-wrought, carefully formed works of art and literature should be approached with caution due not only to what he calls the constitutive "moral ambiguity of the aesthetic," but to the deeper fact that savoring high culture could make them look like out-of-touch (cultural) aristocrats (1027). Hart's argument maps on perfectly to Bourdieu's argument that the "tastes of freedom can only assert themselves as such in relation to tastes of necessity, which are thereby brought to the level of the aesthetic and so defined as vulgar" (*Distinction,* 46). In the conservative fight for "Judeo-Christian civilization," an existential battle crystalized in the revolutionary events of 1968, neither the leisure time necessary to interpret demanding literary forms nor the moral complexity of great literature would be a testament to the Western intellectual tradition, as Chambers and Kirk had believed in the immediate postwar period; now, it would be a dangerous luxury, an empty and pretentious habit epitomizing modern liberalism's cultural decadence and moral masochism. Though seemingly in conflict with Chambers and Kirk, Hart inverted the argument only in order to reiterate the very same premise with relation to the ongoing role of literature in the conservative movement: that formal complexity in literary texts was embraced as long as those works seemed to reproduce unequal power relations as normative phenomena, and denounced when those works potentially created imaginative spaces of emancipation for "inferior" classes.

While surprising to some at the time, it is no coincidence in retrospect that this shift in conservative aesthetic ideology brought about a fresh appreciation of Norman Mailer's mid-career books inside the conservative movement. Significantly, the conservative movement's new appreciation of Mailer's work can be pinpointed to a specific year (1965) and to a specific controversial novel (*An American Dream*), which has gone down in the historiography of postwar feminism as the quintessential example of misogyny and, to a lesser extent, racism in the postwar white male literary canon. From the inception of *National Review* in 1955 until 1965, Buckley made it all but official company policy to pillory Mailer when *National Review* had the chance. This tacit policy changed when Buckley decided to give the review of Mailer's new novel to a young, sharp-tongued conservative named Joan Didion, who lavishly praised the book for its "unfashionableness, [its] final refusal to sail with the prevailing winds" of mainstream liberalism (329–30). Buckley reinforced Didion's judgment, publishing a favorable review of his own on the very day he lost his faux-bid for mayor of New York City. Calling Mailer the "single best-known living American writer" of his generation, Buckley said that Mailer should be considered "in his own fashion a conservative" ("'Life' Goes to Norman Mailer," 969). Buckley reached this conclusion by arguing that Mailer "tends to side with the individualist" against "the hegemonies of government and ideology," a tendency borne out by the protagonist of *An American Dream*, Stephen Rojack, a self-reliant John Wayne–style tough guy who "doesn't depend for his salvation on life rafts cast out into the sea of Hope by Marx, Freud, or [Secretary General of the UN] U. Thant" (Buckley, 969). As an aging white author-intellectual recovering from an early infatuation with Marxism – a life story whose trajectory was remarkably similar to those ex-socialists and former Trotskyites on staff at *National Review* – Mailer's innovative "nonfiction novels" were emerging in the late sixties as some of the most persuasive and elegant critiques of liberalism's moral decadence. At this hinge moment in modern conservatism, as the aesthetic criteria conservatives used to judge literary value were in a state of flux, conservatives became attracted to aspects of the "New Journalism" movement. As I explain at length in later chapters of this book, conservatives lionized several of the most prominent New Journalist practitioners – e.g., Mailer, Joan Didion, and especially Tom Wolfe – who produced formally innovative texts highlighting the dangerous absurdities of liberalism, the sixties counterculture, and Black Power, all while disparaging the supposed objectivity of the major media institutions. Combining factual reportage with the techniques of realist fiction, these

New Journalists usually chose subjects that would strike middle-class white readers as unfamiliar, odd, dangerous, or subversively titillating, often ending their pieces with an implicit celebration of conservatism, at least in some generic form (Hollowell, 40). For example, although Tom Wolfe and Joan Didion almost never wrote *explicitly* about conservative politics or ideology, their sometimes satirical (e.g., Wolfe's "Radical Chic"), sometimes heartbreaking (e.g., Didion's "Slouching Towards Bethlehem") essayistic depictions of people swept up in the countercultural Left invoke *implicit* conservative critiques of New York City race relations and drug-induced breakdowns of the traditional family in San Francisco, respectively. Thus, even though Buckley and the conservative movement never fully embraced Mailer, nor Mailer the conservative movement, conservatives noted approvingly that his breakthrough "nonfiction novels" *The Armies of the Night* and *Miami and the Siege of Chicago* coincided with his midlife turn to "Left Conservatism," even though they were also turned off by his mystical conception of conservatism as an existential cauldron of *eros* and anger.

As a so-called "Left Conservative" uncomfortable with both "consensus" liberalism and modern conservatism, Mailer occupied a liminal position in relation to the collapse of the New Deal coalition in the late sixties and the rise of conservatism. Indeed, it was in large part because of this categorical liminality that Mailer was so preoccupied with the nature of a distinctly American form of fascist totalitarianism, which he understood in a crucial double sense: the liberal welfare state with its soft "sexo-technological variety of neo-fascism" and the conservative Goldwaterite Right "whose ghost is that unlaid blood and breath of Nazism" (Mailer, *Armies*, 93; "In the Red Light," 28). As he would for his entire career, Mailer indulged the old Marxist habit of dividing the world into grand dialectical dualisms, not to explain the history of class struggle, but the totalitarian implications of "hard" fascism on the Right and "soft" fascism on the Left: Bloodthirsty, Goldwaterite "Cannibals" versus meek, liberal "Christians." In the introduction to his aptly titled essay collection *Cannibals and Christians* (1966), Mailer defined "Cannibals" as those Americans on the "right wing" who were obsessed with all that was "second-rate" in the nation and believed, like German Nazis, that "one can save the world by killing off what is second-rate" ("Introducing our Argument," 3–4). Conversely, Mailer defined "Christians" not according to any religious heuristic, but as that group of pacifistic, humanitarian-minded liberals who held a variety of beliefs Mailer found dangerously naïve in the wake of World War II and the Holocaust – e.g., humanity's fundamental goodness, an unshakeable faith in reasoned discussion, and the notion that "science is the salvation of the ill" ("Introducing our Argument," 4). In perhaps the collection's most famous essay, "Into the Red Light: A History of the Republican Convention in 1964," Mailer showed off his innovative New Journalist method of importing fictional techniques into political journalism to underscore his own intuitive ambivalence to Goldwater's candidacy. To his self-horror but boundless curiosity, Mailer found that he could readily empathize with Goldwater's supporters inside the convention where "Chimeras of fascism hung like fogbank" ("Red Light," 28). Although Goldwater's version of conservatism repelled Mailer because it was fanatically simple-minded, it simultaneously attracted him because it represented an emotional revolt against the forms of bureaucratic conformity and technical rationality Mailer associated with progressive liberalism. "Like many other whites," Mailer wrote, exploring the devilish part of him that secretly wished to vote for Goldwater, "I had been leading a life which was a trifle too pointless and a trifle too full of guilt and my gullet was close to nausea with the endless compromises of the empty liberal center" (26). For Mailer, Goldwater was not an intellectual challenge to postwar liberalism so much as a pathological symptom of modern liberalism's very failure to provide existential nourishment to its citizens, especially those white citizens who felt a keen sense of dispossession. Perhaps the sole benefit of Goldwater's doomed campaign, Mailer believed, was that it revealed the great cultural chasm between the "Cannibalistic" right-wingers of conservatism and the "Christian" techno-bureaucrats of postwar liberalism, setting them on a collision course. From our contemporary vantage point, Mailer was using New Journalist techniques, in effect, to adumbrate what Nixon would call the Silent Majority.

In Mailer's mind, these two dialectically opposed camps in American politics collided head-on during the 1967 March on the Pentagon, a historic anti–Vietnam War protest which Mailer made the subject of his multi-perspective nonfiction novel *The Armies of the Night*. As many critics point out, the "armies" that Mailer seemed to be most concerned with were the warring factions on the Left: the Old Left and its "sound as brickwork logic of the next step" in the name of old-line Communism or Trotskyism; the empty center of New Deal liberalism and the Cold War consensus years of the Eisenhower administration; and finally the New Left of hippies, SDS activists, anti-Vietnam protestors, and the counterculture more generally (Mailer, *Armies*, 85).[13] While there is, of course, a great deal of truth in this observation, it also misses the crucial conservative dimensions of the book. One of the most celebrated "counterculture" books of the postwar era, winning both a Pulitzer Prize and a National Book Award, *The Armies of the Night* is divided into two long interconnected sections, "Book One: History as a Novel" and "Book Two: The Novel as History." In Book One, Mailer deploys a variety of fictional techniques to follow the real-life adventures during the March on the Pentagon of "Norman Mailer," referred to in the third person throughout, and other writers and intellectuals on the Left such as Noam Chomsky, Paul Goodman, Robert Lowell, Dwight Mcdonald, and Dr. Benjamin Spock, ultimately highlighting the human flaws that underpin their motivations for protesting the war. In Book Two, Mailer takes on the role of a historian, zooming-out and abandoning his novelistic perspective, in order to deliver an illuminating and concise history of twentieth-century American politics, focusing on various manifestations of the Left. However, what usually goes unexamined is the way in which Mailer's analysis of the Left depends on an implicit, "Cannibalistic" definition of the American Right that misses the dynamic shifts happening within the conservative movement, but in a way that is generative of new sociopolitical insights. Ironically, scholarly readings of *Armies* tend to reproduce the very blind spot found in Mailer's own political universe; the dynamic debate seems to occur between the Left and the liberal center against a background held together by Mailer's static, one-dimensional understanding of movement conservatism.

In Book one of *Armies*, Mailer devotes several pages to depicting the right-wing element in American politics as exemplified by two characters: an American neo-Nazi and a US Marshal. In one scene, Mailer is arrested and placed in a Volkswagen camper the authorities are using to apprehend arrested protestors. In the company of the "enemy," Mailer invokes Buckley, writing that his arrest and detention force him "to watch everything with the attention, let us say, of a man like William Buckley spending his first hour in a Harlem bar" (*Armies,* 141). Suddenly, an American Nazi is shoved into the camper next to Mailer, and this fortuitous situation allows Mailer to describe the Nazi in the same terms he described the fervent Goldwater supporters at the 1964 Republican convention: "The American Nazis were all fanatics, yes, poor mad tormented fanatics, their psyches twisted like burning leaves in the fire of their hatred, yes, indeed! but this man's conviction stood in his eyes as if his soul had been focused to a single point of light" (*Armies*, 142). This portrayal of the Nazi's eyes is nearly identical to Mailer's earlier description of Goldwater supporters: "there was a dark blank fanaticism in their eyes" ("Red Light," 21). In the next scene, Mailer completes his representation of the American Right by portraying a jingoistic US Marshal, who is enraged at the imagined communist infiltration and takeover of the United States. In an extended passage, Mailer imagines the US Marshal's fictional backstory and represents his various resentments in a free indirect speech style that inhabits the Marshal's consciousness:

> ... they, yes *they* – the enemies of the Marshal – tried to pass bills to limit the purchase of hunting rifles, so did *they* try to kill America, inch by inch, all the forces of evil, disorder, mess and chaos in the world, and *cowardice!* and city ways, and slick shit ... all the subtle invisible creeping paralyses of Communism which were changing America from a land where blood was red to a land where water was foul – yes in this Marshal's mind – ... the evil was without, America was threatened by a foreign disease ... (*Armies,* 144)

As Mailer had already written elsewhere, this depiction of the cannibalistic right wing is seemingly motivated by bottomless pathologies that are not susceptible to cures or rational justification. According to Barry Leeds, in this scene Mailer suggests that the Marshal's "enraged commitment to this rigid preconception [of Communism] obviates any possibility of communicating logically with him" (Leeds, 260). On the one hand, Mailer's thematic conflation of the American Nazi and the US Marshal who thinks like a Goldwater Republican represents a deep misunderstanding of movement conservatism as blind rage, belying the skillful strategic calculations that were beginning to win conservatives elections. On the other hand, though, when Mailer's Marshal reiterates the platitudes of right-wing conservatism in relation to the New Left protestors, Mailer's New Journalist method allows his readers to see something *Mailer himself misses.* The Marshal is not so much a latent fascist, as a blindly patriotic movement conservative who professes to love "America" and "freedom." And what the Marshal is really enraged at is not worldwide communist infiltration, but something quite different. As Leeds points out, many of the New Left protestors were interested "not in any international movement, but in improving America by redressing social injustices" (261). In other words, the Marshal speaks the liberty-loving language of classical liberalism, like Buckley and Goldwater conservatives, but he abhors the social disturbances in the private regimes of power having to do with racial and gender equality; thus, he sees the New Left protestors as "America-hating" because they dare to demand true social equality, disrupting the private spheres of power that he ignores in favor of the formal faux-freedom of the public sphere.

Usually, most scholarly analysis on the cannibalistic Right in *Armies* ends with these two representations of the American Nazi and US Marshal.

But these two characters, I maintain, represent just a few pieces of a broader trend that Mailer identifies in the American middle class that indicates the rise of movement conservatism. Through his innovative New Journalist method, Mailer believes he has stumbled upon a profound insight: that "the center of America might be insane" (188). Imagining an archetypal white male everyman, Mailer states that the "average American believed in two opposites more profoundly apart than any previous schism in the Christian soul" (188). The American middle class serves two masters in Mailer's mind: the traditions and rituals of Christianity and the technological profit-motive of "corporation-land." This means, Mailer writes, that "the love of the Mystery of Christ . . . and the love of no Mystery whatsoever, had brought the country to a state of suppressed schizophrenia so deep that the foul brutalities of the war in Vietnam were the only temporary cure possible for the condition" (188). What Mailer uncovers, in essence, is a dialectical conception of Christian love and corporate greed that resembles the deep opposition between traditionalism and libertarianism in postwar conservatism. In addition, Mailer conceives of the Vietnam War as the psychic release-valve for the pressure built up by the cognitive dissonance produced by believing simultaneously in conservative protestant Christianity and unfettered, laizze-faire capitalism – i.e., a new mutant version of the Weberian Protestant work ethic gone mad. "America needed the war," Mailer writes. "It would need a war so long as technology expanded on every road of communication, and the cities and corporations spread like cancer; the good Christian Americans needed the war or they would lose their Christ" (189). Mailer implies that Christian Americans can retain the illusion of their Christianity by supporting the war against the godless ideology of communism. Unbeknownst to Mailer, he illuminates the three key strands of postwar conservatism, but he does not realize it because he does not see this movement as a set of fundamentally different philosophical premises that reinforce each other. Mailer certainly identifies a profound sociopolitical insight in *Armies*, but it is not an insight into the schizophrenia of American society so much as the schizophrenic contradictions of a conservative ideology on the verge of sweeping through American society.

In Mailer's best judgment, the insanity of middle America and its outlet in the Vietnam War is a result of what he defines as "technology land" or "corporation land," which are synonymous pejoratives in his vocabulary that grow out of New Deal liberalism. Retrospectively, though, this kind of insanity looks like the irreconcilable contradiction manifested in the conservative movement's "fusion" of capitalists, anticommunists, and traditionalists. "What Mailer did not anticipate," as Sean McCann points out, "was the evisceration of postwar liberalism and the rise to power of the conservative right, whose ideology and whose reorganization of society his fiction [and nonfiction novels] may not be equipped to challenge or to understand" ("The Imperiled Republic," 296). Mailer's problem with postwar liberalism was not that it failed to deliver its promise of material comfort, but that it delivered on its promise all too well. For Mailer, as for conservatives like Buckley, postwar liberalism transformed Americans into soft conformists who were dependent on the state. Mailer could not help but see the American Right as an impulsive, emotional protest to this kind of mind-numbing, soul-killing politics. Thus, Mailer's self-professed political radicalism exploded certain kinds of prejudices concerning sexual freedom, drug use, and violence, but only to reify (what James Baldwin would see as) the deepest and most retrograde American prejudice of them all: the fantasy of autonomous, white male individualism.

Movement conservatives reserved their strongest praise for Mailer when he romanticized white individualism in the late sixties because it used an innovative literary form in a way that mimicked their own efforts to appeal to racial sentimentality in electoral politics while avoiding the conservative movement's overtly racist positions a decade earlier. In February of 1969, Priscilla Buckley, managing editor of *National Review* and sister of William F. Buckley Jr., wrote arguably the most favorable review Mailer ever received in the magazine for *Miami and the Siege of Chicago* (1968), a nonfiction novel narrated by a third-person creation of Mailer dubbed "the reporter" as he experiences the 1968 Republican National Convention in Miami and the disastrous Democratic National Convention in Chicago. Calling the book "very, very good," Priscilla Buckley praised Mailer specifically for his courageous and "uncomfortable admission" that he was growing weary of black civil rights leaders and their endless protests (P. Buckley, 129–30). While waiting to hear a speech at the GOP convention from the former assistant to Martin Luther King Jr. Reverend Ralph Abernathy, Mailer experiences a "curious emotion" that he does not fully understand: "he was getting tired of Negroes and their rights" (51). In Mailer's cosmology of dualisms, this mysterious resentment toward African Americans illustrated how the devilish conservative side, the same side that housed the amoral Freudian *id* that had once made him feel an irrational compulsion to vote for Goldwater in 1964, could overtake the angelical Leftist side of his political identity. A few pages later, Mailer provides a long, incoherent list of things that African Americans were supposedly doing that made him lose his patience and caused him to flirt with labeling himself a Republican, admitting that he was getting "so heartily sick of listening to the tyranny of soul music, so bored with Negroes triumphantly late to appointments . . . so despairing of the smell of booze and pot and used-up hope in blood-shot eyes of Negroes bombed at noon, so envious finally of that liberty to abdicate from the long year-end decade-drowning yokes of work and responsibility that he must have become in some secret part of his flesh a closet Republican" (53). In Mailer, conservatives saw not only a recovering radical giving voice to their own racial anxieties and resentments, but a major American author crystalizing these reactionary thoughts in a literary form (New Journalism) that could plausibly claim a certain degree of highbrow prestige within the literary field.

However, like virtually every other major postwar novelist conservatives sought to recruit as one of their own, Mailer disappointed them with his unorthodox conception of "genuine" conservatism. In the same review, Priscilla Buckley conveniently overlooked how Mailer, as always, made sense of his psychic rebellion against civil rights and black emancipation by equating it not with a legitimate electoral conservatism, but with a ferocious embrace of his deepest darkest self. In his own racial resentments, Mailer recognized that he shared with the movement conservatives on the convention floor "the same torrents which Hitler had freed in the Germans when he exploded their ten-year obsession with whether they had lost the war through betrayal or through material weakness. Through betrayal, Hitler had told them: Germans were actually strong and good" (52). To be a conservative allied with the Republican Party, in Mailer's estimation, was to be in touch with that part of himself that was naturally predisposed to violence, that was dark and angry and delighted in destruction, that was, ultimately, a proto-fascist.[14] From one perspective, the conservative movement's praise for Mailer's innovative literary work and his idiosyncratic, warts-and-all conservatism was consistent with an earlier, traditionalist conservative vision of aesthetic value. Like conservative favorites Eliot and Pound, Mailer was pioneering a new literary form that intersected with traditionalist anxieties about existential alienation, capitalist-fueled technology's increasing domination of society, and the loss of civilization's all-important mystical "roots." And like Faulkner and O'Connor, he was interrogating the darkest places of his own soul, which often led to the discovery of uncomfortable racial prejudices and a series of shifting, ambivalent explanations for those prejudices. Despite these similarities, though, the conservative movement had to drastically temper its praise for Mailer's quasi-conservative turn. Because their electoral strategy rested on a tight correlation between free-market capitalism for the economic elite and cultural populism for the aggrieved white masses, conservatives established an ideological framework that seemed to give them no other choice but to pivot toward a new literary aesthetic that distrusted even a sometimes-conservative writer like Mailer who could garner high cultural prestige while critiquing liberals, but who broke with conservative orthodoxy.

3.5 Interrogating Postwar Conservatism, Parodying Protest Fiction: Baldwin's *Tell Me How Long the Train's Been Gone*

If Mailer helped pioneer formal literary innovations in New Journalism that reified the deepest prejudices of postwar conservatism in the late sixties, then his rival Baldwin worked to rework the aesthetic assumptions underpinning the most preeminent literary form of the era – the American novel – to disrupt the category of whiteness housed in the nation's racial strongbox of custom. At this moment in the late sixties, Baldwin was struggling with earlier assumptions about the relationship between politics and high cultural literary form – i.e., the prevailing set of normative conventions that had congealed in the thirties that tended to frame didactic protest fiction as progressive political literature and Anglophone modernist novels as incompatible with leftist politics, especially when racial politics "contaminated" great literary texts. For Baldwin, the strongbox of custom metaphor he had identified in his early nonfiction manifested in highbrow culture as a strongbox of *literary* custom that Baldwin eventually recognized and sought to unravel in *Tell Me How Long the Train's Been Gone* by parodying the protest novel genre.

From the early fifties through the early sixties, Baldwin had a reputation for being a major essayist and a minor, though promising, novelist. Upon the publication of Baldwin's third novel, *Another Country*, which was greeted with mixed reviews, Lionel Trilling declared: "There is probably no literary career in America today that matches James Baldwin's in the degree of interest it commands" (qtd. in Campbell, 182). By the late sixties, Baldwin's essays were widely seen as prophetic works that predicted the rise of Black Power and the extreme polarization over American race relations, a common perception that only increased the anticipation for the publication of his fourth novel, *Tell Me How Long The Train's Been Gone* (1968). If there was ever a moment for Baldwin to emerge as a major American novelist, to combine and reinvigorate the novel form's aesthetic and political potential the way Ralph Ellison had with *Invisible Man* in the early fifties, the already-historic year 1968 seemed to be that moment.

Although Baldwin's longest and most ambitious novel to date, when *Tell Me How Long* was published roughly two weeks after the assassination of Martin Luther King, critics such as Irving Howe, Granville Hicks, Nelson Algren, and *National Review*'s Guy Davenport eviscerated it, describing it as the propagandistic ramblings of an embittered black writer. In his widely circulated review for the *New York Times*, Mario Puzo summed up the grim reception of the novel: it "is a simpleminded, one-dimensional novel with mostly cardboard characters, a polemical rather than narrative tone, weak invention and poor selection of incident" (5). This critical judgment persisted for the rest of Baldwin's career, and even endured after his death in the work of a staunch Baldwin defender like Henry Louis Gates Jr., who conceded in 1992 that *Tell Me How Long* was still Baldwin's "least successful" novel because the "connoisseur of complexity tried his hand at being an ideologue" ("The Fire Last Time"). In this familiar narrative of Baldwin's career, *Tell Me How Long* marks the end of Baldwin's place as an original moral voice in American prose, and the beginning of his rhetorical descent into apocalyptic condemnations of the country.

One problem with this account, as more recent Baldwin scholars have pointed out, is that it belies both the novel's formal ingenuity and its groundbreaking representation of sexuality – e.g., the Baldwin-like protagonist Leo Proudhamer and the minor character of "Black Christopher," a Black Power revolutionary who is also bisexual.[15] But even these recuperation efforts, I contend, miss something crucial about the fuller political context surrounding the composition of *Tell Me How Long*, which Baldwin foregrounds continually throughout the novel: the rise of conservatism as a potent, dynamic force in American culture. For many scholars, *Tell Me How Long* represents Baldwin's definitive break with American liberalism and his qualified affirmation of revolutionary movements like Black Power. The novel's "critique of American liberalism," writes Lynn O. Scott, one of the foremost authorities on Baldwin's late novels, "is most evident in its revision of the American success story and its revision of black autobiographical narratives that celebrate individual achievement as representations of racial progress" (24). While this description accurately sums up a major theme of the novel, it overlooks Baldwin's engagement with American conservatives like Buckley who had quickly become the most vocal champions of Horatio Alger–style, rags-to-riches tales of "black opportunity" under the rubric of free-market capitalism. From this perspective, *Tell Me How Long* should be seen as a continuation of Baldwin's long debate with American conservatism and his strongest, most honest assessment of that ideology's implications for literary form. Starting work on the novel just a few months after his debate with Buckley, Baldwin constructed a plot that reads like a direct rebuttal to Buckley's "bootstraps argument" while exploring the shifting metrics of aesthetic value and merit, and the possibility of transgressive black novelists accumulating cultural capital within a changing literary field.

Narrated in the first person by the protagonist Leo Proudhammer, a rich and successful bisexual black actor who hails from Harlem and is active in the civil rights movement, the novel begins with Leo in a hospital room recovering from a sudden onstage heart attack. After establishing this frame narrative, Leo continually shuttles readers back and forth in time, mostly retelling his autobiography in long flashbacks, but occasionally returning to the present in order to chronicle his recovery. In the flashback scenes, Leo focuses on several important people in his life, all of whom serve as recognizable archetypes in Baldwin's fictional *oeuvre*: Leo's nameless father, "a ruined Barbados peasant, exiled in a Harlem which he loathed," who drinks too much and sublimates his anger by spinning fantasies about his long-lost royal Caribbean bloodline; Leo's older brother, Caleb, a World War II veteran who despises white people but channels his frustrations into a fervent attachment to fundamentalist Christianity; Leo's occasional lover, the young Christopher Hall, known throughout the novel as "Black Christopher" for his militant Black Power activism, who serves as a vivid contrast to the dogmatic Christian Caleb and gives voice to Baldwin's own radical sentiments, talking freely of the imminent gas ovens and concentration camps being arranged for African Americans; and finally, Leo's best friend and other occasional lover, Barbara King, a white woman from Kentucky who moves to New York to become an actress and rises to fortune and fame with Leo (*Tell Me How Long,* 14). With this cast of characters, Baldwin highlights the levels of systemic racism Leo and other black characters encounter, presenting Leo's life as just one arbitrary success story in a sea of other life stories stunted by discrimination, prejudice, and lack of opportunity. Ironically, the young Leo drifts aimlessly around New York and his midlife success is largely a result of luck and sympathetic white paternalism, while the black characters most driven to succeed and assert their individuality, such as Caleb and Black Christopher, are penalized for breaking the racial taboo of acting like autonomous white men. Individual achievement for African Americans, Baldwin implies, *contra* Buckley, is only possible if African Americans relinquish their individuality and conform to white stereotypes, meaning that socioeconomic advancement for African Americans is acceptable under the condition that they soothe white consciences in the process.

While this summary could make the novel sound like little more than a plodding "social problem" narrative, Baldwin uses the formal device of the frame narrative to transform the righteous moralism of his most politicized characters. Via the narration of his artist-protagonist Leo, Baldwin threads a series of meta-commentaries throughout the novel on the relationship between aesthetics and politics, leaving no self-righteous statement unchallenged. Reflecting on his childhood, for instance, Leo remembers listening to his father regale him with tales of an ancient black "race greater and nobler than Rome or Judea, mightier than Egypt . . . who had never been slaves" (14). Contemplating his father's words as an adult, Leo describes his slow, painful realization that these stories were not just battle cries galvanizing his community and heralding Black Power, but also his father's personal defense mechanisms. "If our father was of royal blood and we were royal children," Leo says, underscoring how deeply embedded discrimination can deflate revolutionary rhetoric, "our father was certainly the only person in the world who knew it. The landlord did not know it and we observed that our father never mentioned royal blood to *him*. Not at all" (15). Eventually, Leo concludes that these stories were both political narratives about injustice and psychological fantasies steeped in aesthetic pleasure. Imagining his father's stories to be metaphorical rooms, he says that living inside them as a child was like stumbling "about, stubbing our toes . . . on rubies, scraping our shins on golden caskets, bringing down, with a childish cry, the splendid purple tapestry on which, in pounding gold and scarlet, our destinies and our inheritance were figured" (15). From an early age, Leo understands that while no aesthetic work is totally apolitical, no political assertion is devoid of aesthetic qualities either. As a young man deciding to become an actor, Leo realizes that the act of fiction-making, on stage or on film, throws into relief "the great question of where the boundaries of reality were truly to be formed," highlighting the inextricability of art and politics (83).

In his adult life, though, Leo is adamant that the formal characteristics of an artwork must take precedence over any single political message. Recalling a time when he spoke at a civil rights rally with Black Christopher, he claims that the "disguises which an artist wears are his means, not of fleeing from the truth, but of attempting to approach it" (112). But now, looking back on that afternoon, he remembers "facing the people with no recognizable disguise . . . and I was very frightened" (113). Without a proper disguise, a basic mediating fiction, Leo is unable to transform his anger concerning systemic racial injustice into a moving speech, failing to redefine the boundaries of social reality for his audience. Later in the novel, Baldwin underscores this same point in a flashback scene that anticipates precisely those critics who charged *Tell Me How Long* with being mere protest fiction. While training to become actors at an artist colony in rural New England, Barbara and Leo practice together in front of their workshop class and teacher, the novel's famous acting coach Saul San-Marquand. At one point, Barbara explains why she and Leo picked a certain scene from a political play, saying that they both liked it because "it made a connection—between a private love story—and—a—well, between a private sorrow and a public, a *revolutionary* situation" (296). When Saul asks, rather skeptically, if they had personal motives for choosing the scene, Barbara says that one's motives "are always personal." Ventriloquizing Baldwin's own perspective, Saul responds by saying that an actor's personal motives "are one thing – but one's execution of those motives . . . these must be quite something else again," and that Barbara and Leo clearly became "somewhat carried away by [their] motives" (296–97). Saul then clarifies his position on politics and art, privileging the formal qualities of the latter field: "Do not misunderstand us. We admire your motives. We were revolutionaries before you were born, Miss King . . . But we must question your execution. That is what we are here for" (297). With this meta-commentary on his own novel, Baldwin foregrounds the implicit metric by which works of art are judged according to political criteria. All art is of course political, Baldwin implies, but how can political concerns about injustice and inequality be weaved into a literary text without becoming one-dimensional propaganda, preaching only to the already converted? As the famous critic of the "protest novel," Baldwin believed that the failure of the ham-fisted, politically didactic left-wing novel "lies in its rejection of life, the human being, the denial of his beauty, dread, power, in its insistence that it is his categorization alone which is real and which cannot be transcended" (*CE*, "Everybody's Protest Novel," 18). For Baldwin, one of the central problems with protest fiction's one-dimensionality is that it tacitly assumes that reactionary ideology is also one-dimensional, static, and inert. After his debate with Buckley, Baldwin realized that this assumption was fundamentally flawed because conservative ideology – an *apologia*, no doubt, for a version of the racial status quo – was nonetheless changing before his eyes, and was thus perpetually under construction.

From this perspective, the importance of *Tell Me How Long* for postwar American literary history stems not so much from its success or failure as an exceptionally well-made aesthetic object, or from any one particularly penetrating ideological critique, but rather from its trenchant exploration of the changing socio-aesthetic valances of the category of highbrow "literary fiction" itself as a repository of cultural capital during the rise of the American Right. On the one hand, As Lionel Trilling famously noted, Baldwin knew that vaunted literary lions such as Faulkner, Hemingway, Pound, and Eliot, whose novels and poems were said to possess formal aesthetic "excellence," rarely produced works that functioned as imaginative spaces for progressive politics, a common belief that traditionalist conservatives routinely pointed out with pride. But on the other hand, Baldwin also saw that conservatives were deemphasizing traditionalist conservatism and its openly noxious stance on civil rights, along with its embrace of formally complex literature, to accentuate their vision of small-government conservatism and their populist, dog-whistle rhetoric on race.

In this shift toward conservative populism, Baldwin saw a corresponding shift in conservative perceptions of aesthetic value occurring as well, which amounted to a move away from the tragic pessimism of traditionalists like Chambers and Kirk and toward the white moral innocence of Reaganism. In one flashback, Leo anticipates this shift and recalls going to the movie theater with Caleb during his teenage years to see *King's Row* starring Ronald Reagan, an actor whom Leo admits "I couldn't stand" (227). Although the young Leo believes the cast of the film could not "act their way out of a sieve," he notes ironically that the "lights and makeup and an innocence as brutal as it was despairing did marvelous things for these sons and daughters of the one and only God, and very nearly reconciled me to Ronald Reagan's teeth" (228). Looking around the theater, Leo observes the white audience as they watch Reagan, and he sees a process of infantilization occurring, Reagan's performance turning them into "children, children forever, children not as a biological fact, but as a perpetual condition" (229). Years later, in the present time of the novel, Leo implies that Reagan successfully channeled that kind of white innocence into the political sphere, allowing him to capitalize on racial anxieties to win the California governorship. In the California of the late sixties, where John Birch Society members and Black Panthers were living side by side, Leo sees a form of American Fascism growing that shares important similarities with German Nazism, but also crucial differences. "I've often thought," Leo muses, "that if Hitler had had the California police working for him, he would surely be in business still – not that I am persuaded that he ever retired; the business was his in name only" (325). Picking up a familiar theme from his essays here, Baldwin suggests that the principal danger in the United States is not so much militant whiteness, as it had been in Nazi Germany, as it is an illusion of whiteness that demands to be protected militantly, a multivalent form of whiteness signifying individual independence undergirded by a pure, coherent identity. For Baldwin, the violence of the police in urban spaces like Harlem, lauded by conservative pundits and politicians such as Buckley and Nixon as the implementation of "law and order," is not an effect of white hatred, but of white terror and ignorance.

Thus, the electoral rise of conservatism is coextensive with the rise of American Fascism, Baldwin suggests, not because white Americans seek to implement an extermination policy akin to Nazi Germany's, but because they have decided that black lives are just as precarious and expendable in postwar America as they were in antebellum America and Jim Crow America. From the perspective of many African Americans, though, Baldwin is at pains to point out that this kind of acceptable ignorance and neglect will tend to look like an active, conspiratorial policy of black genocide. Toward the end of the novel, while Leo listens to his much younger lover Black Christopher discuss politics with his friends, he hears Christopher say: "We are not going to walk to the gas ovens . . . and we are not going to march to the concentration camps. We have to make the mothers know that" (456). But Leo does not take this seemingly paranoid allegation at face value, seeing it instead as a predictable result of Christopher being the victim of police violence for his entire short life. In Leo's mind, Christopher's warning about gas chambers and concentration camps uses the iconography of fascism to express the same resentment toward police that Leo felt growing up in Harlem, a mixture of anger and fear that once prompted a young Leo to ask his older brother the haunting question: "Caleb, are white people people? . . . I mean—are white people—*people*? People like us?" (60). While Black Christopher's conflation of white Americans and German Nazis may be appealing to some, Baldwin stresses that the analogy is too crude to do justice to the actual process of white disavowal well underway, which conservatives have seized on and redirected into an electoral strategy.

In the novel's final climactic episode, Baldwin illustrates the complex entanglement of white disavowal and conservative ideology when Barbara's conservative family from Kentucky visits her in New York at Leo's apartment, where Black Christopher also happens to be staying. Almost immediately, this combustible group bursts into a heated argument about race, politics, and civil rights, beginning with Black Christopher accusing white people of killing off native Americans and robbing blacks for centuries "while you all sat on your big, fat, white behinds and got rich" (464). For anyone familiar with the Baldwin–Buckley debate in 1965, it becomes increasingly clear that Baldwin rewrites the basic arguments of each side, with Black Christopher and Barbara defending Baldwin's position and Barbara's family defending Buckley's position. As a choir of conservative voices, each member of Barbara's family speaks up to make the same case. "We don't care about the color of a person's skin – we never have done," Barbara's mother pleads. "My daddy used to say, God made us *all*. We're *all* here for the same reason" (464–65). The claim that white Southerners have never cared about skin color is obviously disingenuous, but Baldwin does not put these words into the mouth of Mrs. King simply to expose her hypocrisy. The next move she makes is crucial because it shows how her ahistorical belief links up to her conviction that God created everyone, black and white, equally. A key trope in several Flannery O'Connor short stories exploring racial upheaval, the notion that "all races are equal under God" was an essential premise of the traditionalist argument for segregation, as each person was entitled to an equal chance at salvation, but only if she fulfilled her natural role – which, for an African American, was a subservient one – in the social hierarchy here on earth. By displacing the universalist dimension of the argument from the metaphysical world to the physical, Mrs. King unwittingly leaves a trace of the evolving genealogy of the conservative positions on race, mimicking the underlying shift from a belief in God-given black inferiority to a belief in the cultural inferiority of the black family.

As the debate in Leo's apartment continues, Ken and Bennett – Barbara's brother and his good friend, respectively – pick up where Mrs. King leaves off, forcefully articulating the "bootstraps argument" popularized by Buckley with its corresponding assumption of colorblind individualism. Look at the rich and famous Leo Proudhammer, Bennett says, "you made it, all right, didn't you? Why, I bet you make more money than I do . . . And I bet you don't do it sitting around, feeling sorry for yourself, did you?" (465). Carrying Bennett's argument to its logical conclusion, Ken chimes in to explain the implications of Leo's success: "Hell no, he just made his own way. And *anybody* can make his own way in this country, no matter *what* color he is" (465). Infuriated by her family, Barbara calls Ken's claim "pure bullshit" and points out that the black men who do manual labor under his supervision will never be able "to make their own way" in Kentucky since they cannot even join the whites-only union. After watching this scene of fruitless debate play out for several minutes, with each side talking over the other and misunderstanding their basic premises, Leo speaks up and puts an end to it. "You can't imagine my life, and I won't discuss it," he says, "I don't make as much money as you think I do, and I don't work as often as I would if I were white. Those are the facts. The point is that the Negroes of this country are treated as none of you would dream of treating a dog or cat . . . And I don't feel like talking about it anymore, and I won't. This *is* my house" (467). On the level of plot, Leo acts as the intermediary out of respect for Barbara, defusing the tension in the room and triggering the scene's dénouement, in which they all begin to calm down, listen to music, and eat before Barbara's family departs peaceably. But on another level, Baldwin uses Leo's interjection to pause the argument momentarily between progressives and conservatives in an attempt to highlight the shifting, protean logic of modern conservatism as it toggles between the double register of libertarian individualism and traditionalist social order.

Toward the end of the scene in the apartment, by focalizing the falling action through Leo's cool gaze, Baldwin brackets off his own fiery political sentiments, personified to some extent by Black Christopher, to examine the psychological intricacies of this emerging reactionary discourse. Following the impromptu debate, Leo notes that, "surprisingly enough, it turned out not to be such an awful afternoon, after all" (468). Christopher's acerbic critiques, Leo realizes with a mixture of relief and sorrow, had not breached the ideological defenses of Barbara's family, but rather "had released them" in some "curious way" (468). "I watched Christopher watching [Barbara's family] from the heights of an unassailable contempt," Leo says, which also serves as a metonymy for Baldwin-the-novelist observing Baldwin-the-polemicist, "as they become more and more themselves, more and more human, and less and less attractive. They could not know how much they revealed, how pathetic and tawdry they were – this master race. But they were dangerous, too, unutterably so. They knew nothing about themselves at all" (468). What Leo learns watching Christopher is the same lesson Baldwin eventually learned after his debate with Buckley, a dramatic battle that Baldwin certainly won in 1965, but perhaps, Baldwin seems to fear in 1968, at the expense of losing the broader war.

For Buckley and the conservative movement, Baldwin comes to understand, the ultimate goal was less about winning intellectual arguments concerning black opportunity and equality, and more about winning cultural arguments that resonated with white voters who were increasingly imagining themselves as the hardworking Silent Majority.[16] As the tension lingers between Black Christopher and Barbara's family just before their departure, Leo experiences a minor epiphany, seeing now that saving

Christopher should be his primary motivation, not just unmasking this cadre of Southern conservatives. These people "were not my concern. Christopher was my concern," Leo affirms, and the "problem was how to prevent these Christians from once again destroying this pagan" (468). While Baldwin inserts penetrating, almost essayistic arguments into the novel, suggesting the undeniable need to critique reactionary thought, Baldwin's decision to include an abridged reenactment of his debate with Buckley, in which the voices for black equality fail to persuade their right-wing opponents, reframes this necessity as more complicated than just debunking falsehoods and demystifying white false consciousness. Baldwin showcases Black Christopher's many legitimate political grievances, ostensibly following the rigid schema of the protest novel genre, but largely to signal his inability to persuade white Americans who are not already convinced of the magnitude of black suffering, and are gradually drifting toward the new, racially colorblind version of small-government conservatism. In this reading, *Tell Me How Long* is hardly legible as a radical progressive critique, but as a novel fixated on the sociopolitical crisis of the late-sixties that flirts with the protest novel genre, to be sure, *only to fail by design*. In their late- sixties configurations, Baldwin suggests, some progressive emancipation movements tended to discount the psychologically complex and argument-based dynamism of conservatism. At this unique moment in American history, Baldwin believed that what progressives needed on the cultural front were novels – outlined only in a kind of photographic negative in *Tell Me How Long* – that were both formally innovative and imaginatively capacious enough to shed light on the deep-seated prejudices that were driving the perversely brilliant evolution of conservative thought.

3.6 The Age of Reagan Cometh: Anticipating the Conservative Turn

At the end of *The Armies of the Night*, Mailer reflected on the anti–Vietnam War March on the Pentagon, personifying the United States as a woman "heavy with child" on the verge of giving birth to an unclear future (288). Will she deliver "the most fearsome totalitarianism the world has ever known," Mailer asked with his signature hyperbole, or "a babe of a new world brave and tender, artful and wild?" (288). In hindsight, of course, Mailer's grand Manichean prophecy missed how the upheavals of the sixties gave birth to a cultural future that saw new manifestations of progressive social movements, but also a political future that saw undeniable evidence of a major conservative ascendance that would reach its apex in the Reaganism of the eighties.[17] In Mailer's story of American politics, the sudden electoral appearance of conservatism in the late sixties was supposed to flame out rather quickly. Although conservative white Protestants were still the strongest force in America, Mailer wrote in *Miami and the Siege of Chicago*, they were "a psychic island" who needed to find a bridge to the new America inaugurated by the sixties; otherwise, they would "only grow more insane each year, like a rich nobleman in an empty castle chasing elves and ogres with his stick" (62). By late 1972, though, as Nixon was preparing for a landslide victory over George McGovern at the Republican National Convention, Mailer was unable to account for the resilience of conservatism, forcing himself to conclude unconvincingly that Nixon was a new media genius, "the first social engineer" to truly grasp "the near to illimitable totalitarian resources of television" (*St. George and the Godfather,* 179). For Mailer, one should approach conservatism in the same way Mailer famously approached hipsterism: not as a dry configuration of organizational alliances or as an interesting sociological subgroup, respectively, but as a self-annihilating dive into an ideology that could strip away one's bourgeois niceties and reveal an authentic, primitive identity. The Goldwater-Nixon conservatism of electoral politics, Mailer thought, was too stagnant, mindlessly conventional, and bitter to remain a potent electoral force – and yet its ideological discourse continued, puzzlingly, to gain widespread legitimacy.

Conversely, Baldwin knew from firsthand experience that the endurance of conservatism in the early seventies was due, in no small part, to its strategic versatility, ideological adaptability, and surprising self-reflexivity. Appropriating the deep racial prejudices of American history, some too ingrained even for perspicacious writers like Mailer to appreciate, conservative discourse revealed something shameful about white Americans, Baldwin wrote in his autobiography *No Name in the Street* (1972), that "is very accurately and abjectly summed up by the present, so-called Nixon administration" (*CE,* 409). For Baldwin, the premise of postwar conservatism, whether in its earlier traditionalist bent or in its later libertarian emphasis, was an incredulity toward the existence of black suffering that was tantamount to a form of genocide, a point he drives home with increasing intensity throughout the seventies and eighties with imagery pilfered from popular collective memory of German and Italian Fascism to draw a moral equivalence to the fascistic tendencies of the American Right. As a committed novelist, though, Baldwin held out ambivalent hope that new forms of highbrow fiction would still have the capacity to affect that intimate sphere of individual interiority wherein racial prejudices dwelled. If every "society is really governed by hidden laws, by unspoken but profound assumptions on the part of the people," Baldwin declared in *Nobody Knows My Name*, reiterating his faith in the high cultural literary *illusio*, then it was "up to the American writer to find out what these laws and assumptions are. In a society much given to smashing taboos without thereby managing to be liberated from them, it will be no easy matter" ("The Discovery of What It Means," *CE*, 142). Although Baldwin himself would not be remembered as the defining novelist of his generation, writers such as Toni Morrison would take up his prophetic vision of formally difficult literary fiction as a realm of progressive politics that must engage with the double registers of postwar conservative discourse, eventually playing a key role in reshaping the socio-aesthetics of literary prestige during the culture wars of the second half of the twentieth century.

In the next chapter, I turn my focus to two other major American novelists of the seventies and eighties, Thomas Pynchon and Saul Bellow, to examine how and why prestigious "literary fiction" became so thoroughly aligned with American liberalism and the Left, while movement conservatives were busy making two seemingly contradictory moves within the literary field: *both* lionizing a dwindling list of well-established canonical texts associated with highbrow literature and its attendant, older form of bourgeois cultural capital, *and* increasingly embracing popular fiction genres such as the spy tale and the geopolitical thriller novel that gave voice to white populist resentment. In the process, I investigate the correlation between the rise of Reagan and the New Right, the apex of literary postmodernism, with its apparent commitment to the emancipatory ethos of the sixties, and the narrowing ways critics and scholars politically categorized American novelists, a seemingly inexplicable process which would leave a Nobel Prize winner like Bellow something of a pariah on the literary Left and an awkward, untrustworthy fellow-traveler on the neoconservative Right. In short, I take stock of the understudied impact of modern American conservatism, at its electoral pinnacle, on post-sixties American fiction.

CHAPTER 4

Movement Conservatism, Neoconservatism, and the New Right

Saul Bellow and Thomas Pynchon in the Age of Reagan, 1970–1990

4.1 Introduction: "Echoes of the High Rot of the End of Rome"

In 1970, as the sixties came to an official calendric end, William F. Buckley Jr. ran a series of articles in *National Review* sketching out the lineaments of an early, conservative assessment of the tumultuous decade's worthwhile literary contributions to American culture. In January, Buckley wrote that he found little creativity to celebrate in the field of American literature, especially when compared to the bold originality of emerging economic theories of free-market capitalism: "Though literature and, especially literary criticism were mostly third-rate, and philosophy and theology were somnolent, a single determined and intelligent man (Milton Friedman) reversed an entire economic trend" ("Two Cheers for the Sixties," 14). Reiterating a leitmotif of his New York City mayoral run in 1965, Buckley stressed what would become an increasingly salient theme in post-sixties conservatism: that the dynamism of the "American imagination" in the sixties began a steady migration from the literary Left to the economic Right.[1]

Later that year, in an article titled "Apocalypse Next Exit," a long survey of the supposedly devolving quality of contemporary American fiction, Guy Davenport lamented that even though a handful of novelists valiantly searched "for the vertebrae under the fat of the Pepsi Generation, hoping to find it organized into a spine" – for example, Flannery O'Connor, John O'Hara, the virtually unknown Cormac McCarthy, John Updike, Bernard Malamud, and Saul Bellow – the final verdict on American literature in the sixties remained grim: The novel itself was "going through what seems to be a new decadent period like that at the end of the last century. This movement is just beginning; one can detect the autumnal seriousness, a certain ripeness of decay, echoes of the high rot of the end of Rome" (1303–1304). Tapping into the conservative truism that the social disturbances of the sixties mirrored the early stages of Ancient Rome's decline, Davenport suggested that the deteriorating quality of the contemporary novel was due, in no small part, to its irreconcilability with the conservative movement's own crisis-of-civilization discourse vis-à-vis the New Left and the counterculture more generally.

Although declension narratives about the novel were certainly nothing new, and for many critics had become routine by the early seventies, it is important to see how the conservative declension narrative was fundamentally different in order to grasp the argumentative stakes of this chapter. As Kathleen Fitzpatrick points out, critics have been bemoaning the "death of the novel" for almost as long as the novel itself has existed since the end of the sixteenth century (13). Fitzpatrick argues that, more often than not, the cyclical nature of this lamentation in the post-1945 era – whether Lionel Trilling in the pages of *Partisan Review* in the late forties, or John Barth in "The Literature of Exhaustion" (1967) – "reveals the key to the cultural function of the death-of-the-novel discourse: it is endlessly productive of more discourse," and thus, of more novels (24). Typically, even for writers as dissimilar as Trilling and Barth, the death-of-the-novel discourse was undergirded by conceptual metaphors borrowed from media technology – obsolescence, formal compatibility, reusability, and so on – that were ultimately generative for the novel form. But unlike the death-of-the-novel proclamations made by more liberal literary figures, when conservatives declared that the American novel was dying, that a once important cultural form in the intellectual life of the nation was decomposing, they truly meant it. Davenport's language reveals how the conservative death-of-the-novel discourse was founded on conceptual metaphors of putrefaction – "decay," "rot," degeneration, and so on – that echoed the broader conservative critique of the New Left as a social pathology that had infected postwar culture. From a larger socio-aesthetic perspective, in McGurl's words, Barthian discourse and even Barth's brand of metafiction are symptomatic "of what happens when modernism gets what it wants: a heightened (never total) autonomy from an all-engulfing mass market, and from its traffic in realist representations" (*Novel Art*, 181). But whereas seventies postmodernists such as Barth ironized his absorption into the semiautonomous realm of the postwar university, producing more fiction precisely by aestheticizing the professional-technical discourse of academia, movement conservatives interpreted this same kind of relative literary autonomy as self-indulgent decadence.

Throughout the seventies and eighties, for reasons I explain at length subsequently, American conservatives gradually saw the contemporary literary novel not merely as an obsolete medium but as a disease-carrying agent sustained by university institutions that bore the virus of the New Left, and whose classic symptom was the compulsive need to radically question, critique, and interrogate "America" as a supposedly exceptional nation. From this perspective, it is tempting – but ultimately misleading, I think – to say simply that serious interest in the literary novel declined within the conservative movement at precisely the moment when (from the conservative point of view) potent countercultural movements appeared on the scene brandishing literary fiction as a Gramscian weapon of hegemonic struggle. The multifaceted set of causal factors driving this shift in literary taste across the political spectrum was neither self-evident nor inevitable, and its continued vagueness and obscurity in literary studies today contributes to inelegant overgeneralizations about conservatism being inherently at odds with reified (and politically coded) terms such as the "imagination," the "creative faculty," or the "artistic impulse."

Using this understudied correlation in American literary history as a point of departure, Chapter 4 investigates how and why the cultural capital of "literary fiction" – that is, the kinds of postwar novels that professional critics and scholars thought possess literary merit, that were reviewed in prominent newspapers and journals, that were nominated for major literary prizes, that ended up on a college syllabus as representations of capital-L "Literature" in the United States, and so on – increasingly became aligned with liberalism and the Left in the seventies and eighties. In conducting this inquiry, I introduce a unique historical perspective to the scholarly discussion of post-sixties literature and politics, moving away from the well-trodden narratives about how modern liberalism, the sixties counterculture, or the New Left altered the landscape of literary fiction, and toward a broader political narrative that interrogates the narrow, though powerful, impact of conservatism as an electoral and ideological force on American fiction after the so-called "big-bang-effect" of the sixties on US culture. Such a perspective, I argue, adds one more causal factor into the already complex matrix of causes that scholars have identified which were responsible for the shift in literary taste among different political factions, which range from ideological changes in political discourse to large institutional shifts, such as the conservative movement's unrelenting neo-populist attack on cultural "elites" and the emergence of neoconservatism, to the explosion of conservative think tanks beginning in the seventies and the simultaneous rise of what Mark McGurl calls "The Program

Era," respectively. While conservative institution-building efforts were certainly part of a well-organized political strategy, I stress that they were not part of a direct, coordinated effort to transform conservative views on aesthetics. The shift in conservative literary taste – which, at bottom, almost always functioned as a proxy for the postwar conservative conceptualization of literary cultural capital – was a historical contingency, a largely unintended by-product of three major strains of the post-sixties American Right – the triptych of William F. Buckley's movement conservatism, Irving Kristol's neoconservatism, and the reactionary populist New Right – aligning themselves against liberal-Leftist enemies at certain moments, and clashing bitterly over ideas and policies at other moments.

To advance my argument, I concentrate primarily on the writings of Saul Bellow and Thomas Pynchon, two major postwar novelists who wrote several of the most critically acclaimed works of the era, but who were eventually seen as occupying very different positions in the political literary fields: Bellow's literary prestige declining as he was aligned (largely against his will) with neoconservativism and the American Right, and Pynchon's literary prestige increasing as he was aligned with various strands of the New Left and the broader counterculture. In regards to Bellow, the main figure in this chapter, my central contention is that his post-sixties fiction represents something of an apex of the traditionalist conservative aesthetic and its concomitant association with the cultural capital of the old bourgeoisie, which emphasized complexity, mystery, human foibles, and the frequent failures of Enlightenment reason to manipulate the world to maximize human happiness. As the conservative movement ascended electorally in post-sixties America, and Bellow reiterated the conservative commonplace that the New Left portended totalitarian fascism, Bellow's work became legible almost solely within the rubric of "conservatism," both in a generic sense and a historically specific sense of that term. Yet at the same time, Bellow was often left at the margins of political categorization in the literary and cultural histories of post-sixties America, for he was a sophisticated literary novelist who was trying to conserve elite traditions of cultural prestige at precisely the moment when modern American conservatism was on the verge of embracing neoliberal capitalism, the (at times) high intellectual critiques of Black Power from neoconservatives, and the neo-populist rhetoric of the seventies "New Right." Likewise, I argue that the shifting perceptions of literary cultural capital within the modern conservative movement is a more salient ideological presence, and persistent problem, in Pynchon's mid-career novels than scholars have realized heretofore. Toward this end, I trace Pynchon's shifting representation of fascism in his novels from an all-encompassing trope for a technological–military–industrial complex that dominates postwar life – irrespective of political affiliations or labels – to a more specific trope for a reactionary brand of conservatism personified most saliently by Ronald Reagan. Although Pynchon's explicit interest in modern conservatism begins early in his career, where it represents a set of political beliefs that seem like a comically misguided symptom of an emerging technological order that threatens individuality; by the seventies and eighties Pynchon directly identifies Nixon–Reagan conservatism as an agent of American Fascism, although he grows skeptical of a certain mode of leftist satirical irony that casts conservatives merely as lowbrow fools. What accounts for this shift, I maintain, is not just the way in which the trajectory of postwar American politics transforms Pynchon's conception and deployment of fascism as a complex trope within postmodernism but a deeper authorial self-critique: Pynchon's anxiety about turning into a critically acclaimed novelist who may be just savoring his own moral self-righteousness and high-status distinction without catalyzing any real-world sociopolitical change.

By examining each novelist's fraught relationship with modern conservatism, I demonstrate the under-theorized cultural effects of the modern Right on US literary fiction, even as conservative ideology seemed to be distancing itself from "highbrow" literature as such and embracing popular, mass-market genre fiction, beginning with the launch of William F. Buckley's "Blackford Oakes" spy novels in the late seventies. In the process, I cast fresh light on several obstinate conundrums in postwar American literary studies: Bellow's puzzling status as a virtual pariah in the American academy and wider literary field, particularly *after* his Nobel Prize win in 1976; Pynchon's late-career shift toward more robust normative values and a new appreciation for the traditional family unit within the domestic sphere; and ultimately, the status of literary postmodernism as an ostensibly progressive movement emerging and evolving during the electoral apex of modern conservatism.

4.2 Visions of Weimar America: Saul Bellow and the Aesthetic Rift between Movement Conservatism and Neoconservatism

In the early seventies, the increasingly conservative Saul Bellow and the countercultural icon Thomas Pynchon published major, award-winning novels – *Mr. Sammler's Planet* (1970) and *Gravity's Rainbow* (1973), respectively – which provided sophisticated representations of the anxieties, on both the Right and Left, concerning how the sixties could usher in an illegitimate political system resembling fascist authoritarianism. But it is not so much the specter of Nazi Fascism that haunts *Mr. Sammler's Planet* and *Gravity's Rainbow*, as it is the collapse of the Weimar Republic and sociopolitical conditions of possibility that would enable the ascent of a new kind of fascism in America. While both novels imply that the fall of the Weimar Republic and the rise of the Third Reich are historical events that foreshadow the United States' emergence from the upheavals of the sixties, each work casts the adherents of various political factions in opposite roles. For Pynchon, the counterculture and the New Left are doomed freedom-lovers akin to the noble, inter-war Weimarians, and the Nixon administration with its conservative minions are the malevolent fascists determined to carry out an imperial war abroad against racialized Others and an internal war at home against leftist subversives. For Bellow, by contrast, the high cultural Weimar intellectuals are the shrewd anti-Stalinist liberals from the fifties who have crossed over – or, in many cases, been thrust – into the realm of neoconservatism, and the New Leftists are the irrational nihilists reminiscent of revolting German university students in the early thirties who were unwittingly sowing the seeds of totalitarianism. With these diametrically opposed narrative premises, each novel was designed to appeal to two different intellectual audiences – Pynchon's countercultural readers beginning to base themselves in American universities, and Bellow's disaffected ex-liberals and neoconservatives headquartered in magazines and journals such as *National Review*, *Commentary*, and *The Public Interest*. Despite the fact that these were two of the most highly celebrated novels of the early seventies, the respective audiences they were directed toward received them in strikingly different ways: Pynchon's novel grew into a kind of secular gospel for the scattered remnants of the sixties Left, and Bellow's novel was disparaged by movement conservatives and became a largely forgotten text in the archives of American conservatism.[2]

In contrast to their negative reception of Bellow's post-sixties fiction, movement conservatives were enthusiastic supporters of Bellow's early novels, since his resistance to rigid political categorization and his preoccupation with high intellectual culture via Robert Maynard Hutchins's "Great Books" program at the University of Chicago easily linked up with the conservative movement's midcentury conviction that great literature was inherently conservative because it supposedly transcended the ideologically driven literature of the twentieth-century Left. In Bellow's celebrated novel *The Adventures of Augie March* (1953), when the protagonist Augie claims to "go at things as I have taught myself, free-style" and moves through different jobs as if learning through occupation-based experimentation, conservatives saw not the obvious allusions to John Dewey's pragmatism but implicit similarities to Edmund Burke's disavowal of abstraction and embrace of contextual empiricism (3). In addition, Augie's pragmatic attitude is tempered by an admiration for his "Five-Foot Shelf of Classics" that serves as his intellectual and moral ballast, a clear reference to the Great Books program that Bellow studied as an undergraduate at Chicago and later worked on as an editor indexing Mortimer Adler's massive anthology *The Great Ideas: A Synopticon of Great Books of the Western World* (Bellow, *Augie*, 188). While a perceptive literary scholar and cultural historian like Mark Greif has pointed out that *Augie March* merges the seemingly incompatible theories of Hutchins (the notion of a transcendent human nature found in the Great Books) and Dewey (progressive, "learning through experience" pragmatism), conservatives would see a different merger: Burkean skepticism toward modern ideological abstractions and, as a way of modulating skepticism's potentially corrosive social effects, a redeeming faith in the trans-historical stability of human nature (Greif, 195). Bellow's novels, in other words, marshaled the cultural capital of highbrow literature to perform the exact kind of cultural work that movement conservatives were looking for in the fifties. Bellow "found a way of storytelling," Robert Phelps wrote in his review of *Henderson the Rain King* (1959) in *National Review*, comparing Bellow to Twain and Joyce, "which can deal with ideas and yet sacrifice nothing in the way of racy actuality" (622). Although great distances of all kinds separated Bellow from conservatism in the immediate postwar period, his vision of the American novel – that is, the "novel of ideas" genre combined with character-driven, modernist-influenced complexity – was irresistible to high cultural traditionalists like Russell Kirk who shaped literary taste in the early conservative movement.[3] However, the conservative reception of Bellow's work shifted dramatically between the publication of *Herzog* (1964), which *National Review* fawned over, and the string of negative reviews from movement conservatives that started with *Mr. Sammler's Planet*, even though this was also the moment that Bellow was becoming increasingly associated with the high cultural intellectualism of neoconsevatism.

To solve this conundrum, it is useful to examine *Mr. Sammler's Planet* itself, noting the places that reveal not just the overlapping ideological continuities between neoconservatives and movement conservatives, but also their areas of disagreement and conflict, in order to highlight how neoconservatives continued to lionize contemporary literary fiction in ways that movement conservatives once had in the fifties but were rapidly abandoning in the early seventies. By the late sixties, the most obvious point of agreement between movement conservatives and neoconservatives was visible in Bellow's critique of the so-called "new class" congealing in the late sixties and its cultivation of an "adversary culture," in Lionel Trilling's famous phrase. Recasting the "neoconservative mantra," in Andrew Hartman's words, that "the United States manifested conditions precariously similar to those of Weimar Germany," Bellow created the protagonist Artur Sammler, a Polish Holocaust survivor who sees in the political radicalism of the sixties a reprise of the thirties in Western Europe, and the looming resurrection of fascism (Hartman, *War for the Soul of America*, 56). "Like many people who had seen the world collapse once," Bellow writes early in the novel, "Mr. Sammler entertained the possibility that it might collapse twice. He did not agree with refugee friends that this doom was inevitable, but liberal beliefs did not seem capable of self-defense, and you could smell the decay" (26). Looking upon New York City as the epicenter of civilizational decay, Sammler wonders "whether the worst enemies of civilization might not prove to be its petted intellectuals who attacked it at its weakest points" (26). Echoing neoconservatives like Irving Kristol and Norman Podhoretz, Sammler sees America's liberal "petted intellectuals" as a professional-managerial "new class" made up of university-educated workers who dealt primarily in knowledge and information, but who consciously distanced themselves from the crass materialism and repressive social mores of the traditional bourgeoisie. As Trilling observed in *Beyond Culture* (1965), this financially comfortable "new class" attacked bourgeois society using not one of the many ideological strands of socialism, but the aesthetics of literary modernism, a movement that intensified the bohemian feeling that "a primary function of art and thought is to liberate the individual from the tyranny of his culture in the environmental sense and to permit him to stand beyond it in an autonomy of perception and judgment" (Trilling, xiii). Somewhere between "the end of the first quarter of this century and the present time," Trilling wrote, "there has grown up a populous group whose members take for granted the idea of the adversary culture" (viii). For Trilling, the adversary culture emerging in the sixties, principally its knee-jerk tendency to demystify normative social assumptions, was a direct outgrowth of literary modernism – but *modernism gone politically awry*.

Although Trilling never self-identified as a neoconservative, he nonetheless invented a powerful phrase that neoconservatives adopted, more so than movement conservatives, in order to explain the New Left's scathing anti-American critiques. Neoconservatives saw Trilling's claim about the literary foundation of the adversary culture as especially appealing because it simultaneously reinforced their axiomatic belief that a New Leftist outlook was a stylistic pose rather than an intellectually substantive position, and their deeply ingrained self-perception as shrewd interpreters of highbrow literature who were authorized to adjudicate literary prestige. For neoconservatives and loosely affiliated fellow travelers like Bellow, the primary concern was the institutional processes that transferred high culture to the popular masses, and the important nuances that were perhaps inevitably lost in translation. In *Mr. Sammler's Planet*, Bellow's protagonist agonizes over this precise question: whether "the [avant-garde] minority civilization could be transmitted to the great masses, and that orderly conditions for this transmission were possible" (176). The irrational romanticism of the New Left, in Sammler's view, throws the possibility of this transmission into doubt, turning modernism's medicinal properties for Western civilization into the autoimmune-like sickness of (what would eventually be labeled) postmodernism.

In the neoconservative imagination, while the great literary modernists certainly trained a critical gaze on bourgeois commercialism and normative morality, they wrote not for the untutored masses but for a relatively small, well-educated audience who possessed enough money and leisure time to appreciate complex texts and thus had a vested interest in using those critiques to reform society gradually. In this neoconservative revisionist literary history, reading early twentieth-century modernists was akin to participating in a sociopolitical inoculation process, as multifaceted radical critiques could be introduced to small cadres of elites, seriously discussed, and ultimately revealed as sustaining the culture values of Western modernity all along. "It is not uncommon that a culture [in the West] will be critical of the civilization that sustains it," Irving Kristol explained, "and always critical of the failure of this civilization to realize perfectly the ideals that it claims as inspiration. . . . But culture as a whole has always been assigned the task of, and invariably accepted responsibility for, sustaining and celebrating those values. Indeed, it is a premise of modern sociological and anthropological theory that it is the essence of culture to be 'functional' in this way" ("The Adversary Culture of Intellectuals," 106–107). For Kristol, this built-in process of self-critique testified to the greatness of the Western intellectual tradition, which is why he saw the new, mass adversary culture of the sixties as an existential threat to – what he, and other neoconservatives, majestically termed – "Western civilization."

The intensification of the adversary culture in the late sixties, in the eyes of neoconservatives, could be blamed on a mode of critique, cultivated in American universities, which took "an adversary posture toward the ideals" of modernity itself, pushing it to the verge of nihilism (Kristol, 106). At the heart of the adversary culture, neoconservatives believed, was an odd alliance between individuals and institutions, since its primary catalysts were pseudo-intellectuals who romanticized rebellious individualism, but who had ironically taken refuge in the ossified bureaucracy of the American university system. The great irony, Kristol argued, was that while the "tremendous expansion – especially after World War II – of postsecondary education provided a powerful institutional milieu for modernist tastes and attitudes among the mass of both teachers and students," these institutions functioned like an assembly line that mass produced "the vulgar version of modernism that soon became the mass counterculture among their students who, as consumers, converted it into a pseudobohemian [sic] lifestyle" (118). The practical result was an uncouth adversarial attitude that replaced the "utopian rationalism" of socialism and Trotskyism, ideologies that many neoconservatives had once supported and still found somewhat intellectually respectable, with a "utopian romanticism" that reflexively criticized traditions, social norms, and rationality itself in a nihilistic language drenched in lowbrow sexual perversion and juvenile narcissism (Kristol, 118).

In a famous early scene in *Mr. Sammler's Planet*, Bellow dramatizes just how far left-wing student rhetoric has fallen from its mythical heights in the universities of the thirties, where fabled debates took place between Stalinists and Trotskyites in lunchrooms stretching from Bellow's University of Chicago to Kristol's City College of New York. While giving a lecture at Columbia University, Sammler recounts his time in interwar London as an associate of the Bloomsbury group, specifically his work with H. G. Wells on the utopian "Cosmopolis" project to build one global state, which Sammler now believes was little more than a "kind-hearted, ingenuous, stupid scheme" (33). The project, Sammler says, was premised on "the building of a planned, orderly, and beautiful world society; abolishing national sovereignty, outlawing war . . . offering free universal education, personal freedom (compatible with community welfare) to the utmost degree; a service society based on a rational scientific attitude toward life" (33). As Sammler begins to explain the inherent flaws in utopian progressivism, a New Left ideologue interrupts him, looks around at the audience and shouts: "Why do you listen to this effete old shit? What has he got to tell you? His balls are dry. He's dead. He can't come" (34). This outburst, inspired by a real-life encounter Bellow had while giving a speech at San Francisco State College in 1968, supports Sammler's neoconservative theory that debating standards at American universities have declined because the New Left has rejected the mythical discourse of "Western civilization." Instead, Sammler thinks to himself, student radicals have fooled themselves into accepting "excrement as a standard," which accounts for all of "this confused sex-excrement-militancy, explosiveness, abusiveness, tooth-showing, Barbary ape howling. Or like the spider monkeys in the trees, as Sammler once had read, defecating into their hands, and shrieking, pelting the explorers below" (34). Using the outmoded discourse of colonial-age anthropology, Sammler compares New Left activists to African animals, and tacitly equates himself with the white explorer, in order to highlight their low cultural incivility and intellectual barbarism.

For Bellow, though, this intellectual barbarism could not simply stay contained in the university. As a former socialist convinced of the power of big ideas to change the world, Bellow still assumed that a direct relationship existed between the decline of intellectual discourse in the university and the breakdown of order in New York City. It is no coincidence, then, that the novel's next scene is the controversial "pickpocket" scene, one of the most infamous in postwar American fiction, in which a well-dressed black pickpocket, realizing that Sammler has seen him steal an elderly man's Social Security card on a public bus, follows Sammler home and sexually intimidates Sammler in his own apartment building. "The black man had opened his fly and taken out his penis," Bellow writes, "It was displayed with great oval testicles, a large tan-and-purple uncircumcised thing – a tube, a snake" (39). Significantly, the pickpocket never speaks during the assault, which causes Sammler to liken him to a puma, but merely displays his penis in silence "with mystifying certitude" (41). As critics have been pointing out since the novel's publication, Bellow seems to employ acutely racist language in this scene in an attempt to conflate blackness with animality, sexual perversion, criminality, and general social chaos. According to literary critic Adam Kirsch, it "is especially disastrous that this should take place in a novel that is partly about the Holocaust, because exactly this technique was used by anti-Semites to demonize Jews. To the Nazis, it was the Jews who were instinctively licentious, who were emblems of 'sexual Jewhood.' But instead of drawing the conclusion that this sort of racism is inherently false and cruel, Bellow simply reverses the polarities" ("Flower Children"). Cast as a hypocrite in this reading, Bellow is unwittingly guilty of perpetuating an insidious form of racism that shares a family resemblance with Nazism, for he uses the symbolic capital and moral authority of the Holocaust survivor to denounce anti-Semitism while simultaneously reinforcing anti-black sentiments which have been historically cultivated by the American Right. Bellow's hypocrisy, these critics usually imply, stems from his failure to learn the central moral lesson of postwar liberalism that all forms of racial prejudice are wrong. This ostensible racist blind spot helps explain why critics pinpoint the black pickpocket scene in particular, and *Mr. Sammler's Planet* in general, as the moment in his career when Bellow's authorial image transformed, in the words of one Bellow biographer, from an amiable "Herzogian character resisting the complacent political atmosphere of the late fifties and early sixties into a full-blown reactionary" (Atlas, *Bellow*, 388).

However, the typical reading of this scene and the novel tend to mistakenly conflate Bellow with his protagonist Sammler. The result is that they fail to take into account how Bellow deployed the neoconservative mantra of fascism emerging in America from the New Left not as a firmly held ideological theory but as a classic Bellovian intellectual thought experiment whose very provisionality was designed to break free of any political crusade seeking to narrow Bellow's novelistic possibilities. While my argument neither excuses nor endorses Bellow's thoroughly racist imagery, it does show a more complex neoconservative vision than the prevailing notion that Bellow cannot grasp the progressive liberal truism that racism is morally wrong. Throughout *Mr. Sammler's Planet*, Bellow examines the countercultural trope of unfettered black sexuality – invented largely by white writers, such as the young Norman Mailer in "The White Negro" – as a synecdoche for the sexual revolution itself, and he finds that this ideology fails to imagine the unsavory aspects of human nature unleashed by rapid social change. As Sammler obsessively ponders the pickpocket encounter, noting that "a sexual madness was overwhelming the Western world," he suddenly remembers "hearing that a President of the United States was supposed to have shown himself in a similar way to the representatives of the press (asking the ladies to leave), and demanding to know whether a man so well hung could not be trusted to lead his country" (53). This thinly disguised president is Lyndon Johnson, of course, the crude Texan who ushered in Great Society Liberalism and signed controversial legislation like the Civil Rights Act and Voting Rights Act, and who also serves as a model of (illegitimate) politico-phallic authority that *predates* the black pickpocket's sexual bullying. If toward the end of the sixties the pickpocket comes to see his penis as "a symbol of superlegitimacy [*sic*] or sovereignty," in Bellow's words, it is not simply because black hyper-sexuality codified as hipness catalyzed Great Society Liberalism, as Michal Szalay argues (Bellow, 44; Szalay, *Hip Figures*, 225). Rather, Bellow suggests that Great Society Liberalism legitimized decadent sexual pathologies, especially in the black lower classes, because it sought to maximize material comfort without taking into account the dark side of the human soul. Make "Nature your God," Sammler reasons silently to himself, trying to puzzle out what ideology produced the black pickpocket, "elevate creatureliness [*sic*], and you can count on gross results" (44). Sammler concludes, in short, that the classic axiom of traditionalist, Burkean-style conservatism is true: although modern revolutions have invariably been made in the name of human freedom and welfare, their "last state was always more nihilistic than the first" (61).

From Bellow's perspective, the symbolic authority of Sammler-as-Holocaust-survivor is rooted not in a simple-minded, moralistic objection to the counterculture, but in the notion that the New Left is yet another revolutionary movement that misunderstood the human condition as one marked by radical imperfection, a theory that manifested itself in the literary field by seeking to constrict the full spectrum of artistic expression. While liberals sympathetic to the aims of the counterculture would see this as a distinction without a difference, conservative-minded critics like Bellow did not. In fact, Bellow communicates this theme in the novel by examining how nakedness became a sexual trope in the sixties, instead of a signifier for human vulnerability, as it tended to be in Holocaust literature. Perhaps the most disorienting feature of the sexual revolution for Sammler is the ideological premise that nakedness signifies sexual desire and pleasure, and thus emancipation from repressive bourgeois norms. Sammler's bewilderment stems from the most traumatic episode of his Holocaust experience, one that he cannot help but replay continually in his mind, when he and his wife were rounded up with other Jews in Poland and ordered by Nazis to remove all their clothes and dig their own mass grave before being shot to death. "When they were as naked as children from the womb," Bellow writes, implicitly mocking the countercultural conflation of nakedness and innocent purity, "and the hole was supposedly deep enough, the guns began to blast" (226). Once Sammler claws himself out of the mass graves hours later, he realizes that a blow from a rifle-butt just before falling into the hole has left him permanently blinded in one eye, which transforms him into a Tiresias-like figure whose loss of physical vision only augments a deeper philosophical vision of humanity. Marked by profound pessimism, this vision is thrown into relief when Sammler wanders onto the property of Cieslakiewicz, a Polish man who hides Sammler from the Nazis in an abandoned mausoleum even though Sammler disgusts him. The two men "didn't like each other," Bellow writes, but what "had there been to like in Sammler? – half-naked, famished, caked hair and beard, crawling out of the forest" (74). Notably, Cieslakiewicz's reaction to seeing a victim of Nazi brutality mimics Bellow's own personal reaction to seeing newsreels of the concentration camps in the immediate aftermath of the war. As Bellow explained in an essay about the stakes of being a Jewish novelist in the postwar United States, "American bulldozers pushed naked corpses toward a mass grave ditch. Limbs fell away and heads dropped from disintegrating bodies. My reaction to this was ... a deeply troubling sense of disgrace or human demotion, as if by such afflictions the Jews had lost the respect of the rest of humankind ... The world would see these dead with a pity that placed them at the margin of humanity" ("A Jewish Writer in America," 366). In *Mr. Sammler's Planet*, Bellow explores the uncomfortable possibility that this kind of pity and revulsion is bound up with the idea that the Holocaust exposed the lack of "human-ness" residing not just in European Jewry but in humanity itself. Perhaps the Nazis merely reduced their victims to the animalized bodies that already defined the essence of everyone? The central flaw of the sixties counterculture, from Sammler's Tiresiasian perspective, is that it blithely asserts that the "right to be uninhibited, spontaneous, urinating, defecating, belching, coupling in all positions" will reveal humanity's inherent goodness instead of its metaphysical helplessness and abjection (25).

To Sammler's horror, countercultural youths do not even need to be brutalized into accepting their subhuman status, since they actively degrade themselves with sexual acts that were once seen by "civilized" Westerners as sources of embarrassment and humiliation. In one scene, Sammler listens to the moral anguish of Walter Bruch, a distant nephew who also survived the Holocaust but now is worried about his sexually "perverse" habit of following around female strangers with "beautiful arms" in New York City and surreptitiously masturbating in public. At first, Sammler jokes with Walter by ventriloquizing countercultural hipness, asking him: "Isn't it a comfort that there is no more isolated Victorian sex suffering?" (48). But when Sammler turns serious and tells Walter that he will pray for him, Walter is startled that Sammler would actually admit that he prays, and suddenly Walter laughs wildly, "swinging his trunk comically back and forth, holding both his sides," revealing the influence of the American counterculture in a society where prayer is more shameful than public masturbation (51). In another scene in which Sammler plays the part of countercultural sex pathologist, his niece Angela Gruner asks for advice about how to win back her fiancé, Wharton Horricker, who has had second thoughts about marrying her after she agreed to participate in an orgy during their vacation in Mexico. Short on advice but long on philosophical musings, Sammler explains how stunned he is "that things poor professionals once had to do for a living, performing for bachelor parties, or tourist sex-circuses on the Place Pigalle, ordinary people, housewives, filing-clerks, students, now do just to be sociable. . . . Is it an effort to 'liberalize' human existence and show that nothing that happens between people is really loathsome?" (130). For Sammler, these acts of sexual self-debasement lead the American countercultural to embark on a crude, pseudo-Nietzschean investigation of the genealogy of Western morals, and their supposedly unprecedented social revolution merely opens up the same kind of nihilistic void that German youths discovered in the thirties.

Channeling Dostoyevsky's famous critique of anarchistic socialism and nineteenth-century rationalism in *The Possessed* and *The Brothers Karamazov* – and even Whittaker Chambers's updated Dostoyevskian critique of Soviet Communism and atheism in *Witness* – Bellow portrays Sammler as a traditionalist-minded conservative who hopes to avert nihilism and political authoritarianism by voicing hard truths about the vaunted liberal ideal of "equality." Retaining the basic outline of Marxist class categories, Sammler theorizes that "the right to murder with impunity" exists for bourgeois elites because they control the legal system and the levers of punishment. This amoral political fact, Sammler asserts, is "what revolutions were really about. In a revolution you took away the privileges of an aristocracy and redistributed them. What did equality mean? Did it mean all men were friends and brothers? No, it meant that all belonged to the elite. Killing was an ancient privilege. This was why revolutions plunged into blood" (118). Just as Edmund Burke believed that the French Revolution revealed how noble-sounding terms like "equality" and "liberty" were not absolute, inherent social goods when "stripped of every relation, in all the nakedness and solitude of metaphysical abstraction," Sammler also believes that the New Left turns society upside down in the pursuit of a dangerous utopian project (*Reflections on the Revolution in France*, 7). Ultimately, this vision of conservatism helps explain why the infamous black pickpocket scene is so central to the novel. The black pickpocket is the personification of every form of countercultural "equality" in Sammler's view – the nexus of sexual pathology, moral nihilism, and hip criminality – which is meant to confuse readers at the very beginning of the novel when they encounter the kind of ideological subject produced by utopian abstractions. The black pickpocket, then, is not a person to be understood so much as a stereotype of equality (supposedly created by progressives) to be decoded.

Contrary to the assertions of modern liberalism, though, Bellow suggested that the stereotype of the black criminal had not been formed by white supremacy or structural racism, but by a combination of the adversary culture and the destructive identity politics of the New Left. Toward the end of the novel, in a scene few critics explicate while charging Bellow with racism, Sammler and Eisen – Sammler's son-in-law who is a World War II veteran and makes iron art medallions – spot the pickpocket on the street and Eisen beats the pickpocket over the head with a bag of his medallions, almost crushing the man's skull. Instead of framing this encounter as the pickpocket getting his comeuppance, Bellow portrays Sammler as horrified by the ferocious violence unleashed by Eisen, which Bellow relates in the close third person: "And how much Sammler sympathized with [the pickpocket] – how much he would have done to prevent such atrocious blows!" (243). But if Sammler associates this attack on the pickpocket with his own blinding from a Nazi rifle-butt thirty years earlier, causing him to empathize with the pickpocket's suffering, Eisen draws a completely different lesson from his war experience. "You can't hit a man like this once," Eisen explains to Sammler. "When you hit him you must really hit him. Otherwise he'll kill you. You know. We both fought in the war. You were a partisan. You had a gun," a form of kill-or-be-killed reasoning that sinks "Sammler's heart completely" (241–42). This final scene with the pickpocket is crucial for understanding the neoconservative vision of how totalitarian fascism could arise in America. As Stanley Crouch points out, Sammler does not "forgive the pickpocket his sins, assuming that 'society' gave him no choice and that he shouldn't be punished," which Crouch sees as the standard liberal account of the relationship between structural racism and crime in the early seventies, but rather that "the thief is on the receiving end of force so excessive that it reduces the potency of the law to a ruthless werewolf of totalitarianism" ("Introduction," xxiv). Similar to other postwar American novelists whom movement conservatives applauded in the fifties and sixties for criticizing liberalism's governmental crusade against racism – for example, William Faulkner's tirades during the civil rights movement against Northern white troublemakers ignorant of the intricacies of Southern history, or Flannery O'Connor's formally complex stories that displace real-world racism into the sphere of Christian metaphysics – Bellow essentially accuses the white counterculture of inventing the conditions of social nihilism that created not only the black pickpocket but also the reactionary backlash that nearly killed him. Bellow indicates that the left-wing adversary culture's radical critique of all Western values – supposedly in the service of a progressive quest for racial justice, but really just a strategy to accrue symbolic capital associated with an anti-racist stance – ends up undermining the social order so profoundly that only uncontainable violence remains, which amounts to a kind of right-wing argumentative blueprint for how fascism arises from the preternaturally naïve sixties Left.

Considering the polemical attacks Bellow launched against the New Left in *Mr. Sammler's Planet*, including a rather nuanced conservative theorization of totalitarian fascism, one might have predicted that the novel would become an instant canonical text within the American conservative movement, especially since Bellow was echoing the very sentiments Republican politicians were using to court voters belonging to Nixon's recently coined "Silent Majority." Coming from a major writer routinely heralded by this time as "the premier American novelist," as Joseph Epstein declared in his review of *Mr. Sammler's Planet* for the *New York Times Book Review*, here was a novel that seemed to brilliantly enlist the formal inventiveness and literary prestige of modernist fiction in the conservative cause of post-sixties counterrevolution (Epstein qtd. in Atlas, 394). Written in the idiom of highbrow literature but incessantly registering the visceral disgust of the women's movement and the Black Power movement, the novel produced a rare, double rhetorical effect that epitomized the neoconservative "intellectualization of the white working-class ethos" (Hartman, 53). For a typical Buckley-minded conservative who had been reading *National Review* since the mid-fifties, a magazine founded with the express purpose of alchemizing certain forms of cultural grievance into intellectual respectability, *Mr. Sammler's Planet* seemed to be the closest thing to the great conservative novel they had been waiting for all these years.

Remarkably, though, in a disagreement about the aesthetic merits of *Mr. Sammler's Planet* that revealed deeper ideological rifts within conservatism about the cultural value of the "literary" as such, neoconservatives lavished the novel with praise while movement conservatives actively condemned it. Writing in the neoconservative flagship *Commentary*, Irvin Stock believed it was a major novel of the postwar era, explaining that Bellow had once again created his signature intellectual Jewish protagonist in Sammler, but this time he made him "a man educated not only by books, for he has learned at first hand the chief lessons of our time" (90). The novel, Stock concluded, was "a beautiful defense of our common humanity against all the bogus idealism as well as the frank savagery" that bubbled up out of the counterculture, making Bellow the most important novelist of the post-sixties era (94). Conversely, the assessment of *Mr. Sammler's Planet* run by Buckley in *National Review* took an entirely different view of Bellow's project. Instead of seeing the striking similarities between neoconservatism and traditionalist conservatism in the novel, John Braine's review was framed around the imagined sins Bellow committed against both plot-driven, readerly pleasure and movement conservative orthodoxy. While it was once common for *National Review* writers to applaud the epistemological ambiguities of modernist narrative forms, Braine now criticized the novel's non-linearity, claiming that it produced a seemingly meaningless story where "nothing actually happens to Mr. Sammler" (265). "However deep a novel goes," Braine continued, outlining the implicit expectations of a popular (and conservative populist) reading audience, "it has to be crammed with surprises or otherwise it ceases to be a novel" (265). Compounding its first offense against easy reading, the novel also seemed to Braine to be a parody of "true" conservatism, for no matter Bellow's intention in creating the black pickpocket, that character only reinforced the countercultural fantasies of black men's "superior vitality" and "vivid spontaneous sexuality" (265). Similarly, Braine highlighted another ideological heresy in the novel – that is, not being sufficiently anti-communist – when he pointed to a minor flashback scene in which Sammler travels to Israel during the 1967 Six-Day War and recounts "the smell of rotting flesh, the ugly debris of war," comparing the piles of Muslim corpses killed by advanced Israeli weaponry to the stacks of Jewish bodies shot by Nazis and thrown into mass graves (qtd. in Braine, 266). When analyzed in context, Sammler sees the Six-Day War not through the foreign policy lens of movement conservatives, who neatly categorize Cold War conflicts according to either pro-American or anti-American proxy states, but through a broader philosophical conservative lens that sees war as evidence of humanity's imperfection. Tellingly, Braine can only conclude that Bellow's decline is the result of him becoming an unofficial member of "the Family," the pejorative nickname given to midcentury New York Intellectuals such as Lionel and Diana Trilling, Dwight McDonald, Mary McCarthy, Philip Rahv, and Irving Howe whose commitment to explicating difficult, highbrow literature made them deeply thoughtful, morally ambivalent, allergic to declarations of political certainty, and thus difficult to pin down ideologically (264). From the perspective of *National Review*, then, Bellow's formal virtuosity as a writer and his philosophical depth as a thinker familiar with the various ideas in the Great Books tradition made him not an ideological asset but a liability with unpredictable political sympathies. Whereas movement conservatives had once searched in the fifties and early sixties for great conservative literature marked by moral ambivalence, epistemological ambiguity over ideological rigidity, and a distrust of human-made solutions to intractable social problems, they were increasingly making aesthetic judgments using a hardening set of ideological axioms that *National Review* stamped with the authenticating term "conservative" in order to purge those who did not further the Buckley-defined cause for political power via the Republican Party.[4]

Although difficult to see at the time, the advantage of hindsight helps one grasp how *National Review*'s seemingly odd critical reaction to *Mr. Sammler's Planet* marked an important step in the conservative movement's ongoing shift away from the highbrow literary field as a semiautonomous site of sociopolitical significance and value. In his December 1970 *National Review* article "Secession of the Intellectuals," senior editor Jeffrey Hart exemplified this shift when he appropriated the neoconservative notion of an adversary culture but then revamped it to fit the highly specific definition of conservatism propagated at *National Review*. At first, Hart reiterated the neoconservative story of how the literary adversary culture was once a healthy phenomenon during a mythical golden age of modernism. At that time, the audience for the adversary culture knew how to use the antagonistic nature of highbrow modernist literature "without permitting it to destroy through its very critical power and its mythogenic capacities what Yeats called 'the common good of life' . . . [making] the adversary art function as it should within society" (Hart, 1280). But with the post–World War II higher education boom, the literary "avant garde, vastly expanded and coarsened, has become a kind of mass adversary culture, and it has become institutionalized" in the American university. Now, "[i]nsofar as the mass adversary culture feels the need to translate attitude and [literary] style into formulation and idea," Hart lamented, "it reaches for the most readily available structures of critical political ideas: to liberalism and radicalism" (1280). The problem with literary fiction in the wake of the sixties, Hart implied, was that its unique form of cultural capital had become inextricably linked with the university-based adversary culture and its cadre of "liberal elites" who sought to radically demystify the beloved mythical "America" of conservatives.

What Hart revealed here was the crucial difference between how neoconservatives and movement conservatives were deploying the phrase "adversary culture" in relation to postwar fiction. For neoconservatives, the sixties adversary culture was a distortion of literary modernism that could be corrected by retaining and policing the boundary between a high culture nourished by an intellectual elite and a disconcerting low culture weakened by mass entertainment via the capitalist marketplace. Since capitalism was a practical, effective system but with many inherent flaws and unwanted social byproducts, as Irving Kristol famously argued in *Two Cheers for Capitalism* (1978), it should be given only "two cheers" instead of a full-throated three. As ex-socialists weary of utopian fervor, Kristol and other neoconservatives saw "the impulse to give three cheers for any social, economic, or political system as expressing a dangerous – because it is misplaced – enthusiasm" (*Two Cheers*, ix). Neoconservatives believed that if movement conservatives continued to treat capitalism as an ideal system of social order, they would unwittingly undermine the very traditions they purported to conserve.[5] Similar to traditionalists like Russell Kirk and Whittaker Chambers, neoconservatives thought capitalism must be subordinated to what Bellow calls the "essentials," such as religiously inflected moral duties and values, social cohesion, and deep-rooted cultural habits, all of which were transcendent themes best represented indirectly in the semiautonomous field of highbrow literature (*Mr. Sammler's Planet*, 216). For movement conservatives, on the other hand, the adversary culture was part and parcel of a shadowy network of liberal cultural institutions and media enterprises that were preventing them from exercising political power precisely because troublesome countercultural bohemians used highbrow literary prestige to attack capitalism and mock middle-class philistinism. In an internal White House memo sent to President Nixon in 1970, though, even the neoconservative-minded politician Daniel Patrick Moynihan illustrated the deep suspicion of the adversary culture at the highest levels of conservative power. "No doubt there is a struggle going on in this country of the kind the Germans used to call a *Kulturkampf* [culture struggle]. The adversary culture which dominates all channels of information transfer and opinion formulation has never been stronger," Moynihan wrote, tacitly referencing the American university, major newspapers and journals, and the sphere of American arts and letters, "and as best I can tell it has come near silencing the representatives of traditional America" (qtd. in Hartman, 51). In a crucial inversion of the neoconservative reverence for the sacredness of capital-L "Literature," movement conservatives used the term adversary culture to undermine the hallowed aura of highbrow fiction itself. By exposing the snobbish, stereotypical progressive's taste in complex literary texts that interrogate the status quo as little more than an effect of a given liberal's privileged subject position in the educated "new class," movement conservatives were solidifying their double register of literary value that could, and gradually would, alternate strategically between highbrow elite taste and lowbrow populist grievance.

4.3 Thomas Pynchon's Genealogies of Fascism in Postwar Conservatism and the Hazards of Literary Prestige

If one understands this split in the post-sixties American Right regarding the relationship between the adversary culture and highbrow literary forms, it is easier to grasp their even more divergent reactions to Thomas Pynchon's early career *oeuvre* in general and to the publication of *Gravity's Rainbow* in particular, a watershed text in highbrow postmodernism and, for conservatives of all stripes, the most prominent incarnation of the adversary culture's literary strategy of reshaping the political valences of highbrow cultural capital. Released in 1973 just as conservative traditionalism and its appreciation of "great literature" was being eclipsed by free-market individualism as the animating force of movement conservatism, *Gravity's Rainbow* was largely ignored by Buckley and the staff at *National Review*, failing even to receive a standard-length review in the back of the magazine, despite the fact that Pynchon was well known to *National Review* since the beginning of his career.[6] By the early seventies, the conservative death-of-the-novel discourse, which I outlined earlier in this chapter, had so thoroughly saturated the conservative movement that *Gravity's Rainbow* was barely visible on its cultural radar, a remarkable departure from Buckley's insistence in the mid-fifties that the intellectual reputation of *National Review* was bound up with its aesthetic judgments of new, important American literature.[7]

For neoconservatives, by contrast, *Gravity's Rainbow* was an important book to be reckoned with, despite their various aesthetic and political critiques of Pynchon as a novelist of the adversary culture. "The acclaim conferred upon Thomas Pynchon's *Gravity's Rainbow* probably reveals more about the uncertain state of our literary culture," David Thorburn wrote in "A Dissent on Pynchon," his *Commentary* review of *Gravity's Rainbow*, "than about Pynchon's novel itself, which is brilliant in parts but confused and exceedingly tedious as a whole" (68). Published as the social conflagrations of the sixties were flaming out, *Gravity's Rainbow* emerged,

Thorburn argued, just as left-wing "reviewers sympathetic to that fashionable radicalism whose chief features are a contempt for 'established' culture and a blind devotion to apocalyptic styles and gestures" were searching for an epic literary testament to subversive forms of sociopolitical freedom (68). Since publishing *V.* (1963), Thorburn noted, Pynchon's primary concern had always been "human freedom, or perhaps more accurately the absence of human freedom," a theme that led Pynchon to "expose the men and especially the theoretical systems that stand in totalitarian opposition to individual fulfillment" (69). Thorburn claimed that this thematic anxiety in Pynchon's work compelled him to make each character a flat, hollow "human cipher whose inner life is in essence almost indistinguishable from that of other characters in this [novel's] obsessively self-ratifying world" (70). Thorburn argued that the ultimate effect of the novel's one-dimensional characters – despite a progressive, Pynchonian vision that raged against injustice and man-made suffering – seemed "to ally him with the characters he wishes to condemn and expose," such as the appalling Nazi SS officer Captain Blicero included in both *V.* and *Gravity's Rainbow* (70). Just as Nazis "manipulate and encage their victims," Thorburn concluded, subtly threading the trope of New Leftist fascism into his critique, "so Pynchon the novelist rules his characters, denying or reducing their potential for individuation out of an unyielding and systematic need to fit them to general meanings that collide with or, at best, simply ignore their allegedly individual natures" (70). Thorburn admitted that even though Pynchon's immense talents "justify comparison with Dickens and Joyce," his novels had yet to yield "fully to the claims of art" because he did not include serious objections to his own set of ideological commitments (70). Instead, Thorburn implied, Pynchon chose to write experimentally interesting novels, to be sure, but ones whose left-wing didacticism did not appreciate the properly semiautonomous nature of the literary field, and thus the processes and forms of cultural prestige internal to that field. From this neoconservative perspective, Pynchon's literary project ostensibly dovetailed with the cultural authoritarianism of twentieth-century totalitarian movements that contaminated high art with political propaganda, a socio-aesthetic desecration that ultimately demystified forms of bourgeois selfhood rooted in the discourse of Western humanism.

While I maintain that this neoconservative interpretation of Pynchon's literary project established in the immediate wake of *Gravity's Rainbow* is shortsighted and flawed, I wish to draw attention to how it nevertheless opens up an underappreciated dimension of Pynchon's work – namely, how Pynchon not only indexed the rise of modern conservatism in his writings, but also how he would confront his own flawed assumptions about the American Right during its electoral rise to power, leading him to reimagine some of the key thematic and formal elements of postmodernism that conservatives learned to exploit for their own ends in relation to the paradoxical double register of conservative literary taste. For most of Pynchon's career, critics have rightly started from the premise that his political sympathies are somewhere on the Left, broadly construed, and then they have gone on to trace the gaps and incongruities in his overarching progressive vision.[8] Within the sphere of professional literary studies, the desire to map the specific cultural politics of Pynchon's writings has taken center stage in recent decades.[9] In the most significant contributions to the "Political Pynchon" turn in Pynchon studies – for example, Cyrus R. K. Patell's *Negative Liberties: Morrison, Pynchon, and the Problem of Liberal Ideology* (2001), Samuel Thomas's *Pynchon and the Political* (2011), Joanna Freer's *Thomas Pynchon and American Counterculture* (2014), and Sean Carswell's *Occupy Pynchon: Politics After* Gravity's Rainbow (2017) – the relationship between Pynchon and American politics is usually contextualized within and against the sixties countercultural Left. In other words, the left-wing ideological labels that critics usually apply to Pynchon tend to be fluctuating variables whose very legibility depends on the American Right as a seemingly solid rhetorical constant. Training my focus more exclusively on Pynchon and the modern Right, by contrast, I aim to interrogate not only the basic assumptions that allow American conservatism to serve as the background against which these intra-ideological debates concerning Pynchon's leftism are enacted, but also to illuminate the nagging problem in the "political Pynchon" scholarly debate concerning Pynchon's skepticism toward real-world political procedures and institutions and his ostensible penchant for, in Sean McCann and Michael Szalay's words, "magical thinking" (McCann and Szalay, 468).

Initially, Pynchon's explicit interest in the modern Right began in his first novel, *V.*, wherein he portrays postwar conservatism not just as an amusing, foolish ideology which parrots fascistic rhetoric as it struggles to make sense of an emerging technological order that threatens human autonomy, but also, and most notably for my argument, as an ideology largely for philistine simpletons.[10] The fact that Pynchon concerned himself at all with the American right wing in the early sixties was itself noteworthy, since fifties-style political conservatism was widely seen as a philosophy that had been discredited by Franklin D. Roosevelt's expansive vision of progressive liberalism and essentially rendered obsolete by the Eisenhower administration's preservation and tacit ratification of New Deal welfare programs. Pynchon hinted at this political environment when he wrote about Melvin, a folk singer from the Whole Sick Crew, whose songs are "in militant opposition to Fascism, private capital, the Republican administration and Westbrook Pegler," the latter of whom was a cranky newspaper columnist made famous by his opposition to the New Deal (*V.*, 395). But Pynchon reserved his strongest ridicule for the character Mafia Winsome, a parody of Ayn Rand as the most popular advocate at the time for free-market capitalism in the wake of her bestselling novel *Atlas Shrugged* (1957). On the surface, Pynchon uses Rand's infamous ideological rigidity as comic relief, noting that her deployment of lowbrow genre tropes reveals her own inability to think beyond "anything more demanding than sledgehammer emotions" and "disturbingly predicable" racial stereotypes (132), all characteristics that lead her husband, Rooney Winsome, to admit late in the novel: "My wife ... is a fucking Fascist" (388). Like other liberal-leaning writers, Pynchon invokes a simplified version of the trope of American Fascism to show how an authoritarian right-wing ethos could emerge from the combination of a wealthy elite and the uncultured populist masses. However, below the surface, Pynchon uses Rand and the American Right for more than just easy laughs, and his invocation of right-wing fascism is not quite as flippant as it may seem. Pynchon frequently drifts into the realm of satirical caricature when writing about Mafia Winsome/Ayn Rand, but he also perceptively illustrates the intra-ideological debates in postwar American conservatism through the Winsomes. Although a conservative white Southerner, Rooney Winsome is disturbed when he realizes that his wife thinks that he personally hates African Americans. Mafia, "in nearly total ignorance about the Southern feeling toward Negroes," Rooney laments, "used 'nigger' as a term of hatred" (*V.*, 129). Throughout their marriage, Rooney does not have the heart "to tell her it was not a matter of love, hate, like or not like so much as an inheritance you lived with" (129). By portraying Rooney as representative of the Southern white elite and Mafia as a stand-in for aggrieved white populists, Pynchon allegorizes the racial split in midcentury conservatism in a way that also tracks the cultural division between the benevolent highbrow racism of traditionalist conservatives and the ugly lowbrow prejudice of the Right's paranoid fringe.

For Pynchon, these intra-ideological debates within postwar American conservatism illuminate, in some ways, the genocidal horrors of the mid-twentieth century that make up the unspeakable traumatic core of *V.* (the novel) and V. (the mysterious, reoccurring female character), with all narrative lines either building up to, or moving outward from, World

War II. Echoing Hannah Arendt's famous argument about the imperial roots of the Holocaust in *The Origins of Totalitarianism*, Pynchon writes a chapter set in German-occupied Southwest Africa in the early twenties in which the German characters reminisce about the concentration camps built during the Boer War and the subsequent genocide of Herero and Hottentot peoples in 1904 at the hands of German General Lother von Trotha.[11] As Pynchon's quasi-omniscient third-person narrator notes: "Allowing for natural causes during those unnatural years, von Trotha … is reckoned to have done away with about 60,000 people. This is only 1 percent of six million, but still pretty good" (265). The irony, of course, is that throughout the chapter, the German imperialists see their society as the pinnacle of civilization, replete with humanist mantras about dignity and natural rights; however, an even greater irony is that they do not believe that their genocidal violence invalidates their humanist principles, but that these ostensibly universal principles do not apply universally to certain groups of people on the categorical borderline of humanity. As one character puts it later: "To have humanism we must first be convinced of our humanity" (356). In a fascinating inversion of Bellow's faith in the Great Books tradition, Pynchon implies that when the cultural greatness of "Western civilization" is coupled with the technological rationalism that also emerged out of the same Western intellectual tradition, the result is a proto-fascistic fantasy of state-sanctioned extermination. This familiar Pynchonian theme – a much-discussed literary reiteration of Max Horkheimer and Theodor Adorno's argument in *Dialectic of Enlightenment* that Western rationalism morphs into domination and violence – revealed a crucial paradox about modern American conservatives: On the one hand, they were the self-proclaimed lovers of natural law, individual rights, and human autonomy, proudly fetishizing an imaginary American founding rooted in the bounty of Western civilization; but on other hand, they consistently talked about their alleged subordinates as pests and parasites. "If you ever tried to create [wealth]," Ayn Rand's doppelgänger Mafia Winsome says to her husband during an argument, "instead of live off what other people create, you'd understand" (386). Postwar conservatives, in Pynchon's political cosmology, were another self-righteous and peculiar Christian humanist faction in the genealogy of modern Western political history who were quick to dehumanize and dominate others. At this early point in his career, Pynchon did not just depict modern American conservatism as both a symptom of this "dialectic of enlightenment" and a self-conscious, anxious reaction to its very threat of domination, but he did it using a parodic vocabulary of intellectual superiority that postwar conservatives distained and liberals praised.

Pynchon both deepened his analysis of modern conservatism and reduced the rhetoric of political condescension in his second novel, *The Crying of Lot 49* (1966), a work commonly seen, and taught, as an ur-text of postmodernism, but less commonly regarded as a serious interrogation of modern conservatism, despite the fact that its famous literary protagonist, Oedipa Mass, is a self-proclaimed member of the "Young Republicans" and the novel was published in the same year Reagan was elected governor of California (76).[12] What is important, for my purposes, is how Pynchon's interrogation of the American Right is hidden or nested inside his broader, more recognizable critique of technology, which ultimately illuminates Pynchon's persistent, though transformed, parody of conservatives as philistines trafficking in unsophisticated low cultural discourse. At first glance, in an apparent throwback to *V.*, it appears like Pynchon aims to satirize the American Right's anxiety over "big government" by juxtaposing advances in technology and anxieties over individualism in the character of Oedipa. In Mark Greif's words, Pynchon's central concern in *V.* is that "a confusion was emerging between the inanimate and the human, with a division of human beings into replaceable, insertable parts. In *[Lot 49]*, he starts to show how *removed* parts could be reused, and how they persisted, by themselves, without any context of values" (241). Oedipa, for instance, is worried about how the Volkswagen Beetle – the Nazi "people's car" – migrated from Nazi Germany to the United States "cut off from the values that invented it" (Greif, 242). As a generically conservative suburban housewife in the beginning of the novel confident in the basic continuity between big corporations, powerful military institutions, and unmitigated individual liberty, Oedipa eventually wonders if there is a glitch in her naïve ideological universe, if perhaps individual autonomy, a vaunted American ideal, is not only incompatible with the Cold War military–industrial complex that grew out of World War II, but doomed by the very technology once believed to liberate humanity which had just been put to such deadly use by totalitarian governments.

However, Pynchon does not make Oedipa the sole representative embodiment of the political Right in *Lot 49*, but also Mike Fallopian, a member of the fictional ultra-conservative Peter Pinguid Society, who is suspicious of the American government and thus refuses to use the official national postal service, opting instead for a shadowy underground mail service. On the surface, according to Richard Hofstadter's famous formulation, Fallopian embodies the "paranoid style" associated with the

Goldwater movement, a crude discourse marked by "heated exaggeration, suspiciousness, and conspiratorial fantasy," which conceives of existential threats "directed against a nation, a culture, a way of life whose fate affects not [just the paranoid] himself alone but millions of others" (Hofstadter, 4–5). In this surface-level reading, Fallopian's individualistic defiance against the US government is as misguided as his "left-leaning friends" in the John Birch Society, for Fallopian would simply be engaging in a form of pseudo-resistance that only reinstates the Enlightenment assumptions that gave birth to the sinisterly massive techno-rational governmental apparatus in the first place (*Lot 49*, 50). However, as Fallopian's first conversation with Oedipa and Metzger reveals, Pynchon does not merely depict Fallopian as a right-wing Bircherite buffoon over whom a young, hip (presumably) liberal reading audience should feel morally superior.

Whereas the Birchers named their society after John Birch – supposedly the first casualty of the Cold War, since he was killed by Chinese Communists in August 1945 – Fallopian notes that the Peter Pinguid Society is grounded in a deeper history and a more sophisticated political theory. The Peter Pinguid Society, Fallopian says, was named after the eponymous captain of a Confederate warship who battled a Russian vessel in 1864, and who eventually became "appalled at what had to be some military alliance between abolitionist Russia . . . and a Union that paid lip-service to abolition while it kept its own industrial laborers in a kind of wage-slavery" (*Lot 49*, 50). When Metzger interrupts the conversation, noting that Fallopian makes it sound like Peter Pinguid was "against industrial capitalism," which would obviously "disqualify [Pinguid] as any kind of anti-Communist figure," Pynchon shows that Metzger has mistakenly aligned Fallopian with the John Birch Society and simplistic, reactionary conservatism in general (50). Correcting Metzger, Fallopian says that his response sounds like the naïve Bircher logic of "good guys and bad guys," which never allows one "to get to any of the underlying truth" (51). Unlike the John Birch Society's uncritical worship of limited government and free markets, the Peter Pinguid Society follows Pinguid in opposing industrial capitalism because it leads to Marxism. "Underneath" industrial capitalism and Marxism, Fallopian explains, "both are part of the same creeping horror" (51). Finally, Metzger understands, realizing that Fallopian is against "industrial *anything*" (51, italics in original). In this scene, then, which is sometimes misread as a critique of Bircherite Goldwaterism via Fallopian, Pynchon actually uses Fallopian to invoke the anti-materialist vein of traditionalist conservatism that echoes Whittaker Chambers's critique of capitalism as intrinsically incompatible with any definition of genuine, tradition-based conservatism: "Conservatism is alien to the very nature of capitalism," Chambers wrote to Buckley in the fifties, "whose love of life and growth is perpetual change ... [and] I claim that capitalism is not, and by its essential nature cannot conceivably be, conservative" (*Odyssey of a Friend*, 228–29).[13] Like Chambers, Fallopian believes that to posit capitalism as the foundation of postwar conservatism, as Birchers and later libertarians attempted, would be to root conservatism in the same kind of materialism that undergirds communism. Pynchon reinforces this point later in the novel during another conversation between Metzger and Fallopian in which Fallopian objects to young engineers signing "over all their [patent] rights to a monster like Yoyodyne" (88). Metzger tells Fallopian that "[y]ou're so right-wing you're left-wing," which only makes sense if "right-wing" is tantamount to corporate capitalism (88). For Pynchon, Fallopian is far from a characterological model for political action – not least of all because his anti-industrialist conservatism is founded on white supremacist Confederate rhetoric, which echoes the language of real postwar American agrarian traditionalists. However, Pynchon implies that Fallopian's materialist analysis should not be ridiculed too quickly, for Fallopian echoes Pynchon's own views in his later essay "Is It O.K. To Be A Luddite?" (which I explore at greater length subsequently in this chapter), identifying genuine problems of transcendence and personal meaning in the postwar United States that also are part and parcel of Oedipa's novel-length quest.[14]

At strategic moments in *Lot 49*, then, Pynchon only seems to ventriloquize Hofstadter's influential, though overly simplistic, argument that the postwar conservatism movement could be explained by anxiety-based "status politics," a pathological form of political "grousing," which expresses itself "more in vindictiveness, in sour memories, in the search for scapegoats, than in realistic proposals for positive action" (Hofstadter, 53–54). However, defying the movement conservative stereotype of the liberal-leaning writer who accrues cultural capital by condescendingly portraying conservatives, Pynchon's depictions of Fallopian and Oedipa forestall the notion that conservatives are merely lowbrow fools whom sophisticated readers of his postmodern novel should mock. In a much-cited moment of narrative metalepsis toward the end of the novel, when the third-person omniscient narrator intrudes into the story to address Oedipa's quest for "a real alternative to the exitlessness, to the absence of surprise to life, that harrows the head of every American you know, and you too, sweetie," Pynchon emphasizes the quiet desperation lurking beneath the vacuous life of "every American" Oedipa knows in her parochial, middle-class conservative social circle (170). But, as Christopher Douglas points out, Pynchon still does not align Oedipa in this passage with Goldwaterite conservatism, for "unlike the Goldwater 'New Right' that, in a paranoid style sought to eliminate a subversive enemy, Oedipa's paranoid style is aimed at finding (and maybe joining) this pre-political conspiratorial group of the dispossessed" (175–76). Pynchon sympathizes with American conservative ennui, validating the anxieties that catalyze their search for larger existential meaning, while simultaneously condemning (usually via satire) the noxious ways in which conservatives convert those anxieties into political action, identifying only with the pseudo-dispossessed of the white middle class. Ultimately, at this unique moment in postwar American political history – *after* Goldwater's spectacular defeat in 1964 but *before* Nixon's miraculous comeback presidential victory in 1968 – Pynchon seems acutely aware, in Casey Shoop's words, that "the New Right poses challenges immanent to the logic of postmodernism," for the form of right-wing paranoia that grips Fallopian and Oedipa "is not simply a condition of interpretative dysfunction or illness but the prospective ground of a new political agency" that must be critiqued carefully (52).

In *Gravity's Rainbow* (1973), Pynchon reiterates the motif of a vicious circle embedded in a specific, triumphalist vision of "Western civilization" championed by movement conservatives, but Pynchon also seems more careful than ever about critiquing the fascistic rhetoric of the American Right without letting himself fall into the conservative scapegoat role of the superior, self-righteous liberal novelist. Set in the final months of World War II, one of the novel's key narrative arcs tracks the development of rocket technology, especially the V-2 rocket, by Nazi scientists such as Wernher von Braun and that technology's eventual voyage across the Atlantic to the United States, along with its Nazi creators. For the third consecutive novel, Pynchon not only highlights the notion that European Fascism had been smuggled into the postwar United States via Nazi scientists and their wartime technology, but also its corollary that Americans, especially modern conservatives, had unwittingly embraced this toxic import and rebranded it "American" with the language of racism and jingoistic nationalism. In this sense, the political fault line between Right and Left in the novel – that is, the fascist "System" on the Right buttressed by large multi-national corporations, and the loose "Counterforce" of misfits on the countercultural Left – is also an allegory for the American political scene of the early seventies, which saw the Nixon-led Right at its peak as the New Left declined. Pynchon encapsulates this seemingly unbridgeable political polarization in one of the quirkiest epigraphs in postwar fiction: "'What?' –

Richard Nixon" (629). Although Pynchon certainly had reservations about political resistance in many of its forms, as Joanna Freer writes, he was compelled nevertheless to commit himself to "the political values and methods of the New Left" against the oblivious nihilism of the Right (45).[15] This commitment seems to have led Pynchon to conceptualize Nazi Fascism in ways that mimicked the familiar New Left and Black Power indictments of postwar America as a latent fascist nation. At different moments in *Gravity's Rainbow*, Pynchon aligns fascism with standardized groupthink, bourgeois cultural normativity that secretly revels in sadomasochistic sexual practices, and obscure machinations by faceless bureaucrats to maintain strict control over social rituals, especially those associated with sexual expression, and plunge the country into war. For instance, the life of Tyrone Slothrop, the novel's nominal protagonist, reads like a New Leftist parable about the evils of authoritarianism lurking in large social institutions and the professionalized discourse of trained experts. As an infant, Slothrop was an object of research for the massive corporation I. G. Farben and his sexual reflexes underwent Pavlovian conditioning, which then caused Slothrop to become an object of inquiry for postwar intelligence agencies in the novel's present because this conditioning mysteriously produced a strong statistical correlation between the places he has sex and the places where German rockets land in London. "His erection hums from a certain distance," Pynchon writes, "like an instrument installed, wired by Them into his body as a colonial outpost here in our raw and clamorous world, another office representing Their white Metropolis far away" (290). By creating Slothrop, whose penis predicts the fall of Germany's rockets resembling "simple steel erection[s]," Pynchon alludes to a wide range of critiques popularized by the New Left and Black Power,[16] all of which culminate in a wide-ranging moral indictment: Not only that the twin military–industrial complexes of the Axis and Allied powers during World War II were reckless systems designed to make money and kill millions, but that this systemic death-drive still animated the conservative Cold War US nation-state (329).

However, as evidenced in both the radically fragmented form and self-critical content of the novel's fourth major section, "The Counterforce," Pynchon reveals profound doubts about the efficacy of his literary-political project, doubts which metaphorically delineate the rhetorical complexity of postwar conservatism's cultural double register of highbrow elite taste and lowbrow populism. A political denouement that symbolically interrogates the dissolution of the sixties counterculture, "The Counterforce" section is Pynchon's attempt to show that the counterforce fails, according to Cyrus Patell, because it "ends up merely replicating the military-industrial complex that it was formed to combat" (97). In his incisive work on this countercultural declension theme, Jeffrey S. Baker argues that "the Counterforce's effort, like that of the committed radicals of the sixties' counterculture, is highly problematized, on the one hand, by their inability to conceive of an organizational alternative to the binary pair of Their rationalized systems, and, on the other hand, by a complete lack of structure and organization" (109). While these scholars make good historical-political points, the failure of the Counterforce should also be read as authorial self-critique in relation to Pynchon's own compromised role in the larger literary field. In his critical work on Pynchon and race, David Witzling outlines the problem well: "To write an encyclopedic narrative is to participate in a politics of knowledge that is difficult to separate conceptually or practically from the powerful economic and political institutions of contemporary nation-states, a notion that is encoded in postmodern fiction's frequently radical yet also cavalier irony" (14). Witzling correctly argues not only that Pynchon's privileged cultural authority as a "highbrow" white male author is inextricable from a historical type of cultural capital associated with the old bourgeoisie, but that evidence exists within the very form of Pynchon's postmodern fiction which suggests that he is aware of this cultural-political dilemma.[17]

On the one hand, what Witzling identifies as the radical dimension of postmodern irony is apparent when Pynchon, always suspicious of the strict divide between a conservative modernist "high culture" and popular "low culture," inserts his signature silly songs and reoccurring gags into *Gravity's Rainbow* to draw attention to the familiar countercultural tactics of comic transgression and anarchic subversion characteristic of Yippie individualism – what Freer calls Pynchon's Yippie-style "guerilla pranksterism" – pioneered by people like Abbie Hoffmann in order to delegitimize official institutions of power ranging from the family to the federal state (63).[18] Echoing Wilhelm Reich's famous claim in another canonical New Leftist text, *The Mass Psychology of Fascism*, that the heteronormative bourgeois family structure is the "germ cell" of the fascist state, Pynchon suggests that subversive political action begins not in universal abstractions voiced from nowhere but in the private domestic sphere, for he treats the authoritarianism of the traditional patriarchal family as a microcosm latent with the repressive, large-scale violence of fascism (Reich, 104). As one character puts it near the end of the novel, "if S and M could be established universally, at the family level, the state would wither away" (751). Channeling the discourse of the New Left at key points in the narrative,

Pynchon understands both the postwar American nuclear family and the Cold War state's capitalist–military apparatus as interconnected manifestations of the same kind of "fatherland," wherein an authoritarian community threatens human freedom with the techno-industrial madness of state power. In these celebratory countercultural moments in the novel, Pynchon implies that the kind of freedom required is of the philosophically negative sort – as conceived of by the political philosopher Isaiah Berlin – a freedom *from* repressive control imposed on unwilling subjects.

However, on the other hand, Pynchon remains aware of, and troubled by, the more cavalier dimensions of postmodern irony. If countercultural activists are too insouciant, they are apt to conflate not only the kind of negative liberty prized by the counterculture and the specious appeal of capitalist individualism prized by postwar conservatives, but also the radical language of postmodern critique and the arrogant language of liberal cultural elitism. In "The Counterforce" section, Pynchon implies that one of the core reasons for the implosion of the sixties was that its countercultural coalition simultaneously overestimated the practical effects of irony and skepticism in the public sphere and underestimated the power of money and status. Pynchon reveals that progressives, Witzling argues, were too enchanted with "a kind of free-floating irony that is ostensibly threatening to all who encounter it, but that, in practice, is more likely to be exercised and enjoyed by those who are in safely privileged cultural positions" (15–16). In the much-cited Krupp dinner party scene late in the novel, Pynchon's dejected metafictional narrator asserts that the members of the Counterforce are not "in a better position to disarm, de-penis and dismantle the Man" because they "are as schizoid, as double-minded in the massive presence of money, as any of the rest of us" (727). Toward the end of *Gravity's Rainbow*, then, Pynchon leaves readers with visions of "the failed Counterforce, the glamorous ex-rebels, half-suspected but still enjoying the official immunity and sly love, camera-worthy wherever they carry on . . . doomed pet freaks" (727). As Freer rightly notes, Pynchon's sarcastic language of status-conscious glamour bears a striking resemblance to Tom Wolfe's language of conservative satire in Wolfe's "Radical Chic," a widely read essay that appeared in *New York Magazine* (June 1970) and eviscerated rich, white liberals who – in their condescension toward the striving, conservative middle class – professed an intense, romanticized identification with primitive, lower-class "radicals." Written in a comic style that "consolidated many Americans' distrust of the kind of cross-racial identifications that characterized late sixties liberalism," Stephen Schryer writes, Wolfe narrates an absurdist account of how the composer Leonard

Bernstein held a fundraising party for the Black Panthers in order "to differentiate himself from the middle class" (*Maximum Feasible Participation*, 113). Since radical chic "is only radical in style," Wolfe points out, not in political ideology, "in its heart it is part of Society and its traditions" of social climbing (79).

While Pynchon does not agree with Wolfe's reactionary point in substance, he nevertheless acknowledges the power of Wolfe's rhetorical framing, for in this infamous essay black radicals become the "doomed pet freaks" of conservative discourse, and their white liberal sympathizers little more than "camera-worthy [posers] wherever they carry on" (727). What Pynchon seems to appreciate in Wolfe's essay is the germ of a literary-sociological point that Bourdieu would later elucidate theoretically regarding the apparent structural homology in subject positions between the literary avant-garde and the economically dominated political vanguard. The highbrow "cultural producers, who occupy the economically dominated and symbolically dominant position within the field of cultural production," Bourdieu writes, "tend to feel solidarity with the occupants of the economically and culturally dominated positions within the field of class relations ... [However,] [s]uch alliances, based on homologies of position combined with profound differences in condition, are not exempt from misunderstandings and even bad faith" (*Field of Cultural Production*, 44). From the early seventies to the end of the twentieth century, Wolfe would be lauded by movement conservatives for a type of satirical New Journalism that highlighted the frequent misunderstandings and occasional bad faith practices that occurred between white liberal cultural elites and their economically dominated allies. However, the rhetorical power of Wolfe's satires was also not lost on Pynchon. As Pynchon explains in relation to the fall of the Counterforce: "The Man has a branch office in each of our brains, his corporate emblem is a white albatross, each local rep has a cover known as the Ego, and their mission in this world is Bad Shit" (727). For Pynchon, acutely aware of the various cultural and institutional barriers to radical change, Wolfe's distinctive brand of reactionary satire was a mode of conservative discourse that trafficked in populist resentment, to be sure, but one that still had to be taken seriously since countercultural figures were as susceptible as anyone else when it came to ego-worship and savoring their own social prestige. From this perspective, one can see why Pynchon composes the Krupp dinner party scene as a rewrite of Wolfe's "Radical Chic," but with a few crucial differences. Whereas Wolfe mocks white liberal elites' oblivious admiration for black radicals, Pynchon reconfigures the sociopolitical class lines – transforming Wolfe's liberal elite into a conservative German elite and the Black Panthers into the Counterforce characters Pig Bodine and Roger Mexico – in a way that mimics the satirical spirit of Wolfe's essay, but not Wolfe's underlying conservative politics. The Krupp dinner party ends with a moment of "culinary pranksterism," as Bodine and Roger employ the "repulsive stratagem" to gross out the high-society guests, loudly asking for disgusting dishes made from human snot, pus, menstrual blood, and feces, which causes the guests to abscond in repulsion (729–30). Although some scholars read this scene of Yippie-style transgression as politically redemptive, I want to stress that Pynchon retains a much more uneasy awareness of the co-optive power of conservative discourse.[19] While Roger nauseates the guests, he sees that his lover Jessica leaves the party weeping on the arm of Jeremy. "Does Roger have a second of pain right here?" the narrator asks, and then responds: "Sure. You would too. You might even begin to question your cause" (731). The "cause" in question here, Pynchon implies, is the political efficacy of this coordinated act, for even though it produced some "well-bred gagging," it did not catalyze any real or lasting political efficacy, making it just a minor bright spot in the Counterforce's slow deterioration, a futile flash of *schadenfreude* and leftist back-patting that is vulnerable to Wolfean reactionary satire (730).[20]

In the novel's final pages, Pynchon deepens his skepticism of the efficacy of highbrow fiction to produce lasting change, instead of just "well-bred gagging" in conservative power circles. Pynchon's strongest suggestion that Nazi Fascism migrated to the United States through the unwitting channels of modern conservatism occurs when the Gottfried-Rocket is aimed directly at the Orpheus Theatre in Los Angles, whose night manager is Richard M. Zhlubb. A surreal parody of Richard M. Nixon, Zhlubb is revealed as a distorted version of the President by the nicknames bestowed upon him by friends, who refer to him both as "Dick" and "the Adenoid" in satirical homage to the nasal inflections of Nixon's voice. Shifting suddenly into a second-person narrative mode here, Pynchon writes that Zhlubb "ushers you [the reader] into a black Managerial Volkswagen," a carryover image from *Lot 49* symbolizing how Nazi technology infiltrated America through the managerial bureaucracies of the state. During this ride, Zhlubb says that he wants to let you, the reader, in on a secret "fantasy about how I'll die":

> Listen to this. It's 3 a.m., on the Santa Monica Freeway, a warm night. All my windows are open. I'm doing about 70, 75. The wind blows in, and from the floor in back lifts a thin plastic bag, a common dry-cleaning bag: it comes floating in the air, moving from behind, the mercury lights turning it white as a ghost . . . it wraps around my head, so supine and transparent

> I don't know it's there really until too late. A plastic shroud, smothering me to my death. (771–72)

In Zhlubb's death fantasy, the transparent plastic bag appears from the back of his Nazi-affiliated Volkswagen, thus emerging out of the history of World War II, and slowly kills him. On the one hand, the transparent bag clearly references the Gottfried-Rocket trained on Southern California, as the phrase "it comes floating in the air" brings the novel full circle and evokes the famous opening line about rockets falling on London during the blitz: "A screaming comes across the sky" (771; 3). Dislocating linear time in signature postmodern fashion, Pynchon shows how the rocket's trajectory, the parabolic "gravity's rainbow" of the title, begins in Nazi Germany and ends in postwar America. On the other hand, though, it appears as if the rocket does not land at all; or if it does, it lands in America not with an explosive bang, but an asphyxiating whisper. Out of this ostensible enigma, Pynchon suggests that the rocket's truly destructive power – not the raw, materialist force of an actual explosion so much as the techno-ideology of Western selfhood – has fallen into the postwar United States and is being "driven" by modern conservatives, who are slowly suffocating on its lethal logic and are only vaguely aware of it in the depths of their paranoid dreams. When movement conservatives boasted about all of the supposedly unique characteristics of "American exceptionalism" – technological advancement, militaristic nationalism, global capitalist markets, the racial fetishization of whiteness, transcendental Western selfhood – that allowed the Allies to defeat the fascist-led Axis powers, they unwittingly reinstated the very historical conditions that led to fascism in the first place, and would perhaps culminate in a new form of fascism in postwar America.

As trenchant as this parody of Nixon may be, Pynchon appears to worry that it functions only as a futile irritant at best, and as an unwitting accelerant of populist conservative discourse at worst. At first glance, the Zhlubb character furiously objects to "what he calls [the] 'irresponsible use of the harmonica,'" an instrument with symbolic linkages to various strands of the sixties counterculture, from Bob Dylan–influenced protest music to Slothrop's harmonica in the Malcolm X set piece in *Gravity's Rainbow* (769). A comic sendup of "Nixon's unambiguously divisive commitment to 'law and order,'" Witzling notes, the "specific satirical message of the episode is that Nixon himself is dividing the polity while hastening us to our collective nuclear doom" (153). Upon closer inspection, though, Zhlubb's annoyance of young rebels "playing harmonicas and even *kazoos*, in full disrespect for the Prohibitions" is only half-serious, since his anger is rhetorically strategic

(771, italics in original). To the dismay of Pynchon's second-person audience (the "you" is coded as a hip, anti-Nixon reader), the glove compartment of the convertible has a large collection of tapes labeled in capital letters: "CHEERING [AFFECTIONATE], CHEERING [ABUSIVE], HOSTILE MOB in an assortment of 22 languages, YESES, NOES, NEGRO SUPPORTERS, WOMEN SUPPORTERS" (771). These contentious soundbites, Zhlubb explains, are merely codes: "We have to talk in *some* kind of code, naturally ... We always have. But none of the codes is that hard to break" (771, italics in original). Nixon's indignant, "Silent Majority" coded rhetoric, Pynchon suggests, is not a particularly sophisticated vehicle for populist resentment, but that *lack of sophistication is precisely the point*; it is a cultural code that is designed to be broken by a liberal cultural elite to accelerate conservative resentment, to lure intellectuals into positioning themselves as targets for Wolfe's "radical chic" slur.

Unlike the harsh parodies of Nixon found in novels by his contemporaries – for example, Ishmael Reed's *The Free-Lance Pallbearers* (1967), Philip Roth's *Our Gang* (1971), and Robert Coover's *The Public Burning* (1977) – Pynchon most thoroughly understands that the satirical exposure of conservative hypocrisy leads not to widespread political enlightenment, but to a deeper chasm of polarizing anger between progressives in the professional-managerial class and working-class whites. Thus, Zhlubb's final words, which are spoken as an air raid siren blares indicating the imminent nuclear destruction awaiting readers on the novel's last page, epitomize Pynchon's warning; "I don't think that's a police siren," he says, "*I don't think* – " (772, italics in original). Although Zhlubb is cut off mid-sentence, Pynchon tacitly warns progressive readers that they should resist the obvious, self-congratulatory reading that would revel in the notion that Nixon simply "does not think," connoting the suicidal stupidity of postwar American conservatism. Instead, anticipating the escalation in conservative populist rhetoric under Reaganism, Pynchon challenges his left-leaning audience to find better, more strategic ways of simultaneously asserting their valid criticisms of reactionary politics while stripping off their smug sense of moral superiority.

4.4 Antinomies of Literary Value: Reaganism and the New Right

Due to its commitment to radical critique, *Gravity's Rainbow* would remain a *cause célèbre* in neoconservative circles with relation to literary value and prestige well into the next two decades. Taken as a supreme example of Pynchon's innovative formal project, the novel became a centerpiece in *Commentary* magazine for debates about the explosion of postmodern novels in, what neoconservatives thought should be seen as, the Age of Bellow. In one particularly long and ambitious article, "The New American Novel" (1975), Robert Alter surveyed the most important fiction written between 1960 and 1975 and concluded that several of the most gifted contemporary American novelists – Norman Mailer, Joseph Heller, Kurt Vonnegut, John Barth, Donald Barthelme, and leading them all, Pynchon – had essentially wasted their talents on "a love of pastiche, parody, slapdash invention; a willful neglect of psychological depth and subtly or consecutiveness of character . . . and, underlying all these, a kind of despairing skepticism, tinged with either exhilaration or hysteria, about the validity of language and the very enterprise of fiction" (44). The real concern for anyone who looked to literature as a serious mode of thought, Alter argued, was that these aesthetic qualities had nihilistic political implications, for postmodern novels deconstructed the notion of the human as a unique self with an essential core, allowing writers to forsake deep, realistic characterization altogether. Without rich and vivid characters, Alter worried, the notion of capital-M "Man" in many of these novels, especially Pynchon's, could only be represented as "equally vile everywhere, whether he is a Nazi, an American, or a Soviet Russian, and so Dresden and Hiroshima are, quite without qualification, the exact equivalent of Auschwitz and Dachau" (46). By contrast, Alter argued that Bellow was "the finest writer of his generation" because he intricately depicted "the minute and manifold impingements of the historical moment and of a specific milieu on the consciousness of an individual" protagonist who learned to sift through the external world of ideas and politics to arrive at the quasi-spiritual universals that undergirded human nature, retaining the properly semiautonomous nature of the highbrow literary field (45).

In his 1976 Nobel Prize lecture, Bellow adopted a similar perspective partly inspired by neoconservatism and devoted a substantial portion of his speech to defending his brand of character-driven realism against Anglo-American postmodernism. Singling out Alain Robbe-Grillet, the experimental French writer generally associated with the *Nouveau Roman*, Bellow criticized the aggressive attacks on literary "character" as an old-fashioned relic of bourgeois individualism. But Bellow's aesthetic critique quickly morphed into a political warning against despotism: "Totalitarian ideologies, too, have attacked bourgeois individualism, sometimes identifying it with property. There is a hint of this in M. Robbe-Grillet's argument. Dislike of personality, bad masks, false being have had political results" ("Nobel Lecture" 292). For Bellow, fiction with an ideological agenda designed to "enlighten" readers by punching through the Melvillean pasteboard mask of social artifice amounted, in the end, to second-rate sociology and the cheap intellectual pleasure of highfalutin circular reasoning. While a novelist should be free to redesign the notion of "character" in whatever way he pleases, Bellow said, "it is nonsense to make such a decision on the theoretical ground that the period marked the apogee of the individual, et cetera, is ended ... Should [intellectuals], when they read novels, find in them only the endorsement of their own opinions? Are we here to play such games?" (294). Bellow's answer, of course, was no: "We are much more limber, versatile, better articulated, there is much more to us – we all feel it" (299). Bellow suggested that the irrepressible human-ness of a traditionally well-crafted literary character burns through any theoretical attempts, especially Marxian or psychoanalytic, to pin human beings down to an ideological corkboard, which in his view would desecrate the independent aesthetic category of the "literary" as such.

Using his Nobel Prize lecture as a transatlantic platform, Bellow sketched out a normative framework of literary prestige that would have been instantly legible to many writers of Bellow's era, from his network of acquaintances and supporters in neoconservative circles to traditionalists like Kirk and Chambers in the conservative movement. For them, a constellation of aesthetic assumptions underpinned any serious definition of "good literature": it depicted contemporary particularities in order to gesture toward enduring themes and universal truths; it spoke to a full and continuous core inner self that was too complex for any one political ideology; it promulgated the humane values of Western culture without being overtly propagandistic; and finally, the genius-author harmonized all of these themes and tropes through the text's organic linkage of form and content. The constitutive political feature of this definition, Irving Kristol wrote, took the form of that well-known contradiction articulated by Trilling and seized on by neoconservatives and traditionalists alike: that the modernist paradigm popularized by writers such as Lawrence, Eliot, Yeats, Kafka, and Faulkner "was incompatible with the dominant socialist and liberal worldviews [of the early twentieth century]. ... To put it another way: the metaphysics of modern 'avant-garde' art and the metaphysics of modern 'progressive' politics were at odds with one another" (*Neoconservatism*, 6). At this point in Bellow's career, fresh off a Nobel Prize win that cemented him in the eyes of many as the descendant of these modernist giants, it looked like he was in a unique position to become the premier spokesman for a vision of cultural conservatism that stressed nuance, particularity, and complexity that saved an older, neo-aristocratic form of cultural capital. However, profound shifts in postwar conservatism erased this opportunity for Bellow, leaving him a seemingly bigoted pariah on the Left and an obsolete oddity on the Right, and even caused Pynchon to continue reconsidering, and struggling with, the ostensible linkage between progressive politics and his own experimental fiction.

Throughout the late seventies and into the eighties, as the Reagan era dawned in Washington, DC, and as Bellow and Pynchon became symbolic figureheads in debates about the value of different forms of highbrow fiction, the conservative movement was quietly finalizing a radically new relationship to the American literary field that had begun in the late sixties. During these decades, conservatives began to decry so-called radical professors who were dismantling the white male American canon of "great literature" while simultaneously gravitating toward mass-market genre fiction as they fully embraced the extreme laissez-faire economics of thinkers like Milton Friedman and distanced themselves in part from traditionalist conservatism's roots in the canonical liberal arts. To understand this ostensible contradiction, one must grasp how movement conservatives rose to the upper echelons of power within the Republican Party in the seventies and engaged in an array of network formation practices and institution-building efforts founded on ideological premises that contributed – sometimes willfully, sometimes inadvertently – toward the perception that highbrow fiction was becoming a kind of coded weapon of the adversarial Left.

The origin of this transformation is visible in what has become known in conservative historiography as the "Powell Memo," a confidential though influential memorandum written by the corporate lawyer (and eventual Nixon-nominated Supreme Court Justice) Lewis F. Powell Jr. in 1971 and subtitled "Attack on American Free Enterprise System." Secretly distributed to the US Chamber of Commerce, Powell's memo made the case that free enterprise was under existential assault and that American businessmen needed to learn how to wage political war, an admittedly difficult task as they had never "been trained or equipped to conduct guerrilla warfare with those who propagandize against the system" (Powell, "The Powel Memo"). The critics who had been trained in guerrilla warfare, Powell argued, were university professors whose "chorus of criticism" regularly showed up in "intellectual and *literary journals*" (my emphasis). Powell assured his readers, though, that free-market advocates, instead of remaining disgruntled loners, could appropriate the organizational models that leftist radicals were using in their long, Gramscian march through the universities. "The strength lies in organization," Powell stressed, "in careful long-range planning and implementation, in consistency of action over an indefinite period of years, in the scale of financing available only through joint effort, and in the political power available only through united action and national organizations" (Powell). In this document, Powell strengthened the already familiar rhetorical dichotomy between radical professors embedded in college humanities departments reading postmodernist and multiculturalist novels and free-market apologists entrenched in conservative think tanks reading Ayn Rand.

One of the most important influences on the growth of conservative think tanks in the coming decades, the Powell Memo outlined a strategic blueprint that would help transform the institutional logic of American conservatism and, inadvertently, its basic orientation to the literary field (Phillips-Fein, *Invisible Hands*, 169). If the "history of conservatism in the sixties is essentially institutional history," in the historian James A. Hijiya's words, in which the Goldwater campaign apparatus broke up into loosely affiliated organizations like the collegiate group Young Americans for Freedom (1960) and the American Conservative Union (1964), the history of conservatism in the seventies is the history of how conservatives translated ideology into political action and widespread electoral success through the creation of larger and more powerful networks of conservative institutions – most notably, Phyllis Schlafly's lobbying group the Eagle Forum (1972), the immensely influential think tank the Heritage Foundation (1973), the conservative public interest law firm the Pacific Legal Foundation (1973), the Committee for the Survival of a Free Congress (1974), and the ultraconservative renovation of the Hoover Institute at Stanford University in 1975 (Hijiya, "The Conservative 1960s," 203).

This robust conservative infrastructure was founded and operated by key members of the "New Right" – for example, innovative campaign direct-mail pioneer Richard Viguerie, Young Americans for Freedom cofounder Howard Phillips, Heritage Foundation cofounder and later Moral Majority organizer Paul Weyrich, and Nixon campaign strategist Kevin Phillips – who would go on to advocate for Reaganite conservatism's signature combination of free-market capitalism and right-wing social populism that disparaged high culture as the domain of liberal elites. Throughout the seventies, as Rick Perlstein points out, the Heritage Foundation and other institutions assisted several reactionary populist movements that sought to ban public school textbooks and recommended summer reading literature that promoted atheism, communism, and what the New Right disdainfully called "secular humanism." For the two most well-known conservative education campaigners, a married couple from rural Texas named Mel and Norma Gabler, Kurt Vonnegut's postmodern masterpiece *Slaughterhouse-Five* about the US-led firebombing of Dresden during World War II was "a particular Gabler bête noir" of anti-Americanism (Perlstein, *Invisible Bridge*, 292–93). The Gablers even objected to an anthology of short stories featuring Hemingway and Faulkner, two pillars of American modernism whom traditionalist conservatives at midcentury had regarded with lukewarm respect and profound reverence, respectively (293).

In a 1975 syndicated column, Kevin Phillips made sense of the shifting cultural tastes of the New Right by delineating the features that made up what he called the Buckley-led postwar Old Right and the New Right he had aligned himself with, arguing that the defining difference was the former group's elitism and the latter's populist anger. Phillips claimed that while conservatives who came up through "the older Buckley-oriented 'Conservative Movement' regard ideological conservatism as a surviving high church unhappily now practiced only by the elite handful who have kept uncontaminated by mass culture and politics," the New Right "is designedly anti-elitist – preferring mobilization of Levittown, Georgia, and South Boston to false pretenses of political gentility" (qtd. in Judis, *William F. Buckley, Jr.*, 378). For many in the New Right, a brash group who relished the demagoguery of Nixon's Vice-President Spirow Agnew and George Wallace as they railed against pointy-headed bureaucrats and effete liberal intellectuals, the elitism of earlier postwar conservatives stemmed from their ambivalent relationship with the American university, which functioned as a metaphorical father whom those conservatives rebelled against, but ultimately sought approval from, in the realm of high culture.[21] Conversely, members of the New Right who had come to political power after the sixties tended to see the American university as a chain of institutions that harbored villainous enemies leftover from those days of protest and rage. This antagonistic orientation toward the university caused the New Right, and other conservatives in their wake, to flock to conservative think tanks and related foundations and institutions in such high numbers that by the eighties they had fashioned "a veritable counter-academy" (Hartman, 248). In short, movement conservatives in the immediate postwar era retained a modicum of respect for universities as elite spaces not only of wealth-based authority, but bourgeois cultural authority that fed into an attractive brand of high modernist culture, while New Right conservatives demonized the university as an institutional network that had been captured by the sixties Left.

Significantly for the surviving literary dimension of conservatism, when New Right conservatives plugged into their counter-university system of think tanks and foundations, they were not just advocating for populist causes such as anti-abortion, anti-busing, pro-American textbooks, and the preservation of the Christian family, but for a sweeping vision that subsumed these issues under a paradigm of laissez-faire capitalism that was mostly detached from traditionalist anxieties over literary prestige. For the wealthy backers of these organizations, such as the Coors family of Colorado who bankrolled the Heritage Foundation and other similar political groups, the populist rhetoric around social issues was really a vehicle for popularizing what became known as "supply-side economics," a term meant to signal an implicit departure from the prevailing emphasis on demand in Keynesian economics. As Jason Stahl explains in his historiographical work on conservative think tanks, these organizations were learning how to combine social and economic issues as Reagan ascended to the presidency "in an extremely powerful way by situating those who benefitted the most from American capitalism as its populist underdogs," aligned with a white middle class who also saw themselves as status-underdogs in the realm of culture (93). The long-term effect of this discourse was a displacement of Burkean traditionalists from the center of American conservatism in order to make neoliberal conservatism of free markets the defining attribute of "conservatism" in the Age of Reagan, so much so that even the so-called defenders of "traditional America" in the eighties could almost never openly critique capitalism and still be connected to the conservative power structure. Ultimately, a market-based shift of this magnitude would wreak havoc on the traditionalist conservative vision of highbrow literary value, even though conservatives could not quite bring themselves to totally admit it because they refused to grapple with the cultural effects of capitalism.[22] Considering the ideological synthesis of Reaganite conservatism, a blend of anti-elitist populism contemptuous of the university and a zealous faith in free markets, it is no surprise that the simultaneous rise of conservative think tanks and the electoral rise of "Reagan conservatives" correlated with the decline in esteem for literary fiction within modern conservatism.

On top of such dramatic institutional and electoral changes in conservatism, this moment in American literary history was also marked by the rapid rise of an unprecedented literary patronage system concentrated in American universities: the graduate-level creative writing program. Calling this epoch "the Program Era" in his titular book, Mark McGurl argues that the expansion of "creative writing programs stands as the most important event in postwar American literary history, and that paying attention to the increasingly intimate relation between literary production and practices of higher education is the key to understanding the originality of postwar American literature" (*The Program Era*, ix). The decades in which creative writing programs truly began to take off, McGurl writes, was in the seventies and eighties: "The handful of creative writing programs that existed in the forties had, by 1975, increased to 52 in number. By 1984 there were some 150 graduate degree programs (offering the MA, MFA, or PhD), and as of 2004 there were more than 350 creative writing programs in the United States, all of them staffed by practicing writers, most of whom, by now, are themselves holders of an advanced degree in creative writing" (24). Thus, the rise of creative programs correlated not only with the concomitant electoral rise of American conservatism but also with a strain of post-sixties conservative rhetoric that reinforced their earlier stereotype of the university as a den of liberal iniquities well before the culture wars of the late eighties and nineties. In 1975 even Ronald Reagan, speaking on his post-governorship syndicated radio show that is largely forgotten today, identified creative writing in the humanities by name, complaining bitterly about English instructors who were now teaching "electives like creative writing, filmmaking, mythology, and detective story writing" (qtd. in Perlstein, *Invisible Bridge*, 435).

Although McGurl does not focus on the rise of American conservatism during this era, he does imply that the *modus operandi* of creative writing programs was more compatible with post-sixties liberalism and its rhetoric of tolerance and inclusion than with conservatism's heterodox fusion of white working-class populism and corporate capitalism. Arguably the most important subgenre of literary fiction that creative writing programs produced was "high cultural pluralism," a mode of writing which "joins the high literary values of modernism with a fascination with the experience of cultural difference and the authenticity of the ethnic voice" and was clearly a product of "overlapping institutionalizations of elitist high modernism and cultural pluralism in university English departments of the postwar period" (McGurl, 32; 58). Politically, as McGurl writes, high cultural pluralism is usually read in one of two ways: "either as a partially democratized modernism, which would emphasize the conditioning effect of a liberal-progressive (at least compared to other American institutions) institutional context on an elitist discourse, or, because universities are still a long way from offering unrestricted social access to the masses, as an elitist pluralism in which the lucky ones, among their other privileges, are taught to savor their own open-mindedness" (58). After the publication of *The Program Era*, various progressive writers and scholars have tended to frame the political debate about writing programs around the latter reading and its attendant problems of true universal inclusion. But with the former reading, McGurl inadvertently describes the institutional and cultural conditions that led to the conservative movement's near-total disavowal of literary fiction, for in addition to their ideological problems with that high cultural genre, conservatives imagined it to be irrevocably tainted by the American university as an echo chamber of progressivism.

By the time Reaganism peaked in the eighties, this multifaceted history of numerous institutions and intra-ideological disagreements would give rise to two seemingly irresolvable antinomies of literary value within the conservative movement: on the one hand, a blossoming of contemporary popular genre fiction written by and for conservatives that coincided with a renaissance of Ayn Rand's fiction; while on the other hand, a staunch defense of the traditionally white, male literary canon and the grand thesis of American civilization supposedly at its core against the degrading influence of pop culture, hip postmodernism, and multiculturalism. When examining the first side of this antinomy, it is important to emphasize the influence of Buckley's first novel, a spy thriller entitled *Saving the Queen* (1976), within conservative cultural discourse not only because it was written by arguably the most important figure in postwar conservatism but also because this was the same person who had once thought that the intellectual reputation of *National Review* depended in large part on its taste in highbrow literature and its ability to traffic in the cultural capital of the literary field. As I show in previous chapters, mass-market genre fiction like Rand's *Atlas Shrugged* – a novel with a clear conservative bent – was roundly criticized at the beginning of the conservative movement, and only gradually became more accepted in the late sixties as Nixon-led conservatives bashed the counterculture and seized some forms of electoral power.

But in the wake of the Watergate scandal, the Fall of Saigon in 1975, and the Vietnam War's dishonorable end, and a series of special congressional reports, most notably those published by the Rockefeller and Church committees in 1975, exposing the abuses and crimes of US intelligence agencies, Buckley began to see mass-market fiction as a medium of proselytization that could both spread the congealing orthodoxy of Reaganite conservatism and denigrate stereotypically weak liberals who equivocated in the face of evil. According to Buckley, when he sat down to write his debut novel, he consciously aimed "to commit literary iconoclasm" by composing a work of fiction "in which the good guys and the bad guys were actually distinguishable from one another . . . [I]t would never be in doubt that the CIA is, when all is said and done, not persuasively comparable to the KGB" ("Genesis of Blackford Oakes," 308–9; 310). In a later interview for *The Paris Review*, Buckley expanded on this notion of eradicating moral ambivalence from his novel. "I was determined to avoid one thing, and that was the kind of ambiguity for which Graham Greene and to a certain extent Le Carré became famous," Buckley said. "There you will find that the [secret intelligence] agent of the West is, in the first place, almost necessarily unappealing physically. He drinks too much, he screws too much, and he's always being cuckolded. Then, at some dramatic moment there is the conversation or the moment of reflection in which the reader is asked to contemplate the difficulty in asserting that there is a qualitative difference between Them and Us" ("The Art of Fiction CXLVI," 123). In other words, Buckley, the former disparager of didactic socialist realism, was now consciously weeding out the very formal and thematic features that critics usually cited as evidence in debates about how to differentiate "good," quality literature from partisan, pseudo-literary propaganda.

In *Saving the Queen*, beginning from this intransigent ideological premise, Buckley constructed a story about the handsome protagonist Blackford Oakes, a twenty-three-year-old Yale graduate who served in World War II and is recruited by the CIA out of college, all attributes which resemble Buckley's own biography – although the book is not a *roman à clef* because, in a peculiar moment of meta-fictional self-advertisement, Oakes remarks casually that he enjoyed reading Buckley's own *God and Man at Yale* (*Saving the Queen*, 44). Prefaced by a contemporary frame story, wherein Oakes faces off against the liberal Republican Vice-President, and all-purpose conservative boogeyman, Nelson Rockefeller during a behind-the-scenes meeting for the 1975 Rockefeller Commission, the novel flashes back to 1951 when Oakes first joined the CIA. Immediately upon joining, Oakes finds out that top-secret documents about the US hydrogen bomb are being leaked to the Soviet Union via either an unknown high-ranking official in regular contact with the young fictional Queen Caroline of England, or the Queen herself. While investigating the leak in England, Blackford meets Queen Caroline, charms her, and even manages to have sex with her in the royal palace, before discovering that the real source of the leak is the Queen's crypto-communist cousin Viscount Peregrine Kirk, who dies in a spectacular suicide air-show scene during the novel's climax after Oakes tells him that he can either crash his plane or be shot out of the sky. For Oakes, killing Soviet spies, violating international law, and breaking ethical norms are justified for reasons that cannot be applied equally to Soviet spies who use the same tactics. Contemplating this dilemma, Oakes, Buckley writes,

> felt himself curiously affected by the invisible network being managed at one end by Joseph Stalin, the principle agent – now that Hitler was gone – of human misery; and, at the other, by Washington, D.C., a network of its own, protective of human freedoms in design, but, also, necessarily engaged in the same kind of business: lying, stealing, intimidating, blackmailing, intercepting . . . *Quod licet Jovi, non licet bovi* . . . could be used in defense of indefensible propositions, nevertheless, correctly applied, it was unchallengeable: That which is permitted for Jove to do is not necessarily permitted for a cow to do. We might in secure conscience lie and steal in order to secure the escape of human beings from misery or death; Stalin had no right to lie and steal in order to bring misery and death to others. Yet, viewed without paradigmatic moral coordinates, simpletons would say, simply: *Both sides lied and cheated* – a plague on both their houses. (Buckley, 124)

In this moment, Buckley inverts the typical epiphany scene in a Le Carré novel in which the Western spy draws a moral equivalence between himself and his Soviet counterpart, pushing the audience beyond one-dimensional arguments into a polyphonic literary discourse where ideological certitude and skepticism exist in dialectical tension with one another. The reason Buckley inserted such heavy-handed didacticism into his fiction was not because he had totally forgotten his older criteria of aesthetic value – for example, Buckley still dropped Victorian literary allusions and professed his love for Mozart – but because he was a zealously reenergized Cold Warrior who believed that the threat posed by communism in general and the Soviet Union in particular was still existential in nature, and that Americans had lost this sense of urgency after Watergate, the Vietnam War, and the revelations of government malfeasance. If conservatives once associated midcentury progressive liberalism with socialist realism and conservatism with "great" highbrow literature, Buckley's novel showed just how far conservatives had shifted away from that metric of aesthetic value, as Buckley increasingly aligned left-wing ideology with difficult, morally complex literary fiction and Reaganite conservatism with didactic genre fiction.

Buckley's excursion into spy fiction was part of a broader cultural trend within conservatism during the eighties that quietly reshaped major aspects of conservative taste according to the changing ideological needs of the Reagan administration and its intense focus on supply-side economics.

Ironically, Buckley's increasing conviction that novels written by and for conservatives – a popular mode of entertainment that would harden into a niche genre known as "conservative fiction" and become fully legible in the nineties with the ascent of authors such as Tom Clancy and Christian-apocalyptic novelist Tim LaHaye – should communicate a clear ideological message was reminiscent of *National Review*'s own scathing indictment of Rand's *Atlas Shrugged*. In that famous review, Whittaker Chambers wrote: "*Atlas Shrugged* can be a novel only by devaluing the term. . . . Its story merely serves Miss Rand to get the customers inside the tent, and as a soapbox for delivering her Message. The Message is the thing" (595). Not coincidently, as Maureen Dowd pointed out in a 1987 piece for the *New York Times*, Rand had reemerged from decades of obscurity to become "the novelist laureate" of the Reagan administration, which included fans ranging from Secretary of Commerce William Verity to White House Director of Speechwriting Aram Bakshian to Reagan-appointed Federal Reserve Chairman, and genuine longtime Rand disciple, Alan Greenspan (Dowd, "Where 'Atlas Shrugged'"). For free-market conservatives, Greenspan explained, the attraction to Rand's fiction had less to do with her argument about the practical efficiency of capitalism, which was common in virtually all intellectual defenses of capitalism dating back to Adam Smith, than with her fervent claim that capitalism was also the best system of morality for society – indeed, much better, to the chagrin of traditionalist conservatives, than Christianity (Dowd). At one time, traditionalist Christians like Russell Kirk and Whittaker Chambers saw unrestrained capitalism as a materialistic leveling force that undermined religious morality, and they invoked complex modernist literature as a counterpoint in that intra-ideological debate. But after Reagan's ascent to the presidency, social conservatives began to conceptualize capitalism itself as a God-given absolute, thus shifting movement conservatives toward ideologically motived genre fiction. Ultimately, this shift made conservative literary taste consonant with the basic logic of Reaganism: potboiler fantasies undergirded by free-market capitalism.

From this perspective, one can grasp the meaning of that other side of the conservative antinomy of literary value: the neo-traditionalist defense of literature and the humanities as the necessary cultural groundwork of laissez-faire capitalism against the twin evils of postmodernist relativism and multiculturalist identity politics. First, it should be noted that although Reagan conservatives nominally took up the traditionalist mantle for humanistic education and canonical literature in the eighties, their arguments did not square with the earlier defenses of traditionalists like

Kirk who emphasized mystery, sin, moral doubt, and the perils of appetitive materialism. In several high-profile instances within conservative discourse, the surviving traditionalist conservatives of the early postwar period openly denounced the libertarian direction of movement conservatism, a sub-narrative often obscured even in scholarly accounts of the late twentieth-century "culture wars."[23] In 1980, the most influential living traditionalist in postwar America, Russell Kirk, left *National Review* and criticized the libertarian turn in conservatism with a passionate zeal bordering on the polemical. In one famously divisive essay, "Libertarians: The Chirping Sectaries" (1981), Kirk launched a blistering attack on "libertarian conservatives," a contradiction in terms so offensive to him that he likened the oxymoronic phrase to "a Jewish Nazi" (348). Their "ruinous failing," Kirk argued, "is their fanatic attachment to a simple solitary principle . . . to the notion of personal freedom as the whole end of the civil social order, and indeed of human existence" (345). But the "genuine" Burkean conservative, Kirk asserted, making a literary allusion to Whittaker Chambers's favorite novelist, "will not tolerate ravening liberty; with Dostoevski [*sic*], he knows that those who commence with absolute liberty will end with absolute tyranny" (350). For Kirk, the libertarian worship of free markets was nothing short of a religious heresy with profound implications for literature and society as a whole. In one of his lesser-known late essays, "The Perversity of Recent Fiction" (1982), Kirk fatalistically predicted that "as literature sinks into the perverse, so modern civilization falls into ruin" (48). Instead of finding great works of contemporary literature, Kirk could only perceive mass-marketed products of the "diabolical imagination," which were cynically written by "profiteering 'best-seller' authors" whose greediness had transformed late twentieth-century literature into a "literature of nihilism, of pornography and of sensationalism" (46; 49). Sounding like a staunch defender of the aesthetic disposition articulated by Bourdieu, Kirk castigated Reaganite conservatives for betraying the semi-autonomous realm of "great" literature created by the artist-genius.

Without the chorus of traditionalist voices from the early years of postwar conservatism, those who had defended the humanities and literature in a vocabulary drawn from the New Humanism of Irving Babbitt and the later New Criticism, the conservative cultural warriors of the eighties tended to see the partisan ideology of Reaganism as their primary political and aesthetic compass. For these Reagan conservatives, capitalism had very little to do with narcissistic individualism and atomization, hedonistic greed, the decline of organized religion, or the breakdown of communal duty and cultural cohesion – all phenomena which pointed to a sweeping "era of disaggregation" that historian Daniel T. Rodgers calls our "Age of Fracture" (3). Instead, conservatives such as William J. Bennett, Lynne Cheney, Dinesh D'Souza, and Roger Kimball saw social ills through a cultural lens that revealed the sixties as the destructive turning point for "family values," stable race relations, and patriotic pride. And since the cultural legacy of the sixties, at least in the conservative mind, thrived most conspicuously in the university, specifically English departments, conservatives were compelled to continue attacking post-sixties American literature and the institutions that sustained it.

These developments illuminate why William J. Bennett, the Reagan-appointed chair of the National Endowment for the Humanities, fired arguably the first major shot in the "canon wars" when he wrote the NEH pamphlet *To Reclaim a Legacy: A Report on the Humanities in Higher Education* (1984). Identifying the sixties as the beginning of a trend that would prove "undeniably destructive" to humanities pedagogy, he called for a return to the Western canon in the hopes of once again exposing college students, in the Victorian language of Matthew Arnold, to "the best that has been said, thought, written, and otherwise expressed about the human experience" (27; 5). If not, Bennett claimed, the humanities would continue to be a space in higher education where the "curriculum was no longer a statement of what mattered," and essentially remain "the product of a political compromise among competing schools and departments" (28). For Bennett, the sharp decline in college students majoring in the humanities – he cited a 57 percent decrease in English majors and a 62 percent decrease in history majors since 1970 – was rooted in several virulent strains of literary theory ranging from Marxism to multiculturalism to poststructuralism. The NEH study group found that "[s]ometimes the humanities are used as if they were the handmaiden of ideology, subordinated to particular prejudices and valued or rejected on the basis of their relation to a certain social stance," Bennett wrote, and that other times, "the humanities are declared to have no inherent meaning because all meaning is subjective and relative to one's own perspective" (22). Ironically, while Bennett was decrying the politicization of literature in English departments for degrading the superior literary standards of the Western canon, Buckley was busy writing more ideologically driven spy thrillers featuring Blackford Oakes.

Moreover, Bennett's boss President Reagan was becoming a faithful reader of techno-thriller writer Tom Clancy, whose first novel, *The Hunt for Red October* (1984), Reagan enjoyed so much that he not only invited Clancy to dinner at the White House to talk foreign policy but also treated

Clancy's second novel, the feverishly anti-Soviet *Red Storm Rising* (1986) that reads like inverted Soviet realism, as a briefing paper for his Reykjavik summit with Mikhail Gorbachev in October 1986 (Cannon, *President Reagan*, 141; 252).[24] Adding another layer of irony, the perspectival subjectivity and epistemological uncertainty Bennett bemoaned in literary theory mirrored the central reasons why movement conservatives had championed the New Journalism of Tom Wolfe, Joan Didion, and, at times, Norman Mailer, since it was a middlebrow, quasi-prestigious genre that generated radical distrust of the "mainstream media" and the implicit liberal consensus. When seen in relation to the cultural discourse of American conservatism as a whole, what emerged in Bennett's NEH report was a pattern of aesthetic incompatibilities that would recur in many conservative books surveying the "canon wars": on the one hand, a twofold populist attack on snobbish liberal culture and vast swathes of postwar literary fiction; on the other hand, a conventional elitist attack on the leveling effects of postmodernism and multiculturalism, and a histrionic reverence for canonical American literature. The paradox is that this antinomy was produced by an array of institutional actions and organizational strategies that compelled conservatives to engage in their own self-removal from high culture, even though their fervent defense of the canon clearly signaled a residual desire to be associated with highbrow literature.

4.5 Reckoning with Postmodern Conservatism in Late Bellow and Pynchon

Ultimately, the effects of Reaganism on shifting conservative literary taste produced surprising, even sometimes paradoxical, effects on some of America's most celebrated novelists of the era, such as Bellow and Pynchon, who partially anchored the American literary field. For many scholars, it was not surprising that Allan Bloom's *The Closing of the American Mind* (1987) captivated conservatives just as the culture wars were intensifying. But what scholars have not quite delineated – and what the antinomies of literary value sketched out above reveal – is the matrix of ideological reasons conservatives embraced Bloom but virtually ignored his close friend Saul Bellow, who not only encouraged Bloom to write the book, and even authored an original foreword, but who also seemed to manifest in his novels Bloom's high cultural seriousness and distaste for the post-sixties cultural Left better than any other literary writer. In his blockbuster academic book, Bloom sought to expose the insidious influence of "relativism," a remnant of Black Power and the New Left, on America's most prestigious universities and the culture more broadly. Although Bloom was never a full-fledged "movement conservative," a condensed version of his argument was first published in *National Review* in an essay entitled "Our Listless Universities" (1982), whose alarmist first paragraph stoked the fears of conservative readers: "[S]tudents in our best universities do not believe in anything, and those universities are doing nothing about it, nor can they. An easygoing American kind of nihilism has descended upon us, a nihilism without terror of the abyss" (1537).

Five years later, Bloom took the core of this idea and assembled a long, multifaceted argument that linked postmodernist relativism and the open-mindedness of multiculturalism in eighties America with older strains of nihilism found in the philosophy of Nietzsche and the politics of the Weimar Republic. Essentially, Bloom argued that once the value-laden language of the sixties – that is, "authentic life-style" and "genuine identity" – went mainstream, Americans misinterpreted this ostensibly tolerant, emancipatory shift as an opportunity to find "true" self-fulfillment without the archaic encumbrances of traditional morality, family, religion, or social institutions (108). For Bloom, these developments produced a new type of kitschy American nihilism, which he referred to interchangeably as "nihilism with a happy end" and "nihilism without the abyss" (148; 155). Politically, though, Bloom thought that such blissful ignorance had darker, proto-fascist roots: "the new American life-style has become a Disneyland version of the Weimar Republic for the whole family" (147). On the surface, this line could sound like an ironic quip, but later in the book, Bloom used it to develop an in-depth analogy between US universities in the sixties and the Weimar Republic to explain the relativism of the late eighties. "The American university in the sixties was experiencing the same dismantling of the structure of rational inquiry as had the German university in the thirties. No longer believing in their higher vocation, both gave way to a highly ideologized populace" (313). While movement conservatives frequently had been making similar comparisons in offhanded or anecdotal ways for decades, Bloom's book was the first to bring culturally conservative sensibilities, decades of college-level pedagogy, and an expert knowledge of Western ideas to bear on the sixties. Most importantly, Bloom de-emphasized the materialist linkage between capitalism and nihilism, and instead solidified a constellation of symbolic linkages between the sixties Left, nihilism, a hypothetical proto-fascism in America and the decline of postwar US literature – all of which movement conservatives were eager to endorse. Essentially, Bloom used the conservative version of the trope of American Fascism, perfected and epitomized by Tom Wolf in the seventies, to argue that American authoritarianism could emerge from the combination of a liberal culture elite and the racialized (left-wing) populist masses.

However, just as they had consistently in the seventies, conservatives continued to distance themselves from Bellow, the Bloomian novelist *par excellence* in contemporary American fiction. At times in his foreword to *The Closing of the American Mind*, Bellow seemed sympathetic to conservatism, or at least mutually antagonistic toward the institutions and individuals that conservatives also abhorred. Because he had "never viewed the university as a sanctuary or shelter from the 'outer world,'" Bellow believed that he had kept his mind independent enough to "detect the untreated sewage odors of a century of revolutionary rhetoric . . . the odor of which is no more pleasant now than it was in the thirties. There is nothing at all new in the fiery posturing of these agitational [*sic*] and 'activist' writers" (17). But at other times, Bellow's vision revealed points of friction with Reagnite conservatism, especially the reactionary populism that denigrated the autonomy and value of high culture. Sounding not a little like Russell Kirk on the commercialized degeneration of public discourse, Bellow scoffed that "here and there I am probably hard to read, and I am likely to become harder as the illiteracy of the public increases" (15). Always championing the freedom of the serious artist, Bellow saw the human "soul" as a spiritual-aesthetic counterpoint to any kind of orthodoxy: "The soul has to find and hold its ground against hostile forces, sometimes embedded in ideas which frequently deny its very existence, and which indeed often seem to be trying to annul it altogether" (17). For Bellow, the formal and thematic complexities of high modernism allowed him to remain skeptical of ideological extremism and partisan certitude on both the Right and Left, an aesthetic conviction that overlapped with midcentury literary critics as diverse – and, in many quarters, as equally outdated – as Lionel Trilling and Russell Kirk.

From Bellow's late-career perspective, movement conservatives fetishized capitalism and philistine anti-intellectualism while liberals fetishized multiculturalist relativism and victimhood all in ways that restricted the novelist's imagination, which he thought should transcend the petty, partisan politics of the day. In *The Dean's December* (1982), his first novel after winning the Nobel Prize and one that *National Review* derided as "Bellow at his worst," Bellow continued to exhibit a profound ambivalence about capitalism (Evanier, "Bare Bones," 364). As the novel's beleaguered hero Dean Corde believes, capitalism is a system founded on the profit motive and thus "the first axiom of nihilism – the highest values losing their value" (969). But nevertheless, Corde notes stoically, "capitalism is the best because it fits this emptiness best, and is politically the safest, for horrible reasons, and so on" (969–70). Discouraging deep contemplation about suffering and death, a key Bellovian talking point in defining great literature, "conservative capitalism has to temper or conceal its position that classic conditions of competition will bring suffering and death – American conservatism has its own difficulties with the pain level" (*Dean's December*, 981). Later in *Ravelstein* (2000), Bellow's final novel and a *roman à clef* about his friendship with Bloom, Bellow distanced Bloom (and implicitly himself) even further from American conservatism. In a conversation about economics and culture between Chick and Ravelstein, doppelgängers for Bellow and Bloom, respectively, they both agree that as "an economist, Milton Friedman had it over most others, but Friedman was a free-market fanatic and had no use for culture, whereas Keynes had a cultivated intelligence" (10). In the end, Bellow believed, the distinctive ideological certitude of American conservatism blinded its adherents to the aesthetic position necessary to write and appreciate great literature. As he wrote in the early nineties about the intersection between literature and politics: "Those anticommunist intellectuals and publicists with whom I have agreed on issues of the Cold War, though they tend to be high-toned and swollen with cultural pride and *suffisance*, are often philistine in their tastes. Their opposite numbers on the left are, in this respect, a mess entirely" ("Writers, Intellectuals, Politics," 403).

As the previous quote shows, Bellow remained equally dissatisfied with the other side of the political spectrum, too, and he continued his slashing critiques on Black Power activists, campus radicals, and the university adversary culture that, he believed, narrowed literature into little digestible pieces of moral certitude that merely turned literary texts into vehicles for left-wing cultural capital. In one infamous scene in *The Dean's December*, Bellow has Dean Corde ventriloquize a version of Wolfe's "radical chic" thesis when Corde writes a "brave," politically incorrect essay on the attraction between white wealthy college students and black militants: "America no more knew what to do with this black underclass than it knew what to do with its children. It was impossible for it to educate either, or to bind either to life. It was not itself securely attached to life just now. Sensing this, the children attached themselves to the black underclass. . . . It was not so much the inner city slum that threatened us as the slum of innermost being, of which the inner city was perhaps a material representation" (910). Similarly in *Ravelstein*, Bellow wrote that although Ravelstein's job seemed to dovetail with the archetypal radical professor's job "to make you [the college student] aware of the bourgeois upbringing from which your education was supposed to free you," Ravelstein was, in fact, very different; the left-wing "liberated teachers offered themselves as models, sometimes seeing themselves as revolutionaries. They spoke youth gibberish. They wore ponytails, they grew beards. They were Ph.D. hippies and swingers" (43). Finally, Bellow's most infamous remark on multiculturalism in 1987 – that is, "Who is the Tolstoy of the Zulus? The Proust of the Papuans? I'd like to read him" – cemented his alienation from the cultural liberalism of the American university (qtd. in Atlas, 573). In his follow-up response several years later, Bellow fumed that this quote was being used to paint him as "an elitist, a chauvinist, a reactionary and a racist – in a word, a monster," a campaign of vilification that revealed how those on the post-sixties Left were "despots [who] do not accept the autonomy of the literary imagination" ("Papuans and Zulus," 409–10). If he were to acquiesce to their ideological demands, Bellow believed that he had better just start writing "socialist realism," that propagandistic form "that dominated the literate USSR for many decades [and] forced poets, playwrights and novelists to become part of the official falsehood machine" ("Papuans and Zulus," 410). To the very end, Bellow was skeptical of politically didactic literature emanating from any ideology that claimed to have all the answers, a habit of mind he associated symbolically with totalitarianism throughout his career. For this reason, the triumph of Reaganite conservatism rendered Bellow's unique highbrow literary aesthetic unpalatable to the visions of cultural prestige outlined by both the Left and the Right, leaving him a scapegoat for post-sixties liberals and a "persona non grata in the academy today," as Simon During notes, and simultaneously a neglected relic in the literary annals of American conservatism (124).

Reaganite conservatism also continued to play a role in reshaping how Pynchon understood the political implications of his comparatively postmodern novels. In 1984, Pynchon published two nonfiction pieces tracing some of the ways in which the rise of conservatism made him rethink his fiction: the *New York Times* article "Is It O.K. To Be A Luddite?" and the introduction to a collection of his early short stories entitled *Slow Learner*. Essentially, Pynchon realized that the positive effects of the sixties emancipation movements were inextricably tangled up with the negative effects of neoliberal capitalism, and that his brand of postmodernist fiction must offer more inclusive and communal models of affirmation if it wanted to compete culturally against Reaganite conservatism, an ideology which had managed to position itself as a solution (populist resentment, backward-looking nostalgia, and a return to "traditional values") to the very problems engendered by its vision of political economy (unfettered capitalism, rapid social change, and the obsolescence of Fordist forms of labor configured around unions). In his essay on the political implications of Luddism, typically defined as skepticism toward technological change driven by industrial capitalism, Pynchon inverted the reactionary stigma attached to an ostensible "nostalgia" for the past. Noting that the original Luddite movements emerged in early nineteenth-century England because of labor disputes in the textile industry and the rights of workers – not because of irrational fears about technological "progression" – Pynchon recast the roots of Luddism as "open-eyed class war" ("Is It O.K.," 41). An implicit allegory of the eighties, Pynchon's narrative acknowledged that the fears of many conservative voters were legitimate, but that their energies had been redirected into the realm of culture when they should have been redirected into economics – a basic reiteration of the thematic valence, as I argue earlier in this chapter, of the Mike Fallopian character in *Lot 49*. What the "luddite impulse" had always been about, Pynchon argued, was "a definition of 'human' as particularly distinguished from 'machine,'" which was a concern about human community and meaning that united the Left and the traditionalist wing of the Right, even if they had not realized it ("Is It O.K."). As Pynchon implied with his opening reference to 1984 – the actual year and Orwell's novel – the problem with post-sixties conservatism was that it cornered the political market, in classic Orwellian fashion, on humanistic positivity and communal affirmation. Issuing a surprising, if not unaffected, *mea culpa* in his introduction to *Slow Learner*, Pynchon would go on to claim that the kind of fiction he wrote early in his career ironically made the ideological operations of specific strains of conservatism run smoother. "Modern readers," Pynchon writes, meaning a post-sixties audience, "will be, at least, put off by an unacceptable level of racist, sexist and proto-Fascist talk throughout [one of his specific early stories]" (11). Pynchon says that his obvious, amateurish error was his commitment to work almost exclusively in the postwar literary vein of naïve social critique that compelled him "to begin with a theme, symbol or other abstract agent, and then try to force characters and events to conform to it" ("Introduction," 12). But the best fiction, Pynchon notes, offered more than just critique – that is, experiences transformed into something "undeniably authentic by having been found and taken up, always at a cost, from deeper, more shared levels of the life we all really live" (21).

Pynchon realized that hypercritical demystification, an important legacy of the countercultural sixties Left, was a necessary condition for social progress, but not a sufficient one, since free-market capitalism produced similar kinds of demystification that Reaganite conservatives displaced with folksy stories of moral certitude, national redemption, and resentment toward a liberal cultural elite.

With the publication of *Vineland* (1990), a novel chock-full of references to Nixon and Reagan, Pynchon aimed to combine postmodern skepticism with positive progressive themes, fortifying the post-sixties linkage between highbrow fiction and liberal-Left politics. He retained his usual countercultural ethos, but he called for a renewed commitment to communitarianism, emphasizing familial bonds as the necessary groundwork upon which rests a more inclusive, pluralistic conception of the authoritarianism of "Reagan's America" with its counter-emphasis on the patriarchal family, chauvinistic patriotism, and Christian fundamentalism. For some critics, *Vineland* was a disappointing departure from Pynchon's previous sprawling global epics and a "retreat" into domestic sentimentality. However, from the perspective of my argumentative delineation of Pynchon's career, *Vineland* is not a discouraging nadir, but a new and complex culmination of his quarter-century examination of the postwar Right. Set in the fictional county of Vineland, California, in 1984 – the year, again not coincidently, of President Reagan's reelection and Orwellian shorthand for totalitarianism – the novel follows a group of ex-hippies trying to survive the "War on Drugs," a feverish outgrowth of the earlier "Nixonian repression" that transformed America into a "scabland garrison state" (*Vineland*, 71; 314). Whereas he had previously suggested in his first three novels that European Fascism had been smuggled into the United States through Western political discourse and its attendant technologies of domination – a surreptitious displacement that, at times, portrayed American right-wingers as implicit and unconscious agents of historical fascism – Pynchon now reconfigured Reaganite conservatism as openly fascistic, as a set of institutions and discourses that created and sustained a myth-based American Fascism. It's "the whole Reagan program, isn't it?" one ex-radical from the sixties says; "dismantle the New Deal, reverse the effects of World War II, restore fascism at home and around thc world, flcc into thc past" (265).

At first glance, for readers less familiar with the twin themes of fascism and conservatism stretching through Pynchon's novels, it could seem like Pynchon's repeated deployment of the epitaph *fascist* to describe conservatives is hyperbolic, deliberately inflammatory, and, in the end, merely designed to preach to the surviving remnant of post-sixties progressives. But, in a counterintuitive move, Pynchon actually uses the thematic conflation of fascism and conservatism to open up and recalibrate stereotypical understandings of Reaganite conservatism. Pynchon achieves this goal precisely because he *does not* invoke a singular manifestation of historical fascism so much as a discursive array of fascist discourses and signifiers – spliced together, in characteristic postmodern fashion, from different times and places – whose one distinguishing characteristic is the strategic use of a hodgepodge of reactionary positions in an ad hoc fashion. As prominent theorists of fascism attest, fascist regimes are usually underpinned by a seemingly incoherent concoction of different strands of political modernity, from traditionalist authoritarian communalism to corporate capitalist individualism, all in the name of national revitalization.[25] Although early twentieth-century fascism spoke in the language of categorical absolutes, Pynchon suggests that its tactical dynamism and ideological contingency functioned as a kind of proto-postmodernism of the Right, which implied, in turn, that American conservatism in the eighties was a multifaceted incarnation of reactionary postmodernism. For Pynchon, legacies of fascism under Reaganite conservatism could manifest as anything from postmodernist pastiche – one rock band in the novel is known by its comically nonsensical moniker "Fascist Toejam" – to political inspiration for the "Wars on Drugs" as a campaign to purify the narcotics purportedly responsible for depleting the nation's will (18). In one scene, the fictional Karl Bopp, "former Nazi *Luftwaffe* officer and subsequently useful American citizen," leads an antidrug squadron of unmarked governmental aircraft through rural California on a mission to destroy marijuana fields and reclaim "a timeless, defectively imagined future of zero-tolerance drug-free Americans all pulling their weight and all locked in to the official economy, inoffensive music, endless family specials on the Tube, church all week long, and, on special days, for extra good behavior, maybe a cookie" (221–22). By installing a secret Nazi as the antidrug squadron leader, Pynchon implies that the way conservatives scapegoated marijuana, itself a metonymy for the hippies and sixties leftists, was analogous to the way Nazis weaponized scapegoating: Both discourses utilized sets of villains who were framed as agents of corruptions destroying what would have been an otherwise organic, coherent community. Using simplistic tales from television about America's timeless greatness – the nation's real addiction, Pynchon intimates – Reaganite conservatives rhetorically transfigured the social antagonisms of capitalism into vilified left-wing clarion calls for social justice.

One of Pynchon's crucial insights in *Vineland*, which he had eluded to only elliptically in *Gravity's Rainbow*, was that the mere exposure of patriarchy, racism, and capitalist oppression as ontologically groundless and discursively constructed, or as hegemonic *doxa* ripe for denaturalization and deconstruction, was not inherently progressive. Pynchon suggests, in other words, that pointing out the incongruities and illogicalities in Reaganism did not make modern conservatism contradictory but postmodern. However, Pynchon's conception of postmodern conservatism is not tantamount to the notion, already popular among ex-radicals in the eighties, that the once-subversive tactics of the sixties counterculture had been co-opted by the capitalist Right with its strategy of infantilizing the sixties generation, deceiving them into thinking that genuine rebellion and hedonistic pleasure were inextricably linked and fell under the same category of political radicalism. As Reagan rose to the presidency, and "as revolution went blending into commerce," in Pynchon's words, the novel posits that the sixties Left was never much of a threat to the Right in the first place, and that conservatism ascended into the political mainstream *not despite*, but *because of*, the sixties Left (308). Pynchon allegorizes this idea through the passionate, tortured love affair of Frenesi Gates and Brock Vond, a radical feminist filmmaker in the sixties and a sinister, reactionary antidrug prosecutor, respectively. After Frenesi becomes sexually obsessed with Brock, she snitches on the utopian California collective "The People's Republic of Rock and Roll (PR^3)," triggering its downfall. Brock had predicted this development all along, though, since "Brock Vond's genius was to have seen in the activities of the sixties left not threats to order but unacknowledged desires for it. While the Tube was proclaiming youth revolution against parents of all kinds and most viewers were accepting the story, Brock saw the deep . . . need only to stay children forever, safe inside some extended national family" (269). Ironically, Brock's vindictive destruction of the PR^3 essentially forces Frenesi into the federal witness protection program, separating her indefinitely from her husband and daughter, Zoyd and Prairie Wheeler. Finding herself at the mercy of annual federal budgets, Frenesi must continue her sexual relationship with Brock for basic survival. In a passage that inverts the countercultural assumptions that causal sex "subverts" the status quo, Frenesi realizes that Brock's "erect penis had become the joystick with which, hurtling into the future, she would keep trying to steer among hazards and obstacles . . . she would come, year by year to stand before" (292–93). Without a more robust framework of normative values, Pynchon reveals how conservatives could take advantage of the radical uncertainty wrought by the sexual revolution of the sixties and the rise of academic postmodernism, despite the sanguine notion that postmodernism in the arts represented the "unfinished project of the 1960s" (Hutcheon, 10). Instead, Pynchon anticipates Terry Eagleton's critique in *The Illusions of Postmodernism*, who argues that since academic postmodern discourse devolved in the eighties into "a cult of ambiguity and indeterminacy," postmodern intellectuals had "no particularly pressing reason to locate their own social existence within a broader political framework" as they engaged in sterile intellectual games whose stakes were merely in-group, academic cultural capital (7–8). In his representation of the Frenesi-Brock relationship, Pynchon signals his desire to escape some of the worst effects of this discourse: namely, the lack of a strong, affective motive for political action.[26]

As an antidote to the postwar conservative movement's toxic mixture of capitalist individualism and authoritarian communalism, Pynchon not only links the individualism of the counterculture with the progressive communalism of an earlier, socialistic vision of the American Left, but he continues to do it through difficult, highbrow fiction that was radically different than socialist realism. This vision is evident in Pynchon's genealogical account of Frenesi, who descends from a long line of family-based radicalism in the Traverse-Becker clan. By connecting the sixties Left with the longer arc of twentieth-century progressive politics, Pynchon stresses that what these activists have in common across the century is "the dream of One Big Union . . . the commonwealth of toil that is to be" (76). In contrast to the authoritarian communalism of Reaganite conservatism, Pynchon imagines a different communal model in the radical Traverse-Becker family, with whom Frenesi is happily reunited at novel's end. The family unit, no longer suspect as the Reichian "germ cell" of the fascist state in *Gravity's Rainbow*, becomes the institution through which Americans can inoculate themselves against a paradoxical conservative ideology that has infected normative frameworks of value with its very proposals for a cure. In his supposed late-career "descent" into domesticity and sentimentality, Pynchon stresses that nation, community, and family were not automatically code words for "fascism," as the rhetoric of the sixties counterculture and, at times, Pynchon's own earlier fiction had once suggested, but themes ripe for interrogation in his brand of difficult, highbrow fiction.

Ultimately, as Reaganism peaked electorally, Pynchon seems to have remained ambivalent about literary fiction's potential for political change, despite its capacity for generating shrewd cultural insights – an ambivalence particularly haunted by the shifting rhetorical power of postwar conservatism. To take just one thematic example, as Catherine Flay points out, Pynchon illuminates a perversely brilliant tactic by the authoritarian conservative Vond: "Rather than [explicitly] asserting his conservative ideology through traditional values such as the family or defined gender roles, Vond encourages social fragmentation and, in particular, female liberation against a sense of duty toward fulfilling roles within a family" (221). But if Vond and his conservative minions successfully manipulate countercultural individualism and transgressive feminism only to redirect women back into the traditional family unit, how politically radical is Pynchon's *Vineland*? Troublingly, for Flay, "Pynchon's representation of the family as a counter to [neoliberal] capitalism facilitates the diversification of masculinity but limits the kinds of female behavior that can be considered either moral or radical" (210). An astute observer of the American sociopolitical scene, Pynchon is not unaware of these hazardous, trapdoor-like entanglements of modern conservative discourse, which helps explain toward the end of *Vineland* why the characters cannot quite decide "whether the United States still lingered in a prefascist twilight, or whether that darkness had fallen long stupefied years ago, and the light they thought they saw was coming only from millions of Tubes all showing the same bright-colored shadows" (371). From one perspective, Pynchon's subversive individualism aims to strike a blow against traditionalist conservatism; but if readers adjust that sociopolitical perspective only a few degrees, it appears like his valorization of romantic love and familial duty aims to strike a blow against toxic neoliberal individualism. Realizing that he is caught in a late twentieth-century American political landscape structured less by Right and Left than by two different strains of postwar conservatism, Pynchon signals to his left-leaning audience that they should, in Pynchon's famous words in *V.*, "keep cool, but care," a catchphrase that needs to be reinterpreted continually, mimicking the dynamism of postwar conservatism itself (236).[27]

4.6 Conclusion: Pynchon's Highbrow "Socialist Blather"

Predictably, *National Review* pummeled *Vineland* in its full-length review of the novel. But what makes that review significant, for my purposes, is how clearly it demonstrates the shift in the conservative movement's understanding of the cultural politics of literary taste and, more fundamentally, the Bourdieuan literary *illusio*, as conservatives adopted the broader cultural assumption that literary fiction was allied with progressive liberalism and the Left. The reviewer combined the double register of conservative aesthetics, lowbrow populism and highbrow aesthetic excellence, to accuse Pynchon of writing not simply left-wing propaganda, but didactic fiction in the form of difficult, highbrow postmodernism. On the one hand, J. O. Tate wrote, Pynchon tarnished (apolitical) literary excellence by parroting the line of "the professional victim" and thumped the reader over the head with "feminist jargon" and "socialist blather" (59). But on the other hand, suddenly adopting the populist ethos of an outraged everyman fed up with snobbish elites, Tate complained about the formal complexity of the novel and the sustained mental effort required to understand it, calling it "a bore and a chore" to read, and finally concluding that "little pleasure or intellectual profit is to be derived from reading *Vineland*" (59). This review typifies how conservatives approached literary fiction with a paradoxical set of assumptions about aesthetic merit and value; while they consciously sought to cultivate an image of themselves as guardians of highbrow literature, conservatives were also building partisan institutions and structuring ideologically rigid organizations that distanced them ever further from the major literary institutions and people who sustained the production of literary fiction. By the late eighties, conservative discourse had established its now-familiar framework of aesthetic judgment: volatile rhetorical careening from a sincere belief in the literary *illusio* to a deep cynicism of the stakes of the highbrow literary game. At its deepest level, this suspension between belief and disbelief was bound up with the fantasy that serious literature should function as a static reservoir of "civilization" outside of capitalist disturbance and political change.

For Bellow and Pynchon, two of the most decorated and influential postwar novelists, the rise of Reaganite conservatism transformed the sociopolitical topography of the United States in ways that had unavoidable – and, at times, unpredictable – consequences for the cultural politics of the literary field. In the next and final chapter, I continue to examine this transformation by juxtaposing the novels of Toni Morrison with the simultaneous rise of "conservative popular fiction" to shed light on another paradox of contemporary American fiction. As Reaganite conservatism peaked toward the end of the century, Morrison was appropriating the experimental modernism of Faulkner, once seen as the conservative formal aesthetic *par excellence*, at precisely the moment self-proclaimed conservatives were embracing the conventional literary aesthetics of social realism and mass-market genre fiction. In the final chapter, I complete my central argument that a more thorough investigation into the politics of literary form and cultural distinction in contemporary American fiction must include an investigation into modern American conservatism.

CHAPTER 5

The American Novel and the Reagan Revolution *The Ascent of Toni Morrison in the Age of Conservative Pop Fiction, 1987–2000*

5.1 Introduction: Highbrow Literature as Domestic Defense and Internal Threat

In the years immediately following Ronald Reagan's presidency, while liberal pundits were bemoaning what appeared to be an unequivocal rightward shift in American politics, movement conservatives were tempering their electoral triumphalism with portentous jeremiads on the moral degeneration of American culture. For conservatives, the accomplishments of the Reagan administration, notably its role in ending the Cold War and promoting free-market capitalism around the world, were tainted by its failure to rescue America from cultural decline linked to (in the antiquated contemporaneous conservative language) abortion, second-wave feminism, gay rights, public funding for the arts, and multiculturalism. In his influential *National Review* essay "Conservatism for the People" (1990), New Right architect Paul Weyrich substituted his typical bombast for a circumspect account of the eighties. The "Reagan Revolution will be just another hiatus in the triumphant march of liberal progress," Weyrich warned, unless a "new conservative agenda" spoke to the feeling on the Right of serious "cultural breakdown" (38). Weyrich imagined Reaganism less as the historical apex of movement conservatism than as a momentary deviation from the kind of social liberalism unleashed by the sixties.

As I showed toward the end of Chapter 4, conservatives such as William J. Bennett, Reagan-appointed chair of the National Endowment for the Humanities (NEH) and author of the alarmist exposé *To Reclaim a Legacy: A Report on the Humanities in Higher Education* (1984), believed that the production and institutional study of literature uniquely registered this cultural breakdown because American literature was a privileged site of cultural edification and civic virtue. In the late eighties and nineties, conservatives vocally supported a cluster of books – Allan Bloom's *The Closing of the American Mind* (1987), E. D. Hirsch's *Cultural Literacy*

(1987), Roger Kimball's *Tenured Radicals* (1990), Dinesh D'Souza's *Illiberal Education* (1991), and Lynne Cheney's *Telling the Truth* (1995) – that not only reproduced and amplified Bennett's fears but also deployed genre conventions derived from investigative journalism that were designed to pique a white middle-class reader's outrage by linking the loss of literary standards with political correctness and other partisan buzzwords. In these tendentious accounts, post-sixties radicals in the academy, and liberal colleagues who were supposedly too cowardly to stand up to them, were philistines whose very ignorance endangered America itself. In one well-known syndicated column, "Literary Politics" (1991), George Will captured the depth of conservative hysteria when he claimed that disputes over the Western canon and university literary standards constituted a "low-visibility, high-intensity war" that effectively made then-NEH chair Lynne Cheney more important than her husband, US Defense Secretary Dick Cheney, in the struggle to protect the republic: "The foreign adversaries her husband, Dick, must keep at bay are less dangerous, in the long run, than the domestic forces with which she must deal" ("Literary Politics"). Another way to put this, Will declared, is to call Lynne Cheney the "secretary of domestic defense."

While literary scholars have thoroughly interrogated these panic-stricken conservative narratives – challenging and debunking them almost as quickly as they were being published, as Gerald Graff did in *Beyond the Culture Wars* (1992) – another side of the post-Reagan debates about literary taste remains relatively under-examined, even though it belongs to the same universe of conservative discourse. If conservatives believed that canonical highbrow American literature stretching roughly from Emerson to Faulkner was a means of domestic defense, they held the simultaneous belief that contemporary highbrow literature constituted an internal threat to the republic. They condemned literary fiction in particular as a catalogue of socio-historical relativism (the high postmodernism of Thomas Pynchon, John Barth, and Don DeLillo), moral despair (the gloomy minimalism of Raymond Carver, Ann Beattie, and Brat Pack novelists Bret Easton Ellis, Tama Janowitz, and Jay McInerney), and propagandistic identity politics (the literary multiculturalism associated with writers such as Leslie Marmon Silko, Maxine Hong Kingston, Sandra Cisneros, Alice Walker, and, most threatening of all, Toni Morrison). In lieu of reading these contemporary authors, conservatives championed mass-market realism embodied in the big social novels of Tom Wolfe, the techno-spy thrillers of William F. Buckley Jr. and Tom Clancy, and the didactic Christianity of the *Left Behind* series. America, according to conservatives, needed somehow to retain both the traditionalist elitism of the liberal arts, whose beating heart was the Western canon, *and* eradicate corrosive liberal elitism embedded in contemporary literary culture by reading bestselling paperbacks about the unequivocal moral superiority of the United States.

While it may seem tempting to accuse conservatives of political bad faith, or even blatant intellectual dishonesty, neither of those formulations captures the complex relationship between conservative aesthetics and conservative politics toward the end of the twentieth century. Building on the excellent scholarship of John Guillory, I argue in this chapter that these conflicting visions of literary value revealed an aesthetic antinomy between lowbrow and highbrow that mimicked the deeper foundational antinomy structuring Reaganite conservatism itself: the creative destruction of free-market capitalism and the Christianized cultural values of traditionalism. Invariably, Reagan conservatives failed to acknowledge, in the words of historian Matthew Lassiter, "that many of the forces buffeting American families flowed from the anti-government agenda they themselves demanded and the hedonistic consumer society in which they participated" ("Inventing Family Values," 28). From this angle, the conservative conceptualization of "great literature" was an overdetermined symptom revealing how two different discourses of literary prestige and value clashed in a futile attempt to reconcile the radical tension between capitalism and traditionalism. Once the anxieties of social change wrought by capitalism were displaced on to the post-sixties cultural Left, the category of "highbrow fiction" became a condensation point of perplexing opposites, combining disparate conservative explanations for social decline. For Reaganite conservatives, highbrow fiction was somehow both an elitist liberal discourse that betrayed traditional American values *and* a great civilizational barricade against the untutored, racialized masses. In the end, conservatives mourned the deterioration of meaningful connection and community produced by capitalism, but they reconfigured this neoliberal nihilism into a left-wing specter that haunted contemporary American fiction and the institutions of higher education that produced and legitimized it.

In this chapter, I examine these ostensible contradictions to demonstrate how two novelists, Toni Morrison and Tom Wolfe, emerged as major, diametrically opposed figures in the cultural politics of American fiction toward the end of the twentieth century. Focusing chiefly on the conservative responses to Morrison and Wolfe, I demonstrate that the conservative movement's simultaneous suspicion of contemporary literary prestige and embrace of popular realist fiction was rooted in a commitment to market-based individualism, nominal colorblindness, and the aestheticization of populist white grievance. This imaginative template was best set down by Wolfe in his early New Journalism and his mid-career novel *The Bonfire of the Vanities* (1987), but radically complicated by Morrison's novelistic career and global, post–Nobel Prize fame. In *Beloved* (1987) Morrison takes modern conservatism as seriously as any other contemporary novelist, carefully examining it in a nuanced, empathetic light before ultimately dissolving aestheticized conservative nostalgia from within. She does this not by simply exposing how Reaganite conservatism is a bundle of contradictions, but by revealing how conservatism is a protean ideology that thrives on contradiction and paradox precisely because it cannot disavow masculine whiteness as its axiomatic foundation. To read Morrison's late twentieth-century fiction against its compositional background during the Reagan Revolution is to discover one of the most significant theorists and critics of American conservatism.

I contend that the intertwined career trajectories of Morrison and Wolfe help explain how, for conservatives, Wolfe became the lone conservative novelist *par excellence* and Morrison became a unique cultural nemesis whose novels marked both the destruction of high literary standards *and* the snobbish, liberal elitism associated with the tripartite institutionalization of modernist aesthetics, multiculturalism, and postmodern theory in the academy. In this way, conservatives unwittingly contributed to the dramatic ascent of Toni Morrison, who was using formal modernist aesthetics for racially progressive ends at the exact moment they were most determined to undermine her cultural influence and authority. Ultimately, the stakes of my final chapter boil down to the assertion that a fuller understanding of how highbrow literary fiction became fully aligned with liberalism in virtually every institution of American cultural life at the end of the twentieth century is necessarily an investigation into the racial politics of modern conservatism.

5.2 Political Inversions of Literary Form: Toni Morrison, Tom Wolfe, and Conservative Racial Amnesia

In 1987, Toni Morrison's *Beloved* and Tom Wolfe's *The Bonfire of the Vanities* stood out not only because they were widely regarded as the year's most important novels but also because their receptions were marked by an odd combination of unbridled applause and mocking disparagement that broke down largely along partisan political lines. For many liberals, *Beloved* was destined to silence any doubts, as Margaret Atwood declared in her *New York Times* review, about Morrison's "stature as a pre-eminent American novelist, of her own or any other generation" ("Jaunted By Their Nightmares"). During the following awards season, after *Beloved* had been passed over by the National Book Awards, 48 left-leaning black writers and scholars – for example, Maya Angelou, Amiri and Amina Baraka, Angela Davis, Houston A. Baker, Jr., Sonia Sanchez, and Alice Walker – collectively signed and published "Black Writers in Praise of Toni Morrison" in the *New York Times*, a public rebuke of white literary tastemakers whose "oversight and harmful whimsy" had to that point denied Morrison either a National Book Award or a Pulitzer Prize for any of her books. *Beloved*, they asserted, was nothing less than a gift to "our community, our country, our [national] conscience" ("Black Writers in Praise"). Conversely, most conservatives read *Beloved* as a mixture of lush sentimentality, feminist propaganda, and hyperbolic black victimhood. In one now-infamous review, Stanley Crouch claimed that *Beloved* amounted to a "blackface holocaust novel," since Morrison's primary aim was to "enter American slavery into the big-time martyr ratings contest" of human history whose ultimate measuring stick was the Nazi Holocaust ("Literary Conjure Woman"). In *Commentary*, the conservative critic Carol Iannone criticized *Beloved* as a "book [that] grows massive and heavy with cumulative and oft-repeated miseries," arguing that Morrison's penchant "for simplistic plight-and-protest has done fitful battle with the more capacious demands of a functioning moral imagination," and that, in the end, *Beloved* failed as a piece of highbrow fiction (63).[1]

Regarding the reception of Wolfe's *The Bonfire of the Vanities*, the critical roles were reversed. In a retrospective article examining the racial politics of *Bonfire* on the twentieth anniversary of its publication, Anne Barnard summed up the feelings of many liberals and leftists at the time: "[*Bonfire*] was a cynical endorsement of racial stereotypes that did not so much critique white paranoia as cater to it" ("No Longer the City of 'Bonfire'"). Wolfe indulged white paranoia, civil rights lawyer Ron Kuby said, by telling an implausible story in which "the Wall Street multimillionaire white folk living in $8 million Manhattan apartments . . . feel themselves oppressed by poor black people" (qtd. in Barnard). Conservatives, though, greeted Wolfe's novel with uninhibited enthusiasm, and they made declarations about Wolfe's generational importance that mimicked the ones liberals were making about Morrison's. In *National Review*, Richard Vigilante claimed not only that *Bonfire* secured

"Wolfe's place as the most important writer of his generation," but that Wolfe was the principal writer "saving American literature" from postmodern "solipsism" (46). George Will also predicted canonical greatness, describing *Bonfire* as "news that will stay news" and continue to be read "a century hence" ("News(s) from Tom Wolfe"). For conservatives, the publication of Wolfe's novel was a singular literary event in their movement's history.

By the mid-2000s, these claims about the future canonicity of *Beloved* and *Bonfire* would be thrown into sharp relief, largely to the chagrin of conservatives. Whereas Wolfe's novel had grown into a curious relic of the eighties for many critics, with the major exception of movement conservatives, the reputation of Morrison's novel had blossomed into the something like the quintessential serious literary novel of the last quarter-century. For the fiftieth anniversary issue of *National Review* in December 2005, when the editors compiled the ten most important books published in that fifty-year span, *Bonfire* was the only work of fiction listed, testifying to its immense prestige among conservatives. In the celebratory rationale for including *Bonfire*, Terry Teachout commended Wolfe for his refusal to bow to political correctness as he went about exposing the interrelated failures of big city liberalism, demagogic black politics, and the corrupt New York City media industry. Conservatives, Teachout claimed without a hint of irony, read *Bonfire* "with the same sense of bedazzled revelation with which George Orwell's Winston Smith read *The Theory and Practice of Oligarchical Collectivism*" (115). In 2006, the Book Review section of the *New York Times* held a similar prestige-measuring contest, asking several hundred writers and critics, "What is the best work of American fiction in the last 25 years?" Morrison's *Beloved* received the most votes and was declared the winner while Wolfe's *Bonfire* failed to receive a single vote ("What is the best work"). If admission into the literary canon meant that a novel garnered increasing critical acclaim over several decades, was regularly placed on college syllabi, and was the object of intense scholarly analysis in peer-reviewed journals, then it was clear that *Beloved* had become a canonical text and *Bonfire* had not.

Instead of adjudicating any competing claims about inherent literary merit or cultural consecration, I wish to draw attention to this debate in order to interrogate the implicit political framework of literary form, which both sides largely took for granted. By the end of the twentieth century, liberal and conservative critics assumed that this debate was a conflict of literary taste in which a modernist-influenced, formally difficult progressive novel (*Beloved*) was pitted against a bestselling, conservative social realist fiction (*Bonfire*). When looking at the history of post-1945 literary criticism that had been institutionalized in American universities, this framing is unsurprising; for decades, prominent critics in the vein of Roland Barthes had been exposing bestseller-style realism as a middlebrow commodity that merely reinforced the bourgeois status quo. But when looking at the trajectory of post-1945 American cultural politics against the background of conservatism's ascent, a striking inversion of literary form comes into view. As I have shown in previous chapters, Cold War liberals of the "vital center" crowd such as Lionel Trilling not only lamented the crude economic didacticism of socialist realism and the one-dimensionality of proletarian fiction but also reckoned with the anti-liberalism of the great Anglophone modernists. At the same postwar moment, movement conservatives seized on Trilling's anxieties and made a conservative virtue out of formal complexity, epistemological uncertainty, and certain forms of modernist irony that poked holes in universal abstractions like equality and social justice.

While the other writers I have examined thus far all played different roles in catalyzing this political inversion of literary form, the writings and critical reception of Morrison and Wolfe ratified it in dramatic fashion toward the end of the century. Although many simultaneous historical causes were present, a central reason was the shift in conservative discourse from an older segregationist position to a market-oriented colorblind position. In the fifties, conservatives had cited Poe, Twain, Faulkner, and O'Connor to highlight the mystical paradoxes surrounding slavery and Jim Crow segregation, arguing not only that the issue was too complex to solve with simple theories about racial equality, but that segregation was the least bad option in the interest of social stability. By the eighties, though, conservatives were pointing to Tom Wolfe's sociological satires of white liberals and black demagogues obsessed with past racial grievances to stress that the ethos of black victimhood was contributing more to America's enduring racial disparities than systemic, material forms of historical injustice. In short, movement conservatives' amnesia regarding the virtues of formally complex, morally ambivalent literary fiction paralleled their racial amnesia regarding the historical realities of slavery and Jim Crow segregation, disconcerting national legacies which threatened the Reaganite rhetoric of moral innocence and American exceptionalism that featured so prominently in bestselling conservative pop fiction.

Under the rubric of Reaganism, this corresponding linkage between the conservative movement's evolving racial positions and its shifting views on literature reached its highpoint. Reagan himself was the most instrumental public figure not just in recasting movement conservatism as a colorblind ideology focused on economic uplift, but in contrasting his position with a post-sixties, color-conscious liberalism that reflexively looked to the federal government to right historical wrongs. As the historian Leah Wright Rigueur documents in *The Loneliness of the Black Republican*, Reagan's 1980 presidential campaign repeatedly used the phrase "colorblind coalition" in ads emphasizing economic mobility that ran on black radio stations and in black magazines (288). As Reagan rose to the presidency, the once-staunch opponent of the 1964 Civil Rights Act had transformed part of his image, and the conservative movement's more broadly, by conceding that federal anti-discrimination legislation had been necessary once, but not anymore since the federal government "was ineffective at creating black wealth" compared to the capitalist market (Wright Rigueur, 289). Reagan completed his appropriation of postwar liberalism's colorblind rhetoric by reconfiguring the legacy of Martin Luther King, Jr. as a proto-Reaganite who also wanted racial considerations banned from public life. In a January 1986 speech on his opposition to minority quotas, Reagan argued that King would have disagreed with color-conscious liberals who had been influenced by Black Power and by (what would eventually be called) critical race theory: "We want a colorblind society, a society that, in the words of Dr. King, judges people 'not by the color of their skin, but by the content of their character'" ("Radio Address to the Nation on Martin Luther King, Jr."). What Reagan intuited about rhetorical framing and racial amnesia was explicitly spelled out in an important 1984 Heritage Foundation report, which advised Republican politicians that since 1964 "the most important battle in the civil rights fields has been for the control of the language" (qtd. in Dillard, 87).

The Reaganite dichotomy between colorblind universalism and context-dependent racial particularity had a significant impact on how conservatives valued language and novelistic form. An avid novel reader as a child, Reagan spoke fondly of texts that presented absolute moral distinctions between good and evil – for example, *The Rover Boys* series, Horatio Alger tales, dime-store novels about the ever-upright character Frank Merriwell, and the didactic Christian novel *That Printer of Udell's: A Story of the Middle West* by Harold Wright Bell – which anticipated his later infatuation with Tom Clancy novels (Perlstein, *Invisible Bridge*, 36). As an adult, Reagan would translate ethically complex novels into the same simplistic moral vocabulary, a template that conservatives were eager to replicate in the late twentieth-century culture wars. A striking example of this template was the way in which Reagan not only interpreted Twain's *The Adventures of Huckleberry Finn*, but also helped transform conservative literary discourse around a canonical work that usually inspired difficult questions about the history of American racism. In his autobiography, Reagan described his childhood in twenties Dixon, Illinois, as "one of those rare Huck Finn-Tom Sawyer idylls" (Reagan and Hubler, 18). As President, Reagan framed the novel as an unambiguous tale about overcoming prejudice and achieving a colorblind society, calling on American educators in one speech to "teach our students the same hatred of bigotry, and love of their fellow men that Huck showed on every page, and especially in his love for his big friend Jim" (qtd. in "Born to Trouble: *Adventures of Huckleberry Finn*"). In *The Book of Virtues* (1993), William J. Bennett picked up on Reagan's moral certainty and wrote about the novel as a source of unadulterated virtue and racial innocence, declaring that *Huckleberry Finn* "deserve[s] to be read by every American child" (399). The irony of framing *Huckleberry Finn* this way, Garry Wills pointed out in his critical book *Reagan's America* (1987), was that Twain's novel directly confronted themes such as "superstition, racism, and crime" (9). However, movement conservatives had not always talked about *Huckleberry Finn* in such naïve moral terms. When pro-segregationist traditionalism was still a prominent feature of movement conservatism in the fifties and early sixties, the racial underpinnings of Huck Finn's moral uncertainty and his infamously cruel behavior toward Jim at the end of the novel were not passed over or ignored but foregrounded as central. In one 1960 *National Review* article, Robert Y. Drake, Jr. used the paradox-loving language of New Criticism to argue that the persistence of Huck Finn's racism, especially at novel's end, should be read as the product of "a complex Southwestern society" (320). The end of *Huckleberry Finn*, Drake continued, presented a racial paradox for readers that was not susceptible to easy liberal answers, and "it is indicative of the stubbornness with which this paradox resists simplification that such [liberal] critics have so often been frustrated in their attempts to whitewash Huck and, in other areas, to make the still unregenerate South ... conform to the 'national' pattern" (321). Ironically, several decades later it would be Reaganite conservatives, not liberals, who would try to "whitewash" Huck Finn, recasting Twain's signature novel as a morally unambiguous children's tale.

5.3 The Black Ghost in the Machine: Toni Morrison's *Beloved*

In light of this specific form of nostalgic racial innocence embedded in Reaganism, it is easy to see why conservatives perceived Morrison's literary project as a serious threat to their vision of American culture in general and literary aesthetics in particular. To continue with the exemplary case of *Huckleberry Finn*, in *Playing in the Dark: Whiteness and the Literary Imagination* (1992), Morrison agreed with those earlier traditionalist conservatives that Twain's novel should be considered a "great," multilayered work because of "the frontal debate [about race] it forces" on readers (*Playing in the Dark*, 57). Unlike traditionalists, though, Morrison argued that its enduring greatness stems not from complex race relations too impenetrable for liberal do-gooders, but from the ways in which the novel confronts the anxieties aroused by the "Africanist presence" of dark un-free bodies and thus "simulates and describes the parasitical nature of white freedom" (57). Ever since the birth of the United States, Morrison contended, from the moment the founding generation "decided that their world view would combine agendas for individual freedom and mechanisms for devastating racial oppression," American literature and culture has been shaped and deformed by representations of blackness as de-historical allegory, fetishistic metonymy, and "metaphoric condensation" – symbolic manifestations which all turn whiteness into an invisible, ahistorical universal (*Playing in the Dark*, xiii; 68). In "Unspeakable Things Unspoken: The Afro-American Presence in American Literature," a 1988 Tanner lecture whose title derives from a passage in *Beloved* and whose argument foreshadows *Playing in the Dark*, Morrison explicitly challenged the Reaganite notion that race no longer mattered because, in the words of Linda Chavez, Reagan's staff director of the US Commission on Civil Rights, "race is an arbitrary concept" (qtd. in Rodgers, *Age of Fracture*, 141). Morrison noted that black Americans had been arguing for hundreds of years that race was a pernicious invention, and that "the people who invented the hierarchy of 'race' when it was convenient for them ought not to be the ones to explain it away, now that it does not suit their purposes for it to exist" ("Unspeakable Things Unspoken," 3). For movement conservatives after Reagan, who found it virtually unthinkable that whiteness could be approached as a historical construction, Morrison's analysis struck at the heart of their recent belief that America was at "the end of racism," as Dinesh D'Souza claimed in his titular 1995 book, making the weight of the past largely irrelevant.

By the late eighties, Morrison had established herself as a trenchant interrogator of the racial shift in conservative politics, revealing in essays and novels, *Beloved* especially, how the whiteness of modern conservatism was a hegemonic imaginative construct, to be sure, but one that was also resilient, dynamic, and historically fluid. Morrison's interrogation of postwar conservative racial rhetoric did not begin, though, with the rise of

Reagan and his "colorblind coalition." Indeed, Morrison's early career as a fiction writer can be seen as a long, implicit investigation of movement conservatism vis-à-vis race up through the publication of *Beloved*, for her career paralleled not only the evolution of conservative racial discourse from pro-segregationist traditionalism to colorblind individualism but also conservatism's shift away from formally difficult fiction. For instance, although scholars routinely read Morrison's first novel, *The Bluest Eye* (1970), as an indictment of the Cold War assimilationist discourse favored by white liberals, it can also be read against the background of the Republican Party's twofold break with overt segregation and high cultural traditionalism. Morrison started writing *The Bluest Eye* in 1965, the same year – as I show in chapter 3 – that William F. Buckley, Jr. began reorienting the conservative movement away from Goldwater's opposition to the Civil Rights Act and toward the colorblind "bootstraps" rhetoric that Buckley deployed in his 1965 New York mayoral run and his debate with James Baldwin. By exposing whiteness as a psychologically damaging cultural construct for the novel's protagonist Pecola Breedlove, Morrison critiqued the underlying premise of Buckley's argument that black Americans should simply imitate other ethnic groups who had assimilated into white, Christian middle-class culture. Significantly, the form of Morrison's critique resembled neither Richard Wright's sincere black protest fiction nor James Baldwin's ironic parody of protest fiction, but the Anglophone modernism of Faulkner, Joyce, and Woolf.

Over the course of the seventies, Morrison's next three novels – *Sula* (1973), *Song of Solomon* (1976), and *Tar Baby* (1981) – would become more thematically ambitious and formally complex, but the central narrative conflict of each one (i.e., the friction between the demands of the black community and the temptations of individual freedom) reflected the conservative movement's own struggles with reconciling communal traditionalism and libertarian individualism. Although tensions would always exist between the traditionalist and libertarian factions of postwar conservatism, Buckley's movement reached something like an ideological equilibrium in the late seventies by adopting the notion of "fusionism," the philosophical fruits of *National Review* editor Frank Meyer's twenty-year project to synthesize traditionalism, free-market libertarianism, and aggressive anti-communism from the early fifties until his death in 1972. To unite the various strains of the conservative movement, Meyer contended, conservatives "must draw upon those who called themselves conservatives in [the nineteenth century] but also those who called themselves liberals," thus combining Burkean conservatism's pre-modern defense of inherited privilege and classical liberalism's modern defense of individual liberty (26). Usually called "ordered liberty" by movement conservatives, this combination implied that what should be conserved was not only the political achievements of classical liberalism that benefitted white male property-owners, but also many of the most retrograde social assumptions embedded in the historical setting that produced classical liberalism. By composing three modernist-influenced novels in the seventies focusing on complex black characters, Morrison revealed the practical and theoretical shortcomings of postwar conservatism's appropriation of nineteenth-century liberalism, as conservatives sought to foreground a universal, race-free male individual that left essentially no space for black Americans in general and black women in particular.[2]

Finally, in "Recitatif" (1983), Morrison's only short story and her last piece of fiction before publishing *Beloved*, she explicitly alluded to movement conservatism's so-called colorblind racial politics, portraying the racial resentment generated by "forced" desegregation busing in the late seventies. On the surface, the story recounts the lifelong friendship of Twyla and Roberta, two women who meet as children in an orphanage, one of whom is white and the other black, though the audience never finds out the race of either character. At the heart of "Recitatif," in Morrison's words, "was an experiment in the removal of all racial codes from a narrative about two characters of different races for whom racial identity is crucial" (*Playing in the Dark*, xi). By foregrounding the busing issue as a central conflict late in the story, Morrison parodies the conservative movement's combination of colorblind individualism and racially coded cultural populism best exemplified in the "southern strategy" sketched out by GOP campaign guru Lee Atwater in an infamous 1981 interview: "You start out in 1954 by saying, 'Nigger, nigger, nigger.' By 1968, you can't say 'nigger' – that hurts you. So you say stuff like forced busing, states' rights and all that stuff. You're getting so abstract now . . . and all these things you're talking about are totally economic things and a byproduct of them is blacks get hurt worse than whites" (qtd. in Perlstein, "Exclusive"). In the very form of her short story, then, Morrison outlines the paradox of blackness in conservative discourse, replicating both its centrality and basic unspeak-ability, an absence so conspicuous that the narrator of "Recitatif" can only experience the "racial strife" of busing as a haunting presence: "It woke you in the morning and from the *Today* show to the eleven o'clock news it kept you an awful company" ("Recitatif," 255). Ultimately, Morrison designed the story as a futile quest for racial signifiers to show not simply that "race matters," but that blackness born of racial strife is "the ghost in the machine," as she put it in her Tanner lecture, that keeps colorblind conservatism operational in the first place ("Unspeakable Things Unspoken," 11).

Taking this perspective on Morrison's early career, one can see that her interrogation of conservatism in *Beloved* was a culmination of her aesthetic and political interests up through the late eighties. In other words, although Beloved is rightly read as one of *the* novels of the black experience in America, it is also a novel about the Reaganite politics of whiteness, the American past, and moral innocence. By telling a neo-Gothic ghost story about the devastating psychological effects of slavery, Morrison literalized the "black ghost in the machine" metaphor concerning race as an invisible presence that had been haunting American literature and culture since the nation's founding, and continued to shape America in the present. Ironically, as Morrison was insisting on the lasting historical impact of slavery and racism, Reagan was proclaiming that the past, and the historical injustices associated with it, could be easily transcended. In his acceptance speech at the 1980 Republican convention, Reagan paraphrased Thomas Paine, the archenemy of Edmund Burke and a distrusted historical figure among traditionalists, saying: "We have it in our power to begin the world over again" ("Address Accepting the Presidential Nomination"). The implications for past racial injustice in Reagan's worldview were further thrown into relief later when he stated in a presidential press conference that his administration would staunchly advocate colorblind equality because "I'm old enough to remember when [minority] quotas existed in the U.S. for the purposes of discrimination. And I don't want to see that happen again" (qtd. in Anderson, *The Pursuit of Fairness*, 165). For Reagan, the American past, especially its bleaker side, did not affect the present in the way Morrison, or even a Burkean traditionalist such as Russell Kirk, imagined; indeed, much of the rhetorical potency of Reagan's nostalgic appeal to a bygone, Edenic America relied on the implicit premise that a terrifying disconnect had occurred between past and present. Conversely, the way the past haunted the present, for Morrison, was best captured not just by Faulkner's oft-repeated line that "the past is never dead [;] It's not even past," but by how Faulkner formally enacted this insight using modernist experiments with various narrative viewpoints, puzzlingly disjunctive interior monologues, and nonlinear storytelling (*Requiem for a Nun*, 69).

Considering these radically different views of America's racial history, and the literary forms best suited to representing that problematic heritage, I maintain that the typical ways critics have conceptualized *Beloved* as an engagement with Reaganite conservatism – for example, the contemporaneous political debates over "welfare queens," affirmative action, abortion and family values, and so on – are relatively less significant for postwar American literary history than Morrison's transformative appropriation of modernist aesthetics for racially progressive ends. In rendering the nineteenth-century past via modernist form, Morrison advanced an aesthetic that seemed to align with Russell Kirk's notion of the "moral imagination," a conservative mode of literary thinking that Kirk took from Burke and cultivated in relation to T. S. Eliot and Faulkner which aims to go beyond the events of the moment to interrogate difficult ethical questions invented by people in the past but addressed to their descendants in the present (Kirk, "The Moral Imagination," 207–8). But Morrison also signaled an awareness that a heavy-handed insistence on the inescapability of the past was uncomfortably close to both protest fiction and a mechanical, reactionary view of history that stifled emancipatory possibilities.

The dilemma, Morrison suggested, was twofold. On the one hand, Reaganite conservatism moved between two different registers, or meta-languages, depending on the issue at hand – that is, abstract individual emancipation or tradition-bound communal authority – and thereby established an ideology of privilege and exclusion that was remarkably adaptable. In a 1988 article on the crisis of American liberalism, the political philosopher Michael Sandel sketched out the first half of Morrison's dilemma in a similar way. Reagan's intuitive "political genius," Sandel concluded, "was to bring together in a single voice two contending strands in American conservatism. The first is individualistic, libertarian, and laissez-faire, the second, communal, traditionalist, and Moral Majoritarian" (21). On the other hand, Morrison repeatedly stressed that black emancipation efforts would have to move between similar meta-languages, appropriating pieces of classical liberalism, with its intense focus on individual liberty and equality, and a premodern communal politics that emphasized continuity with ancestors, rituals of selfless belonging, and even cosmic meaning.[3] For a problem this complex and dynamic, the genre of protest fiction was out of the question because it deployed a set of literary devices that tended to construct an imagined stability and stasis in relation to the conservative ideology it aimed to dismantle. For Morrison, protest fiction was useful against an ideology whose contradictions could be easily exposed, but modern conservatism was an ideology that thrived off the contradictions and paradoxes of whiteness, meaning that a more supple and sophisticated literary aesthetic was needed. Ultimately, then, Morrison's aesthetic-political project aimed to turn Reaganism on its head.

In *Beloved*, Morrison delineated the scope of her project by constructing two basic orientations toward the history of American slavery: the past counts for almost nothing versus the past explains virtually everything. Underpinned by a belief in unencumbered human agency, the first stance has political roots in certain Revolutionary Era principles espoused by classical liberal figures such as Thomas Paine and Thomas Jefferson, and it was a position widely taken up by white liberals during the Civil Rights Era, only to be appropriated by Reaganite conservatives in the so-called "post-racist" eighties. Conversely, stressing the weight or influence of the past, the second stance descends politically from Burke – who famously theorized that generations of social experimentation shaped many of our unthinking habits and everyday assumptions – and was adopted by twentieth-century conservative traditionalists, but was later reconfigured by social progressives in the wake of Black Power to emphasize certain forms of continuity between past oppressions and present ones. In *Beloved*, one stance is not unequivocally better (morally or philosophically) than the other, nor does this dichotomy constitute a fully coherent or comprehensive historical dialectic. Instead, Morrison constructed these opposing positions to foreground the complicated conservative discourse about individual freedom and traditional authority, and thus generate better questions about the history of race and gender to envision a more inclusive common good. As Morrison noted in her famous 1984 essay "Rootedness: The Ancestor as Foundation," this kind of critical thinking represents the ultimate purpose of the serious contemporary novel. While the American literary novel should be aesthetically beautiful, Morrison argued, it should also "have something in it that enlightens; something in it that opens the door and points the way. Something in it that suggests what the conflicts are, what the problems are. But it need not solve those problems because it is not a case study, it is not a recipe book" (58–59). In the midst of the Reagan Revolution, Morrison suggested, these conflicts and problems were inseparable from the changing ways Americans both reimagined and repressed the nation's discomforting past.

In the opening sections of *Beloved*, Morrison depicts several characters and scenes that represent the first orientation toward the American past as an unfortunate, though now largely irrelevant, saga of oppression that can be either aggressively ignored or safely repressed. When Paul D arrives at Sethe's home, one of the first actions he performs is to exorcise the disembodied ghost haunting Sethe and her daughter Denver. After he commands Beloved to "Get the hell out," the ghost launches a table at him and Paul D does "not stop whipping the table around until everything was rock quiet. . . . It was gone" (22). In this early scene, as Keith Byerman points out, Paul D "reads the past as divided off from the present and having only the relevance one chooses to grant it. He will not share the present with an embodiment of the past" (31). But after this supposed exorcism, during the novel's famous explication of Sethe's theory of "rememory," Sethe foreshadows Beloved's embodied return when she tells Denver that traumatic memories are like ghosts that "never die" and continue to haunt the present even after the original victim is gone (43). "If a house burns down, it's gone, but the place – the picture of it – stays, and not just in my rememory, but out there, in the world," Sethe explains. "I mean, even if I don't think it, even if I die, the picture of what I did, or knew, or saw is still out there. . . . The picture is still there and what's more, if you go there – you who never was there – if you go there an stand in the place where it was, it will happen again" (43–44). As Kathleen Brogan argues in her work on cultural haunting, rememory is a reconfiguration of personal memory "as an external reality that can take possession of [Sethe]" ("American Stories," 153). According to the novel's framework of rememory, then, trauma is not simply a private individual experience, but a collective, trans-historical experience that can seize the minds of future generations without their full awareness. The disturbing upshot, from Sethe's viewpoint, is that trauma fractures chronological time, making the future "a matter of keeping the past at bay" (51). Paradoxically, if traumatic rememory puts the past in front of the victim and her offspring, Sethe's job as a mother becomes "keeping [Denver] from the past that was still waiting for her" (51). In *Beloved*, the past haunts the characters not by chasing them from behind, but by lying in wait. Although this paradox of the "past-as-future" has been profitably read through psychoanalytic theorists such as Freud and Lacan, its most underappreciated political discourse partner is Reagan, who spoke incessantly about restoring not just America's present, but its future. According to the political scientist Cory Robin, modern conservatives are counter-revolutionaries who are nonetheless deeply influence by revolutionary habits of mind. As a result, "the conservative develops a particular attitude toward political time, a belief in the power of men and women to shape history, to propel it forward or backward; and by virtue of that belief, he comes to adopt the future as his preferred tense" (*Reactionary Mind*, 54). By repositioning the appalling memories of American slavery as future-oriented events, Morrison employs a combination of modernist form (nonlinear narration fragmented by trauma) and magical realism (Beloved's enigmatic embodiment as an adult women) to draw attention to Reaganism's nostalgia for a bygone past that never was and a future that is on the brink of restoring that ahistorical fantasy.

For many critics and scholars, it should be noted, the notion that Beloved's return personifies the unspeakable horrors of slavery and thus functions as a critique of Reaganism was evident from the beginning, and in the ensuing decades it became a routine way of contextualizing *Beloved*'s cultural politics. However, an intense debate has raged over the seemingly reactionary presuppositions built into Morrison's political critique, particularly in relation to the titular character as the key figure through whom colorblind conservatism is indicted. Essentially, some critics ask: in critiquing Reaganism's historical amnesia and colorblind innocence, does Morrison unknowingly adopt a different kind of reactionary position with regard to American racial history? Although I ultimately disagree with these critical stances, it is necessary to understand the terms and assumptions of their arguments to grasp Morrison's unique, complex engagement with Reaganite conservatism. As Trudier Harris noted in the first wave of scholarship on the novel, after Sethe and Paul D take in Beloved and nurture her, Beloved begins to act less like a ghost who haunts the present in the Gothic tradition and more like a vampire or demonic succubus who is animated by "a desire for vengeance" against Sethe (*Fiction and Folklore*, 157). Once Beloved seduces Paul D and then drives him out of Sethe's house, Beloved convinces Sethe that she is her murdered daughter and attaches herself to Sethe in increasingly parasitic ways, manifesting an insatiable desire for food and attention. Taking advantage of Sethe's profound sense of guilt, Beloved makes so many demands that the compulsion to consume eventually outweighs the desired objects themselves. "Anything [Beloved] wanted she got," Morrison writes, "and when Sethe ran out of things to give her, Beloved invented desire" (283). As Sethe fully engrosses herself in a destructive relationship with Beloved, in Keith Byerman's words, Sethe "becomes less and less capable of living in the present," which implies a profound lack of agency and a paralyzing sense of victimization that understands "the negative aspects of [contemporary] African American life [as] the result of this holocaust experience" (34). For these critics, then, Beloved's return and parasitic relationship with Sethe represents a thematic overreaction on Morrison's part, an uneasy political slippage between correcting amnesia and promoting a disabling obsession with the past.

Among these critics, Walter Benn Michaels offers not only the most sophisticated critique of the ostensibly reactionary usages of the past in

Beloved, but one that is inaccurate in a way that nevertheless illuminates Morrison's true project. While the reincarnation of the ghost can be seen, Michaels states, "as a figure for the way in which race can make the past present, another way to regard the ghost is as the figure for a certain anxiety about the very idea of race that is being called upon to perform this function" (*Shape of the Signifier*, 137). According to Michaels, Morrison weaves the Gothic literary device of the ghost into a twentieth-century neo-slave narrative to rebuke Reaganite colorblind individuality, but she quickly encounters the problem of racial essentialism latent in post-sixties, color-conscious liberalism. Morrison's ingenious solution is to harness a basic premise of multiculturalism – that is, that racial identity is not a biological phenomenon, but a historico-political construction – to translate ongoing racial oppression into a question of cultural remembering or forgetting, which means that "although no white or black people now living ever experienced it, slavery can be and must be either remembered or forgotten" (135). As the thematic core of *Beloved*, Michaels concludes, the ghost is not simply a figure for race's intrusion into the present but "a figure instead for a process, for history itself; *Beloved* is, in this respect, not only a historical but a historicist novel. It is historical in that it's about the historical past; it's historicist in that – setting out to remember the 'disremembered' – it redescribes something we have never known as something we have forgotten and thus makes the historical past a part of our own experience" (137). Michaels calls this stance "post-historicist identitarianism," a worldview Morrison supposedly shares with other post-sixties social progressives who tout "diversity" and are fundamentally "more interested in experiencing the past (if only by talking about it) than they are in having true beliefs about it" (140). Although Michaels never mentions Edmund Burke by name, he implicitly accuses Morrison of a strategic mistake vis-à-vis Burkean traditionalism, since her move from learning about history to re-experiencing it mirrors the Burkean notion that the past is infinitely complex, difficult to know theoretically, and thus survives via experiential prejudices and customs. For Morrison, Michaels's criticism implies, identity is inherited through specific kinds of Burkean prejudices – that is, those residual experiences from the past that are embedded in a metaphorical body politic and that manifest themselves through complex mechanisms of remembering and forgetting. Ultimately, Michaels assumes that Morrison misinterpreted the individualism/traditionalism double register of conservatism when she substituted "true," empirical knowledge about history for the multicultural trope of repressed memory.

The problem with Michaels's argument, I contend, is that Morrison includes these reactionary historicist elements in *Beloved* not because she confuses them with progressive multiculturalism, but because she uses them to continue investigating the conflicting strains that constitute movement conservatism itself. By criticizing one strain of modern conservatism – that is, colorblind individualism – and its corollary assumption of a Lockean social contract undergirding society, Morrison seems to risk implicitly adopting another strain of conservatism found in traditionalism, even though she sees valuable elements in traditionalism that she aimed to repurpose. Like Burke, Morrison at times frames society as a massive, trans-historical organism that is comprehensible via metaphors of personhood. In Burke's famous words, society is less a voluntary contract between consenting individuals than "a partnership not only between those who are living, but between those who are living, those who are dead, and those who are to be born" (*Reflections*, 194–95). To flesh out his notion of sociopolitical continuity, Burke liked to compare society to a body that never dies. The upshot, for Burke, was that history lived within the everyday actions and unconscious thoughts of people, and that these prejudices were experiential reenactments that could essentially re-member the past. Although Burke and Morrison would certainly differ on the ultimate benefits of past prejudices, the Burkean conception of the past readily maps onto the history-as-memory framework in *Beloved*. Early in the novel, Morrison writes that Denver sees Sethe's house at 124 Bluestone Road – an oft-cited, multivalent symbol for society and history – "as a person rather than a structure. A person that wept, sighed, trembled and fell into fits" (35). It is no coincidence that in the same chapter, Sethe reveals her theory of "rememory" to Denver, which posits that traumatic memories live on independent of victims and always stay "there waiting for you" (44). The notion that history can be recalled reaches its fullest manifestation in a late chapter told from Beloved's fragmented perspective, as she remembers crossing the Middle Passage on a slave ship steered by white people, or "men without skin" (249). As the novel makes clear, Beloved could not have personally experienced the Middle Passage, insofar as she is the reincarnation of Sethe's infant daughter. This narrative fact suggests that Beloved is an allegorical character who stands in for all of slavery's victims. Since Beloved recalls the Middle Passage only from the perspectives of African slaves, it also seems to establish slavery as the inescapable framework of contemporary African American identity formation. For critics such as Michaels, this multicultural identity trope seems progressive on the surface, but it merely reinscribes a traditionalist vision of the past that denies African Americans real, material agency and plays into the hands of conservatives who decry excessive black victimhood.

However, instead of seeing Morrison as stumped by the individualism/traditionalism double register of conservatism, I contend that she actually understands the modern Right better than many of her critics. The crucial point is that when the past comes back with a vengeance in *Beloved*, when the ghost becomes a grotesque presence sucking the life out of Sethe, Morrison is overtly constructing an outlandish conservative stereotype of black consciousness. In other words, Morrison is again deploying a grim parody – her signature modernist device, as I demonstrate earlier in "Recitatif," for examining Reaganism – to darkly burlesque *how conservatives think African Americans imagine the impact of slavery as an all-consuming, all-excusing historical trauma*. For contemporary African Americans, slavery is still "the wound that never healed," Dinesh D'Souza explains in his conservative polemic *The End of Racism*, because liberal black demagogues make it "the moral core of the oppression story that is so fundamental to black identity today" (69). The black conservative Thomas Sowell elaborates on this point: "slavery has served as an all-purpose explanation of many social phenomena [in black communities], ranging from broken families to poor education, lower labor force participation rates, and high rates of crime and violence" (*Black Rednecks*, 56). Using free indirect discourse from Denver's point of view, Morrison ventriloquizes this conservative racial position when Denver goes to the house and sees that Sethe has stopped eating and lost weight, making Beloved look like the mother and Sethe the child. In one important passage, Morrison depicts their inverted relationship:

> The bigger Beloved got, the smaller Sethe became; the brighter Beloved's eyes, the more those eyes that used to never look away became slits of sleeplessness. Sethe no longer combed her hair or splashed her face with water. She sat in the chair licking her lips like a chastised child while Beloved ate up her life, took it, swelled up with it, grew taller on it. And the older woman yielded it up without a murmur. (294–95)

At this late point in the novel, due to Sethe's experiences of "rememory" and her melancholic relationship with Beloved, one could plausibly claim that this confirms the extent to which Sethe's life is defined by the past. Echoing the conservative critique of black cultural pathology, Sethe is two racist stereotypes in one, a child-like victim of slavery represented through images of infantilized dependence *and* a criminalized victimizer who ultimately blames her murderous deeds on systemic historical injustice.

Morrison reveals her parodic design, though, by focalizing these scenes through Denver, the only major character not to have grown up in the Antebellum United States, who begins searching for ways to break Sethe and Beloved out of their mutual solipsism. By adding this layer of perspectival irony, Morrison signals that she is reconstructing another position or node in the contemporary discourse of American racial politics. If Beloved's embodied return represents the color-conscious liberal position that the past still influences the present, and Sethe's behavior mimics the conservative position that the "haunted past" merely rationalizes black dependency, Denver occupies a third position outside of that restrictive, binary argumentative register. Morrison dramatizes this insight once Denver has taken over all of the domestic duties and chores as Beloved and Sethe ignore everything outside their relationship: "[Denver] came to realize that her presence in that house had no influence on what either woman did. She kept them alive and they ignored her. Growled when they chose; sulked, explained, demanded, strutted, cowered, cried and provoked each other to the edge of violence, then over" (296). Denver's epiphany is that these two positions resemble poles in a partisan debate that form a vicious circle, as both sides are fixed in stances that they cannot argue each other out of. Instead of inserting herself into this futile argument, Denver leaves the house to look for work because, if she simply stays home, "there would be no one to save, no one to come home to, and no Denver either. It was a new thought, having a self to look out for and preserve" (297). As she becomes both more self-reliant and more engaged in the community, Denver fashions an identity that is informed by her life with Sethe and her experiences with Beloved, but ultimately independent of them. At one moment, as Denver thanks a neighbor for pitching in and giving her half a pie, she hears him say, "Take care of yourself, Denver." While merely a casual comment, Denver hears "it as though it were what language was made for" (297). Echoing Audre Lorde's famous late-eighties declaration that self-care is political warfare rather than self-indulgence, Morrison posits a form of black female selfhood that strikes at the heart of the conservative movement's ideological foundation in whiteness (Lorde, 131).

Through Denver's maturation, Morrison establishes a set of coordinates for understanding black emancipation that circumvents, but does not naïvely sidestep, the debate between color-conscious progressivism and colorblind conservatism. Morrison suggests that to get caught in the debate between Beloved and Sethe is to get caught in a debate structured less by Right and Left than by the twin registers of modern conservatism –

that is, libertarian individualism and communal traditionalism. The late-eighties debate about race and the American past, Morrison seems to say, easily took the form of a rigid binary that was not susceptible to ideology critique, as conservatives themselves routinely drew attention during the culture wars to so-called "radicals" who aimed to unmask race and whiteness as paired historical constructions. As signaled by Denver's emergence as the protagonist at the end of *Beloved*, Morrison's answer is to introduce a new black template on the very terms modern conservatism offers, a kind of "ordered liberty" fusionism from the perspective of African Americans. In the novel's climax, Denver helps organize a group of black community members to come to her house and exorcise Beloved, an effort that combines Denver's individual resourcefulness and communal effort to thwart another futile cycle of violence. As the women arrive at the house, Mr. Bodwin approaches to pick up Denver for work, and Sethe rushes toward him with an ice pick, for she is in the grip of a "rememory" and mistakes Mr. Bodwin for schoolteacher, the sadistic authority figure on the Sweet Home plantation. When the women tackle Sethe and prevent her from killing an innocent man, Beloved suddenly disappears. In this moment, as critics have pointed out, the black community not only stops Sethe from recreating her tragic decision, they also redeem themselves in some fashion, since they did not help Sethe eighteen years earlier when schoolteacher came and Sethe killed her child. What many readings still miss, though, is Morrison's subtle engagement with postwar conservative discourse. Morrison asserts that America's haunted past embodied by Beloved certainly needs to be exorcised or transcended, as Reaganite conservatives also argued, but that it must be executed by African Americans themselves, not by conservatives who declare that race does not matter anymore. Refusing to get tangled up in a debate about whether or not the past straightforwardly determines the present, Morrison resists the urge to simply unmask modern conservatism. Instead, she reworks it from within, using modernist aesthetics to offer a new model that decenters conservatism's basic masculine whiteness. As Mark McGurl argues, Morrison saw a blind spot in Faulknerian modernism: "an inability to see things from the African American point of view" (*The Program Era*, 354). By adopting a black point of view, Morrison turned "the high modernist tradition in narrative halfway around on its racial-perspectival axis" (354). This model of racially progressive modernism was incompatible with modern conservatism on its own terms of "ordered liberty," thus dissolving the dilemma as rapidly as Beloved dissolves at novel's end.

With the publication of *Beloved*, Morrison played a significant role in completing a half-century shift in American literary politics. In the mid-fifties, conservatives' embrace of high literary culture was inseparable from their movement's powerful strain of segregationist traditionalism. Morrison transcended the rigid categorization of politics and literature that plagued James Baldwin in the sixties, and showed that progressive novelists did not have to refute modern conservatism with protest fiction's heavy-handed arguments, but could neutralize it with high modernism's poetic lyricism and complex narrative designs from a black perspective. By the eighties, then, Morrison cemented the notion that social progressivism and difficult modernist aesthetics were compatible. However, Morrison and other major progressive novelists were not the only active agents in this historical shift. As revealed in the next section, conservatives were finding it difficult to establish a durable literary tradition in their movement, even in the midst of their electoral victories under Reagan. In the literary field, conservatives would respond to the liberalizing influences of the sixties by adopting a position of white male grievance that adopted the very forms of social realism and didactic genre fiction that they once abhorred, but with the important caveat that class struggle was concealed. At the end of the twentieth century, nobody was more important to this conservative literary project than Tom Wolfe.

5.4 The Literary Rosetta Stone of Modern Conservatism: Tom Wolfe's *The Bonfire of the Vanities*

At the end of World War II, the modern conservative movement was interested in claiming fiction writers who enjoyed the kind of intellectual and cultural respectability often associated with highbrow literature in an attempt to naturalize elite wealth and elite taste. But conservatives were generally not able to square this interest with an ideological agenda that, beginning in the late sixties, increasingly embraced racially coded populism, free-market capitalism, unambiguous patriotism, and moral certitude. For a host of reasons examined in previous chapters, conservatives praised certain serious post-1945 novelists for a limited time – for example, Ralph Ellison, Flannery O'Connor, Norman Mailer, and Saul Bellow – but each one was too unorthodox in the end to be a literary torchbearer for the conservative movement in the same way that liberal-leaning novelists were routinely enlisted as intellectual thought leaders in progressive movements. This changed when Tom Wolfe published *The Bonfire of the Vanities* in 1987. Conservatives found their long-awaited literary darling, crowning Wolfe the most important novelist of modern American conservatism, largely because his novel was able to transform historical class conflict into status conflict, and thus imaginatively smooth over class resentments in the Reagan coalition between wealthy white capitalists and the white working class, essentially naturalizing elite wealth and lowbrow taste.

Although Wolfe was never a full-fledged movement conservative, he had a friendly relationship with postwar conservatism, and Buckley and *National Review* had regarded him as a cultural ally ever since the publication of his controversial work *Radical Chic and Mau-Mauing the Flak Catchers* (1970), a short book composed of two earlier New Journalist essays that satirized Great Society liberalism's supposedly paralyzing white guilt before the righteous anger of black revolutionaries and agitators. In his signature piece "Radical Chic," Wolfe attends a fundraiser for the Black Panthers held by Leonard Bernstein in his swanky Park Avenue apartment and mocks wealthy white liberals who support the Black Panthers not because they truly desire radical social change, no matter how sincerely they think they do, but because it is the latest upper-class social trend. While it may seem new, radical chic is merely the reemergence of *nostalgie de la boue* ("nostalgia for the mud"), Wolfe writes, a collection of vacuous political stances and gestures that gripped wealthy New Yorkers in the nineteenth century ("Radical Chic," 27). Wolfe claims that occasionally, at certain moments in America's unique class history, the enlightened elite resent the striving middle class and they feel an intense, romanticized identification with the seemingly primitive lower classes. Paradoxically, since radical chic "is only radical in style," Wolfe says, "in its heart it is part of Society and its traditions" of social climbing (79). For Wolfe, this irony forces a white liberal like Bernstein into a variety of amusing ideological contortions so that he can rhetorically support the Black Panthers, but continue to live in luxury sustained by the very socioeconomic order that the Panthers want to dismantle.

From the perspective of Buckley and other movement conservatives, Wolfe's nonfiction was uniquely appealing in the wake of the sixties. First, Wolfe helped conservatives shift their emphasis when arguing against the excesses of the civil rights movement and Black Power. In the fifties and early sixties, conservatives had focused their attacks directly on popular civil rights leaders such as Martin Luther King, whom Buckley frequently implied was a communist race-baiter, and federal civil rights legislation. But Wolfe showed conservatives how to deploy less explicitly inflammatory language – even if, in the words of James N. Stull, Wolfe always wrote about African Americans "in a sophomoric manner" – and make clueless, intellectual white liberals the primary target of ridicule (Stull, 29).[4] Moreover, Wolfe's *nostalgie de la boue* functioned as a sophisticated intellectualization of the Southern Strategy, for he popularized the term in conservative circles at the same moment when Vice-President Spiro Agnew was decrying "liberal elites" as snobbish do-gooders who wanted to help poor people of color at the expense of hardworking white families. Finally, Wolfe was doing this cultural work as one of the founders of New Journalism, a self-consciously serious and innovative literary movement that he famously declared "would wipe out the novel as literature's main event" precisely when conservatives were losing faith in most major American novelists, whom conservatives saw as beholden to liberal academic and cultural institutions (*The New Journalism*, 9). The great hope of Wolfe and his conservative allies was that "the New Journalism's anti-academic expertise threatened the [liberal] literary establishment," Stephen Schryer explains, perhaps one day "shattering the status system that had governed it since the nineteenth century and exposing it to its outside. In that system, novelists and poets were the aristocrats, critics were the middle class, journalists the proletariat, and feature writers the 'lumpenproles'" (*Maximum Feasible Participation*, 119). So, when Wolfe appeared on Buckley's television show *Firing Line* in December 1970 to promote *Radical Chic and Mau-Mauing the Flak Catchers*, it is hardly surprising in retrospect that Buckley was already calling Wolfe "the most skillful writer in America" and praising him for writing a book that so enraged the Eastern liberal media establishment that Wolfe was in the process of being "publicly excommunicated by the bishops who preside over the *New York Review of Books*" (Buckley, *Firing Line*, "Radical Chic"). As two Buckley co-biographers wrote, Wolfe's appearance on the show transformed him into "a cultural icon of the right" virtually overnight (Bridges and Coyne, 118). At this moment, Buckley and Wolfe struck up an enduring alliance because both men spearheaded insurgent movements that liked to see themselves as rebel bands escaping the institutional conformity and liberal absurdities of American politics and literature, respectively. Throughout the seventies, Wolfe honed a crude, quasi-Bourdieuan critique of liberal elite aesthetic taste that movement conservatives would adopt as a basic template for literary analysis. Epitomizing this mode of satire in his short vignette "Mauve Gloves & Madmen, Clutter & Vine" (1976), Wolfe describes a cocktail party in Martha's Vineyard in which an unnamed high-status New York author discerns "a glimmer of the future" of the American literary field:

> A vison in which America's best minds, her intellectuals, found a common ground, a natural unity, with the enlightened segments of her old aristocracy, her old money ... the two groups bound together by ... but by what? ... he could *almost* see it, but not quite ... it was *presque vu* ... it was somehow a matter of taste ... of sensibility ... of grace, natural grace ... just as he himself had a natural feel for the best British styles, which were after all the source of British manners. (10–11)

Yet another paradigmatic text in the postwar history of conservative cultural aesthetics, Wolfe's essay provides an almost point-by-point dramatization of Bourdieu's concept of a class-based habitus – that is, the notion that highbrow taste is the result of internalized class conditioning, though it is commonly misrecognized as natural aptitude (*Distinction*, 95–96). By arguing that liberal literary elites are bound to an older, decadent American aristocracy through a shared, corrupted form of highbrow "taste," Wolfe implicitly celebrates the emerging cross-class alliance prized by movement conservatives: commercially successful realist authors (and readers) who share the same "taste" as an energetic, *nouveau riche* entrepreneurial capitalist elite.[5]

When *Bonfire* arrived seventeen years after Wolfe's iconic emergence on the Right, conservatives hailed Wolfe's first novel as a watershed text for their movement, since it was a literary work that was conservative, commercially successful, and generally seen by critics as serious fiction. Wolfe, conservatives believed, had gone beyond his satirical, essayistic sketches of liberal absurdism and offered in their place an immense panorama that, no matter his many conflicting intentions as a novelist, captured the cultural perspective of movement conservatism and imaginatively represented it in a compelling way. Considering the conservative movement at midcentury, what is most surprising about the praise Wolfe garnered from conservatives is that it carried with it a newfound enthusiasm for social realism, or what Wolfe famously called "the new social novel." In the first celebratory review of *Bonfire* in *National Review*, Richard Vigilante claimed that the primary reason why Wolfe had secured "his place as the most important writer of his generation" and was genuinely "saving American literature" was because Wolfe had almost singlehandedly re-legitimized social realism with a blockbuster "bestseller" (Vigilante, 46). "Largely because of Wolfe's efforts," Vigilante wrote, without a trace of irony, "it is finally safe to predict that the social-realist novel will soon re-emerge as an accepted and perhaps dominant force on the serious-fiction scene" (46). Bracketing off Vigilante's shaky argument about the role of social realism in postwar literary fiction, this review is significant because it is an exact inversion of earlier conservative movement rhetoric concerning the value of literary form. Once, conservatives had justified their veneration of high modernists like Faulkner and Eliot by juxtaposing them with supposedly second-rate, politically progressive social realists such as Theodore Dreiser, Frank Norris, and John Steinbeck. At that time, conservatives prized modernist texts mainly for reasons that had to do with form; not only did the modernist text's organic complexity mirror the organic complexity of society theorized by Burke, but its attendant readerly difficulties – in textbook Bourdieuan fashion – separated the traditional elite from the ignorant masses. Toward the end of the twentieth century, though, conservatives were supporting Wolfe's call for a new social novel that was readable and popular, as opposed to the stereotypical postmodern novel's un-readability and small, (liberal) academic target audience.

In Wolfe's theoretical companion piece to *Bonfire*, "Stalking the Billion-Footed Beast," one can see why conservatives supported Wolfe's plea for a new social novel, as Wolfe proposed a popular genre that synced up perfectly with the conservative movement's Reaganite turn toward free-market capitalism and colorblind, though racially aggrieved, populism. In his "literary manifesto for the new social novel," Wolfe mocked the contemporaneous literary scene with colorful quips that echoed decades of conservative digs at out-of-touch academic elites ("Stalking," 45). "Writers in the university creative writing programs," Wolfe claimed, do not investigate reality but have "long, phenomenological discussions in which they decided that the act of writing words on a page was the real thing" (49). To revitalize the American novel, Wolfe called for a return to the social realist novel, but stripped of its central preoccupation with class and replaced with the American preoccupation of status. While Wolfe agreed with Lionel Trilling when Trilling argued in the late forties that "what produced great characters in the nineteenth-century European novel was the portrayal of 'class traits modified by personality,'" Wolfe noted that the European class structure did not exist in the United States. Although Trilling partly shared this view, it was a crucial point for Wolfe because he, like other movement conservatives, contended that "class" was not an operative category in the United States, especially not in the way that Marxists and liberals believed it was operative. From this perspective, Wolfe argued that if "we substitute for *class*, in Trilling's formulation, the broader term *status*, [realist] technique has never been more essential in portraying the innermost life of the individual" (51, emphasis in original). The allure of Wolfe's literary rationale for conservatives is easily discernible here: what first appears to be a class conflict is, if properly portrayed in the new social realist novel, actually a status conflict playing out on a cultural battleground. This process of formal substitution does not produce, of course, a return to an earlier class-based social realism, but a form of inverted proletarian or protest fiction. Wolfe, in other words, produces a white "conservative protest fiction" that evacuates class categories, traffics in characterological types, and aspires, above all, to flesh out a reactionary anthropological sociology of status anxiety.

By looking at *Bonfire*'s basic plot structure from two different angles, one can clearly see how this status-for-class substitution yields a kind of conservative protest fiction. On the one hand, the novel's catalyzing plot point seems like the perfect recipe for a midcentury socialist protest novel laced with issues of race and class: a white couple lost in a bad neighborhood hit a young black man with their car, quickly drive away, and leave him severely injured and likely to die in the street. When the young man goes into a coma in his hospital bed, a black "street socialist" from Harlem rallies the black community, ultimately compelling New York politicians and major media institutions to bring these privileged white Manhattanites to justice. On the other hand, a more detailed, accurate plot summary reveals how this narrative premise merely disguises an agonistic struggle between self-interested status seekers: the posh life of Sherman McCoy, a wealthy white New York financier, is shattered after he picks up his mistress, Maria Ruskin, from the airport and takes a wrong turn into a dystopian vision of the Bronx where two young black criminals obstruct a highway ramp with trash in an attempt to rob them. When McCoy and Ruskin justifiably defend themselves, with McCoy fighting them off and Ruskin getting behind the wheel and hitting the one named Henry Lamb, they speed away for their own safety. In the following weeks, representative characters from every major New York institution swoop down like vultures to capitalize on the incident for their own private gain and become stand-ins for the basic corruption of each group – black activists and community organizers (the greedy demagogic "street socialist" Reverend Reginald Bacon); progressive religious organizations that enable these black demagogues (the liberal Episcopal minister Edward Fiske III, who cowers before Reverend Bacon even though Bacon essentially stole $350,000 from the Episcopal diocese); newspaper and television media (the dishonest, alcoholic journalist Peter Fallow who values sensationalism over "truth"); and, most damningly, the New York justice system (Bronx District Attorney Abe Weiss who sees McCoy as the "Great White Defendant" whose conviction could redeem the collective guilty conscience of so many liberal New York prosecutors and assure Weiss reelection). Wolfe does not give these characters much psychological depth or conflicted inner life, but rather paints them all as "big, vivid blots of typology," in James Wood's memorable criticism of Wolfe's fiction ("Tom Wolfe's Shallowness," 210). After Wolfe introduces each static character, the rest of the novel becomes a story of how these stereotypes collide to produce a social satire of big city liberalism that is significantly bleaker than his earlier essays, for each character's racial political correctness merely masquerades as self-righteous virtue and creates an institutional alliance hell-bent on destroying the life of an essentially innocent man (McCoy) marked out for his wealth and whiteness.

What makes *Bonfire* a truly compelling conservative protest novel, though, is the complex way Wolfe negotiates McCoy's class position and racial identity so that whiteness, not wealth, becomes his most salient feature by novel's end. As James Baldwin noted in his famous indictment of protest fiction, the genre's founding law is that it is "categorization alone which is real and which cannot be transcended" (*CE*, 18). Thus, the basic mechanism of protest fiction, in the words of Baldwin scholar Jerry W. Ward, Jr., is a sociological one: "Like sociology, the protest novel [has always] supported a passion for categorizing" (Ward, 175). Wolfe, a proud literary sociologist, uses the novel's prologue to establish a reactionary conception of race as the fundamental category that will govern the book's narrative arc. In this brief opening section, New York's Jewish Mayor is giving a speech when "Bacon's people," black agitators yelling anti-Semitic slurs at the Mayor, disrupt the event in a premeditated attempt to humiliate him in front of the media (5). In his mind, this signals a conflict that can only be understood along antagonistic racial lines: "Back to blood! Them and us!" (6). Then, as the Mayor looks at the television cameras and fantasizes about addressing a wealthy white audience, Wolfe uses free indirect discourse to establish the novel's central question: "Do you really think this is *your* city any longer? Open your eyes! The greatest city of the twentieth century! Do you think *money* will keep it yours? Come down from your swell co-ops, you general partners and merger lawyers! It's the Third World down there! . . . [and] do you really think you're insulated from the *Third World*?" (6–7, emphasis in original). What the Mayor recognizes is not simply that racial categorization trumps class categorization, but that white racial identity includes its own implicit class position. Across the entire postwar American political spectrum, as the sociologist Michael Kimmel argues, class tends to serve as a proxy for race. "When politicians speak of the 'urban poor,'" Kimmel writes, alluding to an infamous Reagan quote, "we know it's a code for black people. When they talk about 'welfare queens,' we know the race of that woman driving the late model Cadillac" (244). But on the political Right specifically, an interesting reversal occurs: *race often serves as a proxy for class.* When movement conservatives, or sometimes even far-right white supremacists, allude to racial whiteness, they are not thinking about all white people. "They don't mean Wall Street bankers and lawyers, though they are pretty much entirely white and male," Kimmel explains, "They mean middle- and working-class white people. Race consciousness is actually class consciousness without actually having to 'see' class" (244–45). In *Bonfire*, employing this premise that race is a proxy for class, Wolfe reconfigures the signature device of protest fiction – that is, a dominant social problem that damages characters in ways they are only vaguely aware of – to dramatize the central conflict of modern conservatism between free-market capitalism and white working-class populism.

Wolfe's commitment to this conservative racial categorization animates McCoy's long character arc over the nearly 700-page novel, for McCoy must realize that whiteness is inextricably bound up with a working-class ethos in order to be saved from the racial Others who want to destroy him. Early in the novel, McCoy thinks of himself as a privileged member of the wealthiest class, a Wall Street "master of the universe" living in New York, a fabled city that McCoy thinks of as "the Rome, the Paris, the London of the twentieth century, the city of ambition . . . the irresistible destination of all those who insist on being *where things are happening* – and he was among the victors!" (75, emphasis in original). After McCoy and his mistress Maria rush back to her apartment after hitting Henry Lamb, McCoy believes that his wealth and class-based status will protect him because the major public institutions were designed to protect people of his class in the first place. When McCoy tells her that they should notify the police and tell them everything, Maria laughs at his innocence and counters with a politically incorrect *Realpolitik* response rooted in white populism. "I'm from South Carolina and I'm going to tell you [what happened] in plain English," Maria says, ventriloquizing the darkest undercurrent of Lee Atwater's Southern Strategy, "Two niggers tried to kill us, and we got away. Two niggers tried to kill us in the jungle, and we got outta the jungle" (90). After their conversation, Maria's neocolonialist "jungle" metaphor proliferates throughout the novel, remerging many times in McCoy's free indirect discourse, and thematically links to the Mayor's previous insistence that the Bronx and other New York boroughs constitute an internal "third world." Later, once the Bronx DA Weiss begins aggressively pushing for McCoy's arrest, McCoy and Maria have another conversation in which she explains to him that the law of the jungle also governs New York's justice system, and every other rotten liberal institution in the city. McCoy may fancy himself a "master of the universe" in the figurative jungle of Wall Street, Maria tells him, but the legal system is a real, life-or-death state of nature. "Laws weren't any kind of threat to you growing up [because] they were your laws," Maria informs him, "Well, I didn't grow up that way ... Right there on the line everybody's an animal – the police, the judges, the criminals, everybody" (257). A symbolic ambassador of the white working class, Maria introduces McCoy to the kind of white populist identity that he will eventually need to adopt to survive the city's systematic corruption, which was created by people who insist on post-sixties color-conscious liberalism.

While Wolfe depicts Maria as a stereotypical Southern bumpkin, he makes it clear that her intuitions about a metaphorical, citywide racial jungle are accurate. In one of the novel's set-pieces, Reverend Bacon and his right-hand man, a muscular black enforcer figure named "Buck," organize the "Open Gates Employment Coalition," which is a group that marches outside upscale restaurants "to break down the walls of apartheid in the job market" (143). Wolfe demonstrates, though, that this is merely another one of Bacon's schemes that uses intimidation and bullying tactics to extort restaurants and labor unions. Significantly, this scheme is almost a point-by-point reproduction of the intimidation practices Wolfe documented in "Mau-Mauing the Flak Catchers." At San Francisco welfare offices in the late sixties, black goons from what Wolfe tellingly called "the ghetto jungle" used intimidation practices gleaned from Kenya's Mau-Mau rebellion to harass and humiliate government functionaries, who "caught their flak" and handed over money in return ("Mau-Mauing," 105). In an interlocking *Bonfire* storyline, the irresponsible journalist Peter Fallow exacerbates Bacon's inflammatory strategy of racial conflict by creating the myth that Henry Lamb was an honor student. After tracking down the teenager's high school teacher, the white instructor tells Fallow that Lamb may have technically been an "honor student," but that such a term held little practical meaning in a school were students "range from cooperative to life-threatening" and teachers doled out grades according to the level of fear a student inspired (214). Once "honor student" is splashed across the front of every newspaper, Abe Weiss and the other white liberals in the Bronx District Attorney's office feel a combination of external and internal pressure to prosecute the "Great White Defendant." Legendary though elusive, the Great White Defendant is not a specific person, but rather an imaginary rich white male for whom prosecutors search for with a monomania comparable only to Melville's Captain Ahab – which is, not incidentally, the moniker low-level DA bureaucrats have given Weiss – in order to satisfy Bacon's demagoguery and redeem their own guilty consciences for spending their entire professional lives "pack[ing] blacks and Latins off to jail" (101). For the prosecutors, Wolfe reminds readers repeatedly, the origin of their intense search is the uncomfortable reality that people of color are little more than "chow" for the "maw of the criminal justice system" (39). As Joshua J. Masters points out, this set of images alludes to anxieties about cannibalism, another classic leitmotif of the neocolonialist imagination, with McCoy as the sacred object of consumption since "his flesh, simultaneously despised and desired, is elevated by the very category of 'whiteness'" (222). The innocent McCoy, in other words, must play the role of the Great White Defendant and be sacrificed so that the justice system can appear rational and fair-minded, instead of the uncivilized "jungle" that, Wolfe strongly implies, it really is.

Once McCoy fully occupies the role of the Great White Defendant, though, he undergoes a figurative death and rebirth that transforms his identity from one primarily rooted in class (Wall Street financier) to one primarily rooted in race (Scotch-Irish), effectively making him a movement conservative archetype. While going through a horrific experience at the police department's Central Booking office, McCoy is put into a cell with the racialized "maggots," and thinks to himself: "It was *not* an ordinary arrest. It was *death*. Every bit of honor, respect, dignity, that he, a creature named Sherman McCoy, might ever have possessed had been removed . . . and it was his dead soul that now stood here" (440, emphasis in original). During this Odyssean journey through the underworld, which Wolfe refers to in free indirect discourse as "the Congo," McCoy sees the true state of things via the experience of social death (434). McCoy's new identity begins to surface for the first time while he sits in his apartment with his gruff Irish lawyer, Thomas Killian, looks down at "Bacon's people" protesting in front of his building, and says he (McCoy) would like to "invite those bastards . . . on up here" (517). Killian responds: "Now you're turning fucking *Irish*. The Irish been living the last twelve hundred years on dreams of revenge" (517, emphasis in original). Later, while standing in Killian's office as the trial date for Henry Lamb's murder nears, McCoy embraces his Scotch-Irish surname by totally renouncing his previous class identity. "I have nothing to do with Wall Street or Park Avenue or Yale," McCoy says, "I'm a different human being. I exist *down here* now" (603, emphasis in original). In this moment, McCoy becomes legible as a conservative populist who understands that race (psychically endangered whiteness) is a proxy for class (a blue-collar socioeconomic position), but his transformation is not truly complete until the end of the novel.

In the final climactic scene, after the judge finds out that the conversation between McCoy and Maria immediately following the hit-and-run was secretly taped, he declares a mistrial and Bacon's protesters explode in anger. As McCoy is hurried out of the courtroom, he encounters Bacon's enforcer, Buck, and instead of cowering in fear or hiding behind a policeman, delivers a devastating punch to his "solar plexus," doubling Buck over and humiliating him, fulfilling the promise of the chapter's title "Into the Solar Plexus" (627). Employing violence, McCoy finally acts according to the law of the racial jungle that Maria first revealed to him. This scene brings the novel full circle because McCoy has implicitly answered the Mayor's question in the prologue – No, McCoy realizes, his wealth will not save him – and he has accepted the racial categories that the Mayor delineated as the basic terms of conflict. To drive home the point one last time that McCoy has become a reactionary populist, Wolfe includes an epilogue written in the form of several *New York Times* articles; in one, Wolfe reports that McCoy lost a civil trial after Henry Lamb died, and McCoy responded in court by raising a clenched-fist in a re-appropriation of the Black Power salute (637). When Killian is asked to comment, he says that if a trial was being held *in foro conscientiae* ("in the court of the conscience"), which is the space Wolfe's readers occupy, then "the defendants would be Abe Weiss, Reginald Bacon, and Peter Fallow," the three major representatives of New York's irredeemably corrupt liberal institutions. At last, McCoy's true identity is revealed: the Great White, Working-Class Victim of progressive liberalism.

In *Bonfire*, the literary Rosetta Stone of modern conservatism, Wolfe utilized the formal template of realism to create something like a "conservative protest fiction" genre in which every well-wrought detail functions as another piece of evidence in a grand, conservative anthropological theory of status that substitutes class conflict for reactionary cultural conflict. Colorfully illustrated through satire, Wolfe's fiction primarily targeted self-righteous white liberals who disdained the white working class, specifically industrious white men. At the heart of Wolfe's novelistic project, then, was an effort to categorize characters according to their respective combination of status anxiety, liberal ideological bent, and self-perceived position in a given sociocultural (as opposed to class) hierarchy – all of which, ultimately, vindicated a movement conservative worldview rooted in free-market capitalism, nominal colorblind individualism, and aggrieved white working-class populism. In the next few decades, conservative pop novelists from Tom Clancy to Tim LaHaye and Jerry B. Jenkins would take inspiration, directly and indirectly, from Wolfe's novelistic project and appropriate his realist mechanism of characterological categorization to write ideologically didactic genre fiction that eagerly and proudly distanced itself from the liberal stench of high culture. Essentially, Wolfe's big sociological novels confirmed the idea, widely held by midcentury writers and critics such as James Baldwin and Irving Howe, that sociology was the highest form, for better or worse, to which protest fiction could aspire. The most sophisticated manifestation of conservative protest fiction in the Age of Reagan, Wolfe's novelistic project remains the indispensable literary object for understanding the conservative movement's peculiar relationship with, and antagonism toward, the contemporary highbrow American novel.

5.5 Conclusion: Fear the Black Madonna, Respect the White Suit

The profound impact of *Beloved* and *Bonfire* not only turned Morrison and Wolfe into the central literary antagonist and protagonist of the conservative movement, respectively, but also cemented the linkage between liberalism and highbrow literary fiction in the last decade of the twentieth century. After winning the Nobel Prize in Literature in 1993, which was awarded to her in no small part because of *Beloved*, Morrison became a singular force in contemporary American literature: the first native-born American novelist to win the Nobel Prize in over thirty years (since John Steinbeck in 1962); a black female author who wrote formally challenging novels and was the face of American literary multiculturalism, but who also had legions of fans and routinely published bestsellers; an outspoken literary critic whose reappraisal of canonical American literature through the lens of race helped popularize the extant surge in African American scholarship by academics such as Henry Louis Gates, Jr. and Houston A. Baker, Jr.; and, to the unique chagrin of conservatives, an eloquent political orator and essayist who criticized Reaganite conservatism from a distinctive position of cultural prestige. Writing in the Spring 1996 edition of the *Review of Contemporary Fiction*, a still relatively unknown novelist named Jonathan Franzen summed up Morrison's post-Nobel Prize reputation: "Today, when I try to think of American novelists who might be heeded as a cultural authority, the list begins and ends with Toni

Morrison" (34). By the mid-nineties, Morrison's reputation had been utterly transformed from its status even just a decade earlier. To many in the upper echelons of the literary establishment, she was now the most important novelist in the United States.

Although American conservatives in the nineties admitted that Morrison's reputation was a truth universally acknowledged in contemporary literature, it aggrieved them nonetheless. While high culture-minded neoconservatives such as Irving Kristol once believed that the seventies should have been seen as the Age of Bellow, movement conservatives twenty years later believed that this was, if properly understood, the literary Age of Wolfe. In the wake of *Bonfire*, movement conservatives bestowed plaudits upon Wolfe that almost tipped into satire. Buckley credited Wolfe with everything from exposing the "modern skin trade" of big city race politics – in which white defendants were used as chess pieces "to incite racial tensions, to gain political leverage, [and] to flex ethnic muscle" – to discrediting the "the L-word" (liberal) with his devastating attacks on political correctness ("The system works," 19; "Lenny Explains," 71). In an article by John O'Sullivan, a former speechwriter for Margaret Thatcher and senior editor of *National Review* through most of the nineties, the British conservative bemoaned the multicultural proliferation of identity categories, and declared that Wolfe had debunked this trend, making him "the greatest living American psychologist" ("Mistaken Identities," 50). By the time Wolfe published his second big social realist novel, *A Man in Full* (1998), writers in *National Review* and other conservative periodicals were referring to him as one of "our most important novelists" virtually as a matter of routine – even when, as Richard Lowry did in his *National Review* piece on *A Man in Full*, they were writing a lukewarm review (Lowry, "A Man in Full," 50). In the conservative imagination, Wolfe, not Morrison, was the most important novelist in the United States. Ironically, Morrison looked to them like a character out of the all-encompassing cultural hieroglyph of a Tom Wolfe novel – that is, the outspoken black dissenter who usurped cultural capital from conservative white men with the aid of guilty white liberals searching for both symbolic redemption and material advancement via large institutions that had recently commoditized "diversity."[6]

What made Wolfe's larger aesthetic-political project so irresistible to movement conservatives in the nineties was precisely what made Morrison's competing aesthetic-political project so threatening and repellent. As supplements to their novels, Wolfe and Morrison drew on their literary reputations to write in various nonfiction genres and give public speeches in which two conflicting political orientations could not be clearer. Charmed by the conservatives' fawning praise of his fiction, Wolfe turned himself into the conservative movement's most famous literary apologist, even though he remained notably cagy about his own personal political commitments. In the final year of Reagan's presidency, Wolfe wrote an article for *National Review* that credited Reagan with intuitively grasping the emergence of a new class formation in the Sunbelt symbolized by the term "California worker," a label signifying someone who no longer thought of himself as "defined (or enslaved) by his job," but as another "owner" within the capitalist paradigm who wanted lower taxes and "freedom from government intrusion" ("Head of the Class," 35).

In a post-*Bonfire* interview with *The Paris Review*, Wolfe further clarified his attitude toward movement conservatism. When he was asked what he thought about people calling him either a "conservative" or a "reactionary," Wolfe responded with Buckley-esque wit: "Those two words, *reactionary* and *conservative*, are part of the etiquette of intellectual life in New York City – simply a way of saying 'you're bad,' or 'I disagree with you'" ("Tom Wolfe, The Art of Fiction"). Buckley and his team at *National Review*, he continued, were noble intellectual nonconformists, very much like Wolfe himself, who "had not gone along with the official gag for the last quarter-century." Finally, as a featured speaker at the 35th anniversary celebration of *National Review*, Wolfe returned some of the flattery that conservatives had bestowed upon him. Using the "train of history" metaphor as a leitmotif throughout his speech, Wolfe declared that "on November 9, 1989 [fall of the Berlin Wall], a date that I think the children of the twenty-first century will be forced to memorize the way they do 1066, 1492, or 1776, the freight train pulled in ... [and] I think a good half of that train belonged to Bill Buckley" (qtd. in Bridges, "The Staff at Work and Play," 104). Wolfe concluded that it was only right to pay "tribute to a man [Buckley] and a magazine that have done so much not only to advance but to safeguard the cause of individual freedom and the sanctity of the human soul" (104). Ending his speech with soaring rhetoric, Wolfe showed that his post-*Bonfire* partnership with Buckley's movement conservatism was both professionally strategic and ideologically sincere.

At the same political moment, Morrison's nonfiction transformed her into, if not the most famous literary antagonist of Buckley's conservative movement – an honor that may have to go to a writer like Gore Vidal – than surely the literary antagonist with the most critical esteem and high cultural prestige. In her early nonfiction, Morrison sprinkled few overt references to movement conservatism, tending to focus instead on promoting young, unknown black authors such as Toni Cade Bambara and Gayl Jones, or stimulating interest in the suppressed history of African Americans as co-editor of *The Black Book* (1974).[7] Only in the early nineties did Morrison begin to openly criticize conservative ideology, a new form of political activism for her that fully emerged when she edited *Race-ing Justice, En-Gendering Power: Essays on Anita Hill, Clarence Thomas, and the Construction of Social Reality* (1992). In her introduction to the essay compilation, Morrison took direct aim at the twin conservative notions of colorblindness and market-based individualism: "In a society with a history of trying to accommodate both slavery and freedom, and a present that wishes both to exploit and deny the pervasiveness of racism, black people are rarely individualized. Even when his [conservative] supporters were extolling the fierce independence and the 'his own man' line about Clarence Thomas, their block and blocked thinking of racial stereotype prevailed" (xiv–xv). After winning the Nobel Prize, Morrison devoted her Nobel lecture to interrogating oppressive language whose key features unambiguously aligned with movement conservatism. It is the kind of language, Morrison said, that "tucks its fascist boots under crinolines of respectability and patriotism as it moves relentlessly toward the bottom line and the bottomed-out mind" (201). Two years later, Morrison again alluded to movement conservative ideology through the trope of fascism in her Howard University Charter Day Convocation. Characterizing it as an ideology that "changes citizens into taxpayers so individuals become rife with anger at the notion of the public good," Morrison claimed that conservatives hoped to enrage and terrify Americans into voting "against the education, against the health care, against the safety from weapons, against the interest of our own children" (168). By the late nineties, Morrison was rebuking conservative Republicans with ever-sharper public denunciations. In the same famous 1998 *New Yorker* piece in which she argued that President Bill Clinton could be considered "the first black president," Morrison registered her disgust with conservatives who were thrilled by Clinton's sex scandals, transmuting themselves into "feral Republicans, smelling blood and a shot at the totalitarian power they believe is rightfully theirs" ("Talk of the Town"). In 2000, while delivering a speech at Princeton on how universities should teach social values, Morrison condemned "post-Reagan business centers [which] have turned much academic and public discourse back to nineteenth-century liberalism," but a rather particular version of nineteenth-century liberalism that was merely "a combination of nostalgia and hypocrisy" ("How Values Can Be Taught," 197). By the turn of the twenty-first century, then, Morrison was not simply a progressive writer who censured modern American conservatism through oblique allusion, but an open and outright adversary.

It is hardly surprising that, after Morrison's Nobel Prize and her increasingly overt attacks on their movement, conservatives saw her as their main cultural nemesis and sought to denigrate the quality of her literary work. What one would not have expected, though, was the paradoxical ways in which conservatives went about disparaging Morrison novels: they were somehow both popular, low-quality works born of politically correct multiculturalism that revealed the decay of serious American fiction *and* exceptionally difficult, fragmented modernist puzzles that only liberal elitists in the academy could decipher and enjoy. In a 1994 *National Review* cover story, the Oxford-educated conservative Tracy Lee Simmons argued that the "intellectual heft" of a university was evident in the kinds of books professors assigned, either "classics" written by the likes of Plato and Aristotle or maudlin, Oprah-backed novels authored by the likes of Morrison (40). In another *National Review* piece on *The Dictionary of Global Culture* (1997), David Gelernter wrote that it was "a bad idea to substitute 'diversity' for merit," as the book's co-editors Kwame Anthony Appiah and Henry Louis Gates, Jr. had done, because it elevated the second-rate work of Lillian Hellman and Toni Morrison (50). However, at the same time, movement conservatives at *National Review* also regularly dismissed Morrison's novels as being extraordinarily difficult modernist texts that were virtually unreadable. In his review of an anthology of crime novels published by the Library of America, Terry Teachout wrote that readers should not thumb their noses at crime fiction, since those novels "are infinitely more readable than the chokingly tedious output of a thousand American writers of impeccably correct reputation," Toni Morrison the most infamous of all ("Crime Novels," 67). The conservative movement's response to Morrison's post-Nobel fame was a manifestation of the antinomy of conservative literary value outlined in this chapter's introduction. In criticizing Morrison, conservatives aimed to combine two competing aesthetic attitudes, highbrow and lowbrow, in ways that mimicked modern conservatism's combination of high cultural traditionalism and anti-elitist, capitalistic consumerism.

The paradox of contemporary conservative literary taste vis-à-vis Morrison reached its apex in a long *National Review* piece ostensibly evaluating *Paradise* (1998), her first, much-anticipated novel since winning the Nobel Prize. In a vituperative article whose title is worth quoting in full, "Black Madonna: Toni Morrison's popularity is less a matter of literary taste than of mass psychology," David Klinghoffer braids together both contradictory aesthetic attitudes in the ongoing conservative project to deprecate Morrison's fiction. First, Klinghoffer criticizes *Paradise* for being too difficult – with its radical narrative fragmentation and confusing shifts in perspective via free indirect discourse – by deploying the well-worn trope of "lunacy," a device critics of James Joyce and other modernists had used since the early days of literary modernism, and one of which Klinghoffer seems wholly unaware.[8] Beginning the review with an anecdote about once encountering "a deranged man" on the street who was yelling nonsense at him, Klinghoffer notes that "hopelessly trying to guess what [deranged people like that] are talking about ... is not unlike the experience of plowing through Toni Morrison's new novel" (30). Morrison's prose mimics the language of "lunatics or senile people," Klinghoffer states, the kind of "people who will introduce names and references to events into their conversations without wondering whether their interlocutor is familiar with any of them" (30). The effect on the reader is that he feels "forced to edit the book as he goes along," Klinghoffer points out, unwittingly reiterating Roland Barthes's description of the highbrow "writerly text" in which the audience actively participates in the construction of meaning (Barthes, *S/Z*, 5). Unlike Barthes, though, Klinghoffer recodes Morrison's invitation to the reader to construct meaning alongside her as an authorial shortcoming, as if she "invited [readers] to do the job her editor at Knopf chose not to do" (30). Though probably unaware of it, Klinghoffer sounds like an early twentieth-century critic who has just stumbled upon modernism and declared it a scandal – a gross violation of the implicit contract authors have with bourgeois readers looking to be entertained.

However, that is precisely what makes the second half of his review so confounding. Pivoting away from this literary populist attitude and suddenly repositioning himself as a high cultural critic, Klinghoffer effortlessly slips into the rhetoric of aesthetic excellence in order to take white liberals to task for elevating Morrison's second-rate fiction in a critical idiom that echoes midcentury conservative attacks on white liberals who praised so-called "negro protest novels" such as Richard Wright's *Native Son*. Calling the arrival of *Paradise* the perfect "occasion to psychoanalyze white liberals," Klinghoffer claims that their admiration shows how "lionizing a black woman writer gives proof of your virtue" (30). The key difference, of course, is that Klinghoffer accuses white liberals of praising *Paradise* not because it simplifies social issues as midcentury protest fiction did, but because it complicates social issues in the tradition of Faulknerian modernism. The only way Klinghoffer's critique of *Paradise* approaches coherence is if "literary merit" signifies the very kind of popular genre fiction that conservatives routinely classified as corrupting the Western canon.[9] Finally, what dismayed Klinghoffer and other conservatives most about Morrison's novelistic project was not simply her ability to synthesize high modernist form with various strands of post-sixties social progressivism; it was also the cultural implications Morrison's influential, literary-political synthesis raised for a conservative movement that was now defined by a vociferously dogmatic ideology and robust organizational activism that seemed to exclude serious, complex literature virtually as a matter of course.

At the turn of the twenty-first century, the works of Toni Morrison and Tom Wolfe, and the reactions their novels engendered from both conservative and liberal circles, epitomized the radical shift I have been tracking throughout this book in the cultural politics of postwar American fiction. At midcentury, Lionel Trilling was troubled by the notion that the best literature of high modernism seemed incompatible with progressive liberalism. Specifically, he worried about the programmatic nature of modern liberalism and its tendency to turn cultural ideas into "pellets of intellection or crystallizations of thought, precise and completed, and defined by their coherence and their procedural recommendations" (*Liberal Imagination*, 302). Postwar American conservatives in the tradition of Burke seized on Trilling's anxieties and claimed highbrow literature as their own, boasting that their movement was anti-dogmatic and that their corresponding literary sensibilities were rooted in moral ambiguity, epistemological uncertainty, and an awareness of human imperfection, but bent toward the ends of racial segregation. Roughly half a century later, though, movement conservatives would purify their fusionist ideology in the pursuit of electoral power, rejecting high modernism along the way and substituting serious literature with a popular realist aesthetic reminiscent of an inverted, class-blind, though status-conscious, protest fiction. The final stage of this shift was most visible in Wolfe's insistence that the American novel should focus exclusively on the contemporary social moment, that it should strive to be both entertaining and commercially popular, and that it should focus on the status anxieties of working- and middle-class white Americans.[10] In that narrow kind of conservative literary imagination, there was little room to genuinely examine the effects of economic class, the romantic stories of self-reliant individualism, the absolute moral superiority of the nation, or, undergirding all of these issues, the historical fantasies of white racial innocence in the United States. As conservatives largely disavowed contemporary highbrow literature and voluntarily removed themselves from the literary field, they inadvertently contributed to the conditions for the ascent of a major novelist like Morrison, who reconfigured specific kinds of literary fiction, especially the modernist novel, as a socially progressive, high-status form.

Epilogue: The Curious (Conservative) Case of Marilynne Robinson

In twenty-first-century American fiction, the political upshot of Marilynne Robinson's work is a curious, even uniquely perplexing, case. Many contemporary scholars and critics, to paraphrase Nathaniel Hawthorne on Herman Melville's tortuous religious equivocations, do not believe that Robinson belongs on the conservative side of US literary culture, but they are not totally comfortable in this unbelief. For movement conservatives, Robinson has essentially replaced Tom Wolfe as the most important living novelist, though nagging doubts persist because of her stern critiques of conservative ideology. For liberals, though, Robinson is a welcomed anomaly in the literary landscape – that is, a novelist of extraordinary skill who takes Christianity seriously – but one whose anomalous religiosity triggers unease, since her deep commitment to faith seems to flirt at times with illiberalism.[1] Tellingly, this uncertainty even persists in literary scholarship on the intersection between Robinson's religious faith and politics. While uncovering the similarities between Robinson's literary novels and the more stridently conservative *Left Behind* series, Amy Hungerford notes that Robinson's work is marked by "its simultaneous religious pluralism and the continuing prominence of belief understood in traditional Protestant ways" (*Postmodern Belief*, 122). Christopher Douglas argues that, although Robinson is in many ways a liberal Christian writer, Douglas nevertheless "place[s] her partly within the cultural politics of the [conservative Christian] resurgence because her fiction and nonfiction take on the project of contesting a secular history that omits or misrepresents Christian contributions to American history – which places her in an unlikely alliance with conservatives in the Christian resurgence such as Jerry Falwell, Francis Schaeffer, and Tim LaHaye" (104). Thus, for a considerable number of critics and scholars, at a time when highbrow literary culture is dominated by progressive liberal and leftist writers, Robinson seems like the only major US novelist who could legitimately represent the conservative movement's deserted highbrow literary wing. And yet she does not.

The modest aim of this brief epilogue, then, is to answer precisely that conundrum of contemporary literary politics: Why is Marilynne Robinson not identified more closely with modern American conservatism? On the one hand, Robinson's views on a variety of issues seem like they would easily place her on the conservative side of the culture wars: She has been a fierce defender of American cultural heritage as specifically Christian ("America is a Christian country," she flatly begins one essay); has criticized the natural selection mechanism posited by Darwinian evolutionists; has emerged as one of the most public critics of the post-9/11 "New Atheism" movement; and mostly importantly, has contested the secularization thesis, which sees historical progress and the loss of religious faith as inextricable, by arguing for the cultural and moral significance of so-called bigoted traditionalists ranging from John Calvin to seventeenth-century American Puritans ("Fear," 124). On the other hand, though, Robinson has consistently disparaged modern American conservatism, accusing conservatives of being jingoistic and intolerant in their patriotism; essentially racist in their sometimes paranoid attitudes toward minorities ("The present configuration of American culture leads us to assume [falsely] that the [conservative] revivalist style of religion must have always been," Robinson states boldly, "presumptively racist"); hypocritical in their undying devotion to free-market capitalism at the expense of Christian charity ("In my Bible, Jesus does *not* say," Robinson writes with acidic irony in the essay "Wondrous Love," "'I was hungry and you fed me, though not in such a way as to interfere with free-market principles'"); and ultimately animated by, in her words, "certitudes [which] do not provide the basis for a complex or nuanced view of either the present or the future" ("Who Was Oberlin?" 172, 169; "Wondrous Love," 139). To shed light on these tensions, I show how my genealogy of post-1945 literature and politics renders legible the friction in Robinson's artistic and political thought. I argue Robinson is an ambitious twenty-first-century novelist who has taken for granted the foundational aesthetic-cultural idea that key elements of highbrow literature – for example, nuance, irony, ambiguity, emotional complexity – are inherently antithetical to modern American conservatism, but not Robinson's own brand of Christianity, for reasons primarily rooted in issues of race. In short, Robinson implies that a Christian-based, highbrow literary aesthetic, shorn of its associations with modern conservatism's fetishized worship of whiteness, can still function as a vehicle for literary prestige that links liberal Christianity with the anti-racist cultural capital of liberation.

Unlike many other major US novelists, Robinson does not suggest that highbrow literature is *necessarily* aligned with progressive liberalism; rather, she tends to imply that highbrow literature is not "conservative" (i.e., postwar American conservatism) virtually by definition. Robinson suggests, in other words, that if one's working definition of conservatism is bound up with the modern conservative movement and its manifestation in the Republican Party, then to call a text "conservative highbrow literature" is to make a kind of category error. Robinson articulates this stance with stunning clarity, perhaps not coincidently, during her historic 2015 interview with then-President Barack Obama. When Obama asks Robinson, seemingly in jest, if she finds herself rooting against the conservative "red team" and cheering for the liberal "blue team," Robinson answers with surprising candor: "Well, I'm going to be honest, I think there are some political candidacies [progressive liberal ones, Robinson makes clear] that are much more humane in their implications and consequences than others. I mean, if suddenly poles were to be reversed and what I see as humanistic came up on the other side, there I'd be" ("President Obama and Marilynne Robinson," 305).[2] We should pause here to note just how remarkable it is that the strongest contender for "greatest living conservative novelist," according to conservatives themselves, accuses conservative ideology as being fundamentally anti-humanistic while talking to her "good friend" President Barack Obama, a fantasmatic scapegoat figure in so much late-2000s conservative discourse. It is no exaggeration, then, to say that this curious friendship between Obama and Robinson – which Obama traces back to when he first read *Gilead* while campaigning in Iowa during his 2007–2008 presidential run – is the symbolic apex of the cultural politics of contemporary American fiction that I have been charting throughout this book: the ostensibly natural and unbreakable linkage between literary fiction and progressive liberalism.

However, Robinson's reply to the question of partisan red and blue teams indicates that her friendship with Obama also reveals the contingent nature of this literary–political linkage. As Robinson readily admits, if modern American conservatism was more humanistic, more open to aesthetic beauty and complexity, and less ideologically rigid, she could just as easily be on the other side. Ironically, as my earlier chapters demonstrate, this was the precise set of attributes that traditionalist conservatives such as Russell Kirk and Flannery O'Connor championed in the early postwar period. Highbrow literature, in the eyes of midcentury traditionalists, epitomized conservatism's "natural" intellectual depth and complexity, an imagination-based political stance that aimed to always go beyond the limiting horizons of ideology.

Indeed, some of Robinson's most memorable aphoristic passages in her nonfiction – which critics such as James Wood tend to compare to Emerson – echo postwar traditionalist conservatives in their rejection of ideology, their fear and trembling before the distortive power of original sin, and their admiration for mystery in the famous "heresy-of-paraphrase" New Critical vein. "Until there is evidence that ideology mattered to Jesus," Robinson writes, sounding like Russell Kirk in the pages of *National Review* circa 1956, "it will be of no interest to me" ("Wondrous Love," 139). And Robinson sounds like O'Connor in her introduction to *A Memoir of Mary Ann*, when Robinson bemoans the arrogance of contemporary intellectuals who subscribe to the secularization thesis, in which religion is regarded as a rightfully discarded myth: "*once we were crude and benighted*," Robinson caricaturizes these intellectuals as saying, "*and in fact a vast majority of us* [i.e., backwards religious people] *remain so, but I and perhaps certain of my friends have escaped this brute condition by turning our backs on our origins with contempt, with contempt and derision*" ("Puritans and Prigs," 154, italics in original). Remarkably, Robinson's profound metaphysical and aesthetic similarities to traditionalist conservatives even cause her to flirt with their political argument which conflates Soviet Communism and German Nazism. Echoing traditionalists such as O'Connor, Robinsons asserts that most human efforts to actualize God's perfect love on earth are hubristic, and can easily morph into early twentieth-century totalitarianism: "We have replaced this [Puritan vision of faith] and other religious visions with an unsystematic, uncritical and in fact unconscious perfectionism, which may have taken root among us while Stalinism still seemed full of promise, and to have been refreshed by the palmy days of National Socialism in Germany" ("Puritans and Prigs," 156). Despite these similarities, though, one major issue still distinguishes Robinson from these postwar traditionalists: the political valences of highbrow literary form in relation to race.

Unlike the metaphysico-racial mystification typified by O'Connor's short stories – those carefully constructed New Critical gems in which real racial conflicts are displaced into Christian theology – Robinson's fiction harnesses a similar, religiously inflected New Critical complexity, but precisely to invert O'Connorian traditionalism and re-politicize midcentury Christian responses to post-1945 racial segregation.[3] As William Deresiewicz rightly points out, Robinson's novels *Gilead* and *Home*, for all their inward-looking theological debates and familial domestic tropes, are also grand representations of "the national passion play of race" ("Homing Patterns"). Set partially in 1956, both novels contain not only repeated references to the Montgomery bus boycott, but a secret, controversial interracial relationship between Jack Boughton, the hell-raising white son of Gilead's Presbyterian minister, Reverend Boughton, and a black woman, Della, whose father forbids her from seeing him. For John Ames, the narrator of *Gilead*, Jack's love for Della epitomizes not just courage, but also beauty. Detailing Jack's admission about courting Della, and clearly voicing Robinson's own viewpoint, Ames tells his son that Jack "is a man about whom you may never hear one good word, and I just don't know another way to let you see the beauty there is in him" (*Gilead*, 232). But Jack's father in *Home*, unaware of Jack's relationship with Della, consistently denigrates the burgeoning civil rights movement. In a nearly identical reproduction of traditionalist conservative discourse in the mid-fifties, Jack's father watches television with Jack and says: "I have nothing against the colored people. I do think they're going to need to improve themselves, though, if they want to be accepted" (155). Obviously, this kind of implicit segregationist rhetoric runs counter to Jack's deepest intuitions and Robinson's repeated claim, voiced here through Ames in *Gilead*, that "we are to love our enemies, not to satisfy some standard of righteousness, but because God their father loves them" (189). Less obviously, though, it shows how Robinson turns O'Connorian traditionalist conservatism on its head: While both Christian writers use highbrow literary form to emphasize the immense value that inheres in every individual made in the image of God, Robinson uses this individuality to make not a segregationist defense of whiteness, but an explicit critique of it.

For Robinson, ever sympathetic to traditionalist Christianity, midcentury conservatives missed this dimension not because they consciously deployed terms like "community" and "tradition" as code words for domination and oppression, like liberals and leftists believed, but because conservative Christians at the time were lacking in charity and love. Significantly, though, if the de facto segregationist rhetoric of Reverend Boughton – and, by way of metonymy, midcentury traditionalist conservatives – is rooted in a simplistic and inadequate understanding of Christian love, then Robinson surreptitiously strips this argument of the aura of highbrow literary culture that it once seemed to possess. Ultimately, by focusing on the debate surrounding the cultural politics of Marilynne Robinson's *oeuvre*, we see that today's seemingly indissoluble linkage between liberalism and highbrow literary fiction in contemporary

American literature is inextricably bound up with modern conservatism, especially that ideology's changing positions on race. The politics of contemporary American fiction – to quote Lionel Trilling and to gesture back to the midcentury moment in which this book began – is yet another temporary, historically conditioned cultural battle that continues to be waged "at the dark and bloody crossroads where literature and politics meet" (*Liberal Imagination*, 11).

Notes

Introduction

1. The uptick in historical scholarship on conservatism in the American academy is usually traced back to Alan Brinkley's 1994 essay for *American Historical Review*, "The Problem of American Conservatism." Beginning around the turn of the twenty-first century, at least partly in response to Brinkley's challenge, US historians' interest in modern conservatism spiked dramatically. In her 2011 article for *The Journal of American History*, "Conservatism: A State of the Field," Kim Philips-Fein testifies to this dramatic increase in scholarship when she offers the following observation on the extant historiography: "Today, instead of decrying the absence of scholarship on conservatism, historians might be forgiven for asking whether there is anything left to study in the history of the Right. The answer is yes" (723).
2. This point aligns with Giles Scott-Smith's argument in *The Politics of Apolitical Culture: The Congress for Cultural Freedom, the CIA, and Postwar American Hegemony* (Routledge, 2002) that the cultural wing of the United States during the Cold War sought to use seemingly "apolitical" modernist literature as a form of politics (1).
3. The full bibliography on the first two areas of scholarship I have outlined is much too vast to document here. However, for key selections related to reactionary modernism, see Malcolm Bradbury and James McFarlane's important, foundational scholarly collection *Modernism: A Guide to European Literature 1890–1930* (Penguin, 1976), which contains several essays that analyze the conservative dimensions of major modernist texts; Michael North's exemplary study *The Political Aesthetic of Yeats, Eliot, and Pound* (Cambridge University Press, 1922); Paul Morrison's *The Poetics of Fascism: Ezra Pound, T.S. Eliot, and Paul de Man* (Oxford University Press, 1996); and Roger Griffin's *Modernism and Fascism: The Sense of a Beginning under Mussolini and Hitler* (Palgrave Macmillan, 2007). For key selections related to the politics of New Criticism, see Mark Jancovich's watershed book *The Cultural Politics of New Criticism* (Cambridge University Press, 1993); Mark Royden Winchell's critic-based study

Cleanth Brooks and the Rise of Modern Criticism (University of Virginia Press, 1996); and Joseph North's exceptional revisionist literary account *Literary Criticism: A Concise Political History* (Harvard University Press, 2017).

4. See Jennie Chapman's *Plotting Apocalypse: Reading, Agency, and Identity in the* Left Behind *Series* (University of Mississippi Press, 2013), a book-length study of the paradoxical tropes of evangelical victimization and prophecy-based empowerment in the *Left Behind* novels; and Amy Hungerford's *Postmodern Belief: American Literature and Religion Since 1960* (Princeton University Press, 2010), a trenchant account of how religious yearning not only inflects but surreptitiously reenchants certain iterations of postmodern fiction at the level of form, and which devotes significant space to analyzing the curious nexus of anxieties around gender, mass-mediated news and information, and conservative theology in the *Left Behind* novels.
5. This trend of including one or two conservative writers in scholarly books mostly dedicated to postwar fiction and liberalism can be found in the excellent scholarship of Andrew Hoberek and Stephen Schryer. In *The Twilight of the Middle Class: Post-World War II American Fiction and White-Collar Work* (Princeton University Press, 2005), Hoberek includes Ayn Rand and Flannery O'Connor in his interrogation of postwar fiction and the politics of white-collar work. Similarly, in *Fantasies of the New Class: Ideologies of Professionalism in Post-World War II American Fiction* (Columbia University Press, 2011), Schryer reserves one chapter for Saul Bellow's *Mr. Sammler's Planet* (1970) and the rise of neoconservatism. In his next book on Lyndon Johnson's "Great Society" version of liberalism, *Maximum Feasible Participation: American Literature and the War on Poverty* (Stanford University Press, 2018), Schryer devotes considerable space in one chapter to Tom Wolfe's distrust of post-sixties liberalism to speak for, or seriously ameliorate the poverty of, African Americans in urban "ghettos."
6. For a similar cultural-political scholarly account on the concepts of hipness and coolness, but with a focus on a broader array of American texts (literature, films, popular music, etc.), see Joel Dinerstein's *The Origins of Cool in Postwar America* (University of Chicago Press, 2017). "In the era between 1943 and 1963," Dinerstein argues, "a new embodied concept and romantic ideal – *being cool* – emanated out of African-American jazz culture to become an umbrella term for the alienated attitude of American rebels" (7). In the epilogue, Dinerstein includes a brief analysis of Tom Wolfe's New Journalist essays on the fraught relationship between the African American culture and the liberal counterculture (Dinerstein, 445–46).
7. For an exemplary case of this in more recent literary scholarship, see Rachel Greenwald Smith's excellent book *Affect and American Literature in the Age of Neoliberalism* (Cambridge University Press, 2015). Smith argues that critics must

begin to challenge the pervasive "affective hypothesis" – which she defines as "the belief that literature is at its most meaningful when it represents and transmits the emotional specificity of personal experience" – because its underlying assumptions are anchored in a form of individualism that reinforces similar premises within the discourse of post-seventies neoliberalism (Smith, 1). Smith singles out Martha Nussbaum for critique as one of the most vocal, and well-known, advocates of the affective hypothesis. To "cultivate the basis for compassion through the fictional exercise of imagination" is urgent, Nussbaum argues, for by becoming close to a person of different race or sexual orientation, one can imagine what it would be like for someone one loves to have such a life" (*Cultivating Humanity*, 92). Smith contends that Nussbaum's approach, especially in the immediate aftermath of the Cold War, "ignores the degree to which individualization" is part and parcel of neoliberalism (3). In a similar way, the specter of modern conservatism also haunts an influential book like Kenneth W. Warren's *What Was African American Literature?* (Harvard University Press, 2012). African American literature arose as a coherent, aspirational literary project within the context of Jim Crow, Warren argues, and thus "with the legal demise of Jim Crow, the coherence of African American literature has been correspondingly ... eroded as well" (2). By the turn of the century, Warren claims that contemporary African American literature functioned merely as a rhetorical tool for a black cultural elite in a neoliberal economy (Warren, 147–48). My book aims to illuminate critical accounts like these ones by showing that what scholars are arguing about, at least in part, are alternative strategies for confronting different manifestations of postwar movement conservatism.

8. For a trenchant critique of this specific literary-sociological approach, see *American Literature and the Free Market, 1945–2000* (Cambridge University Press, 2010) by Michael Clune, who argues that the greatest drawback of this Bourdieu-inspired approach is that "it is able to analyze these practices, and make these distinctions, only by redescribing all economic, aesthetic, and social values as markers in intersubjective competitions" (9).
9. More specifically, Gouldner argued that the expansion of the professional-managerial class posed new challenges to any traditional Marxist class-based analysis of culture: "What is needed for the systematic analysis of the old and new class is a *general theory of capital* in which moneyed capital is seen as part of the whole, as a special case of capital. Conversely, what is required for the understanding of cultural capital is nothing less than a political economy of culture" (Gouldner, 21).
10. Notably, my argument is congruent with, though not identical to, the best recent sociological research on the phenomenon of academic liberalism – or, in other words, on why the American academy has a higher percentage of progressive liberals than virtually every other profession in the United States.

In the book *Why Are Professors Liberal and Why Do Conservatives Care?*, the sociologist Neil Gross argues that the most salient driver of academic liberalism is the process of self-selection. "Academic liberalism has multiple roots," Gross writes, "but to some extent conservatives' criticism of higher education for being politically one-sided has become a self-fulfilling prophecy, reinforcing the occupation's preexisting reputation for liberalism and steering conservatives into other fields, despite rearguard actions by organizations like ISI [i.e., "Intercollegiate Studies Institute"] to nurture conservative students' interests in academic careers" (298).

11. The historiography on modern conservatism is filled with episodes in which a liberal or New Leftist accuses a conservative or conservative-leaning Republican politician – usually Ronald Reagan or Richard Nixon – of being a fascist in the sixties, with the most famous incident occurring between Gore Vidal and William F. Buckley during ABC's coverage of the 1968 Democratic Convention when Gore called Buckley a "crypto-Nazi" (qtd. in Judis, 291). However, these episodes usually overshadow the fact that conservatives were just as likely to accuse liberals and New Leftists of being nascent fascists. For instance, after the Watts Riots in early August of 1965, the August 31 issue of *National Review* compared the violence wrought by African Americans to the kind of nihilistic violence carried out by Hitler ("Untitled"). In June 1967, Max Geltman argued that the Nazi Youth Movement in the twenties was the true historical precursor to the New Left, a movement which channeled "the energies of the nation's youth into a mindlessness of action that [brings] back horrible memories of the Hiterlite years" (635). In July 1968, Kurt Glaser claimed that the dangers posed by the philosophy of Herbert Marcuse stemmed from the New Left guru's "unquestioning acceptance of National Socialism and fascism as 'Rightist' movements" (652). Finally, in the most dramatic denunciation of the left-wing uprisings of 1968, John Dos Passos declared: "In the organized disorder ravaging American cities and disrupting the colleges we begin to recognize what Huey Long meant by American Fascism" (793).
12. During the cultural Cold War, Saunders point outs, the United States and its European allies routinely linked the authoritarian nature of Soviet Communism with fascism; conversely, the Soviet Cominform used cultural forms to push the alternative narrative that "the U.S. and the western democracies are the war-mongers and Fascists and the Kremlin and its stooges the peace-loving democracies" (Saunders, 56).
13. In her influential essay "Fascinating Fascism" (1974), Susan Sontag bolsters this point when she writes that "fascism" for many American writers had become a literary trope largely emptied of any genuine historical connection to Fascist Italy and Nazi Germany; instead, by the

mid-seventies, its main characteristic was rhetorical plasticity. While the trope of "fascism" still signified right-wing "brutishness and terror" for some, Sontag noted, for others it had "become a referent of [deviant] sexual adventurism," since "much of the imagery of far-out sex" was increasingly "placed under the sign of Nazism" (96; 101–2).

1 US Literature and the Modern Right at Midcentury

1. As a lifelong admirer of the literary critic Irving Babbitt and his early twentieth-century "New Humanism" movement, Kirk was fond of quoting Babbitt's maxim that "the only effective conservatism is an imaginative conservatism" (Babbitt, Irving, *Democracy and Leadership,* Boston: Houghton Mifflin, 1924, 114). For an in-depth analysis of Babbitt's influence on Kirk's thought, see Bradley J. Birzer's *Russell Kirk: American Conservative* (2015), pages 30–38.
2. Kirk identified novelists, poets, journalists, literary critics, and professors stretching from the early Republic to the middle part of the twentieth century. These authors included Washington Irving; James Fennimore Cooper; Orestes Brownson; Edgar Allen Poe; Nathaniel Hawthorne, Kirk's touchstone conservative American novelist; James Russell Lowell; Henry Adams; the New Humanists Irving Babbitt and Paul Elmer More; George Santayana; T. S. Eliot, Kirk's exemplary conservative American poet; the Southern Agrarian Donald Davidson; and Whittaker Chambers.
3. It is significant that, for Chambers, not even Khrushchev's explosive speech at the Twentieth Party Congress (1956) revealing the extent of Stalin's totalitarian crimes seriously affected his political or aesthetic worldview. Far from a moral course correction for Soviet Communism, as many American leftists interpreted them, Khrushchev's revelations signaled a new, even more insidious, phase in the Soviet Union's campaign of political aggression. In a bid for young idealistic minds, Chambers wrote, Khrushchev had merely broken up the "ice that froze and paralyzed the messianic spirit of Communism during the long but (in Communist terms) justifiable Stalinist nightmare. Communism is likely to become more, not less, dangerous" ("The End of a Dark Age Ushers in New Dangers" [1996], 289).
4. As I argue in more detail later in the next chapter, Chambers's famous 1957 review of Rand's *Atlas Shrugged* in *National Review* hinges upon the materialist foundation of capitalism and the dangerous similarities Rand's philosophy shares with the very collectivist ideologies she seeks to repudiate.
5. For a trenchant, book-length account of anxieties produced by certain iterations of capitalism in traditionalist conservative discourse, see Peter Kolozi's *Conservatives against Capitalism: From the Industrial Revolution to Globalization* (Columbia University Press, 2017). For traditionalist

conservatives such as Kirk and Viereck, Kolozi usefully points out, classical "liberal social contract theory [whose ultimate economic expression is capitalism] is unsatisfactory because humans have a social nature; that is, they need to belong to something larger than themselves, to be rooted in morality and ethics, which need to be socially enforced ... [Therefore,] without the authority and function of traditional institutions that liberal individualism has undermined, atomized individuals turn to radical doctrines, whether socialism and Communism on the left, or fascism and Nazism on the right, each of which saw the state as a collective salvation" (117–18).

6. From the beginning of their movement, postwar conservatives were concerned – almost to the point of paranoia – about the appeal communism held for African Americans. Conservatives were especially disturbed by Richard Wright's 1944 confessional essay "I Tried to Be a Communist" published in the *Atlantic Monthly*, later collected in the essay collection hailed by Buckley and others *The God That Failed* (1949). In that essay, Wright confirmed conservatives' worst fear, writing that he had joined the Communist Party not because he was rationally persuaded by Marxist economic theory, but because the Party promised social freedom and conferred dignity on African Americans: "It seemed to me that here at last, in the realm of revolutionary expression, Negro experience could find a home, a functioning value and role" (*God That Failed*, 118). Until the end of the sixties, conservatives repeatedly insinuated that the radical social changes brought on by African American progress could be linked to Soviet Communism. In the late fifties, Buckley routinely hinted that Martin Luther King, Jr. could be a communist. Even as late as the eighties, Ronald Reagan claimed that he was skeptical about making King's birthday a Federal holiday because Americans would not know whether King was a communist for another generation or so (Clines, "Reagan's Doubts").
7. Although no single writer was credited with writing this article, it is significant that it appears in the section of the magazine entitled *The Week*. This section appeared at the front of every issue, typically represented the official position of the magazine and, ultimately, had to be approved by Buckley. Buckley's biographer Carl T. Bogus notes that Buckley probably wrote many of the anonymous articles involving race and desegregation in the fifties (Bogus, 156–157).
8. For instance, in the January 1957 *National Review* article "From Budapest to Buchenwald," Willmoore Kendall criticized liberals who were apologizing for the Soviet Union in the wake of the 1956 Hungarian uprising. American liberals would totally disavow the Soviet Union, Kendall claimed, once they realized that communists and fascists shared the same nihilistic ideology: "The break

will come, if it ever does, on the day when Liberals get as sore at the Communists as they once were at the Nazis. That is, when they have travelled the distance from Budapest to Buchenwald" (14).

9. Although I only demonstrate here how movement conservatives used the novels of Orwell, Koestler, and Camus for partisan political ends, the works of these three writers were also appropriated as ideological weapons by Western intellectuals in the much larger cultural Cold War context. For an account of how Orwell, Koestler, and Camus were used in this wider struggle, see Duncan White's *Cold Warriors: The Writers Who Waged the Literary Cold War* (Custom House, 2019).
10. To be clear, Buckley's article defending segregation was not an aberration for late 1950s American conservatives, though their stance would change drastically in the years following Barry Goldwater's 1964 presidential defeat. In *Up From Liberalism* (1959) – which was marketed as a major, book-length articulation of postwar conservative theory in America – Buckley doubled down on the argument that universal suffrage for African Americans was "justified by its works, not by doctrinaire affirmations of an intrinsic goodness" (119).
11. If conservatives had disapproved of literary texts based solely on their unsavory content, Vladimir Nabokov's *Lolita* would have been a scandalous pariah. Surprisingly, though, staff writers at *National Review* praised the 1955 edition of *Lolita*, published only in Paris at that time, for its formal nuance and brilliant prose. See Roger Becket's article "Heartbreaking Farce," published in the April 6, 1957, issue of *National Review*, page 338.
12. Interestingly, writers at *National Review* also criticized anti-communist novels that did not measure up, in their eyes, to the New Critical principle of aesthetic unity over political messaging. In his lukewarm review of the English translation of Boris Pasternak's blockbuster novel *Doctor Zhivago* (1957; English trans. 1958), John Chamberlain claimed that Pasternak had persuasively argued that the Soviet Union had failed as a political system, but he had not achieved literary greatness: "What Pasternak has done is to use the novel form as a platform from which to deliver some 500 pages of inspired criticism" ("A Judgment on Revolution," 216).
13. Ellison's various political stances and viewpoints are famously intricate and complex, but they are not vitally important for my concluding point here. For in-depth analyses of Ellison's politics, see the essay collection *Ralph Ellison and the Raft of Hope: A Political Companion to Invisible Man* (University Press of Kentucky, 2004) edited by Lucas E. Moral. In addition, Arnold Rampersad's definitive biography, *Ralph Ellison: A Biography* (2007), is an

excellent source for tracking Ellison's political shifts over his life. However, I do wish to note that Ellison had a well-known antipathy toward postwar movement conservatism. A vociferous critic of Barry Goldwater in 1964, Ellison was on record expressing his disgust with Reagan's presidency, saying in a 1982 interview that "the Reagan administration's attack on this country's poor, which is threatening to deprive blacks and other minorities not only of their civil and economic rights, but of their very survival" (qtd. in Rampersad, 533).

14. For a sustained analysis of Ellison's portrayal of communism in both the published 1952 version of *Invisible Man* and the novel's previous drafts, see Barbara Foley's *Wrestling with the Left: The Making of Ralph Ellison's Invisible Man* (Duke University Press, 2010).

15. Praise for Ellison would not become more prevalent within postwar conservatism until the Reagan Era, when the movement abandoned its open opposition to desegregation and pivoted toward a version of colorblind individualism as a counterargument to liberal Affirmative Action. The shift is most evident in the work of a black conservative such as Thomas Sowell, who aligned himself with black individuality reminiscent of Ellison. As Sowell once said in the late nineties: "If you have always believed that everyone should play by the same rules and be judged by the same standards, that would have gotten you labeled a radical 60 years ago, a liberal 30 years ago and a racist [conservative] today" (*Controversial Essays*, 319–20). In *Black Rednecks and White Liberals* (2005), Sowell applauded the way "Ellison rejected and derided the idea of a white man defining what a black man should be and attempting to confine individual blacks to that stereotype" (89–90). Overall, though, a deep historical irony pervades postwar conservatism's reception of Ellison. Put simply, in the fifties conservatives admired Ellison's modernist aesthetics but disproved of his support for colorblind equality; in the nineties, his fiction was too difficult and elitist for their populist tastes but they championed a version of his colorblind racial politics.

16. For a good example of how movement conservatives took seriously even those American novels they profoundly disagreed with, consider Buckley's remarks at the Tenth Anniversary Dinner of *National Review* in 1965. Contemplating the previous ten years, Buckley identified works by two novelists, Jack Kerouac and Norman Mailer, as urgent threats to conservatism. These authors were particularly dangerous because they supposedly ignored the enduring lessons of history and, instead, urged Americans to "go on the road" (Kerouac) or "adopt an existential permissiveness" (Mailer) that upended the roots of social order and created a vacuum for totalitarianism (Buckley, "The Heat of Mr. Truman's Kitchen," 95).

2 The Conservative Movement's Foundational Fictions

1. A good example of this early consensus can be found in Miles Orvell's *Invisible Parade: The Fiction of Flannery O'Connor* (1972), one of the earliest book-length studies of O'Connor's work, wherein he argued that it would be intellectually reductive "to read Flannery O'Connor on a chiefly political or social level" (10).
2. Important critical works by scholars and writers who began to read O'Connor's fiction through the lenses of these theories include Alice Walker's groundbreaking essay "Beyond the Peacock: The Reconstruction of Flannery O'Connor" published in *In Search of Our Mothers' Gardens: Womanist Prose* (1983); Louise Westling's *Sacred Groves and Ravaged Gardens: The Fiction of Eudora Welty, Carson McCullers, and Flannery O'Connor* (1985); Robert H. Brinkmeyer, Jr.'s *The Art and Vision of Flannery O'Connor* (1989); James M. Mellard's "Flannery O'Connor's Others: Freud, Lacan, and the Unconscious," *American Literature* 61 (1989): 625–43.
3. As Bacon wrote in *Flannery O'Connor and Cold War Culture* (1993), "I argue . . . that an American Catholic writing for publication during the Cold War participated in a history both political and religious. O'Connor would object, no doubt, to the fact that I stress politics over theology" (6). Similarly, Hoberek's claim in *The Twilight of the Middle Class* (2005) that O'Connor "does not transcend the social at all" because her fictional works actually "underwrite what we might call the identity politics of the postsixties right" implies that Hoberek has unmasked the conservative political content lurking beneath O'Connor's own fantasy of theologico-literary purity (96).
4. This is not to suggest that Rand would fit neatly into any contemporary definition of racial progressivism. While Rand abhorred racial prejudice as a personal vice, she did not recognize as legitimate any larger systematic forces of racism, especially market forces. As she complained in 1971: "Today, racism is regarded as a crime if practiced by a majority – but as an inalienable right if practiced by a minority" ("The Age of Envy" [1999], 142). As a steadfast believer in her own orthodoxy, Rand consistently held to this position when it was unpopular during the early days of the conservative movement and when it became the preferred position after the advent of Affirmative Action.
5. What is surprising, though, is how O'Connor's conflicted relationship with Jim Crow seemed to be at odds with the broader trends of Catholic social teaching on segregation. By the fifties, John T. McGreevy points out in *Catholicism and American Freedom: A History* (2004), the Catholic Church was an unambiguous opponent of segregation. In 1957, the Vatican newspaper *L'Osservatore Romano* declared: "the Church is completely and unalterably opposed to all forms of discrimination – in New Orleans as much as in the Union of South Africa"

(qtd. in McGreevy, 210). According to her biographer, O'Connor's personal stance on Southern race relations was marked by "complex ambivalence," and it "fell basically close to William Faulkner's" – that is, segregation was not inherently good, but he balked at "forced integration" from the North (Gooch, 332, 334). In the words of one Catholic monk close to O'Connor, "I would call Flannery a cultural racist. It wasn't that she didn't know they were children of God redeemed by the blood of Christ .... But the vocabulary she used was typical Southern white. ... She did not hate black people. But she did resent the whiteys from the North coming down and telling us how to handle our problems with blacks" (qtd. in Gooch, 334).

6. Alice Walker posited a similar claim when she analyzed the revisions O'Connor made to her first published story, "The Geranium" (1946), which O'Connor eventually rewrote as "Judgment Day" (1965). In the original story, Walker saw O'Connor's "passive, self-effacing black characters" as largely a reflection of both her youth and her upbringing in the American South before the civil rights movement (Walker, 52–53).
7. When I classify the Shortley family as "petit bourgeois," I am specifically thinking about Mr. Shortley's secret side job as a bootlegger of whiskey. O'Connor's brief description of his venture exemplifies, in Marxist theory, the petit bourgeois merchant who struggles for autonomy without owning the means of production: "He had a small till back in the farthest reaches of the place, on Mrs. McIntyre's land to be sure, but on land that she owned and did not cultivate, on idle land that was not doing anybody any good" (295). For an in-depth overview of the different Marxist theories that emphasize the role of the middle classes in the rise of fascism, see David Woodley's *Fascism and Political Theory: Critical Perspectives on Fascist Ideology* (2010), particularly chapter three, "Fascism and Social Structure."
8. For an example in literary studies, see Sharon Stockton's *The Economics of Fantasy: Rape in Twentieth-Century Literature* (2006), specifically the chapter entitled "Ayn Rand, Ezra Pound, and The Virile Hero." For an example in the field of political science, see Corey Robin's *The Reactionary Mind* (2011), especially the chapter entitled "Garbage and Gravitas."
9. For an excellent account of how conservative businessmen appropriated and adapted Roosevelt's language of Christianity for their own purposes, see Kevin M. Kruse's *One Nation Under God: How Corporate America Invented Christian America* (2015).
10. This shifting conservative orientation toward the literary *illusio* is evident in Buckley's response to two significant events in the final months of 1964: Goldwater's landslide loss to President Johnson and the Nobel Prize Committee's decision to bestow its award in literature on Jean-Paul Sartre, who famously declined to accept the award. On the one hand,

Buckley evinces a deep concern that the unquestionable prestige that the Nobel Prize grants has not been enjoyed by conservative-leaning writers; on the other hand, though, he cannot help but slip into the cynical discourse of "biased" cultural liberal elites: "It was a public scandal that it did not award a prize to Robert Frost, even while handing them out to such mediocrities as Steinbeck. John Dos Passos would certainly have got one if he had been careful not to follow his conscience into the American conservative movement. No one, but no one in our time, has contributed to literary craftsmanship more than Evelyn Waugh – but he is a traditionalist; and so, unqualified. You do come across Yeats and Eliot and Faulkner, but one has the feeling that their overpowering performances required as a matter of self-preservation that the Committee recognize them" ("The Nobel Committee and Sartre," 1004). In the end, Buckley calls for a perhaps semi-serious boycott of the Nobel Prize in Literature, but for decidedly conservative reasons: "Any red-blooded Westerner should think twice before accepting a Nobel award, precisely because to do so is to lend the recipient's prestige not merely to the idiosyncratic criteria the Committee uses, but to its [left-wing] political relativism" (1004).

3 The Strongbox of Custom

1. Most famously, the political scientist Kevin P. Philips argued in *The Emerging Republican Majority* (1969) that culture was the key to understanding the breakup of the New Deal coalition. Throughout the country, Philips claimed, "ethnic, regional and cultural loyalties constitute the principal dynamics of American voting" (19).
2. It is illuminating to see how even the best literary scholars working at the intersection of postwar American fiction and politics, such as Sean McCann and Michael Szalay, reproduce this literary–political alliance. As they maintain in a joint introduction published in 2008 for the *Yale Journal of Criticism*, an easy symbiosis existed between American fiction and progressive social movements. On the one hand, they write, "much of the important literature of the period embraced a recognizably New Leftist style of politics," while, on the other hand, "the new political attitudes so prevalent throughout American society in the sixties likewise reserved a special place for recognizably literary values: the ineffable, the extraordinary, and the mysterious" (McCann and Szalay, "Introduction: Paul Potter and the Cultural Turn" [2005], 213). When seen from this perspective, the "familiar conflict between liberals and conservatives" established in the sixties, McCann and Szalay claim, actually reveals a fundamental clash between "the imaginative and the unimaginative"

(213). McCann and Szalay posit a framework in which the literary events and debates that have truly mattered since the sixties have tended to center on intra-ideological disputes between New Deal liberals and various types of New Leftists. In short, the legibility of American literature, as a subcategory in the larger sphere of cultural politics, seems to presuppose a background that brackets off the ascent of modern conservatism in the late sixties and early seventies.

3. Although Baldwin understood that "custom" could be a kind of cultural transmission device for racism, he also saw some customs within black communities as necessary rituals of survival. In his essay "Many Thousands Gone," Baldwin famously critiqued Richard Wright's *Native Son* for tacitly promoting the belief "that in Negro life there exists no tradition, no field of manners, no possibility of ritual or intercourse, such as may, for example, sustain the Jew even after he has left his father's house" (27). I am grateful to an anonymous reviewer who pointed out Baldwin's dialectical view of custom when this book was still in manuscript form.

4. For instance, Baldwin famously responded to a scene in Kerouac's Beat novel *On The Road* (1957), in which the narrator Sal Paradise describes walking through "the Denver colored section, wishing I were a Negro, feeling that the best the white world had offered was not enough ecstasy for me, not enough life," by calling its implicit premise "absolute nonsense," an idealistic fantasy that would elicit confused laughter from a real-life black audience if Kerouac ever "read this aloud from the stage of Harlem's Apollo Theater" (*CE*, 278). In response to Mailer's more overt racial sentimentality, Baldwin penned an extended critique in *Esquire* entitled "A Black Boy Looks at the White Boy," which was written, Baldwin explained, with the intention not of exposing Mailer as a simple-minded racist but of showing how two literary friends, divided by race, could open up a difficult conversation about the moral hazards of romanticizing black life. In this "love letter," Baldwin lamented the fact that, even for someone as intelligent as Mailer, it "is still true, alas, that to be an American Negro male is also to be a kind of walking phallic symbol: which means that one pays, in one's own personality for the sexual insecurity of others" (*CE*, 270). Essentially, Baldwin thought that American prejudices were so deeply entrenched that even those self-proclaimed radicals, when confronted with the true dimensions of African American equality, still "wanted their romance" (*CE*, 272).

5. Baldwin applied this theory to the South's reaction to the civil rights movement, and in the process examined an event many movement conservatives saw as a vindication of their views on race: William Faulkner's ambivalence toward desegregation. He stated that this insight illuminated the seemingly inexplicable scenes on television in the late fifties of "screaming

people in the South, who are quite incapable of telling you what it is they are afraid of" (*CE* : "In Search of a Majority," 219). It was not so much that these white Southerners were irrational or unhinged, Baldwin thought, as that they were terribly afraid of something that they could not precisely identify. Baldwin noted that this nameless fear even infected white Southerners as supposedly wise and rational as Faulkner, who infamously said in the space of one interview that he was a liberal morally opposed to racial discrimination but that he would shoot "negroes" in the streets if the federal government compelled Mississippi to desegregate (Theresa M. Towner, *Faulkner on the Color Line: The Later Novels*. University Press of Mississippi, 2000). In his short essay "Faulkner and Desegregation," Baldwin insisted that Faulkner's confused claims did not simply amount to hypocrisy, for "Faulkner means everything he says, means them at once, and with very nearly the same intensity" (*CE*, 211). According to Baldwin, when Faulkner prefaced his statements on race by cataloging all of his ancestors who lived for generations in Mississippi, he appealed to "a legend which contains an accusation" that revealed the central neurosis of Southern history but in disguised language: "And that accusation . . . is that the North, in winning the war, left the South only one means of asserting its identity and that means was the Negro" (*CE*, 213). For many white Americans, regardless of whether they were great writers like Faulkner, the fantasy of a unique, inviolate self had always been bound up with traditionalized rituals that dehumanized African Americans.

6. For a thorough examination of the complex constellation of issues surrounding the creation of the New Deal, Southern-based racism, the changing Democratic Party, see Ira Katznelson's *Fear Itself: The New Deal and the Origins of Our Time* (2013). The American South, Katznelson writes, was the central region that "empowered most New Deal initiatives in Congress, all the while holding fast to the ideology and institutions of official racism. The result was a Democratic Party – then the party of governance – that internalized the deepest contradictions of American life" (23).
7. For instance, less than six months into *National Review*'s first year of publication, Frank Meyer criticized the influential book *The Authoritarian Personality* (1950), a sociological study headed up by Theodor W. Adorno that used the methodologies pioneered by the Frankfurt School – a synthesis of Freudian psychoanalysis and neo-classical Marxism – to conclude that the authoritarian personality is particularly susceptible to the right-wing clarion calls of conservatism and fascism. Adorno and his panel of sociologists mistakenly assume, Meyer wrote, "that anyone opposed to the welfare state is likely to be 'unenlightened' about science and religion; to accept the authority of an organic moral order; to hate Jews and Negroes; to have an unconscious desire to grind the faces of the weak; and to respect his parents" ("The

Authoritarian Personality" [1956], 24). As a result, Meyer said that Adorno and his team "lean upon the thesis that conservative political and economic attitudes today have no relation to rational ideas, but are simply the result of a personality structure which is characteristic of the Nazi" (24). Several months later in August of 1956, in his sarcastic essay "A Report from the Publisher: Reflections on the Failure of 'National Review' to Live Up to Liberal Expectations," Buckley mocked "Adorno *et al.*" for their book "in which it was 'discovered' via laboratory techniques, no less, that conservatives of the tough variety are, at heart, little dictators" (12).

8. Even after the publication of *The Fire Next Time*, conservatives would continue to discuss Baldwin's early novels in glowing terms, despite denouncing his politics. Although Buckley disagreed with Baldwin on virtually every political issue, he admitted in June of 1963 that Baldwin was "a great artist" and that he "has greatly raised the prestige of the Negro in American letters" ("The Call to Color Blindness," 488). In the fall of 1964, during the height of Goldwater's presidential campaign, *National Review* writer Nathan Cohen singled out the long first chapter of Baldwin's *Another Country*, claiming it to be "as brilliantly written as anything in American literature" ("A Flawed Talent," 781).

9. The notion that conservatives were uniquely worried about Baldwin as a writer and public intellectual is corroborated by Buckley's campaign strategy when he ran for mayor of New York in July of 1965, a race he entered not with any intention of winning but of increasing the visibility of doctrinaire conservatism and spoiling the chances of another candidate, the liberal Republican Congressman and media-darling John Lindsey. From the moment he publicized his intentions in the pages of *National Review*, Buckley made race the centerpiece of his campaign speeches, and James Baldwin the embodiment of black demagoguery. As one of those "leaders of the Negro people who cherish resentments," Buckley wrote in his official announcement statement, "Mr. Baldwin has said that the Negroes of Harlem who throw garbage out on the streets do so as a form of social protest. It is a much higher form of social protest to denounce such reasoning and the men who make it" ("Statement by Wm. F. Buckley Jr., Announcing His Candidacy," 587). Buckley framed himself as the only candidate to speak honestly about the city's swelling welfare rolls, escalating crime rate, and the supposedly "minor" issue of police brutality against minorities. As one biographer notes, Buckley singled out Baldwin throughout campaign, rarely discussing "the subject of blacks and crime during the election without referring derisively to Baldwin's comments [and writings]" (Judis 243).

10. At first, Buckley was somewhat surprised when the media attached the labels "racist" and "fascist" to Goldwater because of his opposition to the 1964 Civil

Rights Act. As conservatives noted at the time, Goldwater's career record as an advocate for civil rights was comparable to many, if not most, liberal Democrats of the era. As a politician at the state and federal levels, he could boast several accomplishments regarding racial integration: abolishing legal segregation in Phoenix public schools, privately desegregating his family's chain of department stores, founding the Arizona National Guard and desegregating it two years before the federal government desegregated the US military, hiring an African American woman as his first Senate staff assistant, joining his local Phoenix branch of the National Association for the Advancement of Colored People (NAACP), and voting for the federal Civil Rights Act of 1957 (Perlstein, *Before the Storm,* 18; Critchlow and MacLean, *Debating the American Conservative Movement,* 26). In the eyes of conservatives, the notion that Goldwater was akin to a Klansman or a Nazi because he voted against the Civil Rights Act of 1964 on the constitutional grounds of federal overreach could only seem like left-wing demagoguery. Ultimately, movement conservatives knew that Goldwater lost the election for a host of reasons but they would forever take issue with the notion that Goldwater was some kind of "American Fascist" inclined to sympathize with Klansmen and segregationists.

11. In point of fact, Baldwin won in a landslide, as the Cambridge Union Society voted 544 to 164 that the American dream did indeed come at the expense of the American Negro" ("The American Dream and the American Negro" [1965], 89).
12. In his book-length analysis of the Baldwin–Buckley debate *The Fire is Upon Us: James Baldwin, William F. Buckley Jr., and the Debate Over Race in America* (Princeton University Press, 2019) historian Nicolas Buccola perfectly captures this contradictory spirit of Buckley's debate response: "Buckley wanted Baldwin to adopt the posture of a latter-day Booker T. Washington by urging blacks to 'cast down their buckets' and make the most of whatever opportunities those in power decided to bestow on them" (290).
13. In his definitive biography of Mailer, *Norman Mailer: A Double Life* (2013), J. Michael Lennon quotes the political scientist Sandra Vogelgesang to sum up the importance of *Armies* in understanding the evolving nature of the intellectual Left in the late sixties. "Future historians must consult Norman Mailer's *The Armies of the Night,*" Vogelgesang declares, "to understand how and why the American Intellectual Left moved to 'resistance' against Johnson's Vietnam War and, in fact, to comprehend the radicalized intellectual consciousness of the 1960s" (qtd. in Lennon, 387).
14. In one of his lesser-read essays, "Looking for the Meat and Potatoes – Thoughts on Black Power" (1969), Mailer provided even more clarity regarding his own brand of conservatism infused with desperation and desire. According to Mailer, "any real conservatism is founded on regard for the animal, the oak, and the field; it has instinctive detestation of science, of the creation by machine" (258).

The problem with the conservatism of the Republican Party was that when politicians like Goldwater and Nixon sought to strike "the balance between property rights and the rights of men," they "gave at last too much to the land and too little to the living blood" (258). Ultimately, Mailer believed that "conservatism and tradition" would always possess "one last Herculean strength: they were of the marrow, they partook of primitive wisdom" (259).

15. Early practitioners of what would come to be called queer studies performed the first critical reevaluations of *Tell Me How Long*, and Baldwin's late fiction more generally. In *The Homosexual as Hero in Contemporary Fiction* (1980), Stephen Adams noted that there seems "to be some correlation between [Baldwin's] decline in critical esteem and the increasing prominence given to the homosexual theme in his novels" (45). Roughly a decade later, Emmanuel S. Nelson surveyed the reception of Baldwin's fiction from the early fifties through the late seventies and found that homophobia was "at least partly responsible for the mixed criticism it has provoked" (91). More recently, literary scholars such as Lynn O. Scott and Jacqueline Goldsby have argued that the ostensible formlessness of the novel testifies to Baldwin's recognition that formal experientialism was necessary for capturing the changing, multifaceted nature of American racism.

16. During his famous defection from the conservative movement over civil rights and the Vietnam War, Garry Wills provided concrete support for this claim. In an *Esquire* article on his relationship with Buckley published January 2, 1968, Wills recounted a conversation the two had after Buckley's debate with Baldwin. Although Buckley admitted that it was the worst loss he had ever suffered in a debate, a significant admission for a life-long debater, it was also "the most satisfying debate" in which he had participated ("Buckley, Buckley," 72). Believing that the debate was "planned as an orgy of anti-Americanism," Buckley went in with the intention of steadfastly defending American values. "I didn't give them one gaw-damn *inch*!" Wills recorded Buckley as saying, "They were infuriated . . . But I walked out of there tall, so far as self-respect goes" (72). If Buckley could not beat Baldwin on substance, in what would become an oft-repeated strategy by conservatives, he would shore up his support on the fronts of the emerging culture war.

17. Up through the mid-sixties, it became something of a pastime for Mailer to predict the "fall" of postwar, Goldwaterite movement conservatism. In his humorously scathing review of Lyndon Johnson's book *My Hope for America* (1964), Mailer opens with the following sentence: "In 20 years it may be taken for granted that 1964 was the year in which a major party nominated a major pretender to conservatism" (281). The acute irony, of course, is that by 1984 Goldwater would be widely regarded as the first genuine movement conservative in the postwar era, paving the way for Reagan's presidency.

4 Movement Conservatism, Neoconservatism, and the New Right

1. In his autobiographical account of the mayoral race, *The Unmaking of a Mayor* (1966), Buckley emphasized the imaginative component of more market-based political-economic theories, explaining "that the *private* arrangement tends to be superior to the public arrangement because . . . it is more ingenious, in that it encourages a continuing competition for a variety of approaches" (235). In a 1975 speech before the Mont Pelerin Society honoring Friedrich Hayek's Nobel Prize in economics, Buckley noted that the creativity of Hayek's philosophy is one of its main strengths, quoting Hayek's own claim that his economic theory, unlike socialism, "appeals to the imagination" (qtd. in Buckley, "The Courage of Friedrich Hayek," 227).
2. In his work on the relationship between postwar literature and conservatism, Michael Kimmage corroborates this point about the perplexing reception history of *Mr. Sammler's Planet* on the Right. On the one hand, *Mr. Sammler's Planet* is both "significant [within the mainstream canon of postwar fiction] and conservative," a rare combination that some movement conservatives and many neoconservatives refer to with pride in the seventies (940–50). But on the other hand, the novel is rarely touted as a great work of conservative literature today, and "Nixon or Reagan cannot credibly be pictured reading Saul Bellow" (Kimmage, 950). This conspicuous omission is also evident in a retrospective work such as *American Conservatism: An Encyclopedia* (2006), published by the partisan organization the Intercollegiate Studies Institute, wherein a reference is made to Bellow's novel *Ravelstein* (2000), by way of a passage on Allan Bloom and "liberal bias" in American universities, but not to *Mr. Sammler's Planet.*
3. Bellow best articulates this vision is in his major early-career essay "Where Do We Go from Here? The Future of Fiction" (1962). Describing his admiration for Dostoyevsky, a legendary novelist for conservatives, Bellow claimed that the Russian novelist showed how a "novel of ideas" could be a grand aesthetic achievement. "It becomes art when the views most opposite to the author's own are allowed to exist in full strength. Without this a novel of ideas is mere self-indulgence and didacticism is simply axe-grinding" (130). For traditionalist conservatives, Bellow echoed their idea of great literature as multifaceted and nonideological.
4. It should be noted that despite the critical reaction to *Mr. Sammler's Planet* by *National Review* contributors, some of the magazine's readers pushed back on this interpretation. In one letter to the editor, George Kellog argued that Bellow uses "the great intellectual tradition of Western Europe" to deliver devastating, tradition-based attacks on the sixties counterculture and the radical left all while writing in a style not seen "since the best of William Faulkner" (334). In a clairvoyant remark that anticipated the conservative

movement's abandonment of highbrow literature, Kellog asked: "Does *National Review*, via its cultural bureaus, really want to downgrade a literary effort of this complexion and magnitude?" (334).

5. Recent scholars have noted that Bellow depicts "the cultural contradictions of capitalism [as] a nagging undercurrent in *Mr. Sammler's Planet*" (Schryer, *Fantasies*, 135). These contradictions are condensed in the character of Elya Gruner, the wealthy American businessman and family patriarch who brings Sammler and his daughter to the United States after World War II. On the one hand, Elya is a model of bourgeois respectability and Jewish spirituality whom Sammler, in Elya's death-bed scene at novel's end, declares has met "the terms of his contract [with God]. The terms which, in his inmost heart, each man knows" (260). On the other hand, Elya is a former gynecologist who, Sammler eventually finds out, routinely performed secret and illegal abortions for the mafia, a revelation that portrays Elya as a ruthless profiteer in the black market and an unwitting enabler of the morally confused sixties counterculture.
6. For instance, in a 1963 review of the short story anthology *Lonesome Monsters*, which included a reprint of Pynchon's early story "Entropy," *National Review* writer John Leonard singled out "black humorists" Bruce Jay Friedman and Thomas Pynchon as "brilliant writers already moving away from their early influences – Malamud and Nabokov, respectively" ("Monsters, Butter-Pastry, Saltines," 571). Just two years later, though, conservatives had already begun to see the ironic, experimental novel of the so-called "black humor" movement as the epitome of literary decadence, and Pynchon as its main exemplar. Pointing to Pynchon as a leading representative of the "new fiction," Joan Didion wrote that the "hallmark of this kind of fiction is its refusal to follow or think about the consequences, let alone take them; it is content to throw up its hands, cry that outrage surrounds us. . . . To throw a picaresque character into a series of improvised situations is to stay clear of a consistent [moral] point of view as one possibly can" ("Questions About the New Fiction," 1101).
7. Perhaps the most noteworthy, veiled reference a *National Review* staff writer made to Pynchon as the master novelist of paranoia occurred in a 1975 D. Keith Mano article entitled "It's Adversary, But Is It Art?" that began as a nominal review of Gore Vidal's novel *Myron*, but expanded into a denunciation of seventies postmodernism. "Liberal fiction, having no profound symbolic or spiritual roots," Mano declared, meaning experimental fiction that would come to be labeled postmodernist, "nourishes itself with *institutionalized paranoia*. It's adversary art" (51, emphasis added).
8. For many literary scholars, categorizing Pynchon politically, labeling the Pynchonian political project once and for all, is ultimately not as important as highlighting his commitment to social and economic justice. In David Cowart's words, no matter what you call him – anarchist, neo-Marxist, New

Leftist, countercultural radical, eternal hippie – Pynchon is "an author who leaves readers in no doubt regarding his attitude towards racism, oppressive economic practices, genocidal violence, skullduggery in high places, and police-state repression" (84).

9. For an insightful breakdown of three broad phases within the scholarly reception history of Pynchon's eight novels over fifty years, see Hanjo Berressem's chapter "Critical Literature Review" in *Thomas Pynchon in Context* (2019). In the first embryonic phase of Pynchon studies, Berressem notes, critics and scholars were basically attempting to make any kind of sense out of Pynchon's fictional labyrinths "by organizing their complexities and convolutions into meaningful patterns," eventually pinpointing what would become the most familiar Pynchonian themes: entropy, information theory, and paranoia (356–57). If this first phase cast Pynchon as a Spenglerian skeptic predicting civilizational decline, the second phase deployed the insights of Derrida and Foucault to shift Pynchon's reputation from "a prophet of doom . . . into the patron saint of deconstruction and post-modernism" (357). Coinciding with the publication of *Vineland* (1990), the third and current phase downplayed Pynchon's image as "a master of ironic detachment and playfulness" and reimagined him as a writer of deep "affective intensity" and sociopolitical discernment (358).

10. Pynchon's early interest in conservatism as it manifested in the Republican Party is evidenced in one of the working titles for *V.*, as Boris Kachka points out, which Pynchon almost called *The Republican Party Is a Machine* (Kachka). In addition, Kachka notes that Pynchon's father, Thomas R. Pynchon, Sr., was a minor, local Republican politician in "Long Island's mid-century Establishment" (Kachka). In my own archival research conducted at the Nixon Presidential Library, I found that Pynchon's father seems to have actively campaigned for Nixon in 1960. According to archival documentation, Thomas R. Pynchon, Sr. joined other local GOP politicians when he appeared on stage at a campaign event with Nixon at the Nassau County courthouse in Mineola, New York, on September 28, 1960 ("Itinerary of Vice President Nixon: September 25 through October 1, 1960," Box 46, Folder 13).

11. Specifically, Arendt points to the fact that the concept of the concentration camp was not "an invention of totalitarian movements," but rather had emerged "for the first time during the Boer War, at the beginning of the century, and continued to be used in South Africa . . . for 'undesirable elements'" (*Origins*, 440). Moreover, Arendt argues that the imperial South African concentration camps and the Nazi concentration camps of World War II exhibit similar "totalitarian methods of control" because the Nazi camps "utilize, develop and crystallize on the basis of the nihilistic principle

that 'everything is permitted,' which they inherited [from the imperialist camps] and already take for granted" (440).

12. I do not mean to suggest that literary scholars have totally ignored Pynchon's representations of conservatism in *Lot 49*, but rather that they tend to treat the American Right as a set of secondary themes to the primary one of postmodern instability, paranoia, and the politically progressive effects that are assumed to follow from the radical epistemological uncertainty of postmodernism. For an excellent recent reevaluation of the relationship between American conservatism and postmodernism in the novel, see Casey Shoop's article "Thomas Pynchon, Postmodernism, and the Rise of the New Right in California" (*Contemporary Literature* 53.1 (2012): 51–86).
13. As a germane point of fact, the only character in the novel whom Pynchon explicitly aligns with Goldwater is not Fallopian, but the Los Angeles–based philatelist Genghis Cohen, who wears a Goldwater sweatshirt upon meeting Oedipa (94).
14. Pynchon seems to empathize with Fallopian in yet another way. From a literary-sociological perspective, the highbrow Pynchonian novelist's inverted right-wing doppelgänger is Fallopian in the cultural field. Just as the highbrow novelist privileges the formal mode of representation over easily digestible content and publishes her work in a semiautonomous realm outside of the popular, commercial field to gain cultural capital, Fallopian sends and receives letters through an alternative postal system once a week, even though he and its members have no content-specific message to deliver, to increase his status within the group (*Lot 49*, 53). Instead of parodying a system of miscommunication, Pynchon is parodying a closed system of communication that functions according to Bourdieu's argument that highbrow novelists accrue status within a field of cultural production whose logic of prestige inverts the logic of commercial success.
15. Pynchon's most public declaration of support for the New Left appears in a blurb for Kirkpatrick Sale's landmark book on the subject, *SDS: Ten Years Toward a Revolution* (1973), a work which Pynchon called not only "the first great history of the American prerevolution" but also "a source of clarity, energy and sanity for anyone trying to survive the Nixonian reaction" (qtd. in Mead, 44).
16. These countercultural allusion include: Mario Savio's famous assertion during the Free Speech Movement in Berkley that "we're a bunch of raw materials that don't mean to be ... made into any product!"; Herbert Marcuse's claim that a "one-dimensional man" was recognizable by the ways in which modern capitalism harnessed his sexuality for oppressive ends; the move from "protest to resistance," in Todd Gitlin's words, that characterized the upsurge in college demonstrations in the late sixties against

military and Dow Chemical recruiters on American campuses; and objections to state-sanctioned surveillance and harassment voiced by Black Power activists, which would be confirmed as part of an unprecedented "secret war" against Black Power by the FBI in the late seventies (Savio qtd. in R. Cohen, 190; Marcuse, 78; Gitlin, 254; Joseph, 188).

17. The notion that Pynchon is especially suspicious of cultural capital derived from the combination old bourgeois elite taste and elite wealth is on display in *Bleeding Edge*. "Culture, I'm sorry, Hermann Göring was right, every time you hear the word, check your sidearm," the leftist activist March Kelleher complains, "Culture attracts the worst impulses of the moneyed, it has no honor, it begs to be suburbanized and corrupted" (56).
18. For a more in-depth analysis of the importance of Yippie forms of protest in *Gravity's Rainbow*, see Molly Hite's article "'Fun Actually Was Becoming Quite Subversive': Herbert Marcuse, the Yippies, and the Value System of *Gravity's Rainbow*" (*Contemporary Literature* 51.4 (2010): 677–702). Drawing her title quotation from a remark Hoffman made during the 1969 trial of the Chicago Seven, Hite argues that the Yippie politicization of "fun" is a foundational assumption of the novel (677).
19. For a politically redemptive reading of this scene, see Freer's analysis of it toward the end of Chapter 2 in *Thomas Pynchon and American Counterculture*. According to Freer: "In thus staging a conspicuous rejection of both the culture of consumption itself and the hospitality of those who profit therefrom, in undermining the capitalist spectacle and replacing it with their own, the Counterforce regain the revolutionary edge they had lost" (63).
20. In famous set piece in Part 4, "The Story of Byron the Bulb," Pynchon elaborates on his indictment of countercultural futility in relation to postwar conservative discourse by interrogating the presumptive cultural capital of his own authorial position. Born a fully conscious lightbulb with the soul of a revolutionary anarchist, Byron dedicates his entire (immortal) life to destroying a global lightbulb cartel known as "Phoebus." Although he fantasizes about collectively organizing his fellow bulbs and showing them how to fight through "the Strobing tactic," Byron eventually realizes that resistance to Phoebus is practically useless, since "Phoebus has restricted Bulb to this one identity" and sole social role: "conveyer of light-energy alone" (660–61). An allegorical stand-in for Pynchon, Byron is doomed to illuminate problems and provide "the appearance of power, power against the night, without the reality" (660). Ultimately, Byron, "knowing the truth and powerless to change anything," seems destined to become a cult figure of the counterculture whose "anger and frustration will grow without limit, and he will find himself, poor perverse bulb, enjoying it" (668). In this authorial self-critique, Pynchon seems to signal his concern about becoming a difficult,

postmodern novelist who can indulge in moral self-righteousness and literary-cultural distinction without generating any genuine sociopolitical change.

21. For instance, even though Buckley excoriated his alma mater in his first book, *God and Man at Yale* (1951), for the university's passive acceptance of atheism and socialism being taught on campus, Buckley not only famously retained the vocabulary of an Ivy League intellectual, but high cultural references to literature, philosophy, and classical history would always stud his prose. Similarly, Russell Kirk resigned from his academic post at Michigan State in the late fifties, citing the influx of liberal educational doctrines descended from John Dewey, but Kirk would continue to venerate the small, archetypal college campus as a sacred place for the preservation of the liberal arts where students could encounter Eliot, Faulkner, and O'Connor.

22. As the historian Angus Burgin's archival work shows, none other than Ludwig von Mises and Friedrich Hayek understood and predicted these cultural costs best. In 1950, when the French journalist Bertrand de Jouvenel wrote a private letter to Hayek expressing his concern that if "Capitalism triumphs there is, as I see it, a decline in culture," Hayek agreed with his assessment and responded tepidly by saying that perhaps high culture suffers more under socialism: "Of course I agree that capitalism is not necessarily favorable to culture, but it makes cultural growth possible which would probably not be possible under socialism" (Hayek qtd. in Burgin, 114). Similarly, in an unpublished work on the cultural effects of capitalism, Ludwig von Mises admitted that there "is in the structure of a capitalist society, little room left for the activities of the solitary philosopher, the detached poet and the lofty artist. . . . The majority of the buying public has no use for their products. It is these facts with which we have to deal in studying the cultural effects of capitalism" (qtd. in Burgin, 114).

23. In 1979, for instance, Buckley's former protégé Garry Wills wrote a sharp, book-length denunciation of American conservatism entitled *Confessions of a Conservative*, in which he argued that a Burkean conception of conservatism rooted in cultural cohesion and long-term social stability was superior to the libertarian capitalist conception overtaking the conservative movement. Recently, American conservatives had made a basic category mistake, Wills explained, because they assumed that institutions of power were inherently inclined toward stability and social order. But the rise of capitalist markets in the late seventies and the increasing concentration of power in the business community exposed a flaw in this assumption. Conservatives "rather simple-mindedly kept the nexus *power = conservative*, even when the power involved was a revolutionary and unstable one" (Wills, 213). The final result, Wills concluded, was that the "right wing in America is stuck with the paradox of holding a philosophy of 'conserving' and an actual order it does not want to conserve" (211).

24. Thatcher-era records recently released by the UK government testify further to Reagan's deep appreciation of Clancy's fiction. In one document, Margaret Thatcher's foreign affairs advisor Charles Powell wrote that during a phone call, Reagan "strongly commended to the Prime Minister a new book by the author of 'Red October' called (I think) 'Red Storm Rising.' It gave an excellent picture of the Soviet Union's intentions and strategies. He had clearly been much impressed by the book" ("Selections from MT's files as Prime Minster, 1986–88").
25. In his comprehensive *A History of Fascism: 1914–1945* (1996), Stanley G. Payne coins the term "fascist negations" to account for fascism's internal contradictions, noting that fascists were variously anti-liberal, anti-communist, and anti-conservative, but "were willing to undertake temporary alliances with other sections, mostly commonly with the right" (7). According to Roger Griffin, fascism should be understood as "an ideology deeply bound up with modernization and modernity, one which has assumed a considerable variety of external forms to adapt itself to the particular historical and national context in which it appears, and has drawn on a wide range of cultural and intellectual currents, both left and right, anti-modern and pro-modern, to articulate itself as a body of ideas, slogans, and doctrine" ("The Palingenetic Core of Fascist Ideology," 99). For a succinct but insightful definitional analysis of fascism, see Kevin Passmore's *Fascism: A Very Brief Introduction* (Oxford University Press, 2002).
26. Notably, my argument sheds light on a persistent point of contention in Pynchon studies: The notion that Pynchon, for all his apparent postmodern antifoundationalism, consistently represents heterosexual women as being attracted to abusive, authoritarian men, implying a gender essentialist argument for fascism's appeal. "Frenesi's uniform fetishism," as Simon Cook notes, in relation to Brock Vond, "accords with the paranoid theory of the television as the [gendered] political instrument of the cryptofascist right" (139). Cook's argument represents one critical way to read Pynchon's passive-female/strong-male binary, which aligns Pynchon with a mode of politically gendered moral panic. Conversely, my argument reveals the possibility that Frenesi is attracted to an authoritarian man because he represents a specious, reactionary kind of "family values." Pynchon, in other words, is attempting to distinguish between a vision of "family" as defined by Reaganite conservatives and a more salutary one defined by left-leaning socialists and anarchists.
27. My overarching argument helps illuminate the sociopolitical implications of the final, "happy ending" scene of *Vineland* and, by thematic implication, the problem of "magical thinking" outlined by Szalay and McCann. At the end of *Vineland*, Pynchon seems to offer his readers a leftist pastoral dream: with

Brock Vond magically removed from the novel, the Traverse family gathers together safely in the woods, with the last lines describing Zoyd and Frensei's daughter, Prairie, being licked by a cute pet dog. Instead of "resurrect[ing] the American Left" in any real way, as Sean Carswell claims, Pynchon delivers an explicit fantasy that adumbrates robust normative values, but he does not confuse this fantasy with actual political praxis. The final scene, then, should be read both skeptically and sincerely in ways that mirror the challenges posed by the double register of movement conservative discourse (Carswell, 14).

5 The American Novel and the Reagan Revolution

1. For a brilliant literary-sociological reading of the prize controversy surrounding Morrison's *Beloved*, see chapter 10 ("Strategies of Condescension, Strategies of Play") of James English's *The Economy of Prestige* (Harvard University Press, 2005). Morrison's successful strategy "against the organized cultural right," English points out, was "one of negative affirmation, treating the prize as a more false (in particular, more egregiously racist) *and* a more true (more perfectly in correspondence with the 'legitimate' or the 'ultimate') measure of cultural value than its traditional critics would ever allow" (244–45, italics in original).
2. A crucial way Morrison revealed the shortcomings of universality-as-whiteness was by focusing on black (usually female) characters such as the unmarried, headstrong, pleasure-seeking Sula Peace in *Sula*; Milkman Dead and his historical and existential quest for identity in *Song of Solomon*; and Jadine Childs in *Tar Baby*, who feels compelled to choose between "blackening up or universaling out" as an African American woman, and getting married or pursuing a modeling career in Paris (*Tar Baby*, 64).
3. In many of her nonfiction writings, Morrison moves fluidly between these meta-languages. Regarding the notion of liberty found in classical liberalism, Morrison pointed out in 1971 that black women had historically possessed the least amount of freedom in relation to both whites and black men ("What the Black Woman thinks," 24–25). In her foreword to *Sula*, Morrison noted this idea as a basic premise she wanted to investigate as she wrote that novel and published it in 1973. Sula Peace's "resistance to either sacrifice or accommodation" was about female freedom, Morrison wrote, which "always means sexual freedom, even when – especially when – it is seen through the prism of economic freedom" ("Foreword," 2). But Morrison also noted the importance of communal identity and the value of preserving social traditions and customs. In "Rediscovering Black History" (1974), Morrison contended that in the wake of the sixties, black people felt that "something valuable [was] slipping away from us," making it necessary "to find some way to hold on to the useful past without blocking off the possibilities of the future" (42). Similarly,

in "Rootedness: The Ancestor as Foundation" (1984), Morrison saw the primary role of the African American novel as the site where traditional stories and rituals could be passed down through the generations (58).

4. Notably, in some of his lesser-known essays from the period, Wolfe satirizes liberal intellectuals' deployment of the very trope of American Fascism that I have been tracing throughout this book. In "The Intelligent Coed's Guide to America," for instance, Wolfe writes that American academia is full of left-wing professors hysterically denouncing the rise of "Fascism in America" (107). As a result, Wolfe claims, the average undergraduate emerges from the university campus like a "Candide in reverse" (105). Liberal professors keep "warning them that this [America] is 'the worst of all possible worlds,' and they [the students] know it must be true – and yet life keeps getting easier, sunnier, happier" (105).
5. For another important example of Wolfe honing his conservative critique of liberal elite taste, see his short book *The Painted Word* (1975). According to Wolfe, "there is a peculiarly modern reward that the avant-garde artist can give his [wealthy liberal] benefactor: namely, the feeling that he, like his mate the artist, is separate from and aloof from the bourgeoisie, the middle classes . . . or at least an honorary cong guerilla in the vanguard march through the land of the philistines" (19).
6. The conservative movement's early reception of Morrison's fiction is worth noting here. Conservatives essentially ignored Morrison's first two novels, *The Bluest Eye* (1970) and *Sula* (1973), an unsurprising development considering that those works initially failed to garner much mainstream literary media coverage. Despite her literary fame in the wake of *Song of Solomon* (1977), Morrison still did not show up on the conservative movement's cultural radar until she published *Tar Baby* (1981), a much-hyped novel that one *National Review* writer argued was merely a "piece of thinly disguised Black Power propaganda" that literary reviewers in the monolithic liberal media had hyped into an unlikely bestseller (Rodman, 731). Before *Beloved* arrived, conservatives tracked Morrison's rising popularity but did not yet consider her an existential cultural threat. In one 1986 write up of that year's PEN conference, an anonymous *National Review* article displaying the stylistic hallmarks of Buckley accused her of being a fashionable progressive, "a hot ticket on the campus circuit these days," who exemplified how liberal novelists "trafficked in cliché and stupidity, and seemed less interested in writing than in trendy cultural politics" ("PEN Fiasco," 18). Although conservatives vigorously criticized *Beloved*, as shown earlier in this chapter, they did not view Morrison as a unique antagonist in their cultural narrative of decline until after her 1993 Nobel Prize. This period in Morrison's career coincided, not incidentally, with her most overt attacks on Reaganite conservatism, which I analyze in more depth in the following pages.

7. Morrison's most noteworthy critical reference to movement conservatism appears in her 1976 essay "A Slow Walk of Trees," in which she denounces the rhetoric of "forced busing" with its fearful overtones of black men and rape (11). White people who supported a Republican Party energized by movement conservatism proved themselves to be "desperate prisoners of economics," Morrison wrote, "holding on to their dominion with a tenacity and sang-froid that can only be described as Nixonian" (10).
8. Upon the publication of Joyce's *Ulysses* (1922), to highlight an exemplary case in the reception history of modernism, reviewers commonly argued that the book's disjointed structure and confusing prose signaled that the author was "insane." As one reviewer writing under the pseudonym "Aramis" put it in 1922, the novel "appears to have been written by a perverted lunatic" ("Aramis," 192). There is, of course, a large body of scholarship examining how modernist texts deploy unreliable narrators and ostensibly "crazy" social outcasts to formally enact larger themes of irrationality and alienation. For a solid overview of this scholarly discourse, see Stephen Kern's *The Modernist Novel: A Critical Introduction* (Cambridge University Press, 2011), specifically Chapter 7, "Narrator."
9. One of the deepest ironies of Klingerhoffer's review is that *Paradise* can be read as a thoughtful, at times even empathetic, examination of modern American conservatism. Set in the seventies, the novel is about the all-black town of Ruby, Oklahoma, and the male community leaders who despise, and eventually murder, several women who live in an abandoned Convent on the edge of town. As Tessa Roynon notes, the main conflict Morrison constructs can be broken down along a conservative/liberal axis, for it is between "the men of Ruby, who are patriarchal, defensive of racial 'purity,' religiously and morally conservative, inward-looking, and inhospitable, and the women of the Convent, who are self-sufficient without men, whose racial identities are named neither by themselves nor by Morrison, who are liberal in their moral and religious views and practices, and who are welcoming and solicitous to outsiders" (65). However, it is too simplistic to equate Ruby with reactionary conservatism and the Convent with progressive liberalism. Victims of virulent racism, the original men of Ruby establish a small, prosperous community by combining the Emersonian idea of self-reliance and the strict social morality of Christian fundamentalism. Thus, Morrison's representation of this brand of conservatism, which she clearly abhors, is framed in the most empathic way possible: hardworking black families overcoming generations of racism. The downfall of Ruby, in the end, is that the town's men fail to realize that their ideology merely replicates the very kind of conservative ideology they had escaped. As Morrison writes about the Ruby men: "They think they have outfoxed the whiteman [*sic*] when in fact they imitate him" (*Paradise*, 306).

10. In several essays published in his collection *Hooking Up* (2000), Wolfe exemplifies the thematic essence of conservative aesthetic taste at the turn of the century. In "My Three Stooges," a sharp critique of John Updike, Norman Mailer, and John Irving, who all criticized the aesthetic merit of Wolfe's novel *A Man in Full* (1998), Wolfe claims that they are no longer commercially successful, though "heavy with age and literary prestige," because they had abandoned realism in exchange for the academic "game of art" (151; 164). The contemporary American novel, Wolfe declares, "is dying not of obsolescence, but of anorexia" because it does not capture the status anxieties, the "subtle gestures of respect or disrespect," of white conservatives (170; 168). Contemporary American literature, Wolfe argues in "In the Land of the Rococo Marxists," is born out of liberal academic institutions that are (supposedly) desperate to find new oppressed identity groups. Although traditional Marxism is dead, Wolfe writes, imitating the voice of an elite white cultural liberal, "we can find new proletariats . . . which we can use to express our indignation toward the powers that be and our aloofness to their bourgeois [conservative] stooges" (124).

Epilogue: The Curious (Conservative) Case of Marilynne Robinson

1. For instance, Jeffrey Hart, perhaps *National Review*'s most prominent literary critic, called Robinson's 2004 novel *Gilead* a "masterpiece," a rare word for a conservative to use about a major contemporary American novel also praised in liberal circles such as *The New York Times Book Review* (Hart, "Now, a Masterpiece"). By the end of the 2000s, writers at *National Review* would routinely name Robinson and Tom Wolfe as the two most important conservative writers "among our current crop of literary novelists" (Goldblatt). However, conservatives also found ideological faults with Robinson. As one *National Review* writer put it, despite the notion that Robinson is "perhaps our best living novelist" and a voice for certain conservative principles, her critiques of US conservatism are too harsh: "[Robinson] too readily identifies all Republicans with dog-eat-dog exploitation, and she, with NPR listeners and without much evidence, identifies genuinely civilized, cultured Americans today with political progressivism" (Lawler). Conversely, the more liberal critic James Wood praises Robinson's *Gilead* as the closest thing we have to the "Emersonian essay, poised between homily and home, religious exercise and naturalism" ("Marilynne Robinson," 163). But Wood is also quick to point out that readers should not take Robinson's self-described liberal Protestantism at face value; Robinson's "religious sensibility is really far more uncompromising and archaic

than this allows," Wood writes, for "she is illiberal and unfashionably fierce in her devotion to this Protestant tradition" (163–64).

2. It is important to note that in Robinson's nonfiction writings, "humanism" tends to act as a master term for the humanities in general and literature in particular. "Humanism was the particular glory of the Renaissance," Robinson writes in her aptly titled essay "Humanism," and in "muted, expanded, and adapted forms these Renaissance passions live on among us still in the study of the humanities" (3).
3. My point here helps explain, what some critics have described as, Robinson's somewhat perplexing antagonism toward O'Connor. For instance, in an interview with *The New York Times Magazine*, Robinson said that while O'Connor's "prose is beautiful, her imagination appalls me"; and that in O'Connor's whole body of work, "[t]here's a lot of writing about religion with a cold eye, but virtually none with a loving heart" (Mack, "The Revelations of Marilynne Robinson").

Bibliography

Adams, Stephen. *The Homosexual as Hero in Contemporary Fiction*. Vision Press, 1980.

Adler, Les K. and Thomas G. Paterson. "Red Fascism: The Merger of Nazi Germany and Soviet Russia in the American Image of Totalitarianism, 1930s–1950s." *American Historical Review* 75.4 (1970): 1046–64.

"Albert Camus." Obituary in *National Review*, January 16, 1960, p. 33.

Alter, Robert. "The New American Novel." *Commentary* 60 (November 1975): 44–51.

"The American Dream and the American Negro." *New York Times Magazine*, March 7, 1965, pp. 32–33; 87–89.

Anderson, Terry. *The Pursuit of Fairness: A History of Affirmative Action*. Oxford University Press, 2004.

"Aramis." "The Scandal of *Ulysses*." *Sporting Times* (April 1, 1992), repr. in Robert H Deming (ed.), *James Joyce: The Critical Heritage*, 2 vols. Routledge & Kegan Paul, 1970.

Arendt, Hannah. *The Origins of Totalitarianism*. Harcourt, Brace & World, 1973.

Atlas, James. *Bellow: A Biography*. Random House, 2000.

Atwood, Margaret. "Jaunted by Their Nightmares." Review of *Beloved*, by Toni Morrison. *The New York Times*, September 13, 1987, p. 1.

Bacon, Jon Lance. *Flannery O'Connor and Cold War Culture*. Cambridge University Press, 2005.

Baker, Jeffrey S. "A Democratic Pynchon: Counterculture, Counterforce and Participatory Democracy." *Pynchon Notes* 32–33 (1993): 99–131.

Baldwin, James. *James Baldwin: Collected Essays: Notes of Native Son / Nobody Knows My Name / The Fire Next Time / No Name in the Street / The Devil Finds Work / Other Essays*. Ed. Toni Morrison. Library of America, 1998.

Tell Me How Long the Train's Been Gone. 1968. Vintage International, 1998.

Barthes, Roland. *S/Z*. Trans. Richard Howard. Hill and Wang, 1974.

Barnard, Anne. "No Longer the City of 'Bonfire' in Flames." *The New York Times*, December 10, 2007, www.nytimes.com/2007/12/10/nyregion/10bonfire .html. Accessed January 5, 2017.

"Bayonets and the Law." *National Review*, October 12, 1957, pp. 316–17.

Bellow, Adam. "Let Your Right Brain Run Free." *National Review*, July 7, 2014, pp. 26–30.

Bellow, Saul. *The Adventures of Augie March*. Penguin Classics, 2006.

The Dean's December. Bellow: Novels 1970–1982. Ed. James Wood. Library of America, 2010.

"Foreword." *The Closing of American Mind: How Higher Education Has Failed Democracy and Impoverished the Souls of Today's Students*. Ed. Allan Bloom. Simon and Schuster, 1988.

Mr. Sammler's Planet. Penguin Classics, 2004.

"The Nobel Lecture." *There Is Simply Too Much to Think About: Collected Nonfiction*. Ed. Benjamin Taylor. Penguin, 2016.

"Papuans and Zulus." *There Is Simply Too Much to Think About: Collected Nonfiction*. Ed. Benjamin Taylor. Penguin, 2016.

Ravelstein. Penguin, 2001.

"Where Do We Go from Here? The Future of Fiction." *There Is Simply Too Much to Think About: Collected Nonfiction*. Ed. Benjamin Taylor. Penguin, 2016.

"Writers, Intellectuals, Politics." *There Is Simply Too Much to Think About: Collected Nonfiction*. Ed. Benjamin Taylor. Penguin, 2016.

Benjamin, Walter. "Theses on the Philosophy of History." *Illuminations: Essays and Reflections*. Ed. Hannah Arendt. Trans. Harry Zohn. Schocken, 1968.

Bennett, William J. *To Reclaim a Legacy: A Report on the Humanities in Higher Education*. The National Endowment for the Humanities, 1984.

The Book of Virtues: A Treasury of Great Moral Stories. Ed. William J. Bennett. Simon and Schuster, 1993.

Berressem, Hanjo. "Critical Literature Review." *Thomas Pynchon in Context*. Ed. Inger H. Dalsgaard. Cambridge University Press, 2019.

Birzer, Bradley. *Russell Kirk: American Conservative*. The University Press of Kentucky, 2015.

"Black Writers in Praise of Toni Morrison." *New York Times Book Review*, January 24, 1988, p. 36.

Bloom, Allan. *The Closing of American Mind: How Higher Education Has Failed Democracy and Impoverished the Souls of Today's Students*. Simon and Schuster, 1988.

"Out Listless Universities." *National Review*, December 10, 1982, pp. 1537–48.

Bogus, Carl T. *Buckley: William F. Buckley and the Rise of American Conservatism*. Bloomsbury, 2011.

Born to Trouble: Adventures of Huckleberry Finn. Prod. Jill Janows. Boston: WGBH. January 26, 2000. Television Documentary.

Boothe Luce, Clare. "A Politician's Political Fiction." Review of *The Remnant*, by Stephen C. Shadegg. *National Review*, August 27, 1968, pp. 861–62.

Bourdieu, Pierre. *Distinction: A Social Critique of the Judgement of Taste*. Trans. Richard Nice. 2nd ed., Routledge Classics, 2012.

"The Field of Cultural Production, or: The Economic World Reversed." *The Field of Cultural Production: Essays on Art and Literature*. Columbia University Press, 1993.

The Rules of Art: Genesis and Structure of the Literary Field. Trans. Susan Emanuel. Stanford University Press, 1996.

Braine, John. Untitled Review of *Mr. Sammler's Planet*, by Saul Bellow. *National Review*, March 10, 1970, pp. 264–66.

Branden, Barbara. *The Passion of Ayn Rand.* Doubleday, 1986.

Brogan, Kathleen. "American Stories of Cultural Haunting: Tales of Heirs and Ethnographers." *College English* 57.2 (1995): 149–65.

Brooks, Cleanth. "Powerful and Subtle." Review of *Band of Angels*, by Robert Penn Warren. *National Review*, November 26, 1955, p. 28.

"Irony as a Principle of Structure." *Literary Opinion in America: Essays Illustrating the Status, Methods, and Problems of Criticism in the United States in the Twentieth Century*, 3rd ed., vol. II. Ed. Morton D. Zabel. Harper Torchbooks, 1962.

Brooks, Cleanth and Robert Penn Warren. *Understanding Fiction.* 1943. F. S. Croft & Co., 1947.

Buccola, Nicholas. *The Fire is Upon Us: James Baldwin, William F. Buckley Jr., and the Debate over Race in America.* Princeton University Press, 2019.

Buckley, Priscilla. "Seeing It Like Mailer Does." Review of *Miami and the Siege of Chicago: An Informal History of the Republican and Democratic Conventions of 1968*, by Norman Mailer. *National Review*, February 11, 1969, pp. 129–30.

Buckley, William F. , Jr. "A Report from the Publisher: Reflections on the Failure of 'National Review' to Live Up to Liberal Expectations." *National Review*, August 1, 1956, p. 12.

"The Art of Fiction CXLVI." Interview with Sam Vaughan. *The Paris Review* 139, Summer 1996, repr. in *Conversations with William F. Buckley, Jr.* Ed. William F. Meehan III. University Press of Mississippi, 2009.

"The Call to Color Blindness." *National Review*, June 18, 1963, p. 488.

"The Courage of Friedrich Hayek." *Let Us Talk of Many Things: The Collected Speeches.* Basic Books, 2008.

"Genesis of Blackford Oakes." *Let Us Talk of Many Things: The Collected Speeches.* Basic Books, 2008.

God and Man at Yale: The Superstitions of "Academic Freedom." 50th anniversary ed. Gateway, 2002.

"The Heart of Mr. Truman's Kitchen." *Let Us Talk of Many Things: The Collected Speeches.* Basic Books, 2008.

"Lenny Explains." *National Review*, January 27, 1989, p. 89.

"'Life' Goes to Norman Mailer." *National Review*, November 2, 1965, p. 969.

"The Nobel Committee and Sartre." *National Review*, November 17, 1964, p. 1004.

"Radical Chic." *Firing Line with William F. Buckley Jr.* December 17, 1970. Television.

"Our Mission Statement." *National Review*, November 19, 1955.

Saving the Queen. Doubleday, 1976.

"Statement by Wm. F. Buckley Jr., Announcing His Candidacy for Mayor of New York." *National Review*, July 13, 1965, pp. 586–89.

"The System Works." *National Review*, January 22, 1988, p. 19.

"Two Cheers for the Sixties." *National Review*, January 13, 1970, pp. 14; 16.
The Unmaking of a Mayor. 50th anniversary ed. Encounter, 2015.
Up From Liberalism. New York: McDowell Obolensky, 1959.
"Why the South Must Prevail." *National Review*, August 24, 1957, p. 149.
Buell, Lawrence. "Religion on the American Mind." *American Literary History* 19.1 (Spring 2007): 32–55.
Bridges, Linda. "The Staff at Work and Play." *National Review*, November 5, 1990, p. 104.
Bridges, Linda and John R. Coyne, Jr. *Strictly Right: William F. Buckley Jr. and the American Conservative Movement*. John Wiley & Sons, 2007.
Burgin, Angus. *The Great Persuasion: Reinventing Free Markets since the Depression*. Harvard University Press, 2015.
Burke, Edmund. *Reflections on the Revolution in France*. Penguin, 2004.
Burns, Jennifer. *Goddess of the Market: Ayn Rand and the American Right*. Oxford University Press, 2009.
Byerman, Keith. *Remembering the Past in Contemporary African American Fiction*. The University of North Carolina Press, 2005.
Campbell, James. *Talking at the Gates: A Life of James Baldwin*. Viking, 1991.
Cannon, Lou. *President Reagan: The Role of a Lifetime*. Perseus Books, 2000.
Chamberlain, John. "A Judgment on Revolution." Review of *Doctor Zhivago*, by Boris Pasternak. *National Review*, September 27, 1958, pp. 215–16.
"Orwell: Prophet after the Fact." Review of *The Orwell Reader*, by George Orwell. *National Review*, November 10, 1956, pp. 20–21.
"Sex in the Desert." Review of *The Deer Park*, by Norman Mailer. *National Review*, December 7, 1955, p. 28.
"The Business Novel." *National Review*, February 13, 1960, pp. 111–12.
Chambers, Whittaker. "Big Sister is Watching You." Review of *Atlas Shrugged*, by Ayn Rand. *National Review*, December 28, 1957, pp. 594–96.
Odyssey of a Friend: Letters to William F. Buckley, Jr. 1954–1961. Ed. William F. Buckley, Jr. G. P. Putnam's Sons, 1969.
Witness. Random House, 1952.
"The End of a Dark Age Ushers in New Dangers." *Ghosts on the Roof: Selected Essays*. Ed. Terry Teachout. Transaction Publishers, 1996.
Carswell, Sean. *Occupy Pynchon: Politics after Gravity's Rainbow*. University of Georgia Press, 2017.
Clines, Francis X. "Reagan's Doubts on Dr. King Disclosed." *New York Times*, October 22, 1983.
Clune, Michael W. *American Literature and the Free Market, 1945–2000*. Cambridge University Press, 2010.
Cohen, Nathan. "A Flawed Talent." Review of *Blues for Mr. Charlie*, by James Baldwin. *National Review*, September 8, 1964, pp. 780–81.
Cohen, Robert. *Freedom's Orator: Mario Savio and the Radical Legacy of the 1960s*. Oxford University Press, 2009.
Cook, Simon. "'This Set of Holes, Pleasantly Framed': Pynchon the Competent Pornographer and the Female Conduit." *Thomas Pynchon, Sex, and Gender*.

Eds. Ali Chetwynd, Joanna Freer, and Georgios Maragos. University of Georgia Press, 2018.
Cowart. David. *Thomas Pynchon and the Dark Passages of History*. University of Georgia Press, 2011.
Cox Richardson, Heather. *To Make Men Free: A History of the Republican Party*. Basic Books, 2014.
Critchlow, Donald T. and Nancy MacLean. *Debating the American Conservative Movement: 1945 to the Present*. Rowman & Littlefield, 2009.
Crouch, Stanley. "Introduction." *Mr. Sammler's Planet*, by Saul Bellow. Penguin Classics, 2004.
"Literary Conjure Woman." Review of *Beloved*, by Toni Morrison. *The New Republic*, October 19, 1987, p. 38.
Davenport, Guy. "Magic Realism in Prose." Review of *Another Country*, by James Baldwin. *National Review*, August 28, 1962, pp. 153–54.
"Apocalypse New Exit." *National Review*, December 29, 1970, pp. 1302–04.
Davis, Forrest. "The Right to Nullify." *National Review*, April 25 1956, pp. 9–11.
Deresiewicz, William. "Homing Pattern: Marilynne Robinson's Fiction." *The Nation*, September 25, 2008, www.thenation.com/article/homing-patterns-marilynne-robinsons-fiction/. Accessed March 15, 2018.
Díaz, Junot. "MFA vs. POC." Page-Turner. *The New Yorker*, April 30, 2014. www.newyorker.com/books/page-turner/mfa-vs-poc. Accessed December 12, 2016.
Didion, Joan. "A Social Eye." Review *An American Dream*, by Norman Mailer. *National Review*, 20 April 20, 1965, pp. 329–30.
"Questions about the New Fiction." *National Review*, November 30, 1965, pp. 1100–02.
Dillard, Angela D. *Guess Who's Coming to Dinner Now?: Multicultural Conservatism in America*. New York University Press, 2001.
Dinerstein, Joel. *The Origins of Cool in Postwar America*. University of Chicago Press, 2017.
Dos Passos, John. "1968." *National Review*, August 13, 1968, pp. 793–800.
Douglas, Christopher. *If God Meant to Interfere: American Literature and the Rise of the Christian Right*. Cornell University Press, 2016.
Dowd, Maureen. "Where 'Atlas Shrugged' Is Still Read – Forthrightly." *New York Times*, September 13, 1987, p. E5.
Drake, Robert Y. , Jr. "Huck Among Doctors." *Review of Love and Death in the American Novel*, by Leslie Fiedler. *National Review*, October 22, 1960, pp. 320–22.
D'Souza, Dinesh. *The End of Racism: Principles for a Multiracial Society*. Free Press, 1995.
Eagleton, Terry. *The Illusions of Postmodernism*. Blackwell, 1996.
Eliot, Thomas S. *Christianity and Culture*. Mariner Books, 1977.
Ellison, Ralph. *Invisible Man*. Random House, 2004.
English, James. *The Economy of Prestige: Prizes, Awards, and the Circulation of Cultural Value*. Harvard University Press, 2005.

Evans, M. Stanton. "The Gospel According to Ayn Rand." *National Review*, October 3, 1967, pp. 1059–63.
Review of *The Spirit of '76*, by Holmes Alexander. *National Review*, February 7, 1967, p. 155.
Evanier, David. "Bare Bones." Review of *The Dean's December*, by Saul Bellow. *National Review*, April 2, 1982, p. 364.
Ezell, Macel D. *Unequivocal Americanism: Right-Wing Novels in the Cold War Era*. Scarecrow Press, 1977.
Faulkner, William. "Letter to a Northern Editor." *Essays, Speeches & Public Letters*. Ed. James B. Meriwether. Random House, 1965.
Requiem for a Nun. Vintage International, 2012.
Fitzpatrick, Kathleen. *The Anxiety of Obsolescence: The American Novel in the Age of Television*. Vanderbilt University Press, 2006.
Flay, Catherine. "Conservatism as Radicalism: Family and Antifeminism in Vineland." *Thomas Pynchon, Sex, and Gender*. Eds. Ali Chetwynd, Joanna Freer, and Georgios Maragos. University of Georgia Press, 2018.
Foley, Barbara. *Wrestling with the Left: The Making of Ralph Ellison's "Invisible Man."* Duke University Press, 2010.
Foucault, Michel. *History of Sexuality: Volume I: An Introduction*. Trans. Robert Hurley. Vintage, 1990.
Franzen, Jonathan. "I'll be Doing More of the Same." *Review of Contemporary Fiction* 16.1 (1996): 34–38.
Freer, Joanna. *Thomas Pynchon and the American Counterculture*. Cambridge University Press, 2014.
Gates, Henry Louis. , Jr. "The Fire Last Time: What James Baldwin Can and Can't Teach America." *New Republic*, June 1, 1992, pp. 37–43.
Gelernter, David. "The Dictionary of Global Culture." *Review of The Dictionary of Global Culture*, edited by Kwame Anthony Appiah and Henry Louis Gates, Jr. *National Review*, May 19, 1997, p. 50.
Geltman, Max. "The New Left and the Old Right." *National Review*, June 13, 1967, pp. 632–35.
Gitlin, Todd. *The Sixties: Years of Hope, Days of Rage*. Bantam Books, 1987.
Twilight of Common Dreams: Why America Is Wracked by the Culture Wars. Henry Holt, 1995.
Glaser, Kurt. "Marcuse and the German New Left." *National Review*, July 2, 1968, pp. 649–54.
Goldblatt, Mark. "Where are the Conservative Novelists?" *National Review*, November 19, 2014, www.nationalreview.com/2010/11/where-are-conservative-novelists-mark-goldblatt/. Accessed December 15, 2017.
Gooch, Brad. *Flannery: A Life of Flannery O'Connor*. Little Brown, 2009.
Gouldner, Alvin W. *The Future of Intellectuals and the Rise of the New Class*. Palgrave, 1979.
Greif, Mark. *The Age of the Crisis of Man: Thought and Fiction in America, 1933 – 1973*. Princeton University Press, 2015.

Griffin, Roger. "The Palingenetic Core of Generic Fascist Ideology." *Che cos'è il fascismo? Interpretazioni e prospettive di ricerca*. Ideazione Editrice, 2003.

Gross, Neil. *Why are Professors Liberal and Why Do Conservatives Care?* Harvard University Press, 2013.

Guillory, John. *Cultural Capital: The Problem of Literary Canon Formation*. University of Chicago Press, 1993.

Harris, Trudier. *Fiction and Folklore: The Novels of Toni Morrison*. University of Tennessee Press, 1991.

Hart, Jeffrey. "The New Aesthetics of Politics." *National Review*, October 8, 1968, pp. 1008–09; 1027.

"Now, a Masterpiece." Review of *Gilead*, by Marilynne Robinson. *National Review*, March 28, 2005, www.nationalreview.com/2005/05/now-masterpiece-jeffrey-hart. Accessed December 10, 2017.

"Secession of the Intellectuals." *National Review*, December 1, 1970, pp. 1278–82.

Hartman, Andrew. *War for the Soul of America: A History of the Culture Wars*. University of Chicago Press, 2015.

Hayek, Friedrich. *The Road to Serfdom*. University of Chicago Press, 1944.

Hite, Molly. "'Fun Actually Was Becoming Quite Subversive': Herbert Marcuse, the Yippies, and the Value System of Gravity's Rainbow." *Contemporary Literature* 51.4 (2010): 677–702.

Hijiya, James A. "The Conservative 1960s." *Journal of American Studies* 37.2 (2003): 201–27.

Hoberek, Andrew. *The Twilight of the Middle Class: Post-World War II American Fiction and White-Collar Work*. Princeton University Press, 2005.

Hofstadter, Richard. "The Paranoid Style in American Politics." *The Paranoid Style in American Politics*. Vintage Books, 2008.

Hollowell, John. *Fact & Fiction: The New Journalism and the Nonfiction Novel*. University Press of North Carolina, 1977.

"How Much is it Worth?" *National Review*, January 19, 1957, p. 55.

Howe, Irving. *Politics and the Novel. 1957*. Ivan R. Dee, 2002.

Steady Work: Essays in the Politic of Democratic Radicalism. Mariner, 1967.

Hungerford, Amy. *Postmodern Belief: American Literature and Religion since 1960*. Princeton University Press, 2010.

Hutcheon, Linda. *The Politics of Postmodernism*. Routledge, 1989.

Iannone, Carol. "Toni Morrison's Career." *Commentary* 84 (December 1987): 59–63.

"Itinerary of Vice President Nixon: September 25 through October 1, 1960," Richard Nixon Presidential Library Special Files Collection. The Richard Nixon Presidential Library and Museum. Box 46, Folder 13. www.nixonlibrary.gov/sites/default/files/virtuallibrary/documents/whsfreturned/WHSF_Box_46/WHSF46-13.pdf

Jameson, Fredric. *Postmodernism, or, the Cultural Logic of Late Capitalism*. Duke University Press, 1991.

Joseph, Peniel. *Waiting 'Til the Midnight Hour: A Narrative History of Black Power in America*. Holt Paperbacks, 2007.

Judis, John B. *William F. Buckley, Jr.: Patron Saint of Conservatives*. Simon & Schuster, 1988.

Kachka, Boris. "On the Thomas Pynchon Trail: From the Long Island of His Boyhood to the 'Yupper West Side' of His New Novel." *Vulture.com*, August 25, 2013. www.vulture.com/2013/08/thomas-pynchon-bleeding-edge.html

Katznelson, Ira. *Fear Itself: The New Deal and the Origins of Our Time*. W.W. Norton & Co., 2013.

Kellog, George. Untitled Letter. *National Review*, March 24, 1970, p. 334.

Kelly, Adam. "Formally Conventional Fiction." *American Literature in Transition: 2000–2010*. Ed. Rachel Greenwald Smith. Cambridge University Press, 2018.

Kendall, Willmoore. "From Budapest to Buchenwald." *National Review*, January 5, 1957, p. 14.

Kennan, George F. "Totalitarianism in the Modern World." *Totalitarianism*. Ed. Carl J. Friedrich. Grosset & Dunlap, 1964.

Kimmage, Michael *The Conservative Turn: Lionel Trilling, Whittaker Chambers, and the Lessons of Anti-Communism*. Harvard University Press, 2009.

"The Plight of Conservative Literature." *A New Literary History of America*. Ed. Greil Marcus and Werner Sollors. Harvard University Press, 2009.

Kimmel, Michel. *Angry White Men: American Masculinity at the End of an Era*. Perseus Books, 2013.

Kirk, Russell. *A Program for Conservatives*. Henry Publishing, 1954.

The Conservative Mind: From Burke to Santayana. Chicago: Henry Publishing, 1953.

"The Dissolution of Liberalism." *The Essential Russell Kirk: Selected Essays*. Ed. George A. Panichas. ISI Books, 2007.

Enemies of the Permanent Things: Observations of Abnormity in Literature and Politics. Arlington House, 1969.

"English Letters in the Age of Boredom." *Shenandoah* 7.2 (1956): 3–15.

"Flannery O'Connor and the Grotesque Face of God." *The World and I*, January 1987, pp. 431–33.

Untitled Letter. *National Review* February 1, 1958, p. 118.

"Libertarians: The Chirping Sectaries." *Modern Age* 25 (Fall 1981): 345–51.

"The Moral Conservatism of Hawthorne." *Contemporary Review* 182 (1952): 361–66.

"The Moral Imagination." *The Essential Russell Kirk: Selected Essays*. Ed. George A. Panichas. ISI Books, 2007.

"The Perversity of Recent Fiction." *Reclaiming a Patrimony*. The Heritage Foundation, 1982.

The Sword of Imagination: Memoirs of a Half-Century of Literary Conflict. ISI Books, 2002.

Kirsch, Adam. "Flower Children: Saul Bellow's *Mr. Sammler's Planet* is a Document of the Cravings of 1960s America, and an Attempt to Bring the Holocaust to Bear on America." *Tablet*, March 14, 2012, www.tabletmag.com/jewish-arts-and-culture/books/93653/flower-children. Accessed April 4, 2016.

"The Tea Party's New Front in the American Culture Wars: Literature." Tablet, July 10, 2014, www.tabletmag.com/jewish-arts-and-culture/books/178602/tea-party-literature. Accessed May 5, 2015.

Klinghoffer, David. "Black Madonna: Toni Morrison's Popularity is Less a Matter of Literary Taste than of Mass Psychology." Review of *Paradise*, by Toni Morrison. *National Review*, February 9, 1998, pp. 30–31.

Kolozi, Peter. *Conservatives Against Capitalism: From the Industrial Revolution to Globalization*. Columbia University Press, 2017.

Konstantinou, Lee. *Cool Characters: Irony and American Fiction*. Harvard University Press, 2016.

Kristol, Irving. "The Adversary Culture of Intellectuals." *Neoconservatism: The Autobiography of an Idea: Selected Essays 1949–1995*. The Free Press, 1995.

Two Cheers for Capitalism. New American Library, 1978.

Lassiter, Matthew. "Inventing Family Values." *Rightward Bound: Making America Conservative in the 1970s*. Eds. Bruce Schulman and Julian Zelizer. Harvard University Press, 2008.

Latour, Bruno. "Why Has Critique Run Out of Steam? From Matters of Fact to Matters of Concern." *Critical Inquiry* 30.2 (Winter 2004): 225–48.

Leeds, Barry H. *The Structured Vision of Norman Mailer*. New York University Press, 1969.

Lennon, J. Michael. *Norman Mailer: A Double Life*. Simon & Schuster, 2013. Print.

Leonard, John. "Epitaph for the Beat Generation." *National Review*, September 12, 1959, p. 331.

"Monsters, Butter-Pastry, Saltines." Review of *Lonesome Monsters*, ed. Nelson Algren. *National Review*, December 31, 1963, p. 571.

Levine, Lawrence W. *Highbrow/Lowbrow: The Emergence of Cultural Hierarchy in America*. Harvard University Press, 1990.

Lorde, Audre. *A Burst of Light: Essays*. Firebrand Books, 1988.

Lowry, Richard. "A Man in Full." Review of *A Man in Full*, by Tom Wolfe. *National Review*, November 23, 1998, p. 50.

Mailer, Norman. *The Armies of the Night: History as a Novel, The Novel as History*. Plume, 1994.

"The Debate with William Buckley – The Real Meaning of the Right Wing in America." *The Presidential Papers*. G. P. Putnam's Sons, 1963.

"In the Red Light: A History of the Republican Convention in 1964." *Cannibals and Christians*. The Dial Press, 1966.

"Introducing Our Argument." *Cannibals and Christians*. The Dial Press, 1966.

"Looking for the Meat and Potatoes – Thoughts on Black Power." *Mind of an Outlaw: Selected Essays*. Ed. Phillip Sipiora. Random House, 2014.

Miami and the Siege of Chicago: An Informal History of the Republican and Democratic Conventions of 1968. Reprint ed. Random House, 2016.

"My Hope for America: A Review of a Book by Lyndon B. Johnson." *Norman Mailer: Collected Essays of the 1960s*. Ed. J. Michael Lennon. The Library of America, 2018.

St. George and the Godfather. Signet, 1972.
"The White Negro: Superficial Reflections on the Hipster." *Advertisements for Myself*. G. P. Putnam's Sons, 1959.
Mano, D. Keith. "It's Adversary, But Is It Art?" *National Review*, January 17, 1975, p. 51.
Marcuse, Herbert. *One-Dimensional Man: Studies in the Ideology of Advanced Industrial Society*. 2nd ed. Beacon Press, 1991.
Martin, Benjamin G. *The Nazi-Fascist New Order for European Culture*. Harvard University Press, 2016.
Mason, Wyatt. "The Revelations of Marilynne Robinson." *The New York Times Magazine*, October 1, 2014, www.nytimes.com/2014/10/05/magazine/the-revelations-of-marilynne-robinson.html. Accessed January 12, 2018.
Master, Joshua J. "Race and the Infernal City in Tom Wolfe's The Bonfire of the Vanities." *Journal of Narrative Theory* 29.2 (Spring 1999): 208–24.
Max, Daniel T. *Every Love Story is a Ghost Story: A Life of David Foster Wallace*. Viking, 2012.
McCann, Sean. "The Imperiled Republic: Norman Mailer and the Poetics of Anti-Liberalism." *ELH* 67.1 (2000): 293–336.
and Michael Szalay. "Do You Believe in Magic?: Literary Thinking after the New Left." *The Yale Journal of Criticism* 18.2 (2005): 435–68.
McCann, Sean and Michael Szalay. "Introduction: Paul Potter and the Cultural Turn." *The Yale Journal of Criticism* 18.2 (2005): 209–20.
McGirk, James. "The Search for Serious Literary Fiction for Republicans." *The Daily Beast*, November 5, 2012, www.thedailybeast.com/articles/2012/11/05/the-search-for-serious-literary-fiction-for-republicans.html. Accessed March 15, 2014.
McGreevy, John T. *Catholicism and American Freedom: A History*. W.W. Norton & Co., 2004.
McGurl, Mark. *The Novel Art: Elevations of American Fiction after Henry James*. Princeton University Press, 2001.
The Program Era: Postwar Fiction and the Rise of Creative Writing. Harvard University Press, 2009.
Mead, Clifford. *Thomas Pynchon: A Bibliography of Primary and Secondary Materials*. Dalkey Archive Press, 1989.
Meriwether, James B. and Michael Millgate, eds. *Lion in the Garden: Interviews with William Faulkner, 1926–1962*. Random House, 1968.
Meyer, Frank S. "The Authoritarian Personality." *National Review*, February 8, 1956, pp. 23–24
"Freedom, Tradition, Conservatism." *In Defense of Freedom and Related Essays*. Ed. William C. Dennis. Liberty Fund, 1996.
"Why Freedom." *In Defense of Freedom and Related Essays*. Ed. William C. Dennis. Liberty Fund, 1996.
"Of Khrushchev, Stalin, and Sitting Ducks." *National Review*, July 11, 1956, p. 16.
Michaels, Walter Benn. *The Shape of the Signifier: 1967 to the End of History*. Princeton University Press, 2004.

Morrison, Toni. "A Slow Walk of Trees (As Grandmother Would Say), Hopeless (as Grandfather Would Say)." *What Moves at the Margin: Selected Nonfiction.* Ed. Carolyn C. Denard. University Press of Mississippi, 2008.

Beloved. Random House, 2004.

"Foreword." *Sula.* Ed. Toni Morrison. Random House, 2004.

"How Values Can Be Taught in the University." *What Moves at the Margin: Selected Nonfiction.* Ed. Carolyn C. Denard. University Press of Mississippi, 2008.

"Remarks Given at the Howard University Charter Day Convocation." *What Moves at the Margin: Selected Nonfiction.* Ed. Carolyn C. Denard. University Press of Mississippi, 2008.

"Introduction: Friday on the Potomac." *Race-ing Justice, En-Gendering Power: Essays on Anita Hill, Clarence Thomas, and the Construction of Social Reality.* Ed. Toni Morrison. Pantheon Books, 1992.

"The Nobel Lecture in Literature." *What Moves at the Margin: Selected Nonfiction.* Ed. Carolyn C. Denard. University Press of Mississippi, 2008.

Paradise. Knopf, 1997.

Playing in the Dark: Whiteness and the Literary Imagination. Harvard University Press, 1992.

"Recitatif." *Confirmation: An Anthology of African American Women.* Eds. Imamu Amiri Baraka and Amina Baraka. Morrow, 1983.

"Rediscovering Black History." *What Moves at the Margin: Selected Nonfiction.* Ed. Carolyn C. Denard. University Press of Mississippi, 2008.

"Rootedness: The Ancestor as Foundation." *What Moves at the Margin: Selected Nonfiction.* Ed. Carolyn C. Denard. University Press of Mississippi, 2008.

Song of Solomon. Random House, 2004.

Sula. Random House, 2004.

"Talk of the Town." *What Moves at the Margin: Selected Nonfiction.* Ed. Carolyn C. Denard. University Press of Mississippi, 2008.

Tar Baby. Random House, 2004.

"Unspeakable Things Unspoken: The Afro-American Presence in American Literature." *Michigan Quarterly Review* 5.1 (1988): 1–47.

"What the Black Women Thinks about Women's Lib." *What Moves at the Margin: Selected Nonfiction.* Ed. Carolyn C. Denard. University Press of Mississippi, 2008.

Muggeridge, Malcom. "The Great Liberal Death-Wish." *National Review,* June 14, 1966, pp. 573–75.

Nash, George H. *The Conservative Intellectual Movement in America since 1945.* ISI Books, 2006.

Nussbaum, Martha C. *Cultivating Humanity: A Classical Defense of Reform in Liberal Education.* Harvard University Press, 1998.

O'Connor, Flannery. *Flannery O'Connor: Collected Works.* Ed. Sally Fitzgerald. Library of America, 1988.

Habit of Being: Letters of Flannery O'Connor. Ed. Sally Fitzgerald. Farrar, 1979.

"The Nature and Aim of Fiction." *Mystery and Manners: Occasional Prose*. Ed. Sally Fitzgerald and Robert Fitzgerald. Farrar, 1969.

Untitled Review of Beyond the Dreams of Avarice, by Russell Kirk. Comp. Leo Zuber. Ed. Carter W. Martin. University of Georgia Press, 1983.

Orvell, Miles. *Invisible Parade: The Fiction of Flannery O'Connor*. Temple University Press, 1972.

Patell, Cyrus. *Negative Liberties: Morrison, Pynchon, and the Problem of Liberal Ideology*. Duke University Press, 2001.

Payne, Stanley G. *A History of Fascism: 1914 – 1945*. Routledge, 1995.

"PEN Fiasco." *National Review*, February 14, 1986, pp. 18–19.

Perlstein, Rick. *Before the Storm: Barry Goldwater and the Breaking of the American Consensus*. Nation Books, 2001.

"Exclusive: Lee Atwater's Infamous 1981 Interview on the Southern Strategy." *The Nation*, November 13, 2012, www.thenation.com/article/exclusive-lee-atwaters-infamous-1981-interview-southern-strategy/. Accessed on January 3, 2017.

The Invisible Bridge. The Fall of Nixon and the Rise of Reagan. Simon and Schuster, 2014.

Phelps, Robert. "Kind of on a Quest." Review of *Henderson the Rain King*, by Saul Bellow. *National Review*, March 28, 1959, p. 622.

Phillips, Kevin P. *The Emerging Republican Majority. 1969*. Princeton University Press, 2014.

Phillips-Fein, Kim. "Conservatism: A State of the Field." *Journal of American History* 98.3 (2011): 723–43.

Invisible Hands: The Making of the Conservative Movement from the New Deal to Reagan. W.W. Norton and Co., 2010.

Powell, Lewis F. , Jr. "The Powell Memo." *Reclaim Democracy!*, http://reclaim democracy.org/powell_memo_lewis/. Accessed November 15, 2016.

Puzo, Mario. "His Cardboard Lovers." Review of *Tell Me How Long the Train's Been Gone*, by James Baldwin. *New York Times Book Review*, June 23, 1968, pp. 5; 34.

Pynchon, Thomas. *Bleeding Edge*. Penguin, 2013.

The Crying of Lot 49. Penguin, 2012.

Gravity's Rainbow. Penguin Classics, 1995.

"Is It O.K. To Be A Luddite?" *New York Times Book Review*, October 28, 1984, pp. 40–41.

"Introduction." *Slow Learner: Early Stories*. Back Bay Books, 1985.

V. Harper Perennial, 2005.

Vineland. Penguin, 1997.

Rahv, Philip. "The Sense and Nonsense of Whittaker Chambers." *A Partisan Century: Political Writings from Partisan Review*. Ed. Edith Kurzweil. Columbia University Press, 1996.

Rampersad, Arnold. *Ralph Ellison: A Biography*. Random House, 2008.

Rand, Ayn. "The Age of Envy." *Return of the Primitive: The Anti-Industrial Revolution*. Ed. Peter Schwartz. Meridian, 1999.

Atlas Shrugged. 50th anniversary ed. Signet, 2007.

"'Extremism', or The Art of Smearing." *Capitalism: The Unknown Ideal*. Signet, 1986.

"The Fascist New Frontier." *The Ayn Rand Column: Written for the Los Angles Times*. Ed. Peter Schwartz. Second Renaissance Books, 1991.

The Virtue of Selfishness: A New Concept of Egoism. Signet, 1989.

Reagan, Ronald. "Address Accepting the Presidential Nomination at the Republican National Convention in Detroit." July 17, 1980. Online by Gerhard Peters and John T. Woolley. *The American Presidency Project*, www.presidency.ucsb.edu/ws/?pid=25970. Accessed 19 May 2016.

"A Time for Choosing." October 27, 1964. *American Rhetoric*. HTML transcription by Michael E. Eidenmuller, www.americanrhetoric.com/speeches/ronaldreaganatimeforchoosing.htm. Accessed November 10, 2015.

"Radio Address to the Nation on Martin Luther King, Jr., and Black Americans." January 18, 1986. Online by Gerhard Peters and John T. Woolley. *The American Presidency Project*, www.presidency.ucsb.edu/ws/?pid=37302. Accessed October 10, 2016.

and Richard G. Hubler. *Where's the Rest of Me?* Duell, Sloan, and Pearce, 1965.

Reich, Wilhelm. *The Mass Psychology of Fascism*. Eds. Mary Higgins, Chester M. Raphael, and M. D. Farrar, Straus and Giroux, 1970.

Rigueur, Leah Wright. *The Loneliness of the Black Republican*. Princeton University Press, 2014.

Robin, Corey. *The Reactionary Mind: Conservatism from Edmund Burke to Sarah Palin*. Oxford University Press, 2011.

Robinson, Marilynne. "Fear." *The Givenness of Things: Essays*. Picador, 2015.

Gilead. Picador, 2004.

Home. Picador, 2008.

"Humanism." *The Givenness of Things: Essays*. Picador, 2015.

"President Obama and Marilynne Robinson: A Conversation in Iowa, Parts I and II." *The Givenness of Things: Essays*. Picador, 2015.

"Puritans and Prigs." *The Death of Adam: Essays on Modern Thought*. Picador, 1998.

"Who Was Oberlin?" *When I Was a Child I Read Books*. Picador, 2012.

"Wondrous Love." *When I Was a Child I Read Books*. Picador, 2012.

Rodgers, Daniel T. *Age of Fracture*. Harvard University Press, 2011.

Rodman, Seldon. "Whites and Blacks." Review of *Tar Baby*, by Toni Morrison. *National Review*, June 26, 1981, pp. 730–31.

Roynon, Tessa. *The Cambridge Introduction to Toni Morrison*. Cambridge University Press, 2012.

Root, E. Merrill "What About Ayn Rand?" *National Review*, January 30, 1960, pp. 76–77.

Rothbard, Murray N. Letter. *National Review*, January 25, 1958, p. 95.

Sandel, Michael. "Democrats and Community." *New Republic*, February 22, 1988, pp. 20–23.

Saunders, Frances Stonor. *The Cultural Cold War: The CIA and the World of Arts and Letters*. 2nd ed. The New Press, 2013.

Schryer, Stephen. *Fantasies of the New Class: Ideologies of Professionalism in Post-World War II American Fiction*. Columbia University Press, 2011.

Maximum Feasible Participation: American Literature and the War on Poverty. Stanford University Press, 2018.

Scott, Lynn Orilla. *James Baldwin's Later Fiction: Witness to the Journey*. Michigan State University Press, 2002.

Scott-Smith, Giles. *The Politics of Apolitical Culture: The Congress of Cultural Freedom and the Political Economy of American Hegemony, 1945–1955*. Routledge, 2001.

"Selections from MT's files as Prime Minster, 1986–88." *Margaret Thatcher Foundation*, www.margaretthatcher.org/archive/1986tna1.asp. Accessed September 12, 2016.

Shoop, Casey. "Thomas Pynchon, Postmodernism, and the Rise of the New Right in California." *Contemporary Literature* 53.1 (2012): 51–86.

Simmons, Tracy Lee. "Transcendental 'Meditations' (Meditations of Marcus Aurelius)." *National Review*, September 12, 1994, p. 40.

Smith, Rachel Greenwald. *Affect and American Literature in the Age of Neoliberalism*. Cambridge University Press, 2015.

Sontag, Susan. "Fascinating Fascism." *Under the Sign of Saturn*. Vintage, 1981.

Sowell, Thomas. *Black Rednecks and White Liberals*. Encounter Books, 2005.

Controversial Essays. Hoover Institution Press, 2002.

Stahl, Jason. *Right Moves: The Conservative Think Tank in American Political Culture since 1945*. University of North Carolina Press, 2016.

Stock, Irvin. "Man in Culture." Review of *Mr. Sammler's Planet*, by Saul Bellow. *Commentary*, May 1970, 90–93.

Stull, James N. "The Cultural Gamesmanship of Tom Wolfe." *The Journal of American Culture* 14.3 (1991): 25–30.

Szalay, Michael. *Hip Figures: A Literary History of the Democratic Party*. Stanford University Press, 2012.

Tanenhaus, Sam. *Whittaker Chambers: A Biography*. Random House, 1997.

Tate, J. O. "Sufferin' Succotash." Review of *Vineland*, by Thomas Pynchon. *National Review*, April 30, 1990, p. 59.

Taylor, Charles. *A Secular Age*. Harvard University Press, 2007.

Teachout, Terry. "Tom Wolfe: Telling New York." *National Review*, December 19, 2005, p. 115.

"Crime Novels: American Noir of the 1930s and '40s." Review of *Crime Novels: American Noir of the 1930s and '40s*, Library of America. *National Review*, December 22, 1997, p. 67.

Thorburn, David. "A Dissent on Thomas Pynchon." Review of *Gravity's Rainbow*, by Thomas Pynchon. *Commentary*, September 1973, pp. 68–70.

Trilling, Lionel. *Beyond Culture: Essays on Literature and Learning*. Viking, 1965.

The Liberal Imagination: Essays on Literature and Society. New Review of Books Classics, 2008.

Untitled article. *National Review*, August 31, 1965, p. 1.

Veblen, Thorstein. *The Theory of the Leisure Class*. Oxford World's Classics Ed. University Press, 2009.

Viereck, Peter. *Conservatism Revisited: The Revolt Against Ideology*. Transaction Publishers, 2009.

Vigilante, Richard. "The Bonfire of the Vanities." Review of *The Bonfire of the Vanities*, by Tom Wolfe. *National Review*, December 18, 1987, p. 46.

"Voices of Sanity." *National Review*, April 7, 1956, p. 7.

von Mises, Ludwig. *Omnipotent Government*. Yale University Press, 1944.

Walker, Alice. "Beyond the Peacock: The Reconstruction of Flannery O'Connor." *In Search of Our Mothers' Gardens*. Harcourt, Brace, Jovanovich, 1983.

Ward, Jerry W. , Jr. "Everybody's Protest Novel: The Richard Wright Era." *The Cambridge Companion to the African American Novel*. Ed. Maryemma Graham. Cambridge University Press, 2004.

Warren, Kenneth W. *So Black and Blue: Ralph Ellison and the Occasion of Criticism*. University of Chicago Press, 2003.

What Was African American Literature? Harvard University Press, 2012.

Watson, Jay. "Flannery O'Connor." *The Cambridge Companion to American Fiction after 1945*. Ed. John N. Duvall. Cambridge University Press, 2012.

Weaver, Richard. "The Best of Everything." *National Review* February 1, 1956: 21–22.

Weisberg, Jacob. *Ronald Reagan: The American Presidents Series: The 40th President, 1981–1989*. Henry Holt and Company, 2016.

Weyrich, Paul. "Conservatism for the People." *National Review*, September 3, 1990, pp. 24–27.

"What is the Best Work of American Fiction in the Last 25 Years?" *The New York Times*, May 21, 2006, www.nytimes.com/ref/books/fiction-25-years.html. Accessed December 15, 2016.

Will, George. "Literary Politics." *Newsweek*, April 21, 1990, www.newsweek.com/literary-politics-202084. Accessed October 10, 2014.

"New(s) from Tom Wolfe." Review of *The Bonfire of the Vanities*, by Tom Wolfe. The Washington Post, November 22, 1987, www.washingtonpost.com/archive/opinions/1987/11/22/news-from-tom-wolfe/dcf57942-7f64-4fb0-87b7-412d497f1cd3/?utm_term=.cb34e0534d91. Accessed August 14, 2016.

"William Faulkner, RIP." *National Review*, July 31, 1962, p. 54.

Wills, Garry. "Buckley, Buckley, Bow Wow Wow." *Esquire* 69, Jan 1968, pp. 72–76; 155; 158–59.

Confessions of a Conservative. Doubleday, 1979.

"Is Ayn Rand a Conservative." *National Review*, February 27, 1960, p. 139.

Reagan's America: Innocents at Home. Doubleday, 1986.

"What Color is God?" Review of *The Fire Next Time*, by James Baldwin. *National Review*, May 21, 1963, pp. 408–17.

Wright, Richard. "I Tried to be a Communist." *The God That Failed*. Ed. Richard H. Crossman. Columbia University Press, 2001.

Wolfe, Tom. *The Bonfire of the Vanities*. Picador, 2008.

and E. W. Johnson. *The New Journalism*. Harper and Row, 1973.

"Head of the Class." *National Review*, August 5, 1988, p. 35.

"The Intelligent Coed's Guide to America." *Mauve Gloves & Madmen, Clutter & Vine*. Bantam Books, 1976.

"In the Land of the Rococo Marxists." *Hooking Up*. Farrar, Straus, and Giroux, 2000.

"Mauve Gloves & Madmen, Clutter & Vine." *Mauve Gloves & Madmen, Clutter & Vine*. Bantam Books, 1976.

"My Three Stooges." *Hooking Up*. Farrar, Straus, and Giroux, 2000.

The Painted Word. Farrar, Straus, and Giroux, 1975.

Radical Chic and Mau-Mauing the Flak Catchers. Farrar, Straus and Giroux, 1970.

"Stalking the Billion-Footed Beast: A Literary Manifesto for the New Social Novel." *Harper's Magazine* 279.1674, November 1989, pp. 45–56.

"Tom Wolfe, The Art of Fiction No. 123." Interviewed by George Plimpton. *The Paris Review Issue* 118, Spring 1991, www.theparisreview.org/interviews/2226/tom-wolfe-the-art-of-fiction-no-123-tom-wolfe. Accessed November 17, 2015.

Wood, James. "Marilynne Robinson." *The Fun Stuff: And Other Essays*. Farrar, Straus and Giroux, 2012.

"Tom Wolfe's Shallowness, and the Trouble with Information." *The Irresponsible Self: On Laughter and the Novel*. Picador, 2004.

Wood, Ralph C. *Flannery O'Connor and the Christ-Haunted South*. Wm. B. Eerdmans Publishing, 2004.

Žižek, Slavoj. *The Sublime Object of Ideology*. Verso, 2009.

Living in the End Times. Verso, 2010.

Index

Recent Books In This Series *(continued from page ii)*

176. CINDY WEINSTEIN
Time, Tense, and American Literature
175. CODY MARS
Nineteenth-Century American Literature and the Long Civil War
174. STACEY MARGOLIS
Fictions of Mass Democracy in Nineteenth-Century America
173. PAUL DOWNES
Hobbes, Sovereignty, and Early American Literature
172. DAVID BERGMAN
Poetry of Disturbance
171. MARK NOBLE
American Poetic Materialism from Whitman to Stevens
170. JOANNA FREER
Thomas Pynchon and American Counterculture
169. DOMINIC MASTROIANNI
Politics and Skepticism in Antebellum American Literature
168. GAVIN JONES
Failure and the American Writer
167. LENA HILL
Visualizing Blackness and the Creation of the African American Literary Tradition
166. MICHAEL ZISER
Environmental Practice and Early American Literature
165. ANDREW HEBARD
The Poetics of Sovereignty in American Literature, 1885–1910
164. CHRISTOPHER FREEBURG
Melville and the Idea of Blackness
163. TIM ARMSTRONG
The Logic of Slavery
162. JUSTINE MURISON
The Politics of Anxiety in Nineteenth-Century American Literature
161. HSUAN L. HSU
Geography and the Production of Space in Nineteenth-Century American Literature
160. DORRI BEAM
Style, Gender, and Fantasy in Nineteenth Century American Women's Writing
159. YOGITA GOYAL
Romance, Diaspora, and Black Atlantic Literature
158. MICHAEL CLUNE
American Literature and the Free Market, 1945–2000
157. KERRY LARSON
Imagining Equality in Nineteenth-Century American Literature

156. LAWRENCE ROSENWALD
Multilingual America: Language and the Making of American Literature

155. ANITA PATTERSON
Race, American Literature, and Transnational Modernism

154. ELIZABETH RENKER
The Origins of American Literature Studies: An Institutional History

153. THEO DAVIS
Formalism, Experience, and the Making of American Literature in the Nineteenth Century

152. JOAN RICHARDSON
A Natural History of Pragmatism: The Fact of Feeling from Jonathan Edwards to Gertrude Stein

151. EZRA TAWIL
The Making of Racial Sentiment: Slavery and the Birth of the Frontier Romance

150. ARTHUR RISS
Race, Slavery, and Liberalism in Nineteenth-Century American Literature

149. JENNIFER ASHTON
From Modernism to Postmodernism: American Poetry and Theory in the Twentieth Century

148. MAURICE S. LEE
Slavery, Philosophy, and American Literature, 1830–1860

147. CINDY WEINSTEIN
Family, Kinship and Sympathy in Nineteenth-Century American Literature

146. ELIZABETH HEWITT
Correspondence and American Literature, 1770–1865

145. ANNA BRICKHOUSE
Transamerican Literary Relations and the Nineteenth-Century Public Sphere

144. ELIZA RICHARDS
Gender and the Poetics of Reception in Poe's Circle

143. JENNIE A. KASSANOFF
Edith Wharton and the Politics of Race

142. JOHN MCWILLIAMS
New England's Crises and Cultural Memory: Literature, Politics, History, Religion, 1620–1860

141. SUSAN M. GRIFFIN
Anti-Catholicism and Nineteenth-Century Fiction

140. ROBERT E. ABRAMS
Landscape and Ideology in American Renaissance Literature

139. JOHN D. KERKERING
The Poetics of National and Racial Identity in Nineteenth-Century American Literature

138. MICHELE BIRNBAUM
Race, Work and Desire in American Literature, 1860–1930

137. RICHARD GRUSIN
Culture, Technology and the Creation of America's National Parks

136. RALPH BAUER
The Cultural Geography of Colonial American Literatures: Empire, Travel, Modernity

135. MARY ESTEVE
The Asethetics and Politics of the Crowd in American Literature

For EU product safety concerns, contact us at Calle de José Abascal, 56–1°, 28003 Madrid, Spain or eugpsr@cambridge.org.

www.ingramcontent.com/pod-product-compliance
Ingram Content Group UK Ltd.
Pitfield, Milton Keynes, MK11 3LW, UK
UKHW041858190726
13854UKWH00002B/965

* 9 7 8 1 1 0 8 9 3 2 2 0 2 *